Uncle John's BATHROOM READER® PLUNGES INTO THE UNIVERSE

The Bathroom Readers'
Hysterical Society

San Diego, CA

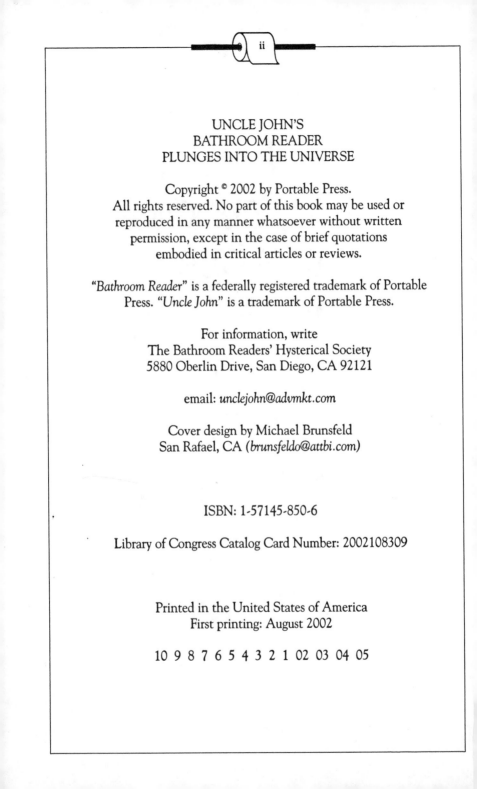
UNCLE JOHN'S
BATHROOM READER
PLUNGES INTO THE UNIVERSE

For information, write
The Bathroom Readers' Hysterical Society
5880 Oberlin Drive, San Diego, CA 92121

email: unclejohn@advmkt.com

Cover design by Michael Brunsfeld
San Rafael, CA (brunsfeldo@attbi.com)

ISBN: 1-57145-850-6

Library of Congress Catalog Card Number: 2002108309

Printed in the United States of America
First printing: August 2002

10 9 8 7 6 5 4 3 2 1 02 03 04 05

Project Team:

Allen Orso, Publisher

JoAnn Padgett, Director, Editorial & Production

Stephanie Spadaccini, Project Editor

Allison Bocksruker, Project Manager

Georgine Lidell, Inventory Manager

THANK YOU!

*The Bathroom Readers' Hysterical Society
sincerely thanks the people whose
advice and assistance made this book possible.*

Bernadette Baillie

Michael Brunsfeld

Victoria Bullman

Michele Crim

Dylan Drake

Rachael Ettelman

Gordon Javna

Brandie Jeffreys

Dan Mansfield

Heinrich Mentius

Mana Monzavi

Janet Nelson

Jay Newman

Mike Nicita

Ellen O'Brien

Ken & Kelly
Padgett

Sydney Stanley

William H. Stoddard

Jennifer Thornton

Charlie & Cindy
Tillinghast

CONTENTS

*Extra-long articles suitable
for an extended sitting session
are marked with an asterisk.*

INTRODUCTION

We've finally made it. Our new book, *Uncle John Plunges Into the Universe*, is a reality. Hmm. What is reality? What is the sound of one hand clapping? How much wood would a woodchuck chuck, if a woodchuck could chuck... but I digress.

It's time for me to write the introduction and then the last page—my favorite, because I look forward to telling you about some of the new and exciting things that we're planning in the future—sort of like visualizing a garden as you plant the seeds. Then we're finished.

JoAnn can go home and sleep for three days (as if!); Allison can remove her intravenous espresso drip; I can reflect on what a crazy and exciting experience it's been to put this latest book together—and wonder how the heck we're going to top this one. We'll certainly give it our very best effort.

And now for a sneak peek at a few of the mind-bending articles we have in store for you when you take the plunge between the covers of *this* book—and I guarantee that they'll keep you on the edge of your seat:

"The Green Flash": Myth or reality? Get the inside info on the best methods for pursuing this elusive and legendary sunset phenomenon, and much more. Remember—don't blink...

What animal has a nose so sensitive that it can detect one odor particle per billion, and whose detective abilities have been used not only to sniff out landmines as well as diag(nose) disease? In "It's Not Just Wet and Cold" we investigate the amazing workings of this incredible schnozz.

We investigate a fascinating form of alternative cuisine popular all around the world in "Waiter! Put More Flies in My Soup!"

We go astrophysical in "How to Make a Black Hole."

We present our theories behind the current explosion of home runs in the major leagues in "Barry Bonds Kicks Ash."

And, finally learn how much wood a woodchuck could chuck in "Ask Uncle John: Zen Questions."

And as for you, our cherished, loyal (and extremely well-informed) readers…

In this vast universe, though there are seemingly billions and billions of fascinating facts to ponder, occasionally we may present an article (or two) on a topic that may seem familiar to you. We try our hardest to avoid this, but sometimes Uncle John and Uncle Al are a little forgetful—and honestly, some of these topics are so darned interesting that we think they can bear examination from another (and possibly new) angle.

That said—your thoughts, opinions, and input on these matters are always appreciated, and if you have specific questions about the *Plunges Into* series, please contact us at *unclejohn@advmkt.com*.

So please bear with us—I think that this book is absolutely crammed with fascinating and unusual facts, a slightly more acerbic viewpoint, and lots of good old-fashioned reading that we hope you'll enjoy as much as we enjoyed putting this book together just for you.

Sit down and be counted.

As always, go with the flow…

—Uncle Al and the
Bathroom Readers'
Hysterical Society

Let your opinions be known! Join us at *www.bathroomreader.com*.

JOURNEY TO THE CENTER OF THE EARTH

And we're not stopping until we get there!

Go get a shovel. Why? Because we're digging—you'll be doing most of the heavy work—right straight down to the very core of the earth. Oh, don't look like that! Your mom told us you tried to dig to China all the time when you were a kid. And this time, we're only going half as far.

The crust: Let's start at the top, which is, conveniently enough, where we are anyway. The earth's crust is where we keep pretty much everything—the oceans, the continents, our cities, ourselves. The crust appears substantial to us, but as far as layers of the earth go, it's both the thinnest (40 miles thick on the continents and as little as 9 miles thick underneath the oceans) and the lightest—made of materials that "floated to the top," as it were. What is in the crust depends on where you are. On the continents, the crust is mostly granitic rock, while the ocean floor is mostly basalt. (Why? Granite is lighter than basalt and "floats" above the heavier rock.

Relative to Earth's size (almost 8,000 miles in diameter), the crust is incredibly thin—much thinner than an eggshell would be if it were shrunk down to the same size. The crust also has a definite boundary, something called the "Mohorovicic discontinuity." The "Moho" (as it's known to geologists who want to sound hip and cool to their grad students) marks the place where seismic waves traveling down through the crust of the earth suddenly speed up. Why? Because right on the other side of the Moho is:

The mantle: Like the crust, the mantle is made up of rocky material. However, there are two major differences. The rocky material in the mantle is denser—this is why the seismic waves speed up—and it's quite a bit hotter: some 1,800°F (982°C) at the top of the mantle and even toastier as you head down. (If we were really digging our way down to the core, we would have basted in our own juices by the time we reached the mantle, not to mention

---

A person takes an average of 16 breaths a minute.

that our shovels would have melted). The heat gives the rocky material in the mantle the consistency of Silly Putty. Unlike the crust, the mantle is impressively thick: some 1,800 miles deep. What's waiting on the other side?

The outer core: The outer core is denser still than the mantle because it's made of molten metal: mostly iron, some nickel, and some sulfur and oxygen tossed in as well, broiling along at a temperature of 6,700°F (3,704°C). All this liquid iron sloshing around in the outer core is what's thought to give the earth its impressive magnetic field: The convection currents in the liquid generate the field. This is good news for us, since our planet's magnetic field deflects a substantial amount of harmful cosmic rays from the Earth's surface. The outer core's environs are hellish, but they help make our planet a paradise for life.

The inner core: Now for the hottest and densest part of the planet. The inner core is almost entirely solid iron, solid despite the infernal heat of 7,700°F (4,260°C). The pressure at the core of the earth is equally intense. Smack-dab in the center of our planet, the pressure is some three million times greater than on the surface. Which make perfect sense, since if you were at the center of the earth, you'd literally have the weight of the world on your shoulders. Here's a dirty secret about the planet's interior. Although we're reasonably sure what the planet's inside looks like, we're not 100 percent sure, mainly because we've never actually looked. The deepest hole humans have dug is less than ten miles deep—not even enough to get through the crust. We get our "view" of the earth's interior by tracking the speed of seismic waves as they travel down into the depths. The model of the earth's interior mentioned here is just one possible option. Some geologists suggest that our planet's core is even stranger than we've imagined. Geophysicist J. Marvin Herndon has suggested that the earth's core isn't made of iron at all, but of uranium and plutonium undergoing a huge, long-lived fission reaction that's been burning underneath our feet for billions of years—which explains why the earth's core has remained so hot for so long.

How can we be sure of what's down there? Grab a shovel. Start digging. Oh, come on, it'll be fun. Just remember we have to close up the hole again once we're done.

The total amount of air both lungs hold when filled to capacity is six liters.

OUT OF AFRICA

Og is a Neanderthal. He stands about 5'6" (168 cm) tall. Although he weighs about 185 pounds (84 kg), it's all muscle. He has a weak chin, a large honker, and a heavy brow line. Ogga looks similar, but is slightly smaller at 5 feet (152 cm) tall and 175 pounds (79 kg). Unfortunately, they're dead now, and so is their entire race. Were they wiped out by natural selection or something more sinister?

Paleoanthropology is the study of human ancestors. You may have recognized the "paleo" from paleontology, the study of ancient animals.

THE CAST OF CHARACTERS

Paleoanthropologists classify humans as both *primates* and *hominids*. Primates are bipedal (two-footed) mammals. Hominids are bipedal primate mammals who walked upright. Apes don't qualify as hominids, because although they're bipedal mammals, they don't walk upright.

A species name has two parts: the genus, which is capitalized, and the species, which is not. The genus is often abbreviated.

Here's human evolution in a nutshell.

AUSTRALOPITHECINES

Australopithecine means "southern ape," but they were no ordinary apes. Australopiths (scientists use that nickname, so we will, too) were distinguished from ordinary apes because they walked upright, like us. Other than that, they looked and acted pretty apelike.

Who: *Ardipithecus ramidus*
When: 4,400,000 years ago
Where: Eastern Africa
The first known hominid. It was very similar to a chimpanzee, except for its teeth (which were smaller) and the fact that it walked. Its teeth had enamel, like the chimps of the same era, suggesting a relationship with the chimpanzee.

A red blood cell lives for 80 to 120 days; white blood cells last an average of only 13 days.

Who: *Australopithecus anamensis*
When: 4,200,000–3,900,000 years ago
Where: Eastern Africa
This hominid also appeared quite apelike except for its bipedal legs. Its teeth had thicker enamel than A. *ramidis*, which may mean it ate much tougher foods.

Who: *Australopithecus afarensis*
When: 3,900,000–3,000,000 years ago
Where: Eastern Africa
Scientists think this hominid spent a lot of time in trees because of its long arms and the way its knees and legs are shaped. It's famous in paleoanthropology circles because the first discovered skeleton of its species, "Lucy," was unusually complete. They named her Lucy because someone on the dig team played the Beatles song, "Lucy in the Sky with Diamonds," over and over again while working.

Who: *Australopithecus africanus*
When: 3,000,000–2,000,000 years ago
Where: South Africa
This was the first australopith ever discovered. It's also thought to be a direct ancestor of modern man because it's less primitive appearing than the other australopiths. Its skull was rounder than its earlier counterparts, and its teeth looked more like ours do today. It, and its clan, probably ate nuts, seeds, and roots.

Who: *Australopithecus garhi*
When: 3,000,000–2,000,000 years ago
Where: Eastern Africa
This newly discovered, somewhat controversial species may be linked to both australopith and homo. Why controversial? Because not all scientists agree that this species is different enough to merit a new species name. It still had long arms like an ape, but its legs were also long, like a human's. Some bones found near the A. *garhi* bones hint that it may have used tools. Some scientists think this is a direct ancestor of modern humans.

Who: *Australopithecus aethiopicus*
When: 2,700,000–2,300,000 years ago

The "Rh" factor was named for the rhesus monkeys used in research to identify blood types.

Where: Eastern Africa
This guy looked a lot like A. *afarensis*, so scientists think it may have evolved along that line. These australopiths were great chewers—their jaws were so powerful that they had ridges on the back of the skull and a greatly elongated face to accommodate all those chewing muscles.

Who: *Australopithecus boisei*
When: 2,300,000–1,400,000 years ago
Where: Eastern Africa
More great chewers. Its face was very wide and caved-in, and its molars were four times larger than ours. What did it find so tasty? Mostly nuts and roots.

Who: *Australopithecus robustus*
When: 1,800,000–1,500,000 years ago
Where: Southern Africa
Yet more chewers with flat or concave faces. This one was different: Tools, such as modified bones, were found with these skeletons, hinting that they may have dug up their food.

HOMO
Homo is our genus, and simply means "human." Our own species is called *Homo sapiens*, meaning "intelligent human," but you might know of some exceptions.

Who: *Homo habilis*
When: 1,800,000–300,000 years ago
Where: Eastern Africa
Homo habilis was another toolmaker and used modified stone tools. Its very name means handyman. Its brain was larger than the australopiths and shaped a lot like ours. In fact, the shape of its skull makes scientists believe that *Homo habilis* may have been capable of speech.

Who: *Homo erectus, Homo egaster, Homo heidelbergensis*
When: 1,800,000–100,000 years ago
Where: Asia (H. *erectus*), Africa (H. *egaster*), and Europe (H. *heidelbergensis*)
There is some controversy over whether or not these are separate

The moon has a 15,000-mile tail of sodium atoms that can only be detected by instruments.

species—that's why we've listed them together. All these species were once known as *H. erectus*. This is the first species that left the African homeland, venturing into the wide unknown world. It had big teeth, a small chin, a long skull, and heavy brow ridges. It used tools as well.

Who: *Homo neanderthalensis*
When: 250,000–30,000 years ago
Where: Europe and central Asia
This most famous primitive man is our closest relative. It had a more massive torso and stronger limbs than we do today. It also had little to no chin, a big nose, and a ridge along its brow line. Other than that, Neanderthals looked quite human and acted very human as well: hunting cooperatively, caring for the elderly and sick, and—a significant sign of civilization—burying their dead. Their stone tools were quite sophisticated. They may have even created artwork. They lived in the very cold climate of Ice Age Europe. Neanderthals lived alongside the first *Homo sapiens*, but most scientists believe that *Homo sapiens* and Neanderthals were incapable of interbreeding.

Who: *Homo sapiens* (in the most modern edition, we're known as *Homo sapiens sapiens*)
When: 100,000–present
Where: Everywhere
Not long after *Homo sapiens* made it onto the scene, all other human races died out. We quickly spread to every part of the globe, flourishing in every climate from Ice Age Europe to sub-Saharan (not that there was a Sahara then) Africa. Modern man is unique in human evolution in that we don't share the earth with any other human species. At least, we didn't for long. Sounds rather suspicious, doesn't it?

* * * * *

"In studying the science of yesteryear one comes upon such interesting notions as gravity, electricity, and the roundness of the earth—while an examination of more recent phenomena shows a strong trend towards spray cheese, stretch denim, and the Moog synthesizer."
—Fran Leibowitz, *Metropolitan Life*

The rocks on the moon are between 3 and 4.6 billion years old.

ASK UNCLE JOHN: DOING THE LAUNDRY

The deep, dark—uhh, we mean white, bright—secrets of laundry.

Dear Uncle John:
How does bleach get my whites their very whitest?

By messing with the chemical composition of stains. Many organic stains, from grass to blood, get their color from chemicals that are known as chromophores. Household bleaches use a chemical called sodium hypochlorite (highly diluted) that interacts with chromophores and breaks them up. No chromophore, no color. Combined with the action of the detergent (which grabs onto dirt and stains) and the agitating motion of your washer (which shakes the dirt and stains off the clothes), your whites become all nice and sparkly. Now, remember not to use your bleach on your colored fabrics, since the same chromophores that make up stains also make up the natural dyes that color your clothes.

What about those newer bleaches that you can use on colors? They aren't bleaches at all but "optical brighteners" that coat your clothes with an ultraviolet-absorbing dye to give your clothes a slightly blue tinge, which your brain perceives as being "brighter." Clothes treated with optical brighteners aren't actually any cleaner than they'd be without the brighteners, mind you. Fun little side effect from using optical brighteners, by the way: Your clothes will glow under black light. Groovy, man!

Dear Uncle John:
What is static cling anyway? And how does fabric softener defeat it?

Static cling is exactly the same stuff that allowed you to rub your feet on the carpet, sneak up on unsuspecting pets and/or siblings, and zap them full of voltage—it's the static electricity that thrives in dry air. When your clothes are tumbling in the dryer, they rub up against each other like high school sweethearts during a slow dance at the winter formal—and in the case of the clothes, that means they're developing static charges. This is what causes your socks to bond so passionately with your skirt, until you tear them asunder with a crackling *rrrrrip*. The poor socks. All they wanted was a little love.

Love, schmove, you say. I just want to get rid of the static cling. That's where your fabric softener comes in. To be blunt about it, fabric softener gives your drying clothes a nice, thorough lube job. It cuts down the amount of static electricity by keeping the clothes slightly moist (and allowing electric charges to flow freely and not get all jammed up). Back to the winter-formal-slow-dance metaphor: If your clothes are hormonal teenagers looking to generate a spark, your fabric softener is the chaperone who makes sure there's eight fingers worth of daylight between them. (And you thought watching your clothes dry would be boring.)

The fabric softener that comes in sheets, incidentally, uses waxy compounds to lube your clothes. That's right, you're waxing your clothes. You just knew that creepy teddy bear wasn't telling you the whole story.

Dear Uncle John:
Are natural, biodegradable detergents as good as the kind that pollute the water?

This is sort of a trick question. First off, detergents are synthetic by definition (although they can use "natural" ingredients) and should be differentiated from soaps, which are created from plant or animal oils. So "natural" detergents are pretty much a contradiction in terms—lots of "natural" detergents are actually soaps. Should this matter to you? Only to the extent that soaps will leave the dreaded "soap scum," a slight film on your clothes that can build up over time, whereas detergents won't. Detergents are harsher on the environment than soaps, but your clothes will stay brighter longer if you use them. Environment versus bright colors? These are the questions that plague modern man.

As for "biodegradable," all soaps and detergents biodegrade eventually, but synthetic detergents take much longer to degrade than most soaps—and certain ingredients of detergents and soaps, such as artificial fragrances, *won't* degrade naturally. Also, it should be noted that the biodegradability depends on several factors, including whether the detergent is in an aerobic (oxygen-filled) or anaerobic (oxygen-deprived) environment, and if there are enough bacteria around to help biodegrade what soap or detergent is in the water supply. Soaps are nicely biodegradable in theory, for example, but if the soap (which would quickly degrade in your basic puddle) is poured into an anaerobic sewer system, along with the soapy water of the rest of a large community, it'll take that "biodegradable" stuff quite a bit longer to break down than it would otherwise. Just something to think about.

Dear Uncle John:
So, what exactly happens when something gets dry-cleaned? How can you clean something if it never gets wet?

Here's the secret: In dry cleaning, you clothes actually do get wet. The difference is the thing they get wet with isn't water, it's a petroleum-based solvent called perchloroethylene (call it "perc" if you want to sound like you've been in the dry cleaning industry). Your clothes are actually immersed in this stuff. If it disturbs you to think your clothes are being washed in stuff that's related to the fuel in your car, consider that in the early days of dry cleaning, the solvents used were actually kerosene or gasoline. Yes, gas was used to dry-clean clothes. Please don't try this at home.

After your clothes are immersed in perchloroethylene and cleaned, they're placed in an "extractor" and all the perc is sucked out. Why? Because perc can be a fairly nasty chemical for people and other living things. It's a carcinogen that in high concentrations can cause major damage to your nervous system and any number of your internal organs. Even the low levels of perc residue left in your clothes can cause irritation of the eyes, nose, and throat. It can also affect your mood and coordination, especially in a small, enclosed space, like your car on the way home from the dry cleaners. This is not to say you shouldn't get your clothes dry-cleaned. Just make sure you've got a good supply of fresh air. Here's *another* secret: A lot of clothes that say "Dry Clean Only" can actually be hand washed gently (or carefully on the gentle cycle of your washing machine). It's just that dry cleaning lessens the chance of them losing their shape or shrinking. If you're willing to take the risk, pull out the Woolite and go to town. The Dry Cleaning Police won't burst through your door and haul you away.

BUMPER STICKERS AROUND THE UNIVERSE

If you can read these, you're probably following too closely behind a scientist.

INTERSTELLAR MATTER IS A GAS

GEOLOGISTS MAKE THE BED ROCK

GRAVITY: NOT JUST A GOOD IDEA...IT'S THE LAW!

STOP CONTINENTAL DRIFT!!!

DO MOLECULAR BIOLOGISTS WEAR DESIGNER GENES?

FRICTION CAN BE A DRAG

BLACK HOLES REALLY SUCK

DO RADIOACTIVE CATS HAVE 18 HALF-LIVES?

QUASARS ARE FAR OUT!

NEUTRINOS HAVE BAD BREADTH

HYPERSPACE: WHERE YOU PARK AT THE SUPERSTORE

POLYMER PHYSICISTS ARE INTO CHAINS

GRAVITY BRINGS ME DOWN

TIME TRAVEL IS POSSIBLE—AT THE SPEED OF ONE SECOND PER SECOND

MOLECULAR BIOLOGISTS ARE SMALL

As long as lightning doesn't cross the heart or spine, a person hit by it will usually survive.

FOOD TERRORS
PART I: MAD COWS

*At the height of the mad cow disease scare, beef sales in Europe
fell 27 percent. That's a lot of steak-and-kidney pies.*

In 1985, a mysterious new disease appeared in British beef
cattle: They called it "bovine spongiform encephalopathy"
or BSE, soon to become famous as "mad cow disease."

The British government has spent billions of pounds trying to
deal with the epidemic. And with a lot of British beef going to
Europe, the disease has started appearing there too, resulting in
the European Union spending billions of Euros on prevention.

But mad cow disease is untreatable, so all that anyone can do
to limit its spread is to test herds and destroy any that cows are
infected. Farmers have gone bankrupt, and the public, understandably enough, is wondering whether to switch to pork, or chicken,
or even Grandpa's old favorite standby: mutton.

A BRAIN LIKE A SPONGE
Mad cow disease can cross species, and the human form,
Creutzfeldt-Jakob disease, does the same thing to people as mad
cow does to cows: It makes holes in the brain, leading to progressive dementia and death. Now the disease has appeared in Japan,
and despite attempts at control, the international food industry is
slowly spreading it all over the world.

SCRAPE THAT LAMBCHOP OFF THE GRILL, BILL
For over 100 years, farmers have known about a disease of sheep
called "scrapie," named for the animal's uncontrollable urge to
scrape itself against trees or fence posts until its flesh is raw, after
which it loses its mind and dies. Scientists mostly agreed it was
caused by some kind of "slow virus"; symptoms took years to
develop. But no one could isolate it, and standard methods of
eliminating virus infections didn't work.

Scrapie wasn't seen as a serious threat, and sheep that died
from it were sold to the animal feed industry along with other

animals that had died from natural causes. Well, this irresponsible practice has come back to bite us on our beef butts. It's believed that mad cow disease began when cows were fed processed feed containing the brains of scrapie-infected sheep.

HISTORY'S MYSTERY

The only historical information about a disease of this type in humans comes from New Guinea, where one tribe—the Fore Highlanders—was found in the 1950s to be suffering from a unique and fatal illness, which they called Kuru, or the Laughing Death. Sufferers would gradually, over many years, develop uncontrollable laughter, until their faces were set in a permanent grin like the Joker in *Batman*. Unable to do anything else, they would laugh themselves helplessly to death.

Investigators found that the tribe practiced ritual cannibalism, where the brains of relatives who died would be eaten as a mark of respect. The brains they were eating had those telltale spongelike holes in them. When scientists persuaded the tribe to stop eating each other's brains, the disease gradually died out.

THE SCIENTIFIC PUZZLE

The scientific mystery was how these diseases could be spread. Infections are usually transmitted by bacteria or viruses, but both in this case had been ruled out. A maverick theory by University of California scientist Stanley Prusiner seems to have provided the answer, though treatment is still not available.

Prusiner had studied Creutzfeldt-Jakob disease, and come to the mind-boggling conclusion that it was normal human proteins, not viruses or bacteria, that caused the disease. Proteins are large molecules, folded up over themselves like a tangle of string, and his idea was that in these diseases the string had somehow gotten tangled up in a different pattern; so it was the same molecule, chemically, but with a different physical shape. Eating infected meat, especially brain tissue, introduced these deviant molecules, and the normal proteins in the infected individual would somehow learn to copy the new squiggly shapes.

SCIENCE EATS ITS HAT

When this theory was first suggested, most scientists rejected it: Come on, they said, infections are caused by life forms like viruses and bacteria. Proteins aren't alive; they don't contain any genetic

A mockingbird can alter its tune almost 90 times in less than 10 minutes.

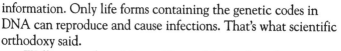

information. Only life forms containing the genetic codes in DNA can reproduce and cause infections. That's what scientific orthodoxy said.

Well, guess what. After millions of dollars have been spent on research over the last 15 years, the protein theory is now accepted as the best available explanation. Prusiner dubbed the shape-shifting proteins "prions"—short for "proteinaceous infectious particles." Scientists are actually relieved to have a theory to explain the mysterious epidemic, even if it's still not clear how these diseases manage to move across species, or exactly what it is that makes the spongelike holes in infected brains.

WHERE'S THE BEEF?

Since deviant protein molecules are chemically identical to normal ones, it's difficult to tell if an individual is infected until symptoms start to appear, which could be 20 years later. You need an electron microscope to look at the physical shape of a protein molecule, and since the proteins in question are in the middle of people's brains, it's only practical to look for them in autopsies of patients who've already died from the disease. Kind of like closing the barn door after the cow has run away.

It's possible that hundreds of millions of people are infected. But some experts think that now that farmers have stopped using scrapie-infected sheep for animal feed, gotten rid of infected beef in their herds, and taken other preventive measures, mad cow and its human relatives will quietly go away again.

I'LL HAVE THE CHICKEN

Meanwhile, it's not that you don't have a choice—that chicken club with bacon and ranch dressing is looking better than ever.

* * * * *

U.S. Red Meat Consumption by Type
Beef: 58%
Pork: 40%
Veal: less than 1%
Lamb and Mutton: less than 1%
—*U.S. Department of Agriculture*

"An average American eats 1,400 chickens, 21 cows, 14 sheep, and 12 pigs during his or her lifetime." —*Kidbits*

Avalanches travel an average of 22 mph.

CREDIT WHERE CREDIT IS DUE
In 1903, the French Academy of Sciences nominated Henri
Becquerel and Pierre—but not Marie—as candidates for the
Nobel Prize in Physics. Eventually, one far-sighted member of the
nominating committee pulled some strings, and Marie was nominated, too. The three physicists won the Nobel Prize in 1903 for
their discovery of natural radioactivity.

HER NEXT NOBEL
After Pierre's death in 1906 (he was run over by a horse-drawn
wagon when he stepped in its path), Marie took over his job at
the Sorbonne, which made her the university's first female faculty
member. But she couldn't give up her work. She continued trying
to isolate pure polonium and pure radium to remove any doubts
about the existence of the new elements. In 1910 she succeeded in
isolating pure radium metal. Her efforts were rewarded with a
second Nobel Prize—this time for Chemistry—in 1911.

WHAT DID THEY KNOW?
Many of the researchers who experimented with these "mysterious
rays" in the early part of the 20th century handled radioactive
materials with their bare hands—Marie and Pierre were no exception. By the end of the 1920s, her fingers severely burned by
radium, Curie began to suffer almost constantly from fatigue, dizziness, and a low-grade fever. She also experienced a continuous
humming in her ears and a gradual loss of eyesight.

On July 4, 1934, Madame Curie succumbed to leukemia, a
disease caused by decades of exposure to the radium that she
devoted her life to. She lived just long enough to see her investigation into uranium give birth to an entirely new scientific
discipline: atomic physics.

NO GIRLS ALLOWED
Only four people have ever won two Nobel Prizes: Linus Pauling
(Chemistry and Peace), Frederick Sanger (Chemistry), John
Bardeen (Physics), and Marie. But despite this accomplishment
(and the fact that she had greatly increased the prestige of France
in the scientific world), Madame Curie was never admitted to the
French Academy of Sciences. (Her hubby, Pierre, was elected to
the Academy in 1905, two years after he *and* Marie had won the
Nobel Prize.)

CURIOUS CAVES

From a cave that moans to a cave that, uh, breaks wind.

SHUT THE CAVE UP!
In 1851, the prospectors who discovered Moaning Cave in California's gold country found a ten-foot-high pile of bones—remains of unwary folks who had accidentally fallen into the cave from a hole above. The prospectors left in disappointment, unaware that they'd discovered a treasure. A skull in the pile was later found to be over 13,000 years old. The cave is famous for wailing sounds, which are caused by rainwater dripping into bottle-shaped formations deep underground. The process creates a low thrumming noise similar to blowing across the top of a half-filled bottle. After the tour, the cavern *does* echo with moans—from tourists who have to climb over 200 stairs back up.

THIS CAVE IS A GAS
China's Yunnan province is home to the Stone Forest, over 64,000 acres of caves and towering limestone pillars that was once an ancient seabed. Over millions of years, rain and wind eroded its limestone formations into their present shapes. A highlight is the Strange Wind Cave. In August and November, a strong wind shoots out of the cave with a thunderous roar. Water from a natural spring inside the cave flows a few yards, then falls abruptly into an underground river. When the spring creates a water level that rises high enough and drops down far enough, it produces the roar of falling water and sends a blast of wind out of the cave.

THE MYSTERY OF KITUM CAVE
Kitum Cave, Kenya, runs 200 feet (61 m) into the side of Mt. Elgon, a dormant volcano. It's a tourist attraction famous for its thousands of bats and for the elephants who bathe in its pools and gouge salty rock from its walls. Kitum went from famous to infamous when scientists realized it held clues to the incurable Ebola virus, which can spread like wildfire and kills up to 90 percent of its victims. Scientists were on high alert when they learned that two unrelated victims of Ebola had visited Kitum Cave. Was the cave a source of Ebola, or was it just a coincidental factor? It turned out that healthy bats can carry Ebola without suffering symptoms, and bat guano sometimes contains the live Ebola virus. Solving the mystery may reduce Ebola's deadly threat, making Kitum one of the world's most important caves.

"WHAT'S THAT SMELL?"

Meats containing lots of fat have a nasty tendency to go rancid. Rancidity (yes, that's a scientific term) is a chemical reaction that breaks down fatty acid molecules into smaller molecular-weight fatty acids. As it does so, some of the molecules evaporate, releasing unpleasant odors. This actually happens with all meat, but the process is faster with fatty meats.

"WHAT'S THAT BLACK STUFF?"

Some spoiled foods are easy to identify. Mold growing on bread looks fuzzy; if you miss it and take a bite anyway, the musty flavor should tip you off. Old milk smells sour and tastes worse—if it gets old enough, it actually curdles. If meat gets old enough, it'll turn brown without the benefit of cooking.

"BUT IT LOOKS FINE TO ME!"

But sometimes you can't tell when food is spoiled, like when bacteria leave an invisible slime on meat. You can check for slime by running a knife blade across the meat. If the blade has cloudy, slippery stuff on it, your meat has been slimed.

It's even harder to tell if an egg is bad. One way you can test it is to put it in a bowl of water. If it sinks, it's fine. If it floats, better get rid of it (preferably without breaking its shell).

OLD MUSTARD NEVER DIES

Not all foods go bad so readily. The yellow mustard that's been in your fridge door for three years, for instance, is a preservative in itself—that's why it won't go bad (though it will lose its flavor).

Then there are antimicrobials (they keep bacteria and fungi from invading your food) and antioxidants (they prevent rancidity, browning, and black spots). Other preservatives absorb water, preserve texture, and prevent trace metals from turning your food strange colors. Some old-fashioned preservatives are salt (to preserve meat and fish), sugar (to preserve fruit), and alcoholic beverages (which is why Aunt Bess's fruitcake can keep for years).

IT CAME FROM THE BACK OF THE FRIDGE

But, as you probably know, not all food can be preserved. And if you've ever neglected to clean out your refrigerator for a while, you've undoubtedly discovered that the stuff that lurks in the back has been doing a slow morph into something alien, evil-smelling, and possibly so dangerous it should come with its own Surgeon General's Warning.

In an ancient Mexican temple, a meteorite was found wrapped in mummy clothes.

YOU'VE GOT RHYTHM

Everyone has rhythm! Circadian rhythm, that is.

I f you've ever tried to stay awake on the night shift or had jet lag, you've felt the effects of the internal clock that tells you when to sleep and when to be alert: your circadian rhythm.

UPS AND DOWNS

"Circadian" means "daily," and your circadian rhythm is the sleep-wake cycle of every day. And night. But it's more than that. Every 24 hours you swing through two high points and two low. Not everyone's timing is exactly the same, but the average person's rhythm goes like this:

10 A.M.

This is the highest point in the day, when most people feel alert. Even if you're really tired, this is probably the best you'll feel all day. It's all downhill from here.

2 P.M.

You've had lunch and now you'd like to go to sleep (but you're probably at work). You've just hit your first low spot of the day. It's only a mild one and if you've had a good night's sleep, you'll probably stay awake.

7 P.M.

You just got home and you're feeling much better. This is your second high for the day. You're not as awake as you were at 10 A.M., but you're much more alert than you were at 2. After 7 though, you're slowly—but very slowly—heading for the major low.

4 A.M.

Usually you're in bed long before this one hits. If you were awake, you'd be finding it very hard to stay that way. After 4 A.M. your cycle starts climbing again toward its morning high at 10. If you stay up all night working, you'll feel awful at 4, start to feel better by 6, and by 10, you'll be wide awake.

In Calama, a town in the Atacama Desert of Chile, it has never rained.

knock any big objects out of its orbital path. Here Pluto fails, as evidenced by the preponderance of Kuiper Belt Objects loitering between it and Neptune. On the other hand, there's a good chance that if Mercury was placed in Pluto's orbit, it wouldn't sweep the lane either. (There are no big objects in Mercury's orbit, but it's also parked next to the Sun, which helps clear things out.)

• Maybe a planet needs an atmosphere? Pluto's got one, at least part of the time—a thin nitrogen atmosphere that freezes out as Pluto moves toward the outer reaches of its orbit. But Mercury doesn't. How about moons? Pluto has Charon, which is half its diameter, making it the biggest moon in the system relative to the size of its planet. Once again Mercury fails, with no moon. Venus also has no moon, but it's indisputably a planet. It's Earth-sized, and has an atmosphere, as well.

• The planet controversy works in the other direction, as well. Jupiter is the largest planet in our solar system by far, but some stars have orbiting balls of hydrogen and helium gas that are several times larger than Jupiter and even generate heat, but are too small to be called stars in their own right. These objects are called "brown dwarfs" rather than planets.

THE LAST WORD, AT LEAST FOR NOW
Ultimately, the definition of a planet is whatever scientists say it is, and for now, that means that Pluto retains its planetary status. In February 1999, the International Astronomical Union put out a press release that stated, "No proposal to change the status of Pluto as the ninth planet in the solar system has been made by any Division, Commission, or Working Group of the IAU responsible for solar system science."

Take that, Rose Center!

* * * * *

"A scientist can discover a new star, but he cannot make one. He would have to ask an engineer to do that."
—Gordon L. Glegg

LITTLE THINGS MEAN A LOT

*Those little things that we take for granted were once
some inventor's bouncing baby brainchild.*

Ballpoint Pen: Invented by a Hungarian who manufactured them in a factory in England, which was eventually taken over by a French company called Bic. (So should we have been pronouncing it "beek" all this time? As in "fleek your beek"?)

Band-Aid: Invented by the husband of an accident-prone woman who was constantly cutting and burning herself in the kitchen.

Baseball Caps: Most players wore straw hats until the late 1860s, when they started wearing visored caps that were based on the Union and Confederate soldiers' uniforms.

Can Opener: Canned food was invented for the British Navy in 1815. The can opener wasn't invented until 50 years later. (While waiting, they used a chisel and a hammer.)

Cellophane: Move over, waxed paper. The inventor was trying to make a stainproof tablecloth and came up with the first clear food wrap instead.

Electric Blankets: Not based as you might think on the electric heating pad, but on the electrically heated flying suits that U.S. Air Force pilots wore during World War II.

Flyswatter: The first was a square piece of wire screen attached to a yardstick. The inventor wanted to call it a fly "bat," but "swatter" fans prevailed.

Jockey Shorts: A Midwestern underwear manufacturer copied the design of men's bathing suits that were popular in France at the time (the 1930s).

Levis: Their creator, Levi Strauss, decided to dye them indigo blue so most stains would disappear into the fabric.

Matches: The first match was a stick that the inventor (who was trying to invent a new kind of explosive) had used to stir his

HOW COLD IS IT?

When you think about an island, you probably imagine it filled with lush tropical vegetation and exotic animals. Wrong!

The island we're talking about is cold enough to solidify the spit in your mouth and freeze the drippings as they emerge from your nose. A place where 32°F (0°C) is considered balmy and –140°F (–96°C) is the average for six to nine months of the year. That's when most vertebrates (or at least the smart ones) leave for warmer climates.

BOTTOM OF THE WORLD, MA!
Antarctica is the biggest island on Earth, the fifth-largest continent, and the only place in the world that doesn't have an indigenous human population. But it wasn't always the frozen wasteland it is now. Fossils of ancient ferns, primitive reptiles, and amphibians prove that the island was once covered with greenery. In fact, it was almost tropical. Hard to believe that a continent covered with 6,000 feet (1,830 m) of ice could ever be warm or host plants other than mosses and lichens. But that's what the scientists say.

WHO'D BE CRAZY ENOUGH TO LIVE THERE?
Scientists are the only vertebrates—other than emperor penguins—who live on the continent year-round. During the winter, all the seals and the other 42 species of birds (of which only seven are penguins) head north to warmer climes. When they come home for the summer, they're happily joined by 40 species of chewing lice, four species of sucking lice, nine species of feather mites, and two species of ticks who feed on them.

HOME SWEET POOP
The rest of Antarctica's permanent animal residents survive because they have glycerol, a kind of antifreeze, in their blood. And who are they? Critters who live in the soil or in bird poop, and who are so tiny you can best see them through a microscope. The big papa of them all is a midge, the *Belgica antarctica*, which grows to a whopping half inch in size.

GOIN' SOUTH?
Now that you've met everyone, if you're ever in the neighborhood, drop by. But don't forget the hot cocoa!

Color-blindness affects 1 in 20 people, mostly males.

SCALPEL, SPONGE, MAGGOTS

In which some very creepy critters stage a medical comeback.

I n the bad old days of medieval medicine, a patient would
fall deathly ill and the doctor would arrive—only to place
blood-sucking leeches on the poor invalid's skin. Out on the
battlefield it was worse. Sanitation was so bad that soldiers'
open wounds crawled with flies and maggots. Sure makes you
glad you live in the modern age, where creepy crawlies are a thing
of the past. Oops, maybe not. Leeches and maggots are making a
medical comeback, and the next hospital patient to have bedbugs
could be you.

A CURE THAT SUCKS

Leeches are segmented worms found mainly in water and swampy
areas (remember *The African Queen?*). They have suckers on
each end of their bodies, and each of those suckers has hundreds
of tiny teeth. Leeches attach themselves to animals and humans,
chomp down, then suck out up to ten times their own body
weight in blood.

At least as far back as ancient Egypt, doctors used these rather
repulsive parasites to heal their patients. Physicians noticed that
taking blood from a sick person, a procedure called a "phle-
botomy," often made a fever go down (though they couldn't tell
you why). By Napoleonic times, leeches were used—without
much justification—to cure everything from aches and pains to
mental illness. As medicine became more hygienic, leeches were
dumped into history's trash can as an antiquated medical mistake.

LEECHES MAKE A COMEBACK

It has now been discovered that microsurgeons can reattach
severed body parts with the help of leeches. When an
appendage—like, say, a finger—is reattached, sutures can
reconnect severed arteries, but damaged veins are harder to
repair because they have thinner walls. As blood clots and
stagnates, the finger turns blue and tissue dies.

A leech placed on damaged veins releases a pharmaceutical cocktail containing painkillers that anesthetize the wound, natural disinfectants to prevent infection, an anticoagulant (hirudin) that keeps the blood from clotting, and a vasodilator that makes blood vessels open. All these chemicals exist, of course, to help blood flow so that the leech can have a good meal. But the chemicals also help the patient by opening blood flow in damaged veins.

FLYING IN THE FACE OF HYGIENE

The fly's four stages of life are egg, larva (also called "maggot" or "grub"), pupa, and finally, fly. And what could be more repulsive than a black, smelly wound swarming with flies and maggots? A black, smelly wound *without* them. Observant physicians like Napoleon's battlefield surgeon, Baron D. J. Larrey, noted that wounds filled with maggots healed better than clean wounds kept free of flies. But modern medicine wasn't paying attention; it was moving in the direction of cleanliness and antibiotics like penicillin. So those repulsive maggots were left behind—until now.

TAKE TWO MAGGOTS AND CALL ME IN THE A.M.

Dr. Ronald Sherman, at the University of California, Irvine Medical Center, has seen maggots cure cases that seemed hopeless. When surgeons were about to amputate a diabetic patient's gangrenous leg, Dr. Sherman decided to try maggot therapy first. He sewed sterilized blowfly maggots into the wound and sealed it with glue and gauze. The maggots weren't quite a millimeter long when they entered the wound, but they came out two to three days later (yikes!) five to ten times larger. They'd feasted on the leg's dead and infected tissue while excreting a natural, ammonia-like disinfectant that protected the healthy tissue. The patient's gangrene healed, and the leg was saved.

DOCS GO BUGGY

Doctors are using maggots to treat problems like bedsores, leg ulcers, and surgical wounds that won't heal. It turns out that maggot therapy heals wounds with minimal scarring, at low cost, and with no anesthesia required. And there seem to be no side effects—except for a certain (shudder) creepy feeling.

So, after centuries of taking the bugs out of medicine, modern physicians are putting them back in.

Citronella irritates a mosquito's feet.

KNOW YOUR PLACE

A quick tour of the Linnaean classification system.
Oh, come on! It'll be fun.

Calling all *Homo sapiens*, and yes, that means you. It's just a name scientists use to describe the human animal. Do you know why you're called a *Homo sapiens*? It's because in the mid-1700s, a Swedish botanist named Carl von Linné (also known by his Latinized name, Carolus Linnaeus) came up with a useful scientific classification system to tell his favorite flower species apart. That's how it all began.

YOU CAN'T BEAT THE SYSTEM

Linné's system eventually shoved every living thing into classification levels (or "taxa," as scientists like to call them) of varying sizes: From kingdoms, which originally separated the plants from the animals, all the way down to species, the smallest box of all, containing a single type of flower, fox, whale, human, or whatever. Humans fit into the box labeled "Homo sapiens"—that's "wise person" in Latin, a rather optimistic assessment of the human race, but you can't blame scientists for being hopeful.

IF IT'S BROKE, FIX IT

Since the 1700s, of course, there've been a few changes to the original setup, as biologists learned more about how life evolved and how the species that are alive today are related to each other. But the basic skeleton is intact and allows scientists to more or less accurately place every species into its own cozy spot in the biosphere.

So where do humans fit into this grand classification system? Let's take a tour of the order of things and see where we end up. We'll start at the top and work our way down.

THE GRAND TOUR

Domain: Domains? What about kingdoms? Aren't kingdoms the top level of the classification system of life? Not anymore—because "life" isn't just about plants and animals, you know. Nowadays many scientists recognize another level of life called the domain. There are three domains: Bacteria, Archaea, and Eukarya. You've heard of Bacteria—they're the single-celled creepies that

Scientists believe that a new star is born every 18 days.

cause a number of diseases in humans (although a few bacteria are good for us, too); Archaea are also single-celled things, most of which live in places where no other life can be found, like in hot springs or alkaline lakes. Humans belong to the domain Eukarya, as do most things we typically think of as "life": plants, animals, fungi, and so on.

Kingdom: Did you think there were only two kingdoms: animal and plants? Surprise! Meet the breakaway kingdoms of Fungi (mushrooms, toadstools) and Protista (various algae). They're not quite plants, not quite animals, and frankly, they were just bringing down the property values in those kingdoms anyway.

Also note that the kingdom Animalia has a new name as well: Metazoa—a "metazoan" being a multicellular animal with organs (which, barring an unfortunate industrial accident, describes you). Don't worry, you can still call it the animal kingdom in casual conversation. Plants are still plants, so far as we know. Ever wonder how we tell the animals from the plants (and fungi and protista)? One word: collagen. Really. We have it, they don't. So it's not just for plumping up wrinkly lips after all!

Phylum: Got a nerve cord? No, don't take it out; we believe you. Congratulations, you're in Chordata, one of the 35 or so phyla in the animal (or Metazoa) kingdom. Phyla are the most basic step of categorization after kingdom, sorting out life by gross evolutionary characteristics. In addition to the chordates, other major animal phyla include Echinodermata (starfish, sea urchins), Arthropoda (crabs, insects), Mollusca (clams, snails), and Annelida (segmented worms). In addition to being chordates, humans are also vertebrates, a rather exclusive subphylum open only to those creatures with spines and skulls. Spine but no skull? Take a hike, pal. Go whine to the Cephalachordates. Maybe they'll let you in.

Class: Within the vertebrate subphylum reside seven classes of animals, which are largely the creatures we think of when we imagine the word "animal." Of these, three classes are fish: Agnatha (jawless fish, like lampreys), Chondrichthyes (sharks and other fish with cartilage instead of bone), and Osteichthyes (fish with bones). Then come the landlubbers: Amphibia (frogs, toads, newts), Reptilia (snakes, lizards, dinosaurs), Aves (birds), and our class, Mammalia (mammals). Birds and mammals are notable for having self-regulating metabolisms (which is a fancy way of saying we're warm-blooded); mammals also have hair and mammary glands (stop that snickering).

Like phyla, classes can be further subdivided. Humans, for example, are part of the mammalian subclass Theria, which includes marsupials and placental mammals, and then also of the infraclass Eutheria, in which those lousy marsupials are given the boot and only the placental mammals remain. Go placentals!

Order: Here's where we start parting out the mammals into broad categories, and you'll find you're familiar with some of these orders right off the bat (bats being of the order Chiroptera, of course). Mice, rats, and squirrels: order Rodentia. Deer, sheep, cows: order Artiodactyla. Lions, tigers, and bears (oh my!): order Carnivora. Rabbits, commonly thought to be rodents, are actually in their own order, Lagomorpha. Horses also have their own order, Perissodactyla.

Humans belong to order Primata, the primates, which we share with lemurs, lorises (small Asian prosimians with big eyes), monkeys, gorillas, and chimpanzees, all of which share our opposable thumbs and forward-looking eyes, for an unbeatable combination of visual depth perception and grabbiness.

Any suborders? There sure are. Humans ditch the lemurs and lorises to hang with the chimps, gorillas, and monkeys in the suborder Anthropoidea, and we further lose some of the monkeys by joining the infraorder Catarrhini.

Family: Sure, if by family you mean family Hominidae. Hominidae are better known for things they lack than the things they have. For example, they lack tails, broad incisors, and fangs. On the other hand, we all also have relatively big brains, complex social structures, and nests (humans call their nests "real estate"). Humans share this family with chimpanzees, gorillas, and orangutans. It's worth noting that until fairly recently, man was all alone in Hominidae, with chimps, gorillas, and orangutans in their own family, Pongidae. But scientists eventually suggested we all belonged in the same family. Think of it as the original family reunion; just don't ask what the chimps put in the potato salad.

Genus: Humans are all alone in their genus of *Homo*, which is known for its big brain and head relative to other primates, its upright stature, and its ability to walk on two legs all the time. But don't get emotional about it—today's humans weren't the only members of genus *Homo* that ever existed. The first man was

Homo habilis (whose name translates to "handyman"), who was playing with tools on the African savanna 2.5 million years ago. After him came *Homo erectus* (stop that!) 1.8 million years ago. Both of these variations of man died out hundreds of thousands of years ago, however, leaving their descendants—us—to carry on the whole human franchise.

Species: *Homo sapiens* (that's us) showed up about 300,000 years ago and are identifiable by their use of complex tools (spears, hoes, computers), the invention of agriculture and shampoo, and the ability to amuse themselves by staring dazedly into a noisy box of electrons during the prime-time hours. Modern man is actually a subspecies of *Homo sapiens*, known as *Homo sapiens sapiens* ("wise wise person," and how's that for being both smug and redundant), who arrived on the scene about 100,000 years ago and have since transformed the world. Remember, however, that it took us 95 percent of that time to figure out how to put a seed in the ground and then have the patience to watch it grow. So don't get too cocky.

HOMO SAPIENS SEEKS SAME

So, to review, you are *Homo sapiens*. But your full taxonomic classification is Eukarya Metazoa Chordata Mammalia Primata Hominidae *Homo sapiens sapiens* [your name here]. Try putting that in a personal ad. Or better yet, memorize it and recite it to a biologist. You'll make a friend for life.

* * * * *

MNEAT MNEMONICS

The Taxonomic Classification for Humans
Eukarya, Metazoa, Chordata, Mammalia, Primata, Hominidae, Homo Sapiens
• Exotic Malaises Can Make People Hate Helping the Sick.

The Biological Groupings Used in Taxonomy
Domain, Kingdom, Phylum, Class, Order, Family, Genus, Species
• Danish Kings Possess Crowns of Fine Gem Stones.
• Dandy King Phillip Came Over for Gene's Special Variety.
• Delighted Kings Play Cards On Fairly Good Soft Velvet.
• Drunken Kings Play Cards On Fat Girls' Stomachs.
• Destructive King Phillip Cuts Open Five Green Snakes.
• Dolphins, Kingfish, Pickerel, Catfish Over-Flowed God's Seas.

The face and head are covered with over 50 small muscles.

KICK-STARTING THE HORSE

How the eohippus *got its start on the long road to horsehood.*

The horse didn't spring full-grown out of the Marlboro Man's head, you know. First there was *eohippus*, meaning "dawn horse." But it was far from the long-legged beast of today.

CHANGING HORSES

Eohippus looked like a horse, but it was two feet (60 cm) long and eight or nine inches (20–23 cm) high at the shoulder—about the size of a beagle. It had four hoofed toes on the front feet, three hoofed toes on each hind foot, and a long skull with 44 teeth. It lived about 50 to 60 million years ago in the Northern Hemisphere during the early Eocene epoch. So there it was, living in the forest, contentedly munching leaves from bushes. Eventually the earth's forests started to shrink and grasslands started to spread. So some of our evolving horses wandered out into the open and started to eat all that grass.

HORSE-FEED

But plants evolve to survive, too, so some of them got harder to eat. Over the next few million years, horses and grasses were locked into an arms race that changed them both.

For instance, endangered "lallang" grasses started including silica—jagged grains of sand—in their leaves. That wore down the horses' teeth, so some of them died off. The horses that had bigger teeth with thicker enamel lived long enough to reproduce. And their offspring developed longer faces with stronger jaws to make even better use of those big, efficient teeth.

RIDING THE OL' PRAIRIE

And you're thinking, but they're still so short! Oh, no. The whole time they were battling the grass—they were out on the wide-open grasslands, remember—they could easily be seen by predators. So they entered into speed races to survive. Each new species was longer-legged, faster, and stronger—and had fewer toes, until they got down to the one toe per hoof of modern horses.

Skin cells live 19 to 34 days.

YOU KNOW THE OLD SAYING

Uncle John debunks a few famous—but overworked— sayings about the animal world

You've heard the saying "sly as a fox." Well, as it turns out, foxes are pretty cunning, based mostly on their well-developed senses of sight, smell, and hearing. But if you believe these other notions, you'll be led astray.

If you want to be thin, eat like a bird.
Birds have a high metabolic rate and must consume more food in proportion to their size than most animals. A warbler might eat 80 percent of its body weight in a day. A hummingbird has to eat constantly or it will die of starvation in a matter of hours. If you want to be thin, it's better to eat like a mayfly: Their mouths aren't fully developed, so they can't feed.

Take care of your vision, or you'll go blind as a bat.
Bats aren't blind, and most species of bats can see very well, thank you. But bats that hunt tiny insects at night don't rely on their vision. Instead they use a system called "echolocation." The bat emits high-frequency sound pulses that strike nearby objects and send "echoes" back to the bat, which it then uses to locate objects and navigate through the dark.

When humans get overheated, they can sweat like a pig.
Pigs have no sweat glands and are unable to sweat; instead, they wallow in mud to cool down. Their mucky appearance gives pigs a reputation for slovenliness. Actually, pigs are some of the cleanest animals around. If given a choice, they refuse to excrete anywhere near their living or eating areas.

If you're really brawny, you're strong as a horse.
Horses have fragile legs and feet for their weight and size. This can make them prone to injury and lameness. If you've ever seen an ox at work, you'll know that "strong as an ox" is much more appropriate.

Sweat produces enough nutrition to feed 65,000 bacteria per square inch of the human body.

When you're feeling good, you're happy as a clam.
As you may have guessed, it's hard to tell when a clam is happy.
The full saying is: "as happy as a clam at high tide." The idea is
that clams are happy at high tide because folks collect them at low
tide. Unfortunately, the clam probably isn't very happy for long
because it's also preyed upon by green crabs, starfish, seabirds, fish,
whelks, and lobsters. With all those predators going after it, you
have to pity the poor, unhappy clam.

Gone 'round the bend? You're as crazy as a loon.
Common loons are shy, solitary water birds. They're beautiful, a
symbol of the North American wilderness—and perfectly sane.
The idea of being crazy as a loon comes from the loon's "tremolo"
call that can heard for miles across the water. The tremolo, which
sounds like a strange (some call it crazy) laugh, can be used to
greet another loon or to signal worry or alarm.

**Don't bother trying to change someone: You can't teach an old
dog new tricks.**
Oh, yes you can. Dogs can learn tricks at any age. If they're smart
enough. Often it's breed, rather than age, that helps a dog learn.
Border Collies, poodles, German Shepherds, and golden retrievers
are said to learn tricks the fastest with the least repetition.

People who pretend to be sad are crying crocodile tears.
The belief that crocodiles wept over their victims before they ate
them dates back to at least the 13th century. Though crocodiles
do have lachrymal (tear) glands, if a croc sheds tears it has nothing to do with phony sadness or remorse, it's because he's been out
of the water long enough for his eyes to need moistening.

**People who ignore things are taking the "ostrich defense" by
burying their heads in the sand.**
At up to 8 feet (2.4 m) tall and 300 pounds (136 kg), the ostrich
has a fine defense against danger that has nothing to do with sand.
Fast enough to easily run away from most predators, the ostrich
also fights them off with nasty kicks from its strong legs and
clawed toes. The idea of the ostrich burying its head may have
come from the fact that when the female is sitting on her eggs,
she'll stretch her head along the ground when danger
approaches—supposedly in an attempt to camouflage herself as a
grassy mound or bush. Also, male ostriches use their bills to dig

A fish's age is determined by its scales, which have growth rings like trees.

shallow nests in the sand and move their eggs around, which might look like the male is sticking his head in the sand.

A brave and noble person is lion-hearted—like the noble King of Beasts.

The King of Beasts is actually something of a bum. The lion's mighty roar is used to scare game in the direction of his mate, who is the real hunter. While the King of Beasts sits around looking brave and noble, it's actually the females in the pride who hunt for food and care for the young. The Lord of the Nap is a better name for him, since the King can snooze for up to 20 hours a day.

* * * * *

THE SURVIVOR

Cockroaches are ugly—flat and oval with long antennae, but they're really only harmful to people with allergies. Most of them range in length from a half inch to more than three inches (8 cm). The biggest cockroach in the world (at about four inches [10 cm]) does not (thankfully!) live in North America. It lives in tropical Madagascar and hisses like a snake in an effort to scare predators. This cockroach is called—you could maybe guess—the Giant Hissing Cockroach.

The most common cockroach in North America is the American cockroach. This black or brown insect is usually no longer than two inches (5 cm). (But it's still a cockroach.)

Most of the breed are scavengers and like to eat decaying plants and animals. The North American variety usually live under rotting logs and vegetation, but a few kinds find their way indoors, where they come out at night (they're repelled by light) to rummage through garbage and unsealed food in kitchen cupboards.

And if you think you can get rid of them permanently, think again. Cockroach fossils have been dated at 55 million years before the dinosaurs. They're survivors.

MYTH EARTH

*Thought you knew everything about our
home planet? These items might surprise you as they
debunk some common myth-conceptions!*

Myth: Mt. Everest is the earth's tallest mountain.
Fact: If you measure from the very bottom of the mountain to its peak, the world's tallest peak is Mauna Koa on the island of Hawaii. It rises 13,784 feet (4,201 m) above sea level, straight from the bottom of the sea. Of course the mountain would seem a lot taller if you could see all of it. But even though 18,000 feet (5,486 m) of the mountain is under the ocean, from its base to its height, Mauna Koa is over 31,000 feet (9,448 m) high. Mt. Everest's peak is a paltry 29,000 feet (8,839 m) high—above sea level.

Myth: The wettest spot on earth is located in the South American rain forest. (That's why they call it the rain forest.)
Fact: Hawaii scores again. The wettest spot is on Mt. Waialeale on the island of Kauai. Waialeale is consistently drenched by rainfall at the rate of nearly 500 inches (1,270 cm) per year.

Myth: The driest spot on earth is in the Saharan desert.
Fact: The driest place on earth is in Chile. It's so dry in Calama, Chile, that 400 years went by without rain; the only source of moisture was the fog in the air. (A torrential rainstorm broke the 400-year dry spell in 1972, but the record remains intact.)

Myth: The Andes is the longest mountain range in the world.
Fact: Actually, the longest mountain range is underwater—in the Atlantic Ocean to be exact. The Mid-Atlantic Ridge runs 10,000 miles (16,093 km), all the way from Iceland to Antarctica.

Myth: There's a hell of a lot of sand at the bottom of the sea.
Fact: The ocean floor is mostly made of basalt rock, formed by the lava spewed up from chains of underwater volcanoes along the midocean ridges.

Myth: Most of the world's plant life is in the dense jungles of Africa and South America.
Fact: The vast majority—85 percent, in fact—of the world's greenery is in the oceans.

The Pacific Ocean comprises 46% of the Earth's water area.

LIGHTS FROM THE DEEP

Strange things are happening thousands of feet below the surface of our oceans. Take a deep breath and come on down.

Thousands and thousands of feet below the ocean waves is a land without light. This strange, dark kingdom is inhabited only by sea creatures who have either evolved to live in utter darkness or who have evolved cunning ways to produce their own light. Down here in the dark, nothing grows and few creatures live, with eternal darkness their lot from birth to death.

But wait a minute.

THE LIGHT AT THE END OF THE AIR-HOSE

That was what scientists always believed, that the deepest parts of the oceans were black as pitch. That is, until 1988, when a source of light was discovered at the bottom of the sea floor—a light that nourishes its own utterly unique forms of life—and possibly even gives us the first example of photosynthesis that doesn't stem from the sun's rays. The discovery has positively *cosmic* implications. If life can flourish around this odd underwater light, why wouldn't it be able to proliferate in equally hostile locations elsewhere?

A SHRIMP TELLS ALL

The lights were discovered by a University of Alaska marine biologist who only intended to study a species of shrimp, *Rimicaris exoculata*. The shrimp was not only blind, but also didn't have any vision organs. It spent its life swimming around its own neighborhood: the warm hydrothermal vents on the mid-Atlantic range of underwater volcanic ridges.

IN HOT WATER

The ridges, formed when edges of the earth's crust pull apart and allow hot magma to seep in between, have small vents that spew volcanically heated liquid. The toxic liquid is as hot as 662°F (350°C), and contains a lot of heavy metal and poisonous compounds. Surrounding that incredibly hot water is intensely cold water just above freezing, with water pressure that would instantly crush a land-dwelling creature. Doesn't sound like much of a homestead to us, but the shrimp seemed to enjoy it.

The biggest snowflake ever reported measured 15 inches across.

A HOT MEAL

Scientists think that the shrimp feed on bacteria that themselves feed on the sulfur compounds in the vent water. But to get at the bacteria, the shrimp have to get awfully close to that superhot vent liquid. If you can cook 'em on the stove, imagine what 662°F (350°C) water could do. How was it the shrimp were staying close enough to the plumes of heat to nibble on bacteria, but at the same time staying far away enough to avoid getting cooked?

EYES IN THE BACK OF ITS SHELL

University of Alaska scientist Cindy Lee Van Dover found one possible reason. After careful study of the exoculata (which means "no eyes") shrimp, her team found that the animal actually did have visual organs, but they were on the back of its shell instead of on its head. And if it did have "eyes," just what exactly did it need them for? Down in the dark ocean there was no light to see. Or was there? Van Dover and a few other scientists began to suspect there was some primitive form of light emerging from the hydrothermal vents. Finally they confirmed it with underwater digital pictures.

ALL AGLOW

The discovery flew in the face of accepted scientific knowledge of the underwater depths. Scientists still aren't sure exactly what causes the haunting glow, but published reports by Van Dover and other scientists suggest four main theories:

- Crystalloluminescence: The chemical brew emitted by the vents spews out at 662°F (350°C) and comes into contact with sea water (at a much colder 36°F [2°C]). As they clash, dissolved minerals in the hot water crystallize and become too heavy for the solution. The energy produced by the crystallization and the "dropping out" of the liquid solution produces light.
- Chemiluminescence: In a reaction similar to crystallolumines-cence, chemical reactions in the vent water release energy in light form.
- Triboluminescence: Mineral crystals in the hot liquid emanate from the vent crack in the cold or bang together to produce light.
- Sonoluminescence: Microscopic bubbles collapse in the hot fluid, emitting a glow.

The Great Barrier Reef is the world's longest reef at 1,250 miles (2,012 km).

GENESIS?

Even though they can't yet pin down the cause of the light, some scientists are becoming curious about what the light means.

One of the great scientific mysteries is our own evolution. How did we come to be here at all? How did the magnificent human brain evolve from a soup of microbes and gases? And perhaps most puzzling, how did we evolve over millions of years as vast asteroids hit the earth and Ice Ages advanced and retreated? Recent evolutionary biology research suggests that hyperthermophiles (microbes that thrive at high temperatures) are ancestral to all organisms alive on the earth today. Could we have evolved from such watery environments?

COSMIC QUESTIONS

The deep-sea light's surprising strength also raises questions surrounding photosynthesis. Do the bacteria that lives nearby, the bacteria on which the shrimp feed, use the light for photosynthesis? Could the lights emanating from the thermal vents actually spark photosynthesis that has nothing to do with the sun's rays? And if it does, does that open up the possibility of life in other environments far from Earth's sun?

Stay tuned.

* * * * *

YOU WOULD THINK...

That water pollution wouldn't be a problem, since the natural water cycle purifies all the water on earth. That's the hydrologic cycle, nature's ongoing way of purifying water. (Did you know that the water we use today is the same water the human race started with? The next glass of water you drink may have once helped fill Cleopatra's bathtub.) The water cycle works thusly. The Sun turns water into vapor, which rises, and when it cools it forms clouds that become heavy with water and rain back to earth—all squeaky clean and purified. But when fossil fuels like coal are burned, releasing sulfur dioxide into the atmosphere, and car exhausts contribute nitrous oxide, the two oxides combine to create sulfuric acid and nitrous acid, which fall back to earth as acid rain, which joins the rest of the earth's water as part of the hydrologic cycle.

The brain uses 20% of the body's total blood supply.

EL NIÑO, A BAD BOY

Naughty little boys get blamed for lots of troubles: spills, broken windows, fires, floods, storms, cholera epidemics...Well, maybe not all little boys.

The weather phenomenon they call El Niño means "the boy," but it wasn't named for a brat. Fishermen off the Peruvian coast noticed a warm current in the ocean that appeared right after Christmas every year, so they named it after the baby Jesus. If they'd known the kind of trouble the kid could get into, they might have called it something else.

A BOUNCING BABY BOY

El Niños are born when the surface of the Pacific Ocean, starting near the equator, gets warmer (no one knows why it happens—it just does). The warm air rises and causes the trade winds, which normally blow to the west, to subside and sometimes even change direction. Weather-wise, all hell breaks loose.

WAIT TILL YOUR FATHER GETS HOME!

In most places, the weather flip-flops. Normally dry areas in both North and South America get drenched with rain and snow; months later the snow melts, which means floods and mudslides that can destroy crops. In poorer countries flooding can lead to the destruction of sewage systems and cholera outbreaks.

Tropical islands like Indonesia and the Philippines get hit with drought; Australia, India, and China get less rain, too. Meanwhile, Hawaii gets more dangerous typhoons and the Atlantic gets fewer hurricanes. In North America, El Niño winters are warm and the springtimes are wetter.

THE BABY-SITTER'S REPORT

Researchers have been keeping an eye on El Niños for 300 years. The usual pattern calls for an El Niño every three to seven years, but for some reason there are more El Niños than ever, most recently in 1986, 1991, 1993, 1994, 1997, and 2002. Science is getting better at predicting them, so that farmers can get a heads-up on the best crops to plant, and everyone in general can get a head start on managing water or stockpiling resources when they know El Niño is coming over to their house for a visit.

History's deadliest cyclone was in 1970 in the Bay of Bengal and killed 30,000 people.

SO YOU THINK YOU'VE SEEN A UFO

A checklist to use before you tell all your buddies at the bar.

Everybody loves a good UFO story. What's not to love? Strange moving lights in the sky, alien abductions, cow dissections, and of course, those famous probings of the human anatomy that aliens just can't seem to get enough of.

Besides, even former President Jimmy Carter has filed a UFO report (in 1973—before he was president, mind you). So seeing a UFO doesn't automatically make you a deranged paranoid who hates *X-Files* reruns because they don't go far enough. You could just be a normal person with an extraordinary experience to share. One that doesn't involve a probe of some sort.

THE CHECKLIST

Well, before you start telling all your friends about your close encounter, keep the following in mind. Because while we would never say you didn't see a UFO, we also want to keep you from enduring a lifetime of mockery from less open-minded "friends."

1. Make sure it's not Venus: Yes, Venus is a famous culprit in many UFO sightings, because it's bright and unblinking and because it can be seen while it's still light out (and, apparently, many people think that a bright, unblinking light just hanging there in the sky while it's still light has just got to be a UFO). Now, you might say to yourself, "Who the heck can't tell the difference between a UFO and a planet millions of miles away?" Well, Jimmy Carter, for one; an examination of the details of the UFO observation he and others made on the night in question rather strongly suggests that the 39th prez was looking at Venus. Jupiter, which can get almost as bright as Venus, is another common planetary UFO culprit.

2. Make sure it's not a meteor: Most meteors streak across the sky and are done with it, but some larger ones can become fireballs and zoom across the sky for a good long time, trailing smoke and sparks behind them and even exploding in midair (when they do that, it's called a "bolis"). Fireballs and bolises can be seen during the day as well, so don't let that fool you.

3. Make sure it's not falling space junk, either: Booster rockets, communications satellites, abandoned space stations—sooner or later they all fall back to earth. Don't be the one that confuses them for aliens making a U-turn on their way back to deep space. Also, be aware that man-made satellites that aren't falling are often mistaken for UFOs because they're bright, starlike objects that cruise across the sky at a good clip.

4. Make sure it's not a cloud: No, we're not trying to insult your intelligence. Certain types of altocumulus clouds take on the traditional "flying saucer" shape and do such a good job of it that people get fooled.

5. Weather balloons are out there: They're released every day all across the U.S.; they're bright and shiny, and they float up tremendously high in the sky (well into the stratosphere), pretty much where you'd suspect there's no man-made object at all. They also make "course changes" depending on the winds up there.

6. Military aircraft can get you: Sure, most people know what a commercial aircraft looks like. But lots of people were fooled in the early days of the SR-71 spy plane, especially when the pilot of said plane did a maneuver called the "Dipsy Doodle," which to a ground observer looks like a UFO diving, hovering for a second, and then taking off at tremendous speeds. More recently, various "stealth" planes have frightened the credulous with their unconventional shapes.

7. Electrical discharges happen: This is the famous "swamp gas" and "St. Elmo's Fire," in which strange but perfectly natural balls of ionized particles bounce and glow and make some people think they're being chased by them crazy ETs. Electrical discharges near high-power lines and power stations have also been known to get a UFO label slapped on them.

8. Your eyes see more than what's there: Here's a dirty little fact about human eyesight—it's not as reliable as people think it is. Involuntary eye movements can make objects that are perfectly

---

Earth's 15 tectonic plates move one inch a year, about the same rate that fingernails grow.

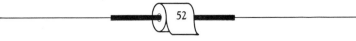

still appear to jerk around in the night sky (this is one of the reasons Venus is so frequently confused for a UFO when it's just sitting there).

Human eyes will also embellish briefly seen objects with details that aren't actually there: People reporting UFOs that turn out to be reentering space junk will often report blinking lights, windows, and purposeful movement, when none of those things were part of the falling debris. This tendency will likely be accentuated if (ahem) you're under the influence of anything.

9. Get Independent Third-Party Verification: One of the really big problems with so many UFO sightings is that no one else is around to see them. Your UFO experience will be much more believable if someone else is experiencing it as well, preferably someone you don't know. There's nothing like having a total stranger come up to you and say, "Did you just see what I just saw?" It won't mean that what you saw is any more a true UFO than it would otherwise be (please review points 1 through 8). But at least you'll have some backup when you go to the bar to tell your friends.

* * * * *

Mnemonics for the spectral classes of stars, hottest to coldest:
O B A F G K M R N S
The astronomer who first classified them in alphabetical order didn't really know what he was doing, so later astronomers had to switch them around, but they kept the letters. That's why the list looks like a spoonful of alphabet soup. So:
- Oh Be A Fine Girl Kiss Me Right Now, Sweetheart.
- Octopus Brains, A Favorite Gastronomical Kitchen Menu, Requires No Sauce.
- Odd Ball Astronomers Find Generally Kooky Mnemonics Really Nifty Stuff.
- Oh Big And Ferocious Gorilla, Kiss My Roommate Next Saturday.
- Oven Baked Ants, Fried Gently, Kept Moist, Retain Natural Succulence.

The elephant is the only mammal with four knees.

TIME TRAVEL MOVIE MARATHON!

Got some time? Here's at least a day's worth of time travel flicks.

Hollywood loves time travel—they're always punting people forward in time or backward in time, or just plopping them into a feedback loop where they relive the same day over and over and over again. Even though time travel is scientifically impossible (sorry to disappoint), it doesn't keep people from making or going to movies about it.

Army of Darkness: Technically the third part of director Sam Raimi's *Evil Dead* series, but it's not like you need a road map for this plot, which features a one-handed discount store salesman (the impossibly lantern-jawed Bruce Campbell) hurled back into the Middle Ages to fight zombies and skeletons and a creepy, man-eating flying book. It's kind of dumb, but all horror freaks love it (and you know how high *their* standards are). It's pretty funny, in a stupid comic-book way. Besides, any movie in which a minimum-wage earner from the future can condescendingly call a castle full of medieval types a bunch of "monkeys" can't be all bad.

Back to the Future: Michael J. Fox goes back to the 1950s and is called "Calvin" because that's the name sewn into his underwear (Calvin Klein underwear—can't believe we need to explain this). The film's still funny in its own right (especially with freaky Crispin Glover as Fox's loser dad), but now it's like two time travel movies in one. First you get the 1950s, which Fox goes back to, then you get the 1980s, which is the "present" for the film. It's enough to give you a shiver (look for the Huey Lewis cameo). There were two more *Back to the Future* films, but unless you've got a thing for Michael J., you needn't bother.

Groundhog Day: Bill Murray goes back in time—exactly one day, over and over again. In the process he turns from obnoxious twit to the perfect man (or at least the perfect man for Andie MacDowell, and who *wouldn't* want to be that man?). It's a fine, fine film, and in addition to being funny, it's actually sweet and even a little serious, and it proved that Murray was a little better of an actor than anyone gave him credit for before. But let's not kid ourselves: If *you* had to live Groundhog Day over and over again, you'd become a little zen yourself to keep from going utterly freakin' insane.

Planet of the Apes: Charlton Heston lands on what he thinks is an alien planet and finds it populated by talking apes who think he's a savage (mind you, this was *before* he became the NRA's alpha male). Ol' Charlie is awesome in this—he grunts, he snarls, he chews scenery like a silverback confronted with a particularly choice bunch of bananas ("Get your stinking paws off me, you damned dirty ape!"). They remade this one recently, but the new version is—how do the French say? Ah yes—un *lame-o stinkeroo*. Stick with Charlie, baby.

Sleeper: This is the movie people are thinking of when they say they liked Woody Allen's movies when he was funny. Freakily enough, many of the wacky things Allen posited about the future in this movie have already come true, like robotic pets and TV with millions of channels. We still don't have an orgasmatron, alas. Something yet to look forward to.

Star Trek IV: The Voyage Home and ***Star Trek: First Contact:*** The crews of the various *Star Trek* series travel in time so much and with such blatant disregard for the Prime Directive that it's entirely possible that Jean-Luc Picard is in your shower stall *right this very instant*. For all that, the two best *Star Trek* movies rely on time travel as plot points: In *Star Trek IV*, the original crew saves the universe by saving the whales, and that means going back to 1980s San Francisco to find some. This features some nice moments with Spock being taken for a hippie burnout, and Kirk being taken for a fatuous windbag (oh—*right*). *First Contact* has Picard's crew going back in time (but still to our future) to keep the evil Borg from assimilating humanity. There are some good action scenes and a disturbingly sexy Borg Queen (Alice Krige) who wants to assimilate (heh heh heh) Data, the friendly android. Speaking of going where no man's gone before.

The *Terminator* Series: The film series that turned Arnold Schwarzenegger's inability to act human into a good thing. In the first film (*The Terminator*), Ah-nold is a killing robot sent from the future to ventilate hapless waitress Sarah Connor (Linda Hamilton); in the second one (*T2*) Arnie helps the now-buff-but-a-bit-insane Sarah battle an advanced shape-shifting Terminator model. The first one was made for roughly the same amount of money it took to cater the second film, but both are superior examples of the action genre, with smart scripting and well-designed mayhem.

Time Bandits: Thieving dwarves steal a map from God and blitz through history causing havoc. This one plays like a Monty Python time-travel film (right down to the distinctly nasty-yet-funny ending: "Mom! Dad! Don't touch that! It's *evil!*"), and there's a good reason for that: It's directed by Python Terry Gilliam and features several of his Monty mates, as well as Sean Connery as Agamemnon (presumably before he left for Troy, since when he got back, he was murdered by his wife. Hey, it's ancient Greece). Kind of freaky, but a real visual feast, and a lot smarter than most.

The Time Machine: Well, duh. How can you *not* include this one? Or these two, actually, since you have your choice: the classic 1960 George Pal version, with Rod Taylor as H. G. Wells, traveling far into the future to find humans divided between the twee, pale Eloi and the brutish, cannibalistic Morlocks, or the 2002 version that features Guy Pearce and a lot of really expensive-looking special effects. (Fun fact: The 2002 version is directed by Simon Wells, H. G. Wells's distant relative.) Neither version quite picks up that the novel *The Time Machine* was a socialist allegory about British class divisions, but, hey, like any of *that's* gonna play at the drive-in.

12 Monkeys: Hey, look, Terry Gilliam's back again, and this time he's sending Bruce Willis hurtling through history, from a depressing stink hole of a future to stop a group of bioterrorists from unleashing a plague that wipes out most of humanity. Willis is damn fine as a disoriented, slightly nutty time traveler who can't quite remember if he's sane or not, and check out Brad Pitt, who plays a cross-eyed scuzzball and ended up picking up an Oscar nomination for it. Overall, really depressing, but in a good way, not unlike Gilliam's *Brazil* or *Blade Runner* (with which this movie shares a screenwriter).

The largest gallstone ever recorded was 13 pounds.

WATT'S SO FUNNY?

How many physical chemists does it take to change a light bulb?
Only one, but he'll change it three times, plot a straight line
through the data, and then extrapolate to zero concentration.
Huh?
Stay with us—they get better.

Q: What did the nuclear physicist have for lunch?
A: Fission chips.

Never lend a geologist money—they consider a million years ago to be recent.

Q: What is an astronomical unit?
A: One helluva big apartment.

Have you heard the one about the chemist who was reading a book on helium and just couldn't put it down?

A mushroom walks into a bar and the bartender says, "Sorry. We don't serve mushrooms here."
        The mushroom replies, "Why? I'm a FUN-GI!"

Two atoms were walking down the street. One turns to the other and says,
        "Oh, no! I think I'm an ion!"
        The other says, "Are you sure?"
        "Yes, I'm positive!"

Q: What's the most important thing to learn in chemistry?
A: Never lick the spoon.

A neutron walks into a bar. "I'd like a beer," he says. The bartender promptly serves up a beer. "How much will that be?" asks the neutron.
        "For you?" replies the bartender, "No charge."

Q: What did one photon say to the other photon?
A: I'm sick and tired of your interference.

THEY CAN'T EVEN SPELL "DUH!"

Worried about your IQ? Relax.
A starfish manages to survive with no brain at all!

KWOLEK'S KEVLAR

As a Washington, D.C., police team was preparing to make a drug bust, a suspect fired a .357 pistol at Officer Gerald L. Awkard, striking him in the back. Aside from severe bruising caused by the bullet hitting his ballistic vest, Awkard was unharmed. And he had Stephanie Kwolek to thank for it.

Stephanie Louise Kwolek had been a research chemist for 18 years with the DuPont Company when, in 1964, she was asked if she could find a new high-performance fabric made of synthetic fibers that were stiffer, tougher, and more heat-resistant than anything that had yet been developed.

THE RIGHT CHEMISTRY
Kwolek knew polymers like you know the back of your hand: She'd spent most of her professional career experimenting with polymers (compounds that are made up of long chains of repeating molecules) and polymerization (the process by which polymers are made). For this project, she concentrated on liquid crystals—polymer solutions in which the molecules all line up pointing in the same direction. (In most polymers, the molecules flow pretty much in any direction they please.)

SOME STRANGE GLOP
During one of her experiments, Kwolek was carefully combining and mixing the polymers with different solvents, just as she did every day. But this day, something strange happened. Instead of turning out viscous (gooey) and clear as she expected, the mixture looked watery and cloudy, sort of like milk. Acting on a hunch, Kwolek rushed to find the person in charge of testing new polymers. He said no—it looked too alien to him—but Kwolek persisted and finally, after days of arguing, she succeeded in convincing him.

Her hunch turned out to be correct. She had just accidentally invented a brand new polymer that weighed very little, but was strong and stiff beyond anyone's imagination.

VESTED INTEREST
What Kwolek had discovered was Kevlar—the material used in the bullet-resistant vest that saved the life of Officer Awkard, as

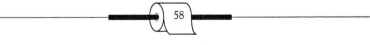

well as the lives of over 2,000 other law enforcement officers over the years.

A vest made with seven layers of Kevlar fibers weighs only 2.5 pounds (1 kg), but it can deflect a knife blade and stop a .38-caliber bullet shot from 10 feet (3 m) away.

BUY KEVLAR! IT'S GOOD FOR YOU!

Kevlar is five times stronger than the same weight of steel, doesn't rust or corrode, and is extremely lightweight. Besides bullet-resistant vests and helmets, Kevlar has been used in the production of over 200 products, ranging from fuel hoses for space vehicles and airplanes, brake pads and radial tires for automobiles, and cut-resistant butchers' and surgeons' gloves. It can also be found in sports equipment: tennis rackets, canoes, and skis. And because it's highly flame-resistant, it's also used to make clothing that protects firefighters, race-car drivers, and jet pilots.

A life-saving discovery—based on a hunch and the right chemistry.

* * * * *

IS IT TRUE THAT PEOPLE CAN GET SO FRIGHTENED THAT THEIR HAIR TURNS WHITE OVERNIGHT?

You've heard the story. Some idiot decides to spend the night alone in a haunted house. The next day he or she is found—now a blithering idiot whose hair has turned completely white. As much as we'd like to believe the yummy horror of it all, the phenomenon is probably legend and nothing more. See, hair is dead tissue and therefore can't turn white until it grows out from the roots. The myth may have its own roots in a condition called "diffuse alopecia areata," which can cause substantial hair loss, but only to pigmented hair. When it occurs in people with a mix of dark and gray/white hair, the only hair left would be the nonpigmented hair, thus giving the impression that someone's hair has turned white overnight. What gives this theory more credence is that the condition is believed to be caused by emotional stress. And what's more stressful than staying alone overnight in a haunted house?

The thickest skin is on the upper back; the thinnest is on the eyelids.

THE ELEMENTAL QUESTIONS

All the questions that you never even knew you had about the elements.

The elements: The fundamental atoms that make up everything from stars to planets to blue whales to that annoying kid down the street. You've got questions about the elements? We've got the answers. Try us.

What elements make a human being? As a child, you were told that girls were made of sugar and spice and everything nice, and that boys were made of snips and snails and puppy dog tails, but let's just say that this list of primary components was, well, a little *off*. Actually, just six elements comprise 99 percent of the mass of every boy and girl. They are (in order of weight): oxygen, carbon, hydrogen, nitrogen, calcium, and phosphorus. Coincidentally, these same elements are major players in snails, spices, sugars, and puppy dog tails. But it's not so much the ingredients, as the way they're put together.

What's the most common element on earth? Oxygen, again. It makes up nearly half the weight of the earth's crust and 62 percent of the total by sheer number of atoms. In the earth's crust, after oxygen, the most abundant elements are (in order of weight): silicon, aluminum, iron, calcium, and sodium. However, before you oxygen partisans get too smug, remind yourselves that in terms of elements in the atmosphere, it ranks a paltry second to nitrogen. Nitrogen is 78 percent of the earth's atmosphere, while oxygen is just 21 percent.

What's the most common element in the universe? Not oxygen, pal, not by a long shot. Roughly three-quarters of the universe is nothing more than hydrogen, the simplest element there is, and most of the rest of it is the only-slightly-more-complex helium. The rest of the naturally occurring elements, from lithium to uranium, make up less than one percent of the universe. Kind of makes you feel small, doesn't it?

Hey, what are some things I really shouldn't do with plutonium? What an excellent question.

1. Don't eat it. Sure, it looks tasty, but swallowing plutonium in

---

Humans possess over 600 muscles; caterpillars have over 2,000.

any appreciable amount—say, over half a gram—will kill you in nasty ways, and even smaller amounts will expose your gastrointestinal tract to heaping doses of radiation. Should it then get into your bloodstream, your liver and bones will also be liberally irradiated and you'll almost certainly get the big C.

2. Don't breathe it, either. Breathing in even a small amount of plutonium will lead to pulmonary edema, which means your lungs will leak and you'll literally drown in your own body fluids. And that's not the way you want to go. How much plutonium do you need to breathe in for this charming demise? Twenty milligrams or so should do the trick.

3. Don't pile a lot of it in one place. You only need 300 grams of plutonium (about two-thirds of a pound) for it to reach critical mass—which is to say, for it to spontaneously explode and turn your hometown into a glowing crater and you into a cloud of disassociated atoms. So keep all your plutonium in very tiny portions, all away from each other.

4. Don't get caught with any. We mean, *duh*. It's not like it's legal for you to have it anyway. Sheesh.

What elements are named for people? They are: rutherfordium (Lord Rutherford, chemist), seaborgium (Glenn Seaborg, physicist and chemist), bohrium (Niels Bohr, who described the atomic structure), meitnerium (physicist Lise Meitner), curium (named for two people, actually: Pierre and Marie Curie), einsteinium (you can guess this one), fermium (Enrico Fermi, physicist), mendelevium (Dmitri Ivanovitch Mendeleyev, who devised the periodic table), nobelium (Alfred Nobel, who invented dynamite and established the Nobel Prizes), and lawrencium (Ernest Lawrence, physicist). One other element, gadolinium, was named for a mineral that was named for chemist Johan Gadolin. Notice how all the elements are named after chemists and physicists. Yes, rock stars get the hot groupies, but scientists get the hot elements.

Can you name the one place on earth that has not one, not two, but four elements named after it? This is one to stump your friends at the next chemistry department mixer you go to. The answer: Ytterby, Sweden, which gave its name to ytterium, erbium, terbium, and ytterbium. The first three of these were found in a quarry near the town, which seems reason enough for their naming; ytterbium, however, was discovered in Switzerland by Jean de Marignac. He named the element after the town because it was a "rare earth" element, and the first rare earth elements discovered were in that quarry outside Ytterby.

Once a hurricane has done excessive damage, its name is retired from the list of future names.

What element are you least likely to find in your everyday life? That would probably be francium, the most highly unstable naturally occurring element (insert your own joke here about the most unstable element being named after France). Less than an ounce is present on the face of the earth at any one time, and none of that in any measurable amounts; it had to be discovered through the decay of actinium, another element entirely.

I have money to blow! Which element is the most expensive? Among the naturally occurring elements, protactinium is likely to be the most expensive, not just because it's rare but also because it's so hard to isolate. In 1961, the British government extracted 125 grams of the stuff from over 60 tons of material at a cost of half a million bucks; in today's money, that works out to $24,000 a gram. But don't start flashing that jewel-encrusted protactinium ring to your friends just yet: It's radioactive and highly toxic, so you probably don't want to carry it on your person.

Why is the chemical symbol for gold "Au"? There's neither an A nor a U in "gold"! Well, no, not in English. However, there is both an *a* and a *u* in *aurum*, the Latin word for gold ("gold," incidentally, comes from the Old English *geolo*, meaning "yellow"). It's just a reminder that, hey, there are other languages out there. Other elements whose chemical symbols don't match their English names include silver (Ag, from *argentum*, Latin), lead (Pb, *plumbum*, Latin), potassium (K, *kalium*, Latin), tungsten (W, *wolfram*, German), and tin (Sn, *stannum*, Latin).

What's the dumbest name for an element? Take your pick: unun-nilium, unununium, or ununbium. These names were given to recently discovered elements after chemists and physicists couldn't play nice and agree on the names these new elements ought to have. In stepped the International Union for Pure and Applied Chemistry, which devised a naming system based on the Latin names for numbers, and the atomic weight of the element. Unun-nilium, for example, has an atomic weight of 110; so, one-one-zero. The Latin word for "one" is "un," and for zero it's "nil"—therefore: un-un-nil-ium. An elegantly scientific answer to a thorny problem, at least until you try to say "Ununilium" or "Unununium." Try it. See? These scientists may be smart, but it doesn't mean their element names can't be dumb.

CINDERELEPHANT

What weighs six tons and wears glass slippers?
How Prince Charming Elephant gets his gal.

lephants live in a segregated society. Females hang out in groups with their female relatives and their children. Adult males sometimes travel with female groups, but that's only for a few days at a time. Mostly they wander alone or in the company of other males. So what happens when Cinderelephant goes into heat and Prince Charming is miles away?

BIG GIRL, SMALL WINDOW OF OPPORTUNITY
A female elephant in heat is a rare thing. It only happens once every three to nine years. And when it does, the cow (as she's called) stays in estrus for only three to six days at time. Once she's pregnant, she carries her calf for nearly two years before she delivers and nurses her little one at least two more years. During all this time, she's unavailable for mating. So when Cinderelephant is actively looking for her prince, it's a big deal.

GET OUTTA THE WAY!
The female herd can go for weeks without seeing the hide or tusk of a male. But just before one of the girls goes into heat, the bulls from miles around come charging in. And the lucky lady knows they're on their way. How does she know? Well, it isn't by smell, and it isn't because there's a definite breeding season.

SOMEDAY MY PRINCE WILL COME
Just before a cow enters estrus, she sings an intense, infrasonic (that is, a low-frequency) song that advertises her come-and-get-it condition and her position to every bull within range—the range being miles. The bulls, in turn, answer her calls with their own low-frequency songs (something by Barry White, probably). The songs tell Cinderelephant a lot about the singer's strength and condition, so even before the males arrive, the female has enough information to at least start the screening process.

Then it's up to her to choose the right man for the job.

ANCIENT ASTRONOMERS

Astronomy wasn't invented a couple of hundred years ago.
The study of the stars is almost as old as humanity itself.

The oldest and most famous cave paintings (16,000 to 20,000 years old) are in Lascaux, France. The animal and human figures in the cave were long thought to be symbols of magic or worship meant to help hunters. Eventually someone noticed that the dots of paint that decorate the animals are actually diagrams of groups of stars. Most of the constellations have different symbols today, but the giant bull (possibly the best-known image in cave art) is actually the constellation we still call Taurus—the bull. His eye is the star Aldebaran, and a V-shaped decoration of dots around it represents the Pleiades star cluster.

NOT JUST A PILE OF STONES

The first ancient monument to be identified as an astronomical observatory was England's Stonehenge. It's attracted a lot of interest from wanna-be Druids over the years, but current researchers think it was built and rebuilt by three separate cultures between 5,000 and 3,000 years ago. While it's not clear exactly what it was used for, the astronomical alignments of the stones are unquestionable. The stones mark out the sunrise at midsummer and midwinter, and the rising and setting of the moon (which repeats in a cycle of 8.6 years). Some people claim to have found many more significant alignments and have suggested that Stonehenge could have been used to predict eclipses—pretty sophisticated stuff. But did the Druids actually make these calculations? We'll probably never know, darn it.

STONEHENGE SOUTH

Just as mysterious is the recently discovered stone circle of Nabta, Egypt, which at 7,000 years old is the oldest astronomical observatory of its kind so far discovered. Like Stonehenge, it marks sunrise and sunset at midsummer, but other than that, no one knows who built it or what else it might be for. The site was abandoned after two thousand years, just before the rise of the Egyptian Old Kingdom. Did the ancient Egyptians get their astronomical knowledge from an older civilization in the Sahara?

Thunder can be heard as far as 20 miles away.

SERIOUS ABOUT SIRIUS

The star Sirius was worshiped by a whole range of ancient peoples, from the Arabs and ancient Egyptians to the West African tribes of the Dogon and the Bozo (don't laugh, they're real). The Egyptians built whole rows of temples pointing at the spot on the horizon where Sirius would rise each year. This was the beginning of their calendar year and marked the flooding of the Nile. For them, Sirius was the resting place of the dead and the most important star in the sky.

THE INVISIBLE SUPERSTAR

Among the Arabs and some tribes in Mali, there was a belief that Sirius had a companion, which the tribesmen called the Eye Star, and which was supposed to have supernatural qualities. Sirius really does have a companion: a small white dwarf called Sirius B, which is not visible to the naked eye. So how did these primitive people know about it? The Dogon have precise astronomical information about its movements, which they celebrate with rituals, even though they admit that it's invisible. (We don't know about you, but we've got chills.) They even had a story about a third star, the Star of Women, which was also invisible. And guess what? In 1995 it was discovered that there really is a third star, a red dwarf that's been named Sirius C.

PYRAMID SCHEME

Because questions remain about the alignment of ancient monuments, the field is wide open for speculation. New Agers (who speculate wildly at least three times before breakfast) will tell you that the Egyptian pyramids are time machines, UFO bases, or gates to other dimensions. Thank heavens (no pun intended) for the Mayans of Mexico, who left detailed written documents to explain the astronomy behind the construction of their pyramids. It turns out that the Mayans had a highly developed calendar system, using astronomical events to fix magical dates for sacrifices and other rituals. Their pyramids were built on alignments that pointed toward the positions of the Sun, Moon, planets, and stars at these special dates. It can't be definitely proven that the Egyptian pyramids, or the similar ziggurats of ancient Mesopotamia, were built on the same kind of idea, but the astronomical alignments are similar, and so far no one has come up with a better explanation.

Tongue prints—as well as fingerprints—are unique to each person.

A FEW OF MAYAN FAVORITE THINGS

For the Mayans, the two most interesting objects in the sky were the planet Venus and the Sun. While Stonehenge and other ancient sites fixed the position of the midsummer sun at dawn, the Mayans used the moment when it was directly overhead. Venus dips below the horizon at a variable date in the year and rises about 50 days later. The Mayans were able to calculate this period, and they were also able to predict eclipses. They marked these occasions with human sacrifices and chose days to go to war by consulting their astronomical calendars.

STONEHENGE, U.S.A.

In the hills of Wyoming, there's an ancient stone construction called the Big Horn Medicine Wheel, which some have called the American Stonehenge. A similar construction is the Moose Mountain Wheel in Alberta, Canada. Both were sacred sites for local Native Americans, but archeologists date them from before the Plains Indians arrived to some unknown indigenous people.

The Big Horn wheel has been dated to A.D. 1000–1400, and Moose Mountain to about 2,000 years ago. The markers—this time neat piles of stones—pick out important events in the sky: the summer solstice and the rising of the bright stars Aldebaran, Rigel, Sirius, and Fomalhaut. There are lots of other medicine wheels and similar constructions in North America, many of which are so damaged that it's impossible to reconstruct their original alignments. But since the positions of dawn and the risings of stars have changed a little over the centuries, it's possible to date the construction of them (and all the others) by accurate scientific methods.

KEEPING AN EYE ON THE SKY

It's not surprising that great civilizations like the Egyptians and the Mayans could develop a kind of astronomy. What's amazing is that people from the Stone Age—or people still living Stone Age lifestyles—also had detailed knowledge of astronomy. Native Americans, nomads in the Sahara Desert, and even genuine cavemen were doing the math and measuring the angles. How many people today could build an astronomical observatory out of lumps of rock?

You over there. Yes, you. Wanna give it a try?

The fireworks you watch usually explode at 1,500 feet.

HOCKEY:
LET'S GET PHYSICAL

Uncle John is a rabid sports fan, but he tends to get distracted by questions like, "Why is ice so slippery?" and "Exactly how fast can a puck travel?" We've slowed down the fastest game on earth just long enough to give you a look at the science behind it.

Ice-skating is the fastest way to travel across the surface of the earth on your feet. When you run, your front foot slows you down every time it hits the ground, but when you're skating, one skate pushes and the other skate glides, so there's hardly any friction to slow you down. In fact, hockey players have been clocked at more than 20 mph (32 kph) in a rink that's just 200 feet (61 m) long.

ICE VS. ICE
Most hockey players prefer "fast ice." It's hard, cold, has a smooth surface, and it makes skating and passing easier. But over the course of a hockey period, fast ice becomes "slow ice." The ice warms up and the surface gets rougher. The puck starts to bounce a little, too, so this is when players become a little more careful— generally they'll try to make a safe play rather than a finesse play.

A-SLIPPIN' AND A-SLIDIN'
You'd think by now that scientists would have nailed down the nature of ice, but there's still some controversy. The long-held belief is that pressure or friction melts the ice and creates a water lubricant that helps skates and pucks to slide. But recent research suggests that skates and pucks don't generate enough pressure to instantly liquefy ice. Instead there's a "quasi-fluid," or waterlike, layer on top of ice that makes it slippery. Even ice that's –250°F (–121°C) or colder has this layer. At that way-below-freezing temperature, the slippery layer is only one molecule thick. As the ice warms, the number of slippery layers increases, so skaters have to slosh through even more molecules, which slows them down.

Unlike an adult, a child aged six or seven months can breathe and swallow at the same time.

HOW COLD WAS IT?

The ideal temperature for hockey is generally considered to be 16°F (–8°C). Figure skaters do best at 22°F (–5.5°C), because the six-degree difference gives them more control and makes for a softer landing.

LOVE ME, LOVE MY HOCKEY STICK

Players take a highly personal approach to their sticks; some prefer longer, straighter sticks, while some like more curve on the blade. Others like to have a different "lie" in the stick (this determines the amount of blade that comes in contact with the ice). They can spend hours preparing their sticks for a game.

Stick material is all-important, too. The newer sticks are made of aluminum or carbon–graphite. They're strong and generally lighter in weight than wooden sticks. Rock elm is the ideal wood, but it's getting scarce because of Dutch elm disease. Some manufacturers have turned to white ash, but it's not nearly as sturdy as elm.

Whatever it's made of, a hockey stick has to be just flexible enough to store as much energy as possible, then release it when it's needed.

WHEN IS A PUCK NOT A PUCK?

The first "pucks" weren't pucks at all. Hockey pioneers would use anything they found lying around: a knot of wood, a stone, an apple—even a piece of frozen cow dung.

The puck as we know it made its debut in Montreal in 1875. The first indoor game was played with a rubber ball, but because it bounced around so much and broke the windows, it cost the rink owners a fortune for repairs. Legend has it that for the next match, one of the owners cut the rounded edges off the ball to reduce the bounce—and inadvertently invented the hockey puck.

A BUCKET OF PUCKS

The 21st century puck is a rubber compound—sulfur-vulcanized rubber—mixed with other materials to give it more strength and to make it less elastic. It's frozen in a bucket of ice before a game to take some of the bounce out of it, and it's even kept frozen between periods for the same reason. When the puck gets warm, it stores more energy and bounces higher, which gives the player

Wind increases in speed the higher it is off the Earth's surface.

less control. Freezing keeps the puck lower to the ground, where the action usually is.

HIT IT!

A slap shot can send that little pucker across the ice at well over 100 mph (160 kph). There are three factors involved:

First, there's the energy produced by the weight that the player transfers to the stick by leaning into it.

Then, there's the "stored elastic energy." Like a pole-vaulter's pole, or an archer's bow, a hockey stick stores energy during a windup. In hockey, the shaft bends slightly during the swing (the end can't keep up with the handle). The stick stores this energy and releases it when it hits the puck. The result is a greater launching speed than you could get from a nonflexible stick. (A stick that's too flexible wouldn't store enough energy.)

Finally, a slight snap of the wrists at the end of the motion releases the puck from the stick. The snap is crucial. It sets the puck to spinning (like a Frisbee), which makes it more stable in flight. If it wasn't spinning it would tend to roll side over side, which would make it follow a more erratic path.

A FLICK OF THE WRIST

Wrist shots aren't as powerful as slap shots, but they've been known to send a puck traveling at 80 to 90 mph (129 to 145 kph). Players say they like the wrist shot because of the control and quick release. Without the windup required for a slap shot, the energy comes from the player pressing down on the stick, then releasing it suddenly with a flick of the wrist. The other factor is the amount of time the puck spends in contact with the blade of the stick, in this case, a much longer amount of time than with a slap shot.

WHEN PANTHERS AND PENGUINS COLLIDE

Hockey stick-meets-puck isn't the only source of energy on the floor of a rink. If a 200-pound (91-kilogram) player was skating across the ice at 50 mph (80 kph), and he just happened to bump into another player of about the same weight, who was also traveling at the same rate of speed, the collision would generate enough energy to light a 60-watt light bulb for 13 seconds.

The U.S. averages 708 tornadoes a year.

DANGER! MAD SCIENTIST AT WORK!

The most brilliant inventor of the 20th century died broke,
friendless, and almost—but not quite—forgotten.

For 40 years before World War II, one of the most famous scientists in the United States was an immigrant from Croatia named Nikola Tesla. He was a genius inventor, but he had serious image problems. In fact, lots of people thought he was nuts.

CERTIFIABLY YOURS
Tesla was a classic obsessive-compulsive who loved pigeons, the dark, and the number three, and was terrified of dirt, germs, and round objects, especially pearls. He sometimes signed his letters with the initials "G. I." for Great Inventor. Other than that, he was just fine. Well, except for the time he announced to the world that he'd received radio messages from people on Mars and Venus. Or that other time when he claimed that if he wanted, he could split the earth in two.

    Some people probably believed him, too. He could produce huge electrical arcs, lightning bolts, earthquakes, sparks running across the ground, and ghostly blue glows in the air. In fact, he was the original mad scientist, the man who all those wild-haired, wild-eyed men in white coats in old Hollywood pictures were based on.

DR. FRANKENSTEIN, I PRESUME
The electricity flashing around Dr. Frankenstein's castle? A direct copy of real-life conditions in Tesla's lab. The classic 1931 Boris Karloff movie *Frankenstein* was the first of many to use real Tesla coils to get those weird arcs of artificial lightning. Even the wacky Dr. Emmett L. Brown in *Back to the Future* is based on Tesla, and besides those same Tesla coils, the antigravity skateboards in *Back to the Future Part II* are based on another of the nutty professor's ideas.

AN ELECTRIC PERSONALITY
Most of his inventions were credited to other people, the reason being that, strange as he was, he was more interested in benefiting

humanity than making money. The alternating current (AC) electricity coming from every wall socket in the world today was invented by Tesla. That single invention could have made him a billionaire, but he tore up his contract with Westinghouse because he claimed his royalty would bankrupt the company. All he wanted was to see unlimited free energy in every home.

AC/DC

This benevolent gesture gave the upper hand to Tesla's arch rival—you may have heard of him—Thomas Edison. Don't be swayed by visions of a kindly Spencer Tracy or a bubbly Mickey Rooney...this is the *real* Thomas Edison we're talking about.

Tesla wanted to establish his AC system, but Edison's company was already committed to its own much more expensive—and unreliable—direct current (DC). Tesla had gotten the idea for AC while a student in Austria, and he came to America to put his idea into practice. He got a job with Edison when he arrived in 1884, but Edison soon came to see the newfangled AC system (and Tesla) as a commercial threat. DC electricity needed thick cables and power stations every mile, while AC electricity could more easily be transmitted over long distances with much thinner and cheaper cables, and without booster stations along the way. So Edison did everything he could to discredit Tesla and his invention.

YOU'LL GET A CHARGE OUT OF THIS

When a New York dentist named Dr. Brown came up with the idea of the electric chair, Edison fairly swooned at the thought of the publicity! Plus, he could use it to rub Tesla's face—and reputation—in the dirt. The electric chair used both DC and AC charges; first there was a jolt of DC to stop the heart, and then a surge of AC to make the heart fibrillate (rapidly contract its muscle fibers). The DC actually killed the subject, but Edison manipulated the facts, telling people that first the criminal got a dose of harmless, safe, all-American DC, followed by the lethal, dangerous AC from the foreign system. "Would you want your wife to be cooking with this?" he asked the public, as he toured around the country electrocuting dogs, cats, horses, an orangutan, and once even an elephant.

Actually, when they eventually tried the electric chair for real, it was a disaster. They miscalculated the necessary charge, and the first subject, an ax murderer named Kemmler, wasn't electrocuted but cooked alive.

The oldest species of tree in the U.S. is the bristlecone pine of Nevada and California.

EDISON 1, TESLA 0
The adverse publicity that Edison organized turned the electricity business away from Tesla and AC for a time, but after a few more demonstrations of its advantages—many organized by Tesla himself—it eventually became clear that AC was the superior system, and the whole world adopted it. Lots of people made lots of money—but not our hero. He was perpetually trying to raise money for his next invention and didn't pay much attention to getting paid for the last one.

TESLA, UNPLUGGED
So forget AC and DC. Tesla had another idea entirely. Why couldn't electricity be transmitted through the air, like radio waves, from public transmission stations, so that everyone would have access to unlimited free electric power? What a nut. At least that's what Edison, Westinghouse, and all their investors thought. Heck, the energy industry was fast developing as the backbone of America's economy. Tesla could have wiped it out overnight.

THERE'S NO MONEY IN FREE STUFF
Tesla's Wireless Broadcasting System was going to use two-hundred-foot high towers with giant 55-ton copper domes on top. The financier J. P. Morgan put up $150,000 for a prototype, but pulled out when he found out about the free electricity angle. The tower was dismantled and sold for scrap to pay Tesla's debts.

STILL CRAZY AFTER ALL THESE YEARS
After that, he never again found serious financial backers for his schemes. He'd seen so many of his great inventions passed off as other people's work—Marconi getting the kudos for radio, and Edison eventually managing to pass off AC as the work of some of his engineers—that Tesla became a recluse.

Every couple of years he'd hold a press conference to announce some amazing new invention, usually with a display of artificial lightning bolts to attract attention. Because he never got the money to develop them, the inventions languished in the lab. Between the two World Wars, Tesla became a long-running joke: the Mad Scientist, always raving about some new earth-shattering invention that never materialized.

Tesla, one of the most brilliant inventors of the 20th century, died at 86, broke, friendless, and almost—but not quite—forgotten.

GOOD REASONS FOR SPITTING

Ancient Greeks and Romans believed spitting was a defense against witchcraft. Maybe that's why spitting is traditionally considered good luck. Some people spit on money for luck, especially the first money earned in the day. In nature, creatures put spit—or a reasonable facsimile—to more practical uses.

A-HUNTING WE WILL GO

Take the lynx spider, for example. It can spit venom at other bugs from as far as eight inches (20 cm) away. Their relatives, the Philippine Scytodes spiders, have an even better weapon. They like to feast on poisonous jumping spiders—prey that could easily turn around and become the predator. So the half-inch-long Scytodes stands back a couple of inches and spits a sticky gum—a combination of poison and glue that holds the catch down while the poison subdues it. Then the Scytodes tiptoes over, wraps his catch in silk, and saves it for a future feast.

WALK? IT TAKES ALL DAY TO PUT HIS SHOES ON

Walking worms shoot a gluelike substance to catch food. These little creatures aren't really worms; you can tell by their 14 to 43 pairs of legs. They're sometimes called velvet worms because of the fine sensory hairs that cover their bodies.

When a walking worm finds something to eat, like a termite or slug, it shoots a stream of gluey slime out of its mouth, which can hit a target nearly 20 inches (50 cm) away. The spit hardens fast, caging the prey and sticking it in place. Then the worm moves in on its many little feet and uses its mandibles (jaws) to poke a hole in the catch through which it injects its own digestive juices, then takes its time sucking out the unfortunate critter's insides.

UNDER THE SHELTERING SPIT

Lots of birds use spit to help hold their nests together (more about one in particular later). And termites use spitballs to build bug

---

Krakatoa volcano's detonation in 1883 was heard as far away as Australia, some 3,000 miles.

palaces that have elaborate tunnels, arches, chimneys, fungus gardens, and lots of rooms, including nursery chambers for babies. The workers who construct termite-mound palaces are blind, but they know what they're doing and where they're spitting.

THE SPIT OF CHAMPIONS

Wasps also spit a lot. They build nests out of water, plant fiber or mud, and spit. After a rainstorm they dry their nests by sucking up excess water and spitting it over the side. Because wasps are endurance champions (they can fly more than 60 miles [96 km] a day), they attracted the attention of some Japanese scientists, who decided that whatever wasps eat might be good for human athletes, too. It turns out that adult wasps don't eat raw food; they feed it to wasp larvae. In return, the larvae spit out saliva. That's what the adult wasps eat.

And that's also what companies have been putting into sports drinks like VAAM (which stands for Vespa amino acid mixture). Vespa, as anyone who owns a motor scooter knows, is Italian (and Latin) for "wasp." According to some human athletes, wasp spit works wonders. It's been credited with at least one Olympic marathon win, and it's been used by athletes in the last three Olympic Games. Because it's 100 percent natural, it doesn't fall foul of Olympic laws against performance-enhancing drugs.

SWALLOWING SWALLOW SPIT

In Southeast Asia, swallowlike birds called swiftlets live deep inside caves. Like bats, they use echolocation—bouncing high-frequency sounds off the cave walls—to find their way around. These birds seldom even try to walk on their tiny little legs, but they can do most anything in the air—including eating, drinking, copulating, and spitting.

Swiftlets have special saliva glands that produce nest-building material. Some kinds of swifts use saliva to glue their nests together and attach them to walls. But the Southeast Asian cave-dwelling branch of the family make their nests entirely out of spaghetti-shaped spit. When it dries, the stuff hardens and becomes translucent. The nests are located high up on cave ceilings and walls, where they're very hard to get at. All the same, people climb hundreds of dangerous feet upward to gather them. That's because the nests are highly valued as a traditional Chinese delicacy—we're talking bird's-nest soup.

Of course, what we're really talking about is spit soup. It's said to cure lung disease and increase sex drive, among other benefits. It's certainly a sign of wealth and status, because it's incredibly expensive. According to one report, good bird's nests sell for almost $3,000 a pound.

JUST PLAIN SALIVA

Spit can work to the spitter's disadvantage, too. That's because plants aren't as dumb as people think. When a bug or caterpillar chews on a plant, it leaves some spit behind. Some plants recognize chemicals in the spit and respond by producing substances that taste bad to bugs. Other plants—such as corn and cotton—respond to a predator's spit by sending chemical messages. They produce chemicals that signal certain kinds of wasps—"Come to lunch!" So the wasps rush to the scene and rescue the plants.

NAMED AFTER SPIT

Spittlebugs are large black leafhoppers with wings, red stripes, and red eyes. Baby spittlebugs, or nymphs, come in other colors but don't yet have their wings. They just sit around all the time and suck the juices out of plants. So they build their own bubbly shelters right where the food is.

Pumping its body up and down, a young spittlebug squirts out fluid. Shooting air from the same orifice, the nymph blows the fluid into bubbles, then uses its back legs to spread the bubbles all over its body. Inside its bubbles, the nymph is safe from predators, and enjoys both temperature and moisture control.

Although this mass of bubbles is commonly called "spittle," both goo and air actually come out of the other end of the bug. Does that count?

* * * * *

SPITTING RECORD

The Guinness World Record for spitting a watermelon seed was first set in 1981 in Luling, Texas. John Wilkinson of Houston spit a seed 65 feet, 4 inches at the Luling Watermelon Thump festival. That record was broken at the 1989 Luling Watermelon Thump by Luling local Lee Wheeler, who spit a seed 68 feet, 9 1/2 inches.

Snakes have been clocked at 12 mph (20 kph).

QUARKS AND LEPTONS AND BOSONS, OH MY!

Let's get really, really, really small...

I n the fourth century B.C. a Greek named Democritus (known as "the laughing philosopher" because he was always making fun of people) proposed a theory of matter that remained uncontested well into the 19th century. (This was before he went mad and blinded himself with hot glass in an effort to heighten his intellectual acuity.)

Anyway, Democritus suggested that all matter is made up of tiny indestructible pieces that he named *atomos*, meaning undivided. Today it's known that atoms can certainly be broken up into subatomic particles, and those particles can be broken into more particles, and so on.

AND THEN THERE WERE THREE

For about 2,200 years, scientists were happy enough with the idea that matter was made up of atoms. This all changed in 1886 when E. Goldstein discovered the positively charged particle that he named "proton," after the Greek root *proto*, meaning "first," since it was the first subatomic particle ever to be discovered.

Shortly after that, in 1897, the English physicist J. J. Thomson (who also only used his initials—is it some sort of club?) discovered negatively charged particles that he called "corpuscles," which today are known as electrons.

In 1932, English scientist Sir James Chadwick (finally, a man with a *real* name!) discovered the neutron, the subatomic particle that lacks a charge.

THREE QUARKS FOR MUSTER MARK!

Of course, scientists were not content to stop at having three subatomic particles—they're funny that way—so they feverishly looked for more. And sure enough, by splitting a proton or a neutron, smaller subatomic particles are created. These particles were named "quarks" in 1964 by scientist Murray Gell-Mann, who got the name from the following quote in James Joyce's novel

The sting of the Australian box jellyfish can kill a person in one to three minutes.

Finnegans Wake: "Three quarks for Muster Mark! Sure he hasn't got much of a bark/And sure any he has it's all beside the mark."

The names of the six "flavors," or types of quarks, are more down to earth. They are: up, down, strange, charmed, top, and bottom. Two "up" quarks and one "down" quark make a proton, and two "down" quarks and one "up" quark make a neutron. And so on.

ELEMENTARY, MY DEAR PARTICLE
In the world of science, you are either an elementary particle or you are a hadron. An elementary particle is one that can't be broken down (yet) into smaller particles. Scientists refer to elementary particles as "fundamental." There are three types of elementary particles: quarks, leptons, and bosons. Hadrons are made of quarks and therefore are not fundamental. Got it?

BOSONS, LEPTONS, AND MORE ONS
The fundamental members of the boson family include photons, gravitons, and gluons. Photons are little packets of electromagnetic radiation, that is, light; gravitons are presumed to be responsible for gravitational force; and gluons are responsible for (you may have guessed this one) gluing and holding together other fundamental particles that comprise hadrons.

The most famous lepton is the electron, from which we get electricity. The other members are the muon (pronounced mew-on, like a cat), tau, electron neutrino, muon neutrino, and tau neutrino. Whew!

THE TRUTH ABOUT HADRONS
There are two main families of hadrons: the baryons and the mesons. Protons and neutrons are part of the baryon family. In the meson family there are several hadrons named mostly after the Greek alphabet (a grudging nod to the laughing philosopher) such as omega, eta, chi, and psi. Mesons are also made up of various combinations of quarks.

SPLITTING HAIRS OVER PARTICLES
How can a teensy-weensy particle be split, anyway? This is not a dumb question. The answer is by using a particle accelerator, of course. A particle accelerator shoots a beam of particles through a closed track. These high-energy beams, along with powerful

Insects outnumber people a million to one.

magnets, cause the particles to move almost as fast as the speed of light. When the particles finally reach top speed, they're slammed into another particle, causing them to break apart into pieces—thus creating new particles that scientists can then name with one of those "on" endings.

There are particle accelerators everywhere (really!), but the largest, called Tevatron, is over four miles (6.4 km) long and can be found at Fermilab in Batavia, Illinois.

ANTIMATTER OF FACT

In addition to all the particles that make up matter, there also exist particles of antimatter. For instance, the antiparticle of the negatively charged electron would be a similar particle with a positive charge, called a positron. There are also antiprotons, antineutrons, and anti almost anything else (though there don't seem to be any antiphotons, but what do you want to bet they turn up someday?). Antimatter was predicted in 1928 by physicist Paul Dirac and later confirmed in 1932.

Matter and antimatter are thought to destroy each other, and scientists believe the universe existing today is made from the remnants of excess matter that was not annihilated by its anti-matter counterpart. A stroke of luck for us!

WHAT'S THE MATTER?

It's invisible. It makes up at least 90 percent of the universe. It is...drum roll, please...dark matter.

See, scientists are still trying to explain the theory that the universe is constantly expanding. If it continues to expand, then there must be a lot of unseen stuff that comprises it. Enter the concept of dark matter.

There are several types of dark matter. And it's here that you begin to notice, hey, scientists are getting much better at naming things. MACHO, for instance, stands for MAssive Compact Halo Object. Scientists witness this form of dark matter by observing the halos that surround stars. WIMP stands for Weakly Interactive Massive Particles, which have yet to actually be discovered but are thought to be the skinny guys at the beach who have sand kicked at them by the MACHO dark matter. There's also hot and cold dark matter, so named for how fast the particles move (the hot ones move faster), and neutrinos, which are the most prolific particles: One billion exist for every single proton and electron.

A queen termite can lay up to 30,000 eggs per day.

MNEMONICS YOU MIGHT MNEED

You mnever mknow.

You think scientists are smart? That's what they'd like you to think. Well, guess what? All this time, they've been using mnemonics. Which, we have to admit, isn't exactly cheating. You probably came across some in school They're pretty excellent devices for remembering lists and necessary (or even unnecessary) facts. They work because new knowledge is more effectively stored in long-term memory if you can associate it with something familiar. Mnemonics focus on association and sometimes the more bizarre or funny your associations, the easier they are to call up when you need to remember something.

FOR EXAMPLE: ASTRONOMY

For remembering the order of the planets according to their distance from the Sun, a lot of people use what are called sentence mnemonics: Taking the first letter of the planets —Mercury, Venus, Earth, Mars, Jupiter, Saturn, Uranus, Neptune, Pluto—and making a new (and occasionally silly) sentence out of it. Like: My Very Excited Mother Just Sold Uncle Ned Pies. Get it? Here's more (including a slightly mnaughty one):

- My Very Educated Mother Just Sent Us Nine Pickles.
- Mother Very Eagerly Made Jelly Sandwiches Under No Protest.
- My Very Earnest Mother Just Served Us Nine Pizzas.
- My Very Educated Mother Just Showed Us Nine Planets.
- Many Very Eager Men Just Sat Under Nine Pines.
- Many Voters Earn Money Just Showing Up Near Polls.
- My Very Eager Mother Just Served Us Nothing.
- Mary's Violet Eyes Make John Stay Up Nights Praying.
- Men Very Easily Make Jugs Serve Useful Nocturnal Purposes.

Did you find the mnaughty one? Good for you. And you know, if you don't like any of our examples, you can make up some of your own (but keep it clean!).

Some insects have up to 4,000 muscles compared to about 600 muscles in a human body.

POKÉMON PANIC

In 1997, hundreds of Japanese children got sick from watching a TV show. Come on, kids, it wasn't that bad! Was it?

To kids all over the world, Pokémon was more than just a game. Originally created for Nintendo's Game Boy, Pokémon was so popular that it spawned comic books, videos, trading cards, clubs, magazines, and even an animated television show.

THE CRAZE
In Japan, the TV series was drawing a huge audience, so that when *Pocket Monsters* (later renamed *Pokémon*) episode 38 aired on December 16, 1997, millions of Japanese kids were watching. This particular episode featured an adventure inside a computer: A creature with electric power tries to stop another creature from detonating a "virus bomb." The explosion was accompanied by a quick series of flashing red and blue lights.

THE CRAZINESS
And therein, apparently, lay the trouble. The flashing lights began at about 6:51 P.M. By 7:30, 618 Japanese children had been taken to hospitals for symptoms ranging from nausea, blurred vision, and dizziness to convulsions, unconsciousness, and vomiting.

THE EVENING NEWS
When the incident was reported on television news the next night, several stations replayed the *Pokémon* sequence in question. Within hours, even more children—and adults—had been rushed to hospitals. Reports vary on how many caught the "second wave," but estimates range all the way up to 12,000.

SAYONARA, *POKÉMON*
Public outcry was at fever pitch. The story was reported throughout the world. Nintendo's shares dropped almost five percentage points on the Tokyo stock market. Video retailers pulled all the Pokémons from their rental shelves.

There is a breed of penguin called Macaroni.

WHEN A LIGHT IS MORE THAN JUST A LIGHT

Meanwhile, Japan's Health and Welfare Ministry held an emergency meeting. The experts were at a loss to explain the *Pokémon* phenomenon. But that didn't stop them from trying.

The most obvious reason they could think of was a well-established phenomenon known as photosensitive epilepsy (PSE), in which seizures are caused by flashing lights. (In fact, part of an electroencepholograph [EEG] test uses strobe lights to test for seizures.) Doctors estimate approximately one in 5,000 people are prone to photosensitive epileptic seizures. And apparently, episode 38 did the trick for at least a few children who were susceptible.

WHEN A LIGHT ISN'T ENOUGH

But this theory didn't sit well with other researchers, or even with *Pokémon* fans. Alternating flashing lights are used in Japanese animation features all the time—there had never been a complaint before. What was it about episode 38 that caused the seizures and other symptoms?

THAT'S HYSTERICAL

Looking back on it now, a lot of experts have come to believe the panic wasn't caused by photosensitive epilepsy. Instead, the major trigger was a mysterious phenomenon known as mass hysteria.

There have been lots of well-documented cases of mass hysteria—including the Salem witch hunts, and the hysteria caused by Orson Welles' radio broadcast of *War of the Worlds* in 1938—but scientists still don't understand the complex causes of what is really a collective delusion.

The symptoms take a standard form: An individual under stress converts the stress into physical symptoms. Family members, friends, coworkers, and others close to the victim seem to "catch" the symptoms and start exhibiting similar ailments. Outbreaks are most common in close-knit, closed environments like schools, hospitals, and workplaces in times of stress. Japan's group-focused society is an ideal environment for hysterical outbreaks. And Japanese schoolchildren were under a great deal of stress the week episode 38 aired—a lot of them were preparing for imminent high-school entrance exams.

Media reports, of course, add more fuel to mass hysteria, a pattern the *Pokémon* panic seems to follow. The first night of the

The largest insect, the 4-inch (10-cm) long Goliath beetle, is the size of a computer mouse.

media reports, about 600 people got sick. Then, after stories about the seizures spread, everybody got on the *Pokémon* bandwagon: a staggering total of 12,000 affected within days.

BLAME IT ON THE MEDIA—YEAH!

The media reports focused excessively on the seizures caused by the episode, even though only about 14–55 children actually suffered seizures. Considering that millions of kids watched that night's episode and about one in 5,000 people are said to have photosensitive epilepsy, the effects of episode 38 don't seem all that terribly alarming. A lot more of the victims were admitted to hospitals with symptoms like dizziness and nausea—the classic symptoms of hysterical reactions.

POSTPANIC

It took about four months for the whole thing to blow over. Come on, said the kids—and their parents—we need our *Pokémon* fix. Nintendo shrugged its shoulders and *Pokémon* was back on the air, where it quickly climbed to third in the ratings.

As a precaution, TV Tokyo put warning labels on all future and past *Pokémon* episodes. The warning says: "Turn off that TV and do your homework!" What? Is our resident translator pulling our collective legs again?

* * * * *

EEK! A MOUSE!

You've probably seen a cartoon of a terrified elephant standing on a wooden stool. (Amazingly, the tiny stool never collapses under the weight of a couple of tons, but hey, it's a cartoon, right?) Gleefully dancing around the base of the stool is a mouse. Although zoologists say elephants aren't afraid of mice as such, they are easily startled by them, and there is a reason for this. Think about where an elephant's eyes are. That's right, on the sides of its head. They're also extremely small compared to the rest of the elephant. Now imagine that your eyes were about the size of your left nostril and located where your ears are. (Yes, this is an exaggeration.) Would you be able to see the cockroach crawling over your toe? Nope. That's how an elephant's vision works. Since its eyes are made for peripheral vision, a mouse becomes a blurry invader threatening the elephant's space.

IN THE CLOUDS

Don't know your cirrus from your cumulonimbus?
You will in a couple of minutes.

They're white and fluffy (except when they're black and angry), and as they puff by on a sunny day, you can see shapes in them, like nature's own Rorschach test. They're clouds, which are just suspended collections of water and ice.

And while you're busy seeing rabbits or twelve-masted schooners in them, you might also wonder what the various types of clouds are called and how they differ from the others. So here are all the types of clouds you need to know. That way, you can say, "That cumulonimbus looks just like Australia," and everyone will be so impressed they'll forget that the cloud actually looks nothing at all like Australia. Let's start from the bottom and work our way up.

Fog: Yes, fog is a kind of cloud, a particularly insidious type that causes 18-wheelers to ram your car off the road, the trucker working on the principle that since he can't see anything in the fog, he should drive faster to get out of it. The simple definition of fog is that it's a cloud of water droplets near ground level, dense enough that horizontal visibility is reduced to less than 3,281 feet (1,000 m). If you can see farther than that, it's not fog, it's haze or mist, although you shouldn't feel like you have to get out the tape measure.

Not all fog is alike; there's:
- "adiabatic expansion" (fog formed when humid air is forced up a mountain)
- advection fog (when humid air flows over a cold surface)
- radiation fog (when the ground loses heat to the atmosphere)
- inversion fog (when a lower part of a stratus cloud hits the ground)
- frontal fog (when rain droplets evaporate and saturate cooler air close to the ground).

But generally speaking, the simple phrase "Hey, look, it's fog" will suffice for most conversational situations.

Stratus: "Stratus" is derived from the Latin word that means layer or blanket, and a big wet blanket is exactly what these clouds are like. These flat, gray clouds can form only a few hundred feet off

---

It takes nectar from around 22 million flowers to make one pound (.5 kg) of honey.

the ground, blot out the sunlight all day long, and cause you to growl into your coffee and snap at coworkers and pets. These clouds don't typically produce rain; they just sit there bringing you down. Clearly the people at Dodge who named a car after these clouds would prefer that you don't think about this too much.

Cumulus: Go ask a four-year-old to draw a picture of a cloud. What you'll get is probably a good approximation of a cumulus cloud. Fluffy and pretty, the delightful yin to the stratus's glowering yang, these clouds are typically only present during the day, due to the mechanics of how they're formed. And they don't last very long: just five minutes to half an hour. You can tell how old a cumulus cloud is by how ragged its edges are (a sign of cloud erosion); new ones look like cotton balls, old cumulus clouds look like cotton balls after they've been shredded by your cat. Cumulus clouds form at altitudes up to 6,500 feet (1,981 m) in most areas (but higher in the tropics, and lower at the poles).

Stratocumulus: If stratus clouds are a thick layer of clouds, and cumulus clouds are fluffy balls, then stratocumulus are…a thick layer of fluffy balls? Works for us. These clouds form anywhere from 1,500 feet (457 m) up (on turbulent days) to 7,000 feet (2,133 m) up (on nice days), and while the view from the ground isn't always so nice (stratocumulus block out the sun and bring down the gray), from above they're actually very lovely, presenting a rolling cloudscape of gentle hills and valleys. Look down sometime while you're on a jet and you'll see what we mean.

Nimbostratus: These clouds have all the depressing grayness of stratus clouds, but this time, you also get rained on. It's a total moisture experience! Cloud tip: Any time you hear "nimbus" or some conjugation thereof being used to describe a cloud, get your umbrella ready, since any cloud with a "nimbus" in it is one that produces rain (remember, "nimbus" means "rainstorm" in Latin).

Altostratus: Up into air we go—"alto" is a prefix used for clouds that form between 6,500 and 23,000 feet (1,981 and 7,010 m). "Alto" is from the Latin meaning "high"—even though clouds with the "alto" prefix aren't actually the highest clouds around. Altostratus clouds provide a high cloud layer that often appears blue or gray, and which sometimes gives you a glimpse of the sun, as if to say, "look what *you* can't have today." Altostratus can produce sustained rain, even though there's no "nimbus" in the name. Don't blame *us* that meteorologists don't believe in consistency.

Altocumulus: These clouds often take on dramatic shapes: Rounded, saucerlike masses that look like (and are sometimes identified as) UFOs, gently undulating rows, or a wavy, ridged cloud cover that looks a little like an M. C. Escher mosaic. If you look up and see an odd-looking cloud that you can't place, think: altocumulus (unless it has a funnel spinning angrily down at you, in which case it's not an altocumulus, and you really ought to get into a basement. Like, *now*).

Cirrocumulus: Up we go again, to between 16,500 to 45,000 feet (5,029 and 13,716 m). At this altitude, clouds are made out of ice, not liquid water. Cirrocumulus appear as a deck of thin, rippled clouds without shading. If you see some and the wind is steady in the southerly up to the northeasterly directions, there's a pretty good chance of rain within 15 or 20 hours. Impress your friends by drawling, "Rain's a-comin'. I feel it in my *bones*."

Cirrostratus: Like cirrocumulus, these clouds are thin and made of ice crystals; they're also transparent, allowing the sun to shine through, which gives them kind of an ethereal look, like maybe heaven's right behind that one on the left. The combo of sunshine and ice crystals produces a "halo" effect around the sun when it shines through a cloud, so when you see a halo in the sky, think "cirrostratus."

Cirrus: The highest of them all, these clouds of ice are thin, wispy, and can be almost hairlike in appearance (that'd be "comb-over hair," not "Fabio hair"). Along with cirrocumulus and cirro-stratus, cirrus clouds help make for spectacular sunsets by catching the setting sun's intense orange, yellow, and red rays.

Cumulonimbus: Every other kind of cloud sticks to its own level of the atmosphere, but not cumulonimbus. These billowy bad boys can reach from near ground level all the way up to cirrus-level, the biggest of them flattening out at the top to form a distinctive anvil shape, as if to say: "Here comes the hammer."

Cumulonimbus clouds carry within them thunderstorms, hail, and tornadoes—all the really destructive atmospheric phenomena that tear through suburban cul-de-sacs like a terrier shreds through a sock. Respect the cumulonimbus, friends. Don't get it angry. You wouldn't like it when it's angry.

Wind is named after the direction from which it blows.

LET'S GET EGGUCATED

Hard-boiled, poached, scrambled, pickled? However you like your eggs, there's no denying that the oval-shaped little beauty that we call the egg is a nutritious powerhouse for us humans.

Eggs are protein-rich, low in sodium, full of vitamins and minerals, and they don't pose the cholesterol dangers that we once thought. So there. Besides, they're inexpensive, delicious, and easy to prepare.

But have you ever wondered how they're actually made? Of course, we all know they come from chickens (or other less popular poultry), but with all the attention paid to the "which came first" debate, many of us have failed to appreciate (or even wonder about) the fascinating process that goes in to producing the humble egg. Never fear—the time for your eggucation has arrived.

THE INCREDIBLE-EDIBLE JOURNEY BEGINS

You probably know that the females of our species, that is, humans, have got a pair of ovaries. Well, lady chickens, that is, hens, have them too. Actually, they've only got one, but it's enough to get the job done. A chicken's ovary is something like a bunch of grapes; the grapes being what are called "follicles" that house an ovum (future egg) while it becomes a yolk. When the chicken ovulates (releases an ovum from a follicle) the almost-finished yolk begins its daylong journey to your breakfast table via a long tube called the oviduct.

A DAY IN THE LIFE OF AN EGG

In the oviduct several amazing things happen. First, the formative egg reaches a section called the infundibulum where, if the chicken has mated, it will be fertilized. (That's what put the "fun" in infundibulum.) Such an egg will produce, not a delicious breakfast, but a cute little chick to ensure the reproduction of the species. Either way...

From here the egg passes to the magnum, where the albumen protein (the egg white) is added. This takes about three hours.

A Virginia forest ranger was struck by lightning seven times from 1942 to 1977.

Then it's on to the isthmus, where two membranes, an inner and an outer, are added to cover the albumin layers. Now the still-soft egg is ready to spend some time in the uterus (yes, hens have those, too). It's a longer stay here: 20 hours or so, while the hard shell is formed.

All eggs are white when they leave the uterus; it's just after this that various colors are formed.

The egg then moves on to the cloaca (hens, like all other birds, have only a single all-purpose outlet "down there") and is expelled by the chicken. The whole process has taken between 24 and 26 hours.

CLUCK...CLUCK...WHEW!

The chicken then takes a well deserved 30-minute break (probably puts her feet up, gossips with the hen next door), and the whole process starts all over again.

So don't underestimate her: Inside that white fluffy exterior, she's a hard-working, lean, mean, egg-making machine.

* * * * *

EGG TRIVIA

- Eggshells contain as many as 17,000 tiny pores over their surface. Through these pores, the egg can absorb flavors and odors (like the rotting vegetables in your refrigerator).

- About 240 million laying hens produce some 5.5 billion dozen eggs per year in the United States.

- Egg yolks are one of the few foods that naturally contain Vitamin D.

- Yolk color depends on the diet of the hen.

- White-shelled eggs are produced by hens with white feathers and ear lobes; brown-shelled eggs are produced by the girls with red feathers and ear lobes.

- If you take some sandpaper to a brown egg and rub a little, you'll be able to see the white underneath.

Tornadoes are dark because they are filled with dust, debris, and dirt.

SPACE JUNK

*There's enough discarded stuff flying around out there
to stock the biggest garage sale in the cosmos.*

Since 1957, the U.S. and the former Soviet Union have carried out approximately 4,000 space launches. Those launches account for the vast majority of the 10,000 large objects and the millions of smaller pieces of debris that orbit aimlessly above the earth. Most of the little stuff is too small to see on radar, but big enough to cause serious injury if it collided with a spacecraft.

With every new space launch—an average of one every four days—the problem gets worse. Yeah, you say, but what are the chances? There's a lot of space in outer space.

A MIR HAPPENSTANCE
Mir, the Russian space station launched in 1986, was hit by a piece of space junk big enough to dent the inner wall of the crew compartment. Even though only four collisions between craft and junk have taken place since the beginning of space flight, scientists predict that the International Space Station, which will be much larger than Mir, will be a "plump target" for wandering debris.

According to a recent study, each decade that it's in orbit, the station will have about a 20 percent chance of a "critical penetration" that could kill a crew member or destroy the station. The chances will increase as more objects are launched into space.

WHAT'S THE DAMAGE?
A small piece of space junk, say two to three inches (5–8 cm) across, would rip a five-inch (12 cm) hole in the wall of a pressurized spacecraft. And because objects in orbit move about six miles (9.6 km) per second (more than 20,000 mph [32,187 kph]), the collision would liquefy both the piece of debris and the wall of the craft. With a flash of heat and blinding light, molten metal would splatter the inside of the cabin. Air would stream out of the hole, leaving any surviving astronauts just a few moments to escape. If the piece of debris were larger, the craft could "unzip," that is, its exterior would come away from the frame like the peel off a

---

Tornadoes occur most often during the months of April, May, and June.

banana, and the contents of the craft would spew out. And, incidentally, add to the space junk tally.

WHAT'S UP?
So what's up there? Here's the short list:
• Used-up satellites
• The rockets that carried the satellites up in the first place
• Discarded fuel tanks
• Various equipment from scientific experiments
• Your basic nuts and bolts
• Lens caps
• Equipment covers
• Thermal blankets
• The coolant from Soviet spy satellites that's congealing into balls about an inch in diameter
• The 400 million tiny and long-obsolete antennas the Air Force released into orbit in 1963 to see if radio waves would bounce off them
• The camera that astronaut Michael Collins "dropped" while on a space walk in 1966

HELLO? HELLO?
And don't think the problem doesn't concern you, earthling. If a piece of space junk collided with the satellite that transmits your cell phone calls or sends you the digital directions to Disneyland, you could be mighty inconvenienced.

Oh, and by the way, that camera that Michael Collins lost his grip on? It reportedly has been found. Everything else is still up there, and as long as it doesn't collide with something and liquefy, the experts say it will probably stay in orbit for thousands or even millions of years.

* * * * *

Myth:
Meteors rarely hit the earth, since they burn up in the atmosphere.
Fact:
Up to 150 tons of meteorite fragments crash into the earth every year. It's a wonder that there are very few known occurrences of people being struck by meteorites. One meteor victim was Mrs. Hewlett Hodges of Alabama. In 1954, a meteorite crashed through her roof, bounced off a radio, and struck her on the hip, giving her a nasty bruise.

WHIZ KIDS

You never know what useful thing a kid is going to invent for a science fair, and the best of them win at the national level. Here's a rundown of some of the inventions that turned up as winners in recent national science fairs.

Who: Ryan Patterson of Central High School, Grand Junction, Colorado
Title of Project: Sign Language Translator
Contest: National Individual Winner, Siemens Westinghouse Science & Technology Competition, and First Place, Intel Science Talent Search (wow!)
The Particulars: Winning one prestigious national science competition wasn't enough for Ryan. His sign language translator looks like a golf glove with a small screen attached. A small computer translates sign language gestures into words on the screen. With this device, a hearing-impaired person does not need to rely on an interpreter. Ryan holds a patent for the device.

Who: Shira Billet and Dora Sosnowik of the Stella K. Abraham High School for Girls, Hewlett Bay Park, New York
Title of Project: Viscometer for Ultra Thin Films
Contest: National Team Winners, Siemens Westinghouse Science & Technology Competition
The Particulars: These smart girls invented a device that measures the viscosity of thin films of lubricants. What exactly is viscosity? We wondered that, too. It's how well a fluid resists flowing freely. (Ketchup is a good example of a high viscosity fluid.) The girls can expect their device to have uses in the many fields of industry where thin films of lubricants are used, from artificial joints to computer disk drives.

Who: Hanna and Heather Craig of East High, Anchorage, Alaska
Title of Project: Ice-Crawler, the Rescue Robot for Snow, Ice, and Glaciers
Contest: $50,000 Scholarship Team Winners, Siemens Westinghouse Science & Technology Competition
The Particulars: These young women invented a robot that they hope will be used to rescue people trapped in remote and wintry

environments. It uses two motors and moves on silicon-reinforced rubber tracks that help it to crawl over snow and ice. They worked on the project for two years before winning all that money.

Who: Branson Sparks, Alexandria Country Day School, Alexandria, Louisiana
Title of Project: Dismissed!
Contest: First Place, 2001 Discovery Channel Young Scientist Challenge
The Particulars: In a contest for younger students, Branson wrote a computer program to coordinate his school's dismissal process. The program, which uses computer sound files to call students' names over the public address system, streamlined the dismissal process, resulting in fewer traffic backups outside his school. It worked so well that the school still uses the system. Branson, the little devil, holds the copyright.

MY KID COULD DO THAT!
If you think your offspring could be the next Edison, encourage him or her to start early. Some of the winners worked on their projects for years. Chances are, your kid's school is already affiliated with a national science fair. If not, we've provided handy web links where you can seek more information. Many of the websites also show what the previous winners did to win.

Contest: Intel International Science and Engineering Fair
Website: http://www.sciserv.org/isef/index.asp
Grade Levels: 9th through 12th
Prizes: Scholarships, tuition grants, scientific equipment, and scientific trips.
This fair operates at the local, regional, state, and national levels. To enter, your kid needs to start at the school level and work his way up. All 50 states and 40 countries participate. The location of the international fair varies from year to year.

Contest: Intel Science Talent Search
Website: http://www.sciserv.org/sts/
Grade Levels: High-school seniors only
Prizes: Scholarships
This is more of a contest than a fair, but past winners have gone

The skin of a polar bear is black and its hair is clear—not white.

on to win no less than the Nobel Prize, as well as numerous other science awards. To enter, submit an entry by mail before the deadline. Forty finalists receive an all-expenses-paid trip to attend the Science Talent Institute in Washington, D.C., where the final winners are chosen.

Contest: Siemens Westinghouse Science & Technology Competition
Website: http://www.siemens-foundation.org/
Grade Levels: For Individual Contest, 12th only; for Team Contest, 9th through 12th
Prizes: Scholarships
This contest also works by submitting an entry, but finalists first have to compete in one of six regional competitions. Regional winners are invited to compete in the National Competition in Washington, D.C.

Contest: Discovery Channel Young Scientist Challenge
Website: http://school.discovery.com/sciencefaircentral/dysc/
Grade Levels: 5th through 8th
Prizes: Scholarships and scientific trips
Similar to the Intel International Science and Engineering Fair, this has contests at local, regional, state, and national levels. So far, most states participate. The final contest is in Washington.

Contest: International Science Olympiads
Website: The Olympiads have multiple websites.
   Mathematics: http://imo.math.ca/ (general info)
   Physics: http://www.jyu.fi/tdk/kastdk/olympiads/
   Chemistry: http://www.icho.sk/
   Biology: http://www.kbinirsnb.be/ibo/ibo.htm
   Informatics: http://olympiads.win.tue.nl/ioi/index.html
   Astronomy: http://issp.ac.ru/univer/astro/ioas_e.html
Grade Levels: High school.
Prizes: gold, silver, or bronze medals
Competitors are given problems to solve and tasks to perform, then their results are judged. Winners are awarded medals, just like in the Olympics. Each nation chooses five or six contestants or team members, depending on the competition. The international competition has a different home every year.

In Greek, *astro* meant "star" and *naut* meant "sailor."

ASK UNCLE JOHN: ABOUT YOUR BODY

Answers to every question you ever had about physiology, provided that every question you ever had is one of these four.

Hey, Uncle John:
What is all this about "left-brained" and "right-brained" people? Does it have a basis in reality? Or is it the new astrology?
The answer is yes to both. The human brain, as you may know, is largely composed of two hemispheres, one left and one right (that would be your left and right, incidentally, not the left and right of someone facing you), each of which is better at certain tasks.

In a very general sense, the left side of your brain is the part that handles most of the "logical" aspects of thinking and process-ing, while the right side handles a lot of the "creative" aspects. So, for example, you do math with your left brain, but you do improv dance numbers with your right. People who are better at logical, reality-based thinking are said to be "left-brained," while people who excel at creative tasks are said to be "right-brained."

So, yes, there's truth to the whole "left-brain, right brain" thing. People have a tendency to grossly oversimplify the concept, which tends to make it like astrology: Whatever scientific under-pinnings there are to their understanding of the subject are over-whelmed by their miscomprehension of the data.

For one thing, no one is wholly "left-brained" or "right-brained"—almost every human is adept at skills from both sides of the hemispheric menu. For another thing, not every brain works the same way. More than 75 percent of people predominately use their left hemisphere for language skills—but that leaves a reason-able chunk of people who have language skills in the right hemi-sphere, or in both hemispheres to some degree. In other words, don't be thinking that someone's left or right hemisphere-ness explains everything about them. They're probably more complicated than that. Incidentally, many people believe that your "handedness" correlates to which side of your brain predominates—so if you're left-handed, you're right-brained (the hemispheres are in charge of the alternate sides of the body, you see). However, this correlation is not at all perfect, either in location of brain activities or in the person's personality. This is why there are left-handed math geeks and right-handed tortured artists.

Dear Uncle John:
Why is your heart on the left side of your body?
It's not. Crack open an anatomy book (or alternately, and only if you're a physician or a med student and have prior permission, crack open a human chest), and you'll notice that the heart is pretty much smack dab in the middle of the chest, nestled between the lungs. What makes people think the heart is to the left is that the heart's left ventricle is quite a bit larger than the right ventricle. This gives the heart its left-leaning shape, so that the heart intrudes farther into the left side of the body than to the right. It also gives the sensation of the heartbeat coming from left of center.

And why is the left ventricle so much larger than the right ventricle? It's because of where the ventricles are pumping blood. The right ventricle receives deoxygenated blood that's just come from the body and sends it off to the lungs to get freshened up; since the lungs are right next to the heart, it's not a very long trip, and not that much effort is required. The left ventricle, however, is sending the now-oxygenated blood to all the rest of the body; this requires a bit more force to get the blood out the door, so to speak. Bigger needs, bigger muscles.

Dear Uncle John:
Just curious: What would have happened to the human race if we hadn't had opposable thumbs?
Well, we wouldn't be as good at pole vaulting, that's for sure. But the meat of the question here is probably not about how good we'd be at pole vaulting, but whether humans would have evolved our big ol' meaty brains, packed as they are with the intelligence that eventually provided us with 24-hour Krispy Kreme stores, if we didn't have a hand on which the fleshy-tipped digit in question could touch its neighbor digits. Since we're unable to go back in time and genetically reengineer the primate who was the first to put its opposable thumb to use, it's really all a matter of specu-

The naked mole rat, the only cold-blooded adult mammal, is not naked, a rat, or a mole.

lation, but if guessing must be done, then it's probably likely that humans (or whatever would have eventually evolved out those first thumbless primates) probably wouldn't even have doughnuts to dunk.

It's likely that human intelligence arose out of the combination of several cognitive functions: Manual dexterity (aided by the opposable thumb) is one part, along with abstract thinking (the ability to use symbols as words), long-term memory, color binocular vision, and so on. Pull out one of the pillars of this intelligence, and you lose some of what makes human intelligence work. And not just human intelligence, but primate intelligence as well, since we share many cognitive functions with our less intellectual ape brethren, including the capacity for abstract thought (which was thought to be a strictly human trait until we observed it in some of the larger apes). We're just better at it than they are, or at the very least, we invent more interesting toys.

Now, if you're asking if humanlike thumbless entities could survive, the answer is sure, just not like we survive, which is literally by our wits. We're all very impressed with our big brains, but from a strictly evolutionary point of view, intelligence is just one adaptation to the world, fundamentally no more successful than the evolutionary advantages that have allowed algae to survive for billions of years. Algae gets along fine without big brains and Krispy Kreme doughnuts. Our dumb and thumb-deprived almost-humans would do the same.

Dear Uncle John:
Do "double-jointed" people actually have two sets of joints?
Eeeeeeew. No. What "double-jointed" people have is a condition known in medical circles as Joint Hypermobility Syndrome. It's not that these people have joints the rest of us don't, it's simply that the joints they do have are more flexible. While "Joint Hypermobility Syndrome" certainly sounds more threatening than just being double-jointed, most of the time it's fairly benign. Doctors say that somewhere between 10 and 15 percent of children have hypermobility, which is something that anyone who has ever been in a classroom of third-graders knows already. Most of these kids will lose their hyperflexibility over time and become normal people who don't gross the rest of us out by bending their

---

In the last century, the average life span has increased by over 30 years.

arms the wrong way. In fairly rare cases, joint hypermobility can be a symptom of Ehlers-Danlos Syndrome, a class of ailments that includes weakened connective tissues at the joints, as well as other weird phenomena such as hyperelastic skin. Kids who have hypermobile joints may also be more susceptible to pulls and sprains, and other more serious ailments such as scoliosis (curvature of the spine).

Finally, a recent study published in the *Journal of Rheumatology* suggests that people who are double-jointed may be slightly more susceptible to fibromyalgia or "fibromyalgia-like syndromes" (fibromyalgia, in case you don't know, is a pain disorder affecting the muscles and bones). So while bending your arms backwards to impress your friends may seem like fun when you're a kid, as an adult you may wish to find some other way to keep your pals entertained.

* * * * *

WOULD YOU LIKE A BREATH MINT? I INSIST.

In your mouth, bacteria thrive in the grooves between teeth, multiply on the tongue, and live under gums. Not a very romantic thought, indeed. But necessary. When you chew your food the bacteria go to work on it. The waste it leaves behind contains volatile sulfur compounds (VSCs). Some common VSCs are hydrogen sulfide (that rotten egg smell) and methyl mercaptan, better known as skunk oil. Some foods that cause VSCs are coffee, dairy products, sugar-containing mints (yes, mints), and even chewing gum.

IT'S THE PITS!

The armpit is a complex region of the body dedicated to keeping you cool. As if one was not enough, there are two types of sweat glands in the armpit: the apocrine glands, which are associated with hair follicles, and the eccrine glands, which release water in the form of sweat for temperature moderation. Most sweat is made of water but the sweat secreted by hair follicles produces a milky white substance that when broken down by bacteria, produces 3-methyl-2-hexanoic acid (Never you mind: It's a stinky chemical). The condition of stinky armpits is referred to as "axillary malodor," if you want to get fancy about it.

THE TWISTER TEST

The truth about tornadoes can be stranger than fiction.
Can you tell the difference?

Every year about a thousand tornadoes whirl across the United States. Most last only a few minutes with winds of less than 112 mph (180 kph), but some have been clocked at over 200 mph, the fastest winds in nature. Twisters can touch down in one place, then completely change direction, and do it over and over again. Or they can pick up a bus and leave the bench at the bus stop untouched.

Okay, that's all the hints you're going to get. Now try these hard-to-believe stories and see if you can find the one and only phony.

1. A tornado swept a toddler out of his bed and set him down safely 50 feet (15 m) away without removing his blankets.
2. A woman walked into her front yard to find a sturdy, 40-foot tree uprooted—even though the lawn furniture remained exactly where she had left it!
3. A tornado picked up a tie rack with 10 ties attached, and carried it for 40 miles (64 km) without removing one tie.
4. While a couple slept, a tornado lifted their cottage then dropped it into a nearby lake. They remembered only a loud bang before they woke up in deep water.
5. Tornadoes have plucked all the feathers off chickens.
6. After a tornado you'll sometimes find straw sticking out of telephone poles.
7. A tornado scooped up five horses that were hitched to a rail, then set the whole arrangement down, intact, horses uninjured, a quarter-mile away.
8. A large rooster was sucked into a small earthenware pitcher with only his head sticking out.
9. In 1987, in China, 12 children walking home from school were sucked up by a tornado and safely deposited 12 miles (19 km) away in sand dunes.
10. After a tornado killed migrating ducks at a migratory bird refuge, it rained dead ducks 40 miles (64 km) away.

TWISTER TEST ANSWER

If you guessed that the rooster (#8) is the phony because tornadoes don't suck large objects into small ones, you win. Your prize—a rooster in an earthenware pitcher—is on its way to your home right now.

Trepanning, or drilling a hole in the skull, is the oldest known operation.

DEAD AS A DODO

Humans aren't bad, really. We just occasionally rub out an entire species for no good reason at all.

As the cause of mass extinctions, human beings don't do half as well as natural phenomena, such as climate changes or the occasional asteroid slamming into the Gulf of Mexico. But it's not that we don't try. We've been directly responsible for the demise of dozens of species over the centuries—by hunting, by introducing predator species, or simply by wrecking the environment of various species. In a lot of cases, we weren't intentionally trying to wipe out these animals; we just didn't think of the long-term consequences. Funny how that happens.

Dodo: The most famous dead bird of all. Here's how it went down. In the 1500s, Portuguese sailors landed on the island of Mauritius, off the east coast of Africa, and discovered a weird-looking, flightless bird wandering around the place. It was fat (up to 50 pounds [22 kg]) and gray, with a huge hooked beak, and it waddled when it walked. It showed absolutely no fear of humans because it had never seen any humans before and didn't know any better. The sailors equated this lack of fear with the bird being stupid, which says a bit more about the Portuguese sailor's perception of the human race than it does about the bird's native intelligence. The bird was dubbed the "dodo," derived either from the Portuguese *doudo*, meaning "foolish," or the Dutch *dodoor*, meaning "sluggard." (Note that the Dutch colonized Mauritius about a hundred years later.) Either way, it's not a very nice name.

The dodo's lack of fear helped kill it, since it wouldn't run away from the hunters who tromped through the forests, bringing back dozens of carcasses at a time (even though no one thought they tasted all that good). Later, when the Dutch moved in, the animals they brought with them—dogs, pigs, monkeys—trampled dodo nests and snacked on both dodo eggs and dodo chicks. Between humans and their domestic animals, the dodo was entirely wiped out by 1693. Of course, it was the dodo's extinction that gave the bird its everlasting fame, since the way most of us first hear about the dodo is as part of the phrase "Dead as a...." Given its druthers, the dodo would probably prefer to be obscure and alive than famous and extinct. But it's not like it was given a choice.

Passenger Pigeon: The second most famous dead bird. Which is kind of funny, because the passenger pigeon was literally the last species anyone ever expected to go extinct. The reason? At one point, it was estimated that there were more passenger pigeons than any other species of bird. Population estimates went as high as five billion passenger pigeons; they accounted for an estimated 40 percent of the total bird population of North America in the early 19th century.

As numerous as they were, they were vulnerable to human incursion into their nesting territory. Passenger pigeon nests were shoddy things, the pigeons laid only one egg at a time, and two weeks after the eggs hatched, the parent pigeons (all of them) would leave their baby pigeons to fend for themselves. Turns out people thought these abandoned baby pigeons were mighty tasty eatin'. First the Native Americans and then the transplanted Europeans came to consider the little birds a great delicacy. And hey, the adult birds weren't so bad, either. When we weren't eating them, we were releasing pigeons from traps to shoot them as they flew away. (Now you know why it's called "trap shooting" and why targets are called "clay pigeons.")

By the 1850s, commercial trapping of passenger pigeons was going full steam, and hundreds of thousands of the birds were harvested every day: On July 23, 1860, for example, 235,000 pigeons were harvested in Grand Rapids, Michigan, alone, to be sent east, where they would be made into popular pigeon pies. More of the pigeons' nesting territory was being cleared away for farming and other uses. As numerous as the passenger pigeons were, they were not an infinite resource. By the 1880s, people started noticing the birds becoming scarce. In the East, the pigeons were gone by 1890. The last passenger pigeons killed in the wild were shot in 1899.

Eventually those billions and billions of birds dwindled down to a single remaining specimen, a passenger pigeon named Martha, who died on September 1, 1914, at 1:00 P.M., at the Cincinnati Zoo. In addition to being the end of an era, it was also the first time humans were able to exactly time the extinction of a species down to the very last minute.

Only females are carriers of hemophilia, but only males contract the disease.

Tasmanian Wolf: Okay, enough extinct birds. Here's not only an extinct mammal, but an extinct marsupial: the Tasmanian wolf, also known as the Tasmanian tiger (but not to be confused with the Tasmanian Devil, which is not extinct...yet). The wolf was the largest marsupial carnivore of recent times, a doglike creature about five feet in length from nose to tail tip. Its fur was yellowish brown with stripes (which is why it was also called a tiger), but its most impressive feature was its jaw, which opened enormously—wider, some zoologists believe, than any other mammal's.

The Tasmanian wolf's days were numbered when Europeans colonized Tasmania (an island directly off the southeast edge of Australia) and introduced sheep to the island in 1824. It didn't take long for the settlers to decide their sheep were more valuable than a marsupial predator; the first bounty for the Tasmanian wolves went out in 1830, and continued for 80 years. By 1910, the animal was nearly extinct; zoos were racing around, trying to get specimens. The last captive Tasmanian wolf died in 1936, the same year the Aussies added the wolf to their list of protected species. The Tasmanian wolf was officially declared extinct in 1986.

BUT, WAIT A MINUTE. It might be that the Tasmanian wolf is the Elvis of endangered species. Hundreds of sightings have been reported, including a report from an actual Parks and Wildlife officer, who spotted one in eastern Tasmania in 1995. However tantalizing these sightings are, there has been no verifiable evidence the wolves are still knocking about. They remain extinct until proven otherwise.

Caribbean Monk Seal: These 10-foot aquatic seals had the honor of being slaughtered by Christopher Columbus himself (or at least his crew, which killed eight of the beasts in 1495), and for several centuries thereafter they were preyed on both commercially and opportunistically by local fishermen. The last confirmed sighting of these seals was in 1952.

Steller's Sea Cow: We ran through these babies pretty darn quick. These massive manatee-like aquatic mammals (35 feet long and three tons or more) were slow-moving, toothless, and showed no fear of the humans who cheerfully slaughtered them for food and leather. Discovered by the stranded crew of Vitus Bering (the guy they named the strait after, and as it happens, that's where the sea cows were found) in 1741, the Steller's Sea Cow was hunted to

Spiders coat their legs with an oily spittle so they are not caught in their own webs.

extinction in just 27 short years. Moral to that story: The slow moving and toothless shouldn't be fearless to boot.

Great Auk: Oh, look, another bird. And here's a heartwarming tale of extinction for you: These large (30 inches or 76 centimeters tall), helpless, penguinlike birds were native to the North Atlantic and were hunted between the 1780s and the 1840s, primarily so people could use their feathers to stuff pillows and mattresses, but also for food and bait. The very last great auks were a mating pair who were killed by two fishermen. The pair had left behind one last great auk egg. The fishermen smashed it.

MORE OF THE SAME

There's lots more: the blue pike of the Great Lakes, the heath hen, the moa (another flightless bird—which goes to prove that if you're going to be a bird, you'd better know how to fly—but even then, there's the dusky seaside sparrow, who from all accounts knew how to fly just fine). And so on...

Environmentalists and their opponents argue about the human potential to exterminate thousands upon thousands of animal and plant species over the next century or so. Whichever side you're on, let's be a little more careful out there, okay?

* * * * *

Is it true that scientists dug up an oversized "velociraptor" after Steven Spielberg created one for *Jurassic Park*?

Actually, a large raptor was discovered two years before the release of *Jurassic Park*, but supposedly the all-powerful and all-seeing Spielberg didn't know it. He just took the raptors that Michael Crichton had used in the book of the same name, and made them bigger and more menacing. The real raptor, which may not have been a pack hunter like the velociraptors in the film, was found in Utah and is now officially called "Utahraptor."

A hummingbird weighs about as much as a copper penny.

LITTLE-BITTY BUCKYBALLS

These odd little carbon molecules in the shape of soccer balls are hollow inside, but if you squash them, they pop right back into shape. And they're so small, you could line up 25 million of them in a one-inch space.

Carbon forms part of more than 90 percent of all the chemical substances we know about, including DNA and proteins. In fact, that's what the field of organic chemistry is about: the study of carbon. For a long time, diamonds and graphite were considered the only pure forms of carbon. Then came buckyballs.

KROTO, SMALLEY, AND CURL, INC.

In 1986, British chemist Harry Kroto and American chemists Richard Smalley and Robert Curl were trying to duplicate high temperatures similar to those found near red giant stars. When they vaporized some graphite with a laser, what they got was a lot of carbon molecules like nobody had ever seen before. Ten years later, they shared the Nobel Prize in Chemistry for their discovery.

HEY, SPORTS FANS!

Buckyballs have exactly the same shape as soccer balls—32 pentagons connected together. They bounce, too. But that's where the similarities end. Buckyballs spin a lot faster—100 million times per second. And they're a lot smaller. Given the coincidences, why weren't they named soccer balls? (Or krotoballs, or smalleyballs, or curlballs after their discoverers?) Because the team had something—or rather, someone—else in mind.

OH, THAT BUCKY!

The three chemists thought the new molecules resembled a geodesic dome, a rounded network of triangles that achieves great structural strength with a minimum of materials. (The shortest distance between any two points on a sphere is a geodesic line.)

The three known blood colors are red for mammals, blue for lobsters, and yellow for insects.

The dome was the brainchild of architect Buckminster "Bucky" Fuller (1895–1983), who designed a 20-story dome for the U.S. Pavilion at Expo '67 in Montreal. Since then, smaller geodesic domes have breen used for everything from weather stations to homes to hot-dog stands. One famous geodesic structure is the 165-foot-diameter Spaceship Earth at Disney's Epcot Center, which is not just a dome, but actually a full geodesic globe. Anyway, the chemists called the new carbon molecules buckminsterfullerenes, or fullerenes for short. The most common one—C_{60}, which has 60 atoms—is usually called a buckyball.

PLAYING WITH BUCKYBALLS
Soon after 1990, other chemists started making buckyballs and other fullerenes in the laboratory. Since then, they've come up with "fuzzyball" fullerenes that have hydrogen atoms attached to them, "giant fullerenes" that have hundreds of carbon atoms, and even "babyballs" that have fewer than 60 atoms.

WHAT ARE THEY GOOD FOR?
Researchers are still investigating potential uses. They speculate that buckyballs might be used as lubricants, rolling around between other molecules like tiny ball bearings. Or they may be super-duper superconductors. Because they're hollow, buckyballs can carry an atom of something else inside, like a little cage. Some think they can be made to break open at just the right time to deliver drugs inside the body, like a capsule, only more high-tech. Buckyballs have already been tested in HIV research; Lou Gehrig's disease is next. They're also the subject of research at NASA, IBM, Xerox, and DuPont, but the truth is, nobody's yet found a practical, cost-effective use for them. The problem is that it's difficult to make buckyballs in large enough quantities to work with.

ALIEN BUCKYBALLS
Besides all these cool things, the possibly coolest thing is that there are buckyballs in outer space—buckyballs have been found in meteorites and asteroid craters.

The migration champion is the Arctic tern, who twice a year makes an 11,000-mile flight.

LIFE'S A BEACH

All beaches are not created equal.

If you think that all beaches are the same, you need to get out and travel a little. The more beaches you encounter, the more you'll realize just how many variations there are.

HOW DO YOU LIKE YOUR SAND?
Black: Typically found in volcanic areas, the coarse black sand comes from ground lava.

Pastel: Pink or other colorful sand is generally the result of offshore coral that's been ground fine.

White: Glistening white beaches are formed from broken seashells that are ground to powder.

GRAIN EXPECTATIONS
Most beaches are made of small, rounded quartz crystals mixed with fine particles of lots of different rock types that range from very coarse to very fine—as big as .08 inches (2 mm) and as tiny as .002 inches (0.06 mm) in size. Any bigger or smaller and they don't qualify as sand.

THAT PERFECT SLOPE
Beaches also differ based on slope shape—and the sand on them differs accordingly. On the steep beaches of British Columbia or Java, Indonesia, the sand is coarse and not tightly packed. Beaches that slope more gradually—or with hardly any slope at all—have finer sand. The water offshore continues to be shallow for a greater distance and the waves will break farther out. Fine sand also packs down solidly—you can even drive a car on it like at Daytona Beach, Florida, home of racing's Daytona 500.

THE SANDS OF TIME
Generally, incoming waves are smaller and gentler in summer and larger and more powerful in winter. Gentler waves tend to push sand up on the beach, whereas stormy waves of winter drag the sand away and deposit it in long sandbars parallel to the beach. When summer's gentler waves return, sandbars tend to disappear as the sand is gradually pushed up on the beach by the waves.

The American opossum's gestation period is 12–13 days; the elephant's is 21.7 months.

GOT GAS? PART I

In which our hero discovers oxygen and other nifty stuff by accident.

Born in 1733 in Yorkshire, England, Joseph Priestley was a child prodigy. By age 16 he'd already mastered Greek, Latin, and Hebrew (didn't everybody?). He went on to teach himself French, Italian, and German. His fascination with chemistry came later in life, as did his career as an English minister and a Dissenter. (The Dissenters, a.k.a. Nonconformists, didn't believe in the doctrines of the Anglican Church, the denomination that most of England belonged to in the 18th century.)

SOMETHING BIG BREWING
When he became a minister, Priestley took lodging next to a brewery. Others might have been repelled by the odor that hung over the place, but Priestley was curious about the "air," that is, the gas that effervesced from the vats of fermenting liquor. This gas, which was actually carbon dioxide, could extinguish a small fire, and when Priestly dissolved it in water, he discovered that it made bubbles.

MR. SODA
Priestley quickly picked up on the idea that this fizzy water might be useful for making sparkling wines. In the course of additional experiments, he succeeded in inventing soda water, making him, in effect, the father of the soft-drink industry. Britain's national academy of science and technology, the Royal Society, gave him a well-deserved medal for it in 1773.

NO LAUGHING MATTER
Priestley was on his way. He constructed a simple but ingenious apparatus consisting of a trough full of mercury over which glass vessels could be inverted to collect a gas. The substance to be heated was placed in a second, smaller glass vessel within the larger one. Priestley then heated the substance by focusing the sun's rays on it using a 12-inch glass lens. Between 1767 and 1773 he discovered four new "airs," including one of our all-time favorites—nitrous oxide, more commonly known to grateful dental patients as "laughing gas."

THE VERY AIR WE BREATHE

But that was nothing compared to Priestley's next discovery: In an experiment on August 1, 1774, Priestley decided to see what would happen if he extracted air from red mercuric oxide. He heated the substance as he'd done in previous experiments until it gave off a gas. Then he added water to see if it would dissolve. It didn't, but what surprised him more than anything was that a nearby candle he'd lit (and which wasn't part of the experiment) began to burn "with a remarkably vigorous air." He was obviously onto something big. But what?

OF MICE AND MEN

After testing the gas on some mice and himself (and enjoying the surge of energy it gave him), Priestley realized that this gas was the component of common air that made both combustion and respiration possible. What Priestley had discovered was, in fact, the gas of gases: none other than oxygen.

However, it wasn't until 1789 that Antoine-Laurent Lavoisier, the famous French chemist, actually gave it the name "oxygen," from the Greek for "acid." (Those crazy French, eh?) In a series of brilliant experiments, Lavoisier showed that air contains 20 percent oxygen and that combustion—the process that produces heat and light—is due to the combination of a combustible substance with oxygen.

To find out more about laughing gas,
see "Got Gas? Part II" on page 174.

* * * * *

Myth:
Life on earth developed because the atmosphere contains oxygen.

Fact:
Life on earth probably developed in an oxygen-free atmosphere, and even today some microorganisms can only live in the absence of oxygen.

THE INVADERS

We're being invaded by creatures that cause untold destruction.
These beasts aren't from outer space; they're from Earth itself.
And they're looking for trouble!

An "invasive species" is any living organism that moves from the environment where it evolved into a new ecosystem. When these organisms arrive in a new area and find no natural enemies waiting for them, they run rampant. Invasive species can be microscopic organisms like bacteria and fungi, or insects, plants, marine creatures, or even animals like birds, snakes, or large mammals.

IT CAME FROM YOUR LUGGAGE

They travel in a various ways: Sometimes they're introduced on purpose—as new crops, livestock, or pets—and then escape into the wild. Usually though, invasive species are introduced by accident. Called "tramp species," they hitch rides with unwary travelers in luggage or in other cargo on airplanes and ships that traverse the globe.

Invasive species can hurt native species in numerous ways: by competing with the locals for food sources, or simply by using the locals for food. Invaders also bring their own luggage: exotic parasites or pathogens that can make local species sick. They can also alter the environment so that local species can no longer survive.

AND IT'S EXPENSIVE

In the U.S. alone, invasive species cost an estimated $100 billion every year, which includes damage to agriculture and the degradation of natural ecosystems. (For example, invader weeds alone cost the economy $35 million.) Out on the range, invasive plants like cheat grass shove aside more nutritious forage plants, cause soil erosion, and poison livestock. Another invader plant, the purple loosestrife, produces nearly 3 million seeds per plant per year and damages wetlands to the tune of over $40 million annually.

NEW KUDZU ON THE BLOCK

Kudzu arrived in America amid a lot of fanfare: It was supposed to be the answer to a gardener's prayers, a fast-growing ornamental vine and ground cover. It settled in the American South, where the weather was just perfect. And it grows like crazy there. The kudzu vine can grow up to one foot per day. Vast parts of the

South are now covered in it. It smothers local plants, kills trees, and crowds out native animals. In fact, kudzu is so tough that some herbicides actually make it grow faster.

DRIVING US BUGGY!

Insects account for more than $30 million in damage per year.

- The glassy winged sharpshooter, recently introduced to California, carries a bacterium that causes a devastating disease in grapes, which is bad news for a wine-producing state (not to mention their customers).
- The Argentine fire ant has become established across the American South and has displaced quite a few native species of ants.
- The famous Africanized honeybee (a.k.a. the killer bee) has moved to the U.S. and threatens native bees in a lot of areas—but at least they've given something back by providing material for movie producers and comedians.
- The most harmful bug of all is the gypsy moth, introduced to America for silk production in the 19th century; it escaped into the wild and continues to destroy native trees even today.

A FUNGUS AMONG US

The threat from invaders doesn't come from bugs alone. Every organism wants to get into the act. In the early 20th century, a fungus that attacks chestnut trees entered the U.S. and within decades virtually wiped the native American chestnut off the map.

SNAKES, WHY DID IT HAVE TO BE SNAKES?

What's more disturbing than having your yard covered with kudzu? How about having your yard covered with 10-foot snakes? Guam has been invaded by the brown tree snake, a native to New Guinea that arrived in Guam after World War II, most likely in military transports. It grows up to 10 feet (3 m) long and in the last half-century it has depleted Guam of most of its native species of lizards and bats, and all of its songbirds. Now that most of its natural prey is gone, the snakes are attacking farm birds and pets.

These snakes also cause thousands of power outages every year by crawling onto electrical lines. They're nocturnal, mildly poisonous, and do bite humans—usually at night while people are sleeping in their beds. It's been estimated that some sections of Guam have nearly 12,000 brown tree snakes per square mile!

TIE ME CANE TOAD DOWN, SPORT

Like Guam, Australia is an island, albeit a much larger one, with serious invasion problems. Australia is under siege—toads, cats, and rabbits are just a few of the invaders that are driving down the populations of Australia's unique native animals that exist nowhere else in the world.

Cane toads—imported originally to eat the cane beetle, a sugarcane pest—breed faster than native frogs. They're bigger, too, so they're now the bosses of the lily pond. And they're a danger to curious or hungry animals like dogs because of their poisonous skin.

Generations of pet kitties have escaped from homes to join the ranks of feral marauders. Cats can kill a wallaby with one paw tied behind their backs, and they thrive in varied environments from deserts to rain forests, just like the domesticated rabbits that escaped into the Aussie bush where they bred like...well, you know. Now there are huge hordes of rabbits devastating the plant life of delicate ecosystems, causing erosion and loss of topsoil, as well as depriving food to native species.

NOT TONIGHT, HONEY, I HAVE A...HONEY!

The good news (yes, there is a little) is increased awareness: Governments worldwide are becoming more and more concerned about the economic and ecological consequences of invasive species. But, sad to say, with the volume of international travel and trade, there's no way to completely prevent the transfer of potentially harmful species between countries and regions of the world. So keep watching the skies! Or you could wake up to find a brown tree snake in your bed.

* * * * *

WILL PLOWING A FIELD AT NIGHT REDUCE WEEDS?

Some initial research has shown remarkable reductions in weed populations when tillage of fields was done at night—as great as 80 percent but generally 50 to 60 percent.

Tilling at night postpones or even prevents some weeds from emerging, leaving them buried so that they're less viable and more prone to attack by soil microbes. If fewer weeds appear, that means fewer tractor trips and reduced herbicide use, the latter a nice thing for us vegetable eaters.

Of course, there are always the exceptions: Large-seeded weeds like velvet-leaf and cocklebur still sprout after night tilling and annual grass species aren't affected at all.

Antarctica was not discovered as a continent until the 1940s.

IT'S A BLINKING MARVEL

You're going to do something about 15,000 times today and for the most part, you aren't even going to be aware of doing it. See? You did it again.

The human eye has been compared to a fully automatic, three-dimensional, self-focusing, full-color, motion-picture camera. When not in use, a camera's delicate lens is covered with a cap. But the eye does better than that. It blinks.

EYES WIDE SHUT
Most of your eye lies protected in its socket, thank goodness. But the remaining 10 percent of its surface is exposed to the hazards of the atmosphere. To protect against this, each eye has a retractable "lens cap" made of the thinnest skin on your body. In snapping shut and then retracting, the eyelid draws a thin film of fluid across the eye, rinsing and polishing at the same time.

THE BLINKING-THINKING CONNECTION
A blink lasts only about a tenth of a second and occurs some 15 times every minute. The rinse and polish job only requires about two blinks per minute, so why all the extra blinks?

Anxiety, for instance, makes you blink more often. If you were cross-examined by a hostile lawyer, your blinkers would work overtime (especially if you were guilty). On the other hand, visual concentration makes you blink less frequently. Imminent danger restricts blinking even further, so the eyes can dart quickly from the main field of view to the periphery and back again (like that shifty-eyed look we've seen in some politicians).

Blinking also takes place at the moment that we stop seeing and start thinking. It serves as a kind of mental punctuation, indicating the transition from information input to information processing.

BLINKETY-BLINK
Our research at BRI has shown that if the female next door has been blinking a mile a minute at you lately, she's either fluttering her eyelashes (which means she likes you), very nervous (which means she likes you, too!), or she has something in her eye.

The first kidney transplant was performed on June 17, 1950.

MYTHS ABOUT MARS

The Martians aren't coming! The Martians aren't coming!

Uh-oh. You've learned everything you know about Mars from old science fiction books, half-heard reports on CNN, and those Warner Bros. cartoons starring Marvin the Martian. Well, hold on to your Illudium Q-36 Explosive Space Modulator because, as it turns out, most of what you know about Mars—or what you think you know—is probably a little off base. We're here to correct that, with the following myths about Mars—and the real facts behind the myths.

Mars Myth #1: Mars is the closest planet to Earth.
Mars Reality #1: Well, sometimes it is, but on average, Venus is the closest planet to Earth. Venus orbits the Sun at an average distance of 67.2 million miles (108.1 million km), while the Earth is parked at 93 million miles (149 million km) and Mars is out there at 141 million miles (226 million km). Pull out your handy calculator, and you'll see that at its closest approach, Venus is about 25 million miles (40 million km) from Earth, while Mars's closest approach is something like 48 million miles (77 million km). (Mars can actually get closer, thanks to its highly eccentric orbit, but never as close as Venus.) When Mars is on the far side of its orbit from Earth, it's so far away that two planets are actually closer to us: Venus and tiny Mercury, which orbits the Sun at a distance of a mere 36 million miles (58 million km). In other words, schlepping to Mars won't be just like going down to the corner store.

Mars Myth #2: Mars is the planet most like Earth.
Mars Reality #2: This depends on what you mean by "most like Earth." It's most like Earth in its surface features and weather, in its annual temperature range, its axial tilt, and its length of day (which is about 24 and a half hours long). But then other planets start intruding in the comparison. In terms of actual size, Venus is closer to Earth's size than Mars. With a radius of 7,500 miles (12,070 km), Venus is just 400 miles (644 km) smaller in diameter than Earth; Mars has a diameter of a mere 4,200 miles (6,759 km). Venus is also closer in terms of gravitational pull—on Venus you'd

weigh 91 percent of what you do on Earth, while on Mars you'd weigh just 38 percent as much. Saturn, Uranus, and Neptune also have similar gravitational pulls to Earth. In terms of water, the planet that is most like Earth is Jupiter's moon Europa, which scientists think may have an ocean of liquid water hidden beneath a massive covering of ice. So while Mars is like Earth in some ways, in many other ways it's not.

Mars Myth #3: Mars is easily habitable by man.
Mars Reality #3: Ha! If you want to know what living on Mars is like, here's what you do. First, move to Antarctica, because that's how cold it is on Mars: The average temperature is a nastily cold –85°F (–65°C). Now, once you've moved to Antarctica, remove 99 percent of the air from the atmosphere—because Mars's atmospheric pressure at the surface is just one percent of what Earth's is. Not that you could use it anyway, since about 95 percent of Mars's atmosphere is carbon dioxide, which you can't breathe. Finally, should you ever land on Mars, you'd be millions upon millions of miles from the nearest 7-11, McDonald's, or Krispy Kreme. Elton John got it right when he said: "Mars ain't the kind of place to raise your kids." He should know; he's the Rocket Man.

Mars Myth #4: They've discovered liquid water on Mars.
Mars Reality #4: Not exactly. In 2002, NASA scientists discovered what they called a "whopping large" hydrogen signal underneath and surrounding the southern pole of Mars—a hydrogen signal that almost certainly means that there is water on Mars, trapped in the Martian soil. This discovery is a good thing, since: a) water is an important ingredient in life as we know it, boosting the chances for life on Mars, and b) it would make it easier for us to visit and even colonize one day. But it's not clear whether any of that water is liquid; given Mars's frigid temperatures, it's more likely that any underground Martian water is frozen. In June 2000, NASA announced that they had found evidence that water might have once flowed on the Martian surface—evidence in the form of gullies that looked a great deal like water-formed gullies on Earth. However, a year later, scientists from the University of Arizona noted that these gullies could have also been created by frozen carbon dioxide—carbon dioxide being the main ingredient of the atmosphere, and frozen carbon dioxide also being present in Mars's ice caps.

Two American engineers invented the microchip in 1959.

Mars Myth #5: Mars's surface is covered with canals.
Mars Reality #5: Nope. The idea of Martian canals got its start with American astronomer Percival Lowell, who in the late 19th century mistranslated comments from an Italian astronomer about the possibility of huge *canali*, or "channels," on the surface of Mars. Lowell thought *canali* meant "canals"—artificial structures made by advanced, intelligent creatures—rather than naturally occurring channels, which was the original idea. The existence of the canals was hotly debated for decades, until a visit from the *Mariner* spacecraft in the 1960s proved without a doubt that no canals (or channels, for that matter), existed at all—and there was no other sign of intelligent life on Mars. So that was that.

However, the canals still pop up from time to time. They're featured in popular science fiction books by Ray Bradbury and Robert Heinlein (both wrote many of their books before the question was settled). They were even a minor plot point in the 1996 movie *Mars Attacks!* By 1996 the filmmakers should have known better, but then it was a movie about Martians attacking Earth, so you can't beat on them for not being factually correct.

Mars Myth #6: NASA spacecraft spotted a face on Mars, evidence of an ancient advanced society.
Mars Reality #6: The famous "face on Mars" was discovered in 1976 when NASA spacecraft *Viking I* snapped a picture of a mesa in the Cydonia region of Mars. The mesa looked disturbingly like an actual human face—a human face two miles (3 km) long, that is. Since then, "the face" has been a popular pop culture icon and was even featured in the really terrible 2000 flick *Mission to Mars* (in which it really *was* a face left there by old, dead Martians). But don't get too excited. In 2001, the Mars Global Surveyor took a finely detailed picture of the "face"—and *this* time it looked like—well, like a big pile of rocks, which is exactly what it is. The "face" on the mesa is really nothing more than a combination of shadows and the poor imaging resolution of the camera attached to the *Viking I* spacecraft. There's also a crater called Galle on Mars that looks like a "happy face." Evidence of a very cheerful, ancient civilization? Probably not.

Mars Myth #7: The Martians sabotaged our spacecraft so we wouldn't find out about them.

Mars Reality #7: Yeah, *that's* it. The spacecraft in question would be 1999's ill-fated Mars *Climate Orbiter* and *Polar Lander* spacecraft, both of which bit the big one after arriving at Mars. As interesting as it would be to say that these spacecraft were knocked out of the sky by Marvin the Martian and his pals taking a little target practice, the fact is that both missions failed because of screwups back on Earth. The former spacecraft burned up in Mars's atmosphere, the latter went plummeting to the surface.

Mars Myth #8: Scientists found microbes from Mars on Earth.

Mars Reality #8: The Martian microbes may or may not be real. What we've got here is a meteor named ALH 84001, found in Antarctica in 1984 and originally from Mars, in which scientists discovered some interesting things: little squiggles that looked similar to fossilized Earth bacteria, carbon (a primary ingredient of life), and some organic molecules. It was enough for NASA to announce in 1996 that there was a possibility of life once existing on Mars. Then the skeptics weighed in: The "squiggles" were too small to have been bacteria, the "fossils" could have been created by chemical processes without the need for living things, and the organic materials in the rock could have come from Antarctica, where the rock has been, after all, for about 13,000 years—plenty of time for contamination. The current status of the "microbes"? Well, they *could* be life. Or they might not be. Your guess (for now, at least) is as good as theirs.

* * * * *

"A man said to the universe
'Sir, I exist!'
'However,' replied the universe,
'The fact has not created in me
A sense of obligation.' "

—Stephen Crane,
War Is Kind, 1899

Yuri Gagarin, a Russian, is the first human to travel in space in 1961.

"YOU THINK I'M MAD, DON'T YOU?"

They're not mad! It's the world that's mad!!
Bwa hah hah hah hah!!!

Look at it from the mad scientist's point of view. All he wants to do is reanimate the dead, or invent a transporter, or maybe just drink a mind-altering potion in the privacy of his own home. But the rest of the world seems to think that's wrong! What do *they* know?!? *They* didn't spend years digging up cadavers, mixing toxic chemicals, or exploring the eighth dimension! *They* probably don't have any advanced degrees! Foolish mortals! See? From the scientist's point of view, it makes perfect sense. Here are ten films to prove they're not mad—just misunderstood.

The Adventures of Buckaroo Bonzai Across the 8th Dimension!

Yes, the exclamation point is part of the title. The mad scientist is Dr. Emilio Lizardo (John Lithgow), who went looking for trouble in the eighth dimension and found it when some goopy-looking alien took over his skull. Now he needs to get back to where he once belonged, and the only thing stopping him is Buckaroo Bonzai: scientist, rock 'n' roll star, and cultural icon. A true cult favorite among the brainy and socially maladapted. (They want to be Buckaroo Banzai, but they smell like Dr. Lizardo.) While it is a little obscure for some, it starts making twisted sense after the fifth or sixth viewing. Stick with it.

Coma

Here's a flick to make you nervous the next time you go in for a tummy tuck. Genevieve Bujold plays a doctor who is investigating her friend's death during minor surgery. One thing leads to another, and the next thing she knows, she's wandering through a big room filled with people hanging from tubes, their organs just waiting to be harvested! Apparently people forgot you could just check the "donor" box on your driver's license application. Michael Douglas plays her love interest and Richard Widmark is the doctor who keeps slipping the patients a little too much gas. So remember, next time you're in, ask for a local.

April 21, 1970, is the first celebration of Earth Day.

Dr. Jekyll and Mr. Hyde

Long before Anthony Hopkins got an Oscar for playing a doctor gone bad in *Silence of the Lambs*, Fredric March copped one in 1932 for this baby. You know how it works: Mild-mannered doctor by day goes drinking and then becomes an evil criminal jerk by night. Yes, it sounds no different than what happens at any convention—but in *this* case Dr. Jekyll isn't tossing back frilly drinks with umbrellas in them. This one's been remade a few times (including as a stoner comedy in the early 1980s, for which karmic punishment will certainly apply), but the Fredric March version is still the best.

Dr. Strangelove, or How I Learned to Stop Worrying and Love the Bomb

Even if the entire film weren't already a brilliant black comedy about the end of the world by way of nuclear holocaust (and it *is*), this would still be worth seeing for the great Peter Seller's portrayal of Dr. Strangelove, an expatriate Nazi scientist (very loosely modeled on Werner von Braun). Strangelove is intensely weird, from the top of his toupéed head to the fingertips of his out-of-control (and self-homicidal) right hand. If actual nuclear scientists were anything like him, we'd all be glowing piles of ash.

The Fly

Jeff Goldblum zaps himself in a transporter of his own making and makes it through to the other side, no problem. Well, *one* problem: The fly that went along for the ride is now in his DNA. Pretty soon he's superstrong and walking on the ceiling, which is cool, but he also loses fingers and teeth and has to vomit on his food to digest it, which is, um, icky. *The Fly* could simply have been a gross-out horrorfest (and it certainly is that—no pregnant woman should *ever* watch the birth scene), but director David Cronenberg makes it surprisingly touching in places. A remake of a 1950s B movie, this one is superior in every way.

Frankenstein

You have two choices: The classic 1931 version starring Colin Clive as Dr. Frankenstein and Boris Karloff as the grunting, rivet-necked monster, or the not-so-classic 1994 version with Kenneth Branagh as the good doctor and Robert De Niro as the monster (which certainly puts a whole new spin on the classic De Niro line, "You lookin' at *me?*"). The 1931 version is indelibly printed onto our cultural memory—the collective image of the Frankenstein monster is Boris Karloff's—but on the other hand, the 1994 version is much more faithful to the original 19th century novel by Mary Shelley. And it's in color! And don't forget *Young Frankenstein*, Mel Brooks's dazzling send-up of *Frankenstein* and classic horror films—a classic in its own right.

Hollow Man
Kevin Bacon turns invisible, and no, this is not an assessment of his movie career. In *Hollow Man* he plays an unethical scientist who uses his own untested process to become invisible. Then, as he must in a movie like this, he goes completely insane and starts sneaking into hot girls' apartments and killing off colleagues. Watch this for the special effects; the story is a bit, er, transparent.

The Island of Dr. Moreau
There are several versions of this tale of a mad scientist combining humans and animals, the most recent starring Marlon Brando as the doctor in question, channeling his *Apocalypse Now* Colonel Kurtz performance. You might prefer the 1977 version with Burt Lancaster—less flab, more acting. The author of the original novel, H. G. Wells, was doing his patented thing of using science fiction to make a social point—this time about the fine line between human and animal nature, but as with the Hollywood versions of *The Time Machine*, good luck finding much of a social point here, especially in the Brando version.

The Nutty Professor
Dr. Jekyll done for comedy. The original *Nutty Professor* had Jerry Lewis turning from maladapted loser/science professor into suave ladies' man, Buddy Love; the Eddie Murphy remake has him as maladapted *and* obese, but still turning into Mr. Love. They both have to bottle Buddy back up: He's suave, but he's also kind of a creep. It's a toss-up which version is better. The Lewis version is beloved by the French, but the Murphy version, filled with potty jokes, is more in line with contemporary tastes.

Re-Animator
In the mood for a really over-the-top splatterfest? *Re-Animator* has got the goods, a nasty—and nastily funny—flick in the *Frankenstein* mode (based on a story by creepmaster H. P. Lovecraft). In a nutshell: Testy medical student Herbert West (Jeffrey Combs) finds a formula to reanimate dead tissue, so he *does*. Hilarious and gory hijinks ensue. Not everyone's cup of tea, to be sure.

SPACE JAMS

One small slip for a man, one huge screwup in space!

Since the first *Sputnik* orbited Earth in October 1957, billions and billions of dollars have been poured into the space race. You probably know about the more spectacular (and some-times tragic) failures. Here are a few lesser-known mishaps. No lives were lost, but one or two jobs in the aerospace industry prob-ably went by the wayside.

1961: The U.S. *Mariner I* interplanetary probe to Venus was forced to self-destruct, even though it was operating normally, due to a combination of faulty hardware and software on the ground.

1964: The U.S. *Mariner 3* was launched toward Mars; it went off course and is now happily orbiting the Sun (with its buddy probes *Mariners 5, 6, 7,* and *10*).

1988: A missing letter from a string of commands radioed to the Russian *Phobos I* probe en route to Mars caused it to self-destruct.

1990: The Hubble Space Telescope mirror was found to be out of focus. It orbited aimlessly for over three years until it was repaired by U.S. astronauts.

1997: Twenty separate glitches occurred on the *Mir* space station, including failures of the main computer, oxygen and power gener-ators, and the air-conditioning system.

1998: The failure of a *Galaxy* communications satellite disabled millions of pagers and interrupted radio broadcasts in the U.S.

1999: The Mars *Climate Orbiter* was lost because of a miscalcula-tion caused by a program (supplied by Lockheed) working in imperial units rather than the metric units expected by the other programs.

Also, in 1999, the Mars *Polar Lander* was sent crashing onto the surface of Mars because a software glitch caused the onboard computer to assume that it had safely landed. It shut down its engines when it was still 132 feet (40 m) above the surface.

2000: Nine international satellites were lost due to launch failures at a cost of about $100 million per launch.

Cellular phones first appeared in cars in 1985.

AARGH! IT'S COMING RIGHT AT US!

*How do 3-D movies make objects pop out of the screen
and head right for the audience?*

Humans need two things to see: an eye and a brain. Both of these features are critical to vision. Light enters the eyeball through the cornea, where it's focused and then sprayed onto a receptor-rich area called the retina. The retina converts it into signals that are sent to the brain via the optic nerve. Then it's the brain's turn to process the information and let you know what it is you're seeing: a familiar face or aliens who have come to give you a duodenal probe (it's how they say hello).

HEY, TWO EYES!
All of this would work even if you only had one eye. With that extra eye, you get a special gift: stereo vision—the ability to gauge, with a fair deal of accuracy, the distance of objects in front of you. This happens because your two eyes are situated slightly apart (two inches [5 cm] is the norm). So even though both eyes are looking at the same scene, each has a different take on whatever it is you're looking at (one a little more to the left, and the other a little more to the right—you get the picture).

THE MOVING FINGER
Both eyes transmit the information to the brain's visual centers, the brain fuses the two pictures together, and you "see" one picture that incorporates those two different perspectives and provides you with depth perception. The melding is skillful enough that you don't even notice that you're really looking at two views of the same scene unless you go out of your way to do so. (Try moving a finger slowly toward the bridge of your nose: You'll see two images of your finger appear because your eyes' separate fields of vision don't overlap there.)

BUILT-IN BINOCULARS
Just having two eyes doesn't automatically guarantee depth perception—eye placement is key as well. Human eyes face

Every day your kidney filters about 200 quarts of fluid.

forward, which provides the eyes with the overlap that they need for truly useful stereo vision. Useful for what? Well, hunting, for one thing—depth perception comes in handy for things like judging where to heft a spear. Many predators who rely on vision for hunting have forward-facing eyes and wide fields of binocular vision, including owls, tigers (whose binocular vision is almost as good as man's), and bears (who are, however, nearsighted). Not coincidentally, quite a few prey animals have eyes to the sides of their heads, giving up depth perception for a wider field of vision to see what's planning to attack and gnaw their tender vittles.

STALKING THE WILD MEATLOAF
Today most people use their binocular vision for hunting around the butcher's counter for the best cut of steak, but we use our stereo vision for plenty of other activities, like playing sports or driving. You can do both without two eyes, but it's more difficult to judge distances between you and other objects, which can be critical when a fastball (or a student driver) is heading at you.

IN THE PATH OF AN ONCOMING TRAIN
One activity that doesn't generally use our 3-D vision capabilities is movie watching. Typically, movies consist of a single image projected onto a large screen; the image is flat, so both eyes get the same information. We can get fooled by an illusion of depth; early moviegoers who watched *The Great Train Robbery* were reported to have jumped out of their chairs to avoid the oncoming train, but true depth perception is usually not on the marquee.

This changed in the 1950s when movie studios, terrified by the prospect of moviegoers staying home to watch TV, started experimenting with different technologies to lure people back into theaters. One of these technologies was 3-D films: films that tricked the eye (and the brain) into thinking that objects were leaping off the screen and jumping right into the moviegoer's lap.

TURKEY FILM FESTIVAL
The technology for 3-D films was fairly simple. Moviegoers were given glasses with one red lens and one blue (or green) lens. The movie projected onto the screen featured two images filmed slightly apart: One of these images was projected in red, and the other in blue (or green). The colored lenses filtered out the images

The shells of cashew nuts contain caustic oil that can blister the skin.

projected in their color while letting the other get through, so each eye received a slightly different image, and the brain put them together like it usually does to provide the 3-D effect. It worked swell, as long as the film was in black and white. People loved it at first, until they realized that most 3-D movies stank.

In the early 1980s, 3-D films made another comeback, this time relying on polarization to work the three-dimensional magic. Filmgoers were given glasses in which each lens had a different polarization—meaning the lens would allow certain types of light in, but not others. Once again, two images were projected onto the screen, each with a different polarity, and the glasses blocked one image while letting the second image through. Polarizing allowed color films to be shown in 3-D. But once again, 3-D was killed, not by the technology, but by rank, fetid movies like *Jaws 3* (a.k.a. *Jaws 3-D*) and *Comin' At Ya!* (Ironically, while most 3-D films of the 1950s were in black and white and used the colored lenses, the very first commercial 3-D movie, 1952's *Bwana Devil*, was in color and used polarized lenses).

3-D MEETS A.D. 2000
These days, you don't go to the movies for the most advanced 3-D systems (although the IMAX large-screen theaters have raised 3-D movies to a new high, literally—one of their productions, *Space Station 3-D*, was shot in orbit above Earth), you go to your computer. The new computerized visualization system uses LCD (liquid crystal display) lenses in the glasses to black out the right and left eye alternately, while the computer screen alternates drawing an image on its screen from slightly different perspectives. Today's computers redraw their screens so quickly that the person wearing the glasses doesn't even notice his or her vision is being blacked out in one eye for a fraction of second, several times faster than the proverbial blink of an eye.

STALKING THE WILD GAMEBOY
One use for these systems: video games, of course. Their advantage over movies is that no one's paying attention to the plot anyway, they're just looking for things to hunt and shoot. And so bleeding-edge 3-D technology brings binocular vision back to one of its original purposes. That's some irony, huh, coming right at you.

NOTHING TO FEAR BUT THE BIOSPHERE

TV's Survivor series has nothing on Biosphere 2. The Biosurvivors suffered near-starvation, chronic overwork, lack of oxygen, and bad press, and still managed to survive.

Biosphere 2 was the prototype of a space colony housed in an airtight 3.15-acre greenhouse on the outskirts of Tucson, Arizona. The idea was to duplicate the natural, self-sufficient ecosystem of Biosphere 1, more commonly known as Earth.

JUST LIKE HOME

The complex was stocked with human beings, animals, insects, and plants—all of which were supposed to coexist in a world made up of miniature ecological communities called "biomes": a mangrove swamp, a desert, a savanna, a rain forest (complete with misting rain), and a one-million-gallon ocean that included a coral reef and lagoon.

Each Biospherian would have a private apartment complete with a bed, storage space, a phone, a TV, and a computer with modem. The bathrooms were equipped with a built-in spray—no toilet paper. Biospherian-waste was recycled as fertilizer for the crops. Water, food scraps, and air were recycled as well.

DAY 1–DAY 730

In September 1991, eight optimistic and healthy environmentalists—four men and four women—trooped into the oversized greenhouse. At the end of two years they emerged, thin and haggard looking. But they were better off than the animals, most of whom didn't make it at all.

YOU SHOULD LIVE SO LONG

The plan had been that the Biospherians would grow their own supplies of fruit and vegetables. They had fish to eat, chickens, and eggs—how hard could it be? Well, one problem was that their farm was designed by the crew's doctor, Roy Walford, the author of *The 120-Year Diet*. The book advocates an extremely low-calorie diet as a means to longevity. As a result, the Biospherians

---

The number one cause of daytime fatigue is a lack of water.

were often hungry—a situation that put everyone but the good doctor on edge—and led to some bang-up arguments in the kitchen and elsewhere.

KILLING THE GOLDEN CHICKENS
Things got so bad in the hunger department that the humans started competing with the chickens for food. Guess who won? When they ran out of chicken feed, they killed the chickens and ate them, which left them with no chickens—and no eggs.

AIR SUPPLY
All the same, the low-fat, low-calorie diet they lived on should have made the Bio-2 humans feel fit, but in fact, they usually felt sluggish. The library went unused because no one had the energy to climb the 100 or so steps to get there. The reason, they eventually realized, was that they were living at the edge of suffocation.

The level of oxygen that the rest of us earthlings breathe contains about 21 percent oxygen. The planners had assumed that the plants and algae growing inside Biosphere 2 and its million-gallon ocean would produce a comparable amount. And they should have. But in reality, a lot of precious oxygen was being consumed by the concrete walls—which hadn't been completely cured—and by microbes in the soil. At times, the oxygen level dropped as low as 14.5 percent, dangerously close to the minimum needed to sustain life. Eventually, oxygen was pumped in from the outside. At the same time, greenhouse gases—carbon dioxide and nitrous oxide—levels soared.

BIRDS, BEES, ETC.
First the emerald-throated hummingbirds and blue finches died. Then all seven species of frogs disappeared. Among the rest of the animals—bats, lizards, and so on—19 of the 25 species of vertebrates became "extinct." This wasn't a surprise to the planners: They'd expected a 30 to 40 percent drop off in species by the end of Biosphere 2's two-year run. As the animal population declined, so did the tropical forest and the coral reef.

THEM
The Biosphere was stocked with three resident species of ants, most of whom soon became extinct. It wasn't long before the complex was invaded by a party-crashing species called "crazy ants." With few predators to eat them, crazy ants took over,

A butterfly's life span ranges from a week to ten days.

living side by side with the other "survivors"—the cockroaches and katydids.

SEX AND OTHER INTERACTIONS
From Herb Caen's column in the *San Francisco Chronicle*, October 4, 1991: "So four men and four women have sealed themselves off inside Biosphere 2. No contraceptives are allowed and if a woman gets pregnant, she's expelled. This is progress? Sounds more like high school in the 1950s." The Biospherians called it "As the Biosphere Recycles," but to our consternation, won't talk about their sex lives, except to make it clear that interpersonal relations were tricky enough without the unnecessary complications of sex.

"SAY AHHH"
They went through the usual assorted health complaints: diarrhea, back pain, eye and urinary-tract infections, and a cold that made the rounds until there was no one left to catch it. The most serious medical episode was when one crew member lost a fingertip in a thresher accident. When the injury failed to heal, she was whisked away for emergency treatment and whisked back in—the only member of the team who had been on the outside in the entire two years of confinement.

AN EXPERIMENT THAT FAILED?
In one sense, Biosphere 2 was a failure. But a lot of scientists who once pooh-poohed it as "unscientific" grudgingly admitted its contributions. Especially as a lab for studying the effects of Biosphere 1's most pressing environmental problem—the proliferation of greenhouse gases.

UNDER NEW MANAGEMENT
In 1994 a new group of colonists were sealed inside the newly cured cement walls of Biosphere 2, but this time just for a six-month stay—two years was deemed too long. Then, in 1995, New York's Columbia University took over Bio-2's management. It's now used for teaching and research.

And if you're ever in Arizona, it's a pretty cool tourist attraction, too.

Male cats that are colored both orange and black are sterile.

GOOD VIBRATIONS

Waves are invisible, so how do we know they exist?

A bell chimes because when the clapper strikes the metal, it vibrates. The vibrations of the bell push against the air around it, causing the vibrations of adjacent air molecules, which cause the vibrations of other nearby molecules, and so on. Those waves of vibrations produce sound. It's that simple.

But if you were to put the bell in a vacuum chamber and ring it, it would still vibrate, but there wouldn't be any sound. That's because there wouldn't be any air for the bell to push against. No air, no wave. No wave, no sound.

FUN WITH PHYSICS

To demonstrate the different types of waves, just go to your local physics lab—or any kid's toy box. First, find a jump rope and tie it to a doorknob. Hold it taut and wave it once. The wave will travel along the rope, bounce off the door, and come back to your hand. You've just created a transverse wave, where the individual particles of the rope move up and down (or side to side, for that matter). Sound waves are transverse waves.

Now dig around for the Slinky and stretch it out on the rug. Give one end a tap. A wave will shiver all across the length of the Slinky and back again. That kind of wave is called a longitudinal wave. It works by compressing the spring and stretching it back out again.

Next, fill up the toy pool, and toss in the rubber ducky. Make some waves. Notice that the ducky moves in small, vertical circles as the waves travel under it. A water wave is an example of a wave that is both longitudinal and transverse, since the individual particles of water both compress and relax while moving up and down (hence the circular motion).

THE ULTIMATE WAVE

Another type of wave, the electromagnetic wave, can be seen just by the virtue of the fact that you can see. Electromagnetic waves (such as light) can travel through the vacuum of space as well as through liquids and solids. Solids, you say? How come light can't

---

Dogs can make around 10 vocal sounds; cats can make over 100.

travel through, say, a bucket? Well, part of the light spectrum—the radio waves—can. Your AM/FM radio would work just as well under the bucket (or in your house for that matter) as out.

RACETRACK PHYSICS

Now let's go to the Indy 500. Here at the track, if a speeding car is moving toward you, the waves moving toward you are compressed, so the sound the car makes seems higher pitched. When it passes you and zooms away from you, the sound jumps to a much lower pitch. This is called the Doppler effect (after the Austrian physicist who first described it), and it applies to any wave—even light. A light wave moving toward you is compressed, so it seems bluer than a stationary light. A light wave moving away is stretched out and seems redder. These are called blue shifts and red shifts.

FASTER THAN A SPEEDING STAR

Something has to be moving really fast for us to notice this—such as a star. Since stars and distant galaxies are redder than we would otherwise expect, we know that they're moving. And since the redness indicates they all are moving away from each other, scientists have concluded that the universe is expanding. This expansion is what led scientists to come up with the Big Bang theory. Cool, huh?

STOP INTERFERING!

But back to the jump rope. Start waving it up and down, and try to time it so the waves appear to stay in place, rather than moving up and down the rope. This is a standing wave. (Back to standing waves in a minute.)

For now, tie one end of the rope to the middle of another rope so you have a Y. Tie the stem end of the Y to the doorknob and hold the other ends in your hands. Wave the rope with both hands moving in opposite directions, while trying to time it so both waves are even on each side. If you do it right, when the waves reach the knot in the middle they'll cancel each other out, and the stem of the Y will not move much at all! This is called destructive interference.

Next, keep the two ends parallel to each other as you wave. Again, if you time it right, the small waves of the two ropes will add up to one big wave in the stem of the Y. This is called constructive interference.

MUSICAL PHYSICS

Standing waves are important in music because the points at which they can exist on a string are called harmonics. If you get the jump rope to move in two standing waves, the stationary point in the middle is a harmonic.

Get out the kid's guitar or violin and give it a twang. Look closely and you'll notice that it doesn't vibrate evenly across the string's length. The whole string shivers across several segments all up and down the string. This is what produces overtones.

Most things that vibrate have overtones, and we actually prefer it that way. The sound of a tuning fork (which is about as close to an overtone-free sound as you can get) is somewhat boring, which is why we don't have bands called the Tuning-Fork Trio (yawn).

BAD VIBRATIONS

Sound waves can be dangerous, even if they aren't particularly loud. Resonance is what causes an object to vibrate sympathetically because another nearby object is vibrating (like crying babies). If you were to take two tuning forks tuned to A, and ring one, the vibrations would cause the other one to ring faintly as well. This happens most dramatically when the sound is the same pitch as the resonating object.

Back in 1940, winds blowing over a suspension bridge in Tacoma, Washington, started a small vibration that built up to twisting standing waves in the bridge surface over 20 feet (6 m) high! The winds were at just the right strength, and hit the bridge at just the right angle, to cause the bridge to resonate. Naturally, the bridge collapsed. Nowadays, engineers know better and build their structures and engines with a healthy respect for the damage waves can cause.

A BIG, DARK, SILENT NOTHING

Who would think that waves could wield such power? Well, they're even more powerful than that. Without them, there'd be no light, no sound. No life at all. No nothing.

In the last century Americans' time spent sleeping has decreased 20%.

KITCHEN CHEMISTRY

*The cavemen creep out of their cave, thanking the gods of fire
for sparing them from the blaze. As they venture into the burned
wasteland, Og stumbles over a burned deer carcass. Never one
to miss an opportunity to eat, he rips off a hunk and stuffs it
into his mouth. To his surprise, the cooked meat is much more
delicious than usual. He calls out to everyone, and they enjoy
an impromptu feast. The science of cooking has begun.*

Could the first cavemen ever have imagined a soufflé? Or a
doughnut? They had to begin somewhere, probably by
dabbling with simple things like meat. So shall we.

A MEATY SUBJECT

What actually happens when meat browns? First, the heat causes
the proteins and sugars in the meat to break down—to literally
separate into the elements they're made up of. (Some elements,
like gold, oxygen, or carbon, can't be broken down, but that's
another story. Back to the kitchen.) Once the proteins and sugars
have broken down, they recombine again and again while the
meat cooks. As they do so, different flavors develop. That's why
rare meat has a different taste than well-done meat.

Aging also produces flavors. This is because when meat is
allowed to sit, it starts to break down—a slower process that gives
it more time to release enzymes that attack the meat fiber, resulting in more tender meat. Of course, you wouldn't want to let it
age too long, as rotting and aging are essentially the same thing.

ACCORDING TO THE EGGS-PERTS

Why do eggs turn white when you cook them? We're glad you
asked. In their transparent, uncooked form, egg-white molecules
are like overdone spaghetti that sticks to itself, proteins that are
made up of strings of amino acids folded and jumbled together. It's
these crosslinks that hold the protein together.

Heating unjoins the links (so does beating them or adding
chemicals, like vinegar). Heating shakes the crosslinks apart, and
the strands unravel and start forming new links with neighboring
strands. As more links form they create a network, only this one is

---

Frogs croak more before a rainstorm.

much tighter than before. The new network is tight enough to block light, which is why eggs lose their transparency and turn white as they cook. And once this network forms, it can't be undone—nothing you can do will make a cooked egg raw again. If you want to see this web, simply overcook your eggs; you'll eventually drive all the moisture out of the egg, and you'll wind up with egg lace.

FLOUR POWER
Flour is an amorphous substance, which means literally that it doesn't dissolve in water (in contrast to crystalline substances like salt and sugar). But it does thicken. And as it does so, the flour granules swell and form a network with other granules. That's why you only have to add a little flour to gravy to make it thicken. If you do the opposite—add only a bit of moisture and a lot of flour, you make the transition from cooking to baking. By definition, baking is the art of making breads and pastries. Both take place in the kitchen, and both involve a lot of the same ingredients. But cooking and baking are separate sciences. A chef is both a cook and a baker, but a baker is a baker is a baker.

BAKIN' AND EGGS
Have you ever wondered how cakes can call for both oil and water when they don't mix? Everyone knows that oil forms bubbles in water, but it doesn't actually mix, it just kind of sits there. You can beat it with a blender until the bubbles are so small you can't see them, but eventually they'll come apart.

The secret to mixing oil and water is an emulsifier—something like eggs—that allows you to thoroughly mix the unmixable. This is because the lecithin in egg whites is attracted to oil molecules at one end and water molecules at the other. Together, they form happy little chains, preventing the oil and water from unmixing. Other emulsifiers are gelatin, nonfat milk, and mustard.

YEAST IS YEAST, BUT...
You've heard that bread rises—you may have even seen it happen. But you may be surprised to learn *how* it happens.

Yeast is kneaded into the bread as it's mixed. Then the whole wad is left to sit in a warm place. While it sits, the yeast is eating

As you age, your thymus gets smaller in size.

the sugar in the bread. As it does so, it leaves behind certain waste products. One of the waste products is carbon dioxide. That's what forms the tiny bubbles in the bread, causing it to rise. The other waste product is sugar alcohol, which burns off when the bread cooks, but adds to the bread's flavor. If this sounds like fermentation to you, you're right. Wine is made the same way.

THE BUN ALSO RISES

Baking soda and baking powder also form bubbles of carbon dioxide, but what's the difference between the two? (Admit it—you've always wondered.) The answer is virtually no difference, since baking powder is just baking soda with a dry acid (calcium acid phosphate) mixed in. The acid produces two chemical reactions. The first one takes place when you add moisture to the mixture. The acid reacts against the baking soda, producing carbon dioxide. Once you place the batter in the oven, the gas expands, and the cake rises.

Baking soda is much stronger than baking powder because it's pure. Recipes that call for baking soda also call for some sort of acid (like lemon or milk). When you mix the two together, the baking soda starts working at once. That's why you have to put batters made with baking soda into the oven immediately, so all the gas bubbles don't escape before the cake is baked.

That's a free tip from Uncle John's kitchen.

* * * * *

Myth:
If you want to lose weight you have to change your diet.
Fact:
You can eat the same amount of the same foods and still lose weight—if you stay away from the North or South Pole and head to the equator. The centrifugal effect at the equator counteracts gravity's pull and makes everything at the equator a bit less weighty. A person who weighed 151 pounds (68 kg) at the North or South Pole is a paltry 150 pounds (68 kg) at the equator.

Lettuce is part of the sunflower family.

ARE YOU MY TYPE?

*Having a blood transfusion used to be like playing
Russian roulette—until the big breakthrough.*

Before blood types were discovered, getting a blood transfusion was risky. There was a very good chance that the new blood would kill you rather than help you. No one knew what made some people's blood incompatible with other people's blood. A biologist named Karl Landsteiner decided to find out.

AHA!

Under his microscope, Landsteiner saw that mixing certain types of blood caused the red blood cells to clump up, while this didn't happen with other types. He devised a simple system of classification based on what he saw, with four kinds of red blood cells, A, B, AB, and O. Later researchers identified two kinds of proteins, type A and type B, on the surfaces of the cells. A cell that had both types was AB; one that had only one was A, or B; one that had neither was O. Simple, huh? Well, not exactly.

THE Rh FACTOR FACTOR

There's another protein, called the Rh factor, to add to the equation. It was found in *rh*esus monkeys (and named for them) years later by Landsteiner and his colleagues. The Rh factor is also found in most humans. If it's there, the blood is said to be positive. If not, the blood is negative. From all this, we have a total of eight different combinations of blood types.

THE ANTIBODY FACTOR

A baby develops the antibody opposite to its blood type shortly after birth. For Type A blood, Type B antibodies form. For Type O blood, both Type A and Type B antibodies form. For Type AB blood, no antibodies form. When it comes to transfusions, if the wrong blood type is administered, the person's antibodies immediately attack the new blood. Antibodies work by attaching themselves to invaders—foreign bacteria and viruses as well as incompatible blood. The antibodies that form against an incompatible blood type cause the foreign cells to clump together. If the clot gets large enough it can stop the blood flow in a vein or artery, causing a heart attack, embolism, or stroke.

Eating celery burns more calories than the celery contains.

DELAYED REACTION

For the Rh factor, the antibodies develop only when a blood transfusion with the wrong Rh factor is administered. Then the antibodies develop more gradually, but the new blood cells will eventually be destroyed. And if another transfusion with the wrong Rh factor is administered, those antibodies will be ready to attack it right away.

THE BOTTOM LINE, BLOOD-WISE

A lucky person with AB+ (positive) blood contains all of the proteins and none of the antibodies, and can therefore receive any type of blood. People with type O blood (no proteins) are called "universal donors"—their blood is in very high demand because they can donate safely to any blood type. Type O negatives are even more desirable: They're the best transfusion type for newborn babies. So what's your type?

* * * * *

MNEMONIC FOR THE FUNCTIONS OF BLOOD

Oxygen transport, Carbon dioxide transport, Food, Heat, Waste, Hormones, Disease, Clotting becomes Old Charlie Foster Hates Women Having Dull Clothes.

IS IT TRUE THAT THERE ARE ONLY "SIX DEGREES OF SEPARATION" BETWEEN ANY TWO PEOPLE?

The concept is based on an experiment designed to see if randomly selected people from all walks of life would be able to find a particular "target" person using only their own network of friends.

It worked like this. A psychologist randomly selected pairs of people and designated one as the "source" and one as the "target." The source's job was to reach the target in the fewest number of steps possible, by using only people he knew. The source sent a letter to the person he knew who was most likely to know the target. If, say, the target lived in Boca Raton, the source would send a letter to a friend who lived in or near there, who in turn might send a letter to a person that she knew would be most likely to know the target. The number of intermediate links ranged from two to 10. The most common number wasn't six, it was five.

The first hominoid fossil found was a skull fragment unearthed in Germany in 1856.

PREHISTORIC ODDITIES

Why should dinosaurs have all the fun? Here are a few prehistoric critters that are every bit as bizarre as the strangest of saurians.

CANCEL THAT SCAMPI!

Opabinia—It might be a distant cousin of shrimp salad or it might be unrelated to anything alive today. Although it looked like something out of a science fiction movie, this weird four-inch-long animal lived in the sea that covered what is now Canada about 530 million years ago. Instead of legs, it had 14 pairs of oarlike gills used for swimming. But the real strangeness was saved for the head. It had five eyes—two pairs on stalks and another sitting in the middle of the top of the head. In front of all these eyes was a long flexible nozzle with a claw at the end. Scientists think the claw captured food and carried it to the mouth.

WHICH WAY DID HE GO?

Hallucigenia—This appropriately named little beast bears no resemblance to any animal alive or dead. Like *Opabinia*, it lived in Canada about 530 million years ago. *Hallucigenia* is so bizarre that scientists are uncertain which end is the front and which side is up. The most-accepted version shows a wormlike body supported by seven pairs of spines. Along the top of the body were seven long tentacles with two-pronged tips. One end had a bulbous feature that looked a bit like a head but with no sign of eyes or mouth. At the other end was a long tube that curved up over the "back," which may have been a mouth or an anus.

WHO NEEDS SYMMETRY?

Carpoids—Virtually all animals have some kind of symmetry—either bilateral like humans where your right hand is the mirror image of your left hand, or radial like a starfish, which looks the same no matter which arm is pointing up. But carpoids were completely asymmetrical. This distant relation of the sand dollar lived in the oceans of the Northern Hemisphere from 500 to about 350 million years ago. It looked something like a misshapen armored tadpole, with a bulging body covered with stony plates and a long, segmented tail that it used for swimming. Some scientists think that carpoids may have been the ancestors of vertebrates.

A baby panda is smaller than a stick of butter.

MORE THAN JUST A WORM
Conodonts—For more than a century scientists kept finding microscopic, teethlike objects in marine rocks dating from 510 to 210 million years ago. They looked like tiny, cone-shaped teeth or combs, but there was no sign of a jaw or any other bit of a skeleton associated with them. There were quite a few theories about what class of animal these conodonts belonged to, but it wasn't until about 20 years ago that a fossil of the whole animal was found. In appearance it was not spectacular. It was long and thin like a worm, but it had eyes and a low dorsal fin, and the teeth were located in the mouth. Many scientists now believe that the conodont may be one of the earliest-known vertebrates.

NICE SKELETON COSTUME!
Ostracoderms—Some of the earliest vertebrates were armored, jawless fish that were most common between 430 and 370 million years ago. These fish had skeletons made of cartilage, but their bodies were covered with plates of bone, so it could be said that they were wearing their skeletons on the outside. Ostracoderms could be up to 3 feet (1 m) long, but most were under a foot. Their heads were usually covered by a semicircular shield with two small holes for eyes. The rest of the body was surrounded by articulated plates that allowed the animal to swim slowly by moving its tail from side to side. These animals preferred a quiet environment like a lagoon where they could drift along the bottom, straining edible particles out of the mud.

HEY, BOOMERANG HEAD!
Diplocaulus—This 3-foot (1 m) long amphibian lived in what is now Texas about 270 million years ago. In most respects it looked like a large salamander, but its head made it unique. The skull was shaped like a boomerang with two small eyes in the front corners and the wings on either side. Scientists are not sure why *Diplocaulus's* head is such an odd shape, but they think it was either to make the animal swim better near the bottom of the lakes and streams it lived in—or the wide head made it more difficult for predators to swallow.

A LIZARD WITH OVERBITE
Lystrosaurus—Before the age of the dinosaurs, there were a lot of strange-looking reptiles, but few odder than *Lystrosaurus*. This 3-foot-long plant-eater had a squat body and splayed legs like a lizard, but its muzzle was shortened a bit like that of a bulldog.

As if this wasn't attractive enough, from the corners of its mouth hung two long tusks. The eyes and nostrils were set high up, making some scientists think that the animal had lived the way hippos do now, but recent findings show that Lystrosaurus could also have lived in arid environments that were common about 230 million years ago.

SEAWORLD, EAT YOUR HEART OUT

Ambulocetus—Halfway between the land-dwelling ancestors of whales and the modern marine mammals, *Ambulocetus* lived in what is now Pakistan about 50 million years ago. This 12-foot-long animal looked a bit like a cross between an otter and an alligator. It had a large head with long jaws and pointed teeth designed for catching and holding fish like an alligator, but the body was more like that of an otter. Scientists think it swam by moving its tail up and down like a modern whale rather than from side to side like a fish.

BIGGER THAN BIG BIRD

Phorurhacos—About 20 million years ago, South America was an island continent with its own unique forms of birds and mammals. Because no large mammalian predators had evolved there, the top carnivore was a bird—*Phorurhacos*. These flightless birds stood up to 10 feet (3 m) tall and had a head the size of that of a horse. Although they couldn't fly, they were very fast runners. They could run down their prey, catch it with their powerful talons, and tear it apart with their long, hooked beaks. These frightening birds survived until about 3 million years ago, when a land bridge formed between North and South America, allowing modern carnivores to invade South America and give *Phorurhacos* a little carnivorish competition.

WHY'D IT HAVE TO BE GIANT WOMBATS?

Diprotodon—Before humans arrived in Australia about 40,000 years ago, marsupials were larger and more varied than they are today. The largest of all was the *Diprotodon*, which was about the size of a hippopotamus. It looked like a gigantic wombat (one of those furry, bearlike things), and it ate leaves and grass. It wasn't a fast runner, but it was too large for any of the native predators to tackle until humans came along. (We're not pointing fingers or anything, but the *Diprotodon* became extinct suspiciously soon after the first humans arrived. A coincidence?)

Dragonflies can fly at speeds up to 35 mph and can move their two sets of wings separately.

BUILT LIKE A TANK

Glyptodon—The most heavily armored mammal of all time has to have been the *Glyptodon*. About the size of a VW Beetle, this distant relation of the armadillo roamed the plains of South America until 15,000 years ago. The first humans in that part of the world encountered these strange beasts and incorporated them into their legends. *Glyptodon* resembled a turtle with patches of fur except that the high, rounded shell was made of many small plates of bone. It had a long tail with a ball at the end of it like the mace of a medieval knight.

WHO NEEDS A ZOO?

Moropus—When scientists first discovered the *Moropus*, they couldn't believe that the horselike head and body belonged with the long claws and massive feet found nearby. This 10-foot-long distant relative of the horse looked like a mixed-up bag of spare parts. The head and neck looked like a stunted giraffe, but the body was more like that of a bear. The front legs were quite a bit longer than the back legs, and all four feet were armed with long claws. Some scientists believe that *Moropus* fed by rearing up on its hind legs and pulling down branches so it could strip off the leaves with its long tongue. This animal lived in tropical Asia until about 12,000 years ago.

WHEN MAMMOTH DOESN'T MEAN BIG

Mammuthus—Everyone knows what a woolly mammoth looked like—a big hairy elephant with long, curling tusks. Everyone also knows that they died out at the end of the last ice age, about 10,000 years ago. Guess again. For one thing, the last mammoths weren't very mammoth; they were about the size of a buffalo. They lived on Wrangel Island, off the northern coast of Siberia, and survived after other mammoths became extinct. Scientists believe that the dwarf mammoths were still around about 4,000 years ago, which makes them younger than the pyramids!

* * * * *

IF I LIVE TO BE 100...

Of all the existing mammals, including the big guys—elephants, gorillas, whales—the human being is the only one who lives to be more than 100 years old. Even in ancient times, before there were great medical advances, human beings were said to have occasionally lived over 100 years.

The Frisbee was first named the Pluto Platter.

SHUTTERBUG SCIENCE

The kids gather reluctantly next to the picnic table. On cue they bare their teeth and chorus "cheese!" Uncle Billy snaps the shot, only to realize that Gracie had her finger up her nose, Timmy had his eyes shut, and Johnny was holding two fingers over Sally's head.

In technology, everything usually starts out big, like the computers that once filled large rooms. Photography was only slightly different: It was a room. A thousand years ago, the first camera was merely a hole drilled in the side of a room. Simple, but it worked. Light entering the room through the hole formed an image—of whatever was outside the hole—on the opposite wall. (Of course, it wasn't a photograph—that refinement was still a few centuries away.) Since Latin was a common language among scientists, they called it a *camera obscura*, which means "dark room." Unimaginative, but apt.

THE INCREDIBLE SHRINKING ROOM
The design was improved upon over the years. There was a hole in the wall with a lens that could focus the light and a diaphragm to control the amount of light entering the room. Eventually, they shrunk the whole thing down so it was small enough to carry around. When a mirror was added to reflect the image down onto a viewing surface, artists took it up as a tool because it allowed them to cheat when making realistic drawings.

CAPTURING THE MOMENT
Soon everyone wanted a way to make the images permanent. Beginning in the 1600s, various enthusiasts started experimenting with silver salts. It all started when Angelo Sala noticed that silver salts darken in the sun. He and the experimenters who followed him played with the technique—but with unsatisfactory results. A major problem was how to stop the silver salts from darkening too much. Once they started darkening, they didn't stop. So the 17th-century camera buffs couldn't figure out how to stop the image from becoming overexposed.

SOMEDAY MY PRINTS WILL COME
Finally, in the 1800s, things started to get moving. A Frenchman named Joseph Niépce made the world's first photograph. It took

eight hours in the back of a camera obscura for the image (a couple of buildings and a tree) to form, but it was a success—fuzzy, but a success. He took it to England and tried to sell the scientists at the Royal Society on it, but they turned him away.

Niépce returned to France, and teamed up with a fellow Frenchman, Louis-Jacques-Mandee Daguerre, who later developed the daguerreotype, an image on a metal plate. Daguerreotypes looked great, but each was one of a kind. This suited most snobs just fine, but the rest of mankind wanted a way to mass-produce photographs. Next at bat was an Englishman named William Henry Fox Talbot, who came up with the first negative, from which unlimited prints could be made.

OVERNIGHT DEVELOPMENTS
After that it was one photographic invention after another all through the mid to late 1800s (similar to how we have one computer invention after another). Eventually, George Eastman came up with the flexible roll film and produced the Brownie camera, which was an instant success. Although refined a great deal over the last century, the process is pretty much the same now as it was then.

SHEDDING LIGHT ON THE SUBJECT
Anything that takes a thousand years to figure out is going to be fantastically complicated, and photography is no exception. It all starts with light shining through the lens. The role of the lens is to direct light onto the film. When light hits a sheet of glass, it's as if the light is diving into water: The glass slows the light down. As it does, it deflects the light into another direction. Throw a rock into water and you can see this for yourself.

When the glass is curved like a lens is, it bends all the light inward toward a focal point. That's the point at which the image is clear. When you focus the camera lens, you're aligning the focal point onto the film. Unless you need glasses, you'll soon get a clear image.

A camera works by exposing photosensitive film to light. The film has layers and layers of chemicals, some of them sensitive to red, green, and blue light. The layers are suspended in gelatin (that's right; just like Jell-O, but without the flavors); that's what holds all the layers together and what's most important during film developing.

CLICK!

When you click the button on the camera, the shutter opens, a curtain slides back, and for a brief instant, the image shines on the film. Then, everything closes back up and the camera advances the film for the next shot. From that point until you take the film into the developer, the film is kept in the dark. Or else.

OFF TO THE CAMERA OBSCURA

Once in the darkroom, the roll of film is placed in a bath that converts the silver ions in the film to silver metal. Remember the gelatin? Once it gets wet, it swells, allowing the chemicals to reach all the layers of the film. The ions that were exposed to light convert faster than unexposed portions, so the film can only be left in this chemical for a short period of time.

The layers that are sensitive to different colors all react by forming a color themselves. The red-sensitive layer creates a cyan (greenish-blue) dye, the green layer creates magenta, and the blue layer creates yellow. You can see colors other than this in the negative because each layer is superimposed upon the other, mixing the colors when light shines through.

A "stop bath" (that long-awaited Holy Grail of photography) prevents the chemicals from developing the negative any further. A "fix bath" removes any unexposed silver grains. The film is then washed and dried. Only now can the film see the light of day without ruining your shots.

A PICTURE OF A PICTURE

Next, the strips of film are loaded into a projector. One by one, the projector shines light through the film onto photographic paper. These papers have some of the same layers as the negative film, including layers that are sensitive to the colors in the negative. A "picture" of the negative is taken onto the print, and the entire development process is repeated with the print. So when you take the picture, the image is reversed onto the negative. To get the print, the image is reversed again. And if you made it through math, you know that two negatives make a positive. That's how you end up with a reproduction of your original scene.

Your prints are ready to be picked up.

If you are a shutterbug and enjoyed this article, see
Uncle John's Supremely Satisfying Bathroom Reader
for a collection of great articles on photography.

CONTINENTAL DRIFT: PART I

*You could probably pick Earth out of a planetary lineup.
But you wouldn't have recognized it a couple of
hundred million years ago.*

Asia, Africa, North America, South America, Antarctica, Europe, and Australia. Right? (And, yeah, we know, sometimes Europe and Asia are counted as one and called Eurasia.) But it wasn't always thus. The continents have changed a lot in the last couple of hundred million years.

OUR JIGSAW-PUZZLE PLANET
Back in 1596, a Dutch mapmaker named Abraham Ortelius noticed that Earth's continents looked like pieces of a puzzle. For example, the east coast of South America and the west coast of Africa would fit together nicely if they weren't separated by the Atlantic Ocean. He saw that—with a little sliding and turning—other continents might fit together, too. Ortelius thought that one big original continent had been torn apart by earthquakes and floods. But nobody believed him.

Over 300 years went by. Most scientists were secure in their "knowledge" that Earth's continents had always been the same. They stubbornly ignored anyone who suggested otherwise—including some very good thinkers.

OTHER SMART GUYS
For example, in 1620, philosopher and all-around brilliant guy Francis Bacon made note of the same fit between the two continents. And in the late 18th century, Benjamin Franklin did, too. Franklin also proposed the unheard-of idea that Earth's crust "floated" on a fluid core.

HOME SWEET PANGAEA
In 1912, German meteorologist Alfred Wegener also came to the conclusion that today's continents had once been all clumped together. He even named the former megacontinent Pangaea

An adult octopus has 2,000 suckers on average.

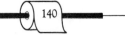

(Greek for "all the land"). Wegener estimated that Pangaea began to come apart about 200 million years ago—at the time when dinosaurs dominated Earth. (The first mammals had also appeared on the scene around then, but they spent most of their time trying to avoid getting trampled or eaten.)

Like Ortelius, Wegener based his theory on the visual fit of the continents. But he had other information to back up his claim. By his time, scientists had identified identical plant and animal fossils in widely separated parts of the world. Wegener figured that this was because living things could easily spread their species around while the continents were still joined. For example, fossils of *Mesosaurus*—a freshwater aquatic reptile that lived before the dinosaurs—were found in both South America and South Africa. It seems unlikely that these ancient creatures swam across the Atlantic, so it made sense that the coastlines must have once been clumped together. This encouraged other scientists to think more seriously about the theory called "continental drift."

BREAKING UP IS HARD TO DO
When the breakup started, Pangaea first split into two parts. That took about ten million years (these things can't be rushed). Scientists call the northern continent—now North America, Europe, and Asia—Laurasia. The southern part was named Gondwanaland—now South America, Africa, India, Australia, and Antarctica. The two continents were divided by a great sea. Before long (geologically speaking), each of those two broke into smaller pieces and went their separate ways. By 65 million years ago, the continents were shaped a lot like those we live on today.

BUT HOW?
"Who're you kidding?" demanded most scientists. "No force on Earth is powerful enough to move huge continents around like that." Unfortunately, Wegener couldn't explain how continental migration could have happened. It would be another 50 years or so before anyone figured it out.

EARTH FLOATS
Benjamin Franklin was right about Earth's floating crust. By the 1960s, there was a new science called plate tectonics (from the Greek "to build"). According to plate tectonics, the ground we walk on—Earth's crust—is made up of huge, floating rock plates.

They usually seem steady enough to those of us who don't live in earthquake territory. The plates are from 50 to 75 miles (80 to 120 km) thick, so we're not usually aware of the molten rock that boils away under our feet. This primordial and very hot soup (called "magma" when it's down there and "lava" up here on the surface) has currents that push the plates around. The plates go both sideways and up and down. They change size and shape as they get squashed together, built up, or pushed down. This causes things like mountains, valleys, seas, deep ocean trenches, earthquakes, and volcanoes. And it causes continental drift.

DID YOU FEEL THAT?
In fact, Earth's continents are still moving. In California's San Andreas Fault, laser measurements show that two major plates are slipping past each other at a rate of about two centimeters a year—nearly one inch. (See? I was sure I felt something.)

If Earth's plates slid along smoothly, we'd never notice. But they can get stuck for years. When they jerk ahead, you've got an earthquake. Sudden San Andreas slips devastated San Francisco in 1906 and again in 1989. Measurements made from satellites show that Europe and North America are still drifting apart—at a rate of about four centimeters a year.

So here we are, suspended in this moment of geological time. But the continents are still on the move.

Want to know the forecast for the next few million years? See Part II of Continental Drift on page 196.

* * * * *

Myth:
It will take a huge drop in temperature to put us into an ice age.
Fact:
It doesn't take a large change in temperature to create an ice age. It only takes slightly colder winters and summers. If more snow falls during a slightly colder winter than can be melted in a slightly cooler summer, the result would be an ice age.

Mosquitoes kill more than a million people annually.

HOW TO SURVIVE AN AVALANCHE

*Look! It's snowing! Soft, powdery snow seems like
such an innocent substance. But when those snowdrifts
are piled high, watch out!*

Avalanches don't just happen in the Alps—around 2,000
are reported to the U.S. Forest Service Avalanche Center
in an average winter. Worldwide, avalanches kill an average of 135 luckless people a year. The swift-moving slides (up to
50 mph [80 kph]) don't stop at burying skiers. They can isolate
towns, block roads and passes, sweep cars from roads, and even
knock down buildings. Just a few recent examples:

- In February 2000, the Alaskan ski resort town of Girdwood was
  isolated for almost a week. Officials had to resort to dynamite to
  blast the roads clear.
- In January 2000, an avalanche in Norway pushed a bus into the
  sea, killing five.
- An avalanche slid into a Quebec Inuit village on New Year's
  Day 1999, collapsing a school gym and killing nine.

Avalanches can happen anywhere, except maybe Florida and
Africa. Read this handy guide so you know what to do just in case.

WALK SOFTLY AND CARRY A BIG SHOVEL
Of course, all this advice goes for you skiers out there, too (though
you probably won't be toting the shovel), but it's mostly for people
who inexplicably want to walk around in the freezing cold. So, if
you're going to be traveling in avalanche-prone areas, be sure to
use caution:

- Travel on ridge tops above avalanche paths, in dense timber,
  and on slopes of 25 degrees or less that aren't topped by
  steeper slopes.
- Cross slopes at the very top when possible.
- Climb or descend the edge of a slope rather than the center.
- Alter your route or go back when you detect unstable snow.

Snakes don't have ears; they "hear" by feeling vibrations from the ground.

- When crossing dangerous areas, split up your group and stay in constant visual or voice contact.
- Never walk up to the edge of a drop-off without first checking it carefully—it's common sense, but thousands have died this way.

You should also carry avalanche rescue gear at all times, including:

- A beacon, a.k.a. an avalanche transceiver
- A shovel
- Collapsible or ski-pole probe
- A day pack with enough equipment to spend the night

WHAT ARE FRIENDS FOR?
In the first place, you should have a partner with you; virtually all avalanche victims are dug out by someone else. With any luck you or your partner will be spared to rescue the other or to go for help. But if you're caught in a snowslide:

- First, try to escape to the side or grab a tree or rock.
- If you're knocked down and sliding with the snow, dump your pack and/or your poles and skis if you've got 'em, all of which weigh you down.
- "Swim" with the avalanche to try to stay on top and avoid trees.

If the worst happens, and you're buried by the snow:

- Rule number one: Try to keep calm (easier said than done, but you'll expire a lot faster if you panic and breathe in snow).
- Dig a breathing space around your face—as large as possible (your breath's heat will form an ice wall around you).
- If you've been knocked down and tumbled around, you may not know which way is up and which direction to dig. Ball up some snow and drop it in your breathing space. A couple of drops will reveal the way as gravity pulls the small ball downward.
- Dig slowly and calmly directly upward, taking care that bits of snow do not plug up your mouth, nose, and eyes.
- Call for help as often and as loudly as you can.

DON'T BE A STATISTIC
That covers the basics. Fewer than half of the avalanche victims who are completely buried survive. Nobody who has been buried deeper than 7 feet (6.4 m) has lived to tell of it.

Cats can jump as high as the length of their tail times five.

THE BEST OFFENSE, A GOOD DEFENSE

We can learn a lot from the way animals defend themselves, and it isn't always the strongest guy who wins.

Not every creature can fight like a tiger or overpower enemies with the strength of a grizzly. There are sneakier ways to succeed at the game of survival.

FLY AWAY HOME

The animal kingdom is filled with critters who just want to live long, peaceable lives. To accomplish that feat, they're often equipped with at least two types of defenses: primary and secondary. A primary defense is always in use, whether or not an enemy is nearby. For instance, a ladybug's primary defense is that she (or he) tastes so disgusting, most birds won't eat her. When threatened, a ladybug uses her secondary defense: She flies away. Why stick around to become a bad taste in some bird's mouth?

HOME SWEET HIDEOUT

If animals were people you'd find plenty of them behind locked gates and bolted doors:

- Moles and earthworms live their entire lives underground.
- The kit fox has from two to 24 entrances to his den so that he can make a quick escape. He also has more than one den so he can move his family if they're threatened.
- The marsh wren builds fake nests to protect its real nest from discovery.
- The underwater entrance to a beaver's lodge discourages predators from dropping in unannounced.

BODY ARMOR

Then there are the guys who get out a lot, but they're not scared of predators because they've got built-in body armor:

- Turtles, tortoises, and terrapins have been around since the Triassic period, approximately 200 million years ago. Which only goes to show how effective the classic shell defense is.
- The porcupine carries an arsenal of over 30,000 barbed quills on

---

Buzz Aldrin and Neil Armstrong's first meal on the moon was roast turkey.

his body. It's a myth that porcupines "throw" their quills, but if attacked, a porcupine uses his quill-covered tail to pound needle-sharp barbs into the predator who was dumb enough to give him any trouble.

- Three-banded armadillos (whose upper bodies are covered with tough plated armor) protect their soft underbellies by rolling into a grapefruit-sized ball.
- A sturgeon's scales are hard enough to deflect a small-caliber bullet.

NOW YOU SEE ME, NOW YOU DON'T
The common chameleon has nothing on these masters of disguise:
- The ermine, the snowshoe rabbit, and the arctic fox all change the color of their coats with the seasons—brown to blend in with dry summer foliage, snow-white to hide in winter.
- You'd think a zebra's distinctive stripes would make it stand out amid the brown and green of the African plain. Not so. At dusk and early dawn (when most predators are out hunting), shadows on white stripes make a zebra hard to spot. If a lioness attacks one zebra in a herd, the group's mass of stripes can create confusion and help the victim get lost in the crowd.
- Green caterpillars spend their time in the green leaves; brown caterpillars prefer brown trunks and twigs.
- The *Stephanopsis altifrons*, an Australian bark-dwelling spider, has knobby growths on its body that imitate the texture of the rough bark found on the trees of its habitat.

THE DISGUISE PRIZE
To get out of trouble, animals can mimic plants, their surroundings, or other animals:
- Because birds don't eat monarch butterflies (which feed on milkweed containing toxic chemicals), the viceroy butterfly mimics the beautiful orange and black pattern of the monarch and the birds leave him alone.
- An opossum goes comatose when frightened. It rolls over on its side and lies limp with its tongue hanging out. Even its heart rate slows. This sudden, involuntary imitation of a corpse turns off the killing instinct in most predators.
- If you've ever wondered why squids eject ink, it's to create a pseudomorph, or "false body," in the water. The inky illusion

distracts enemies long enough for the real squid to propel itself away. A neat trick.

- But the Uncle John Camouflage and Disguise Prize is still reserved for the *Cilix compressa*, a white-and-gray moth. To guarantee undisturbed rest during the day, the little moth uses its coloration to mimic an unappetizing pile of bird droppings.

GETTING NASTY

Animals have been known to forget their manners when forced to defend their lives.

The plesiopid fish shamelessly moons his enemies! If frightened, he sticks his head in a crevice and waves his anal and dorsal fins at the predator. Since the plesiopid's fanny resembles the head of a deadly moray eel, attackers usually scram.

Two very rude snakes from the American Southwest scare away trouble with—flatulence! The Sonoran coral snake and the western hook-nosed snake send rumbling air bubbles out of the cloaca, an opening in their rear ends.

SURVIVAL OF THE STINKIEST

What's worse than flatulent snakes? How about turkey vultures that vomit putrid roadkill on their enemies? Or scared skunks that spray thiols, the same chemicals found in the odors of decomposing flesh and fecal matter?

When trouble arrives, animals may run, hop, swim, or fly from danger, trick their enemies, or show their nasty side—but they don't consult a book of etiquette. The law of the jungle seems to be "safety first with whatever works." Animals know that it isn't always the strongest who survive—sometimes it's the stinkiest.

* * * * *

Myth:
A heavy snowfall obliterates animal or human tracks.
Fact:
Snow won't cover your tracks in the spruce-tree forest of the Canadian Lakes District in central Canada. In some places this forest grows so densely that the winter snow stays on top of the trees and doesn't penetrate to the forest floor.

THE BODY'S SECOND STRING

*These organs and systems don't have the name recognition
of your heart and your brain, but if you don't think they're
important, try living without them.*

Your spleen, your lymphatic system, your integumentary system: Even if you've never heard of them, you've got 'em and they're important. They're the hard-working, quiet guys behind the scenes. Sure, you wouldn't survive very long without your heart or brain, but a life without your integumentary system would be equally short and unpleasant, as you'll soon see.

A BODY SYSTEM UNDERCOVER

Integumentary system: It's all over you! It's...your skin! Well, your skin and the other things that are attached to your skin: hair, nails, eyelashes, sweat glands, that sort of thing. Your skin is actually considered an organ in its own right. Not only that, it's the largest organ of the human body. The average human has about 6 pounds (2.7 kg) of skin; stretched out, there's about two and a half square yards of the stuff.

"Integumentary" comes out of the Latin word for "covering," and that's essentially what the integumentary system does. It covers your body to protect it from disease, dehydration, and the elements. For disease prevention, the skin forms a barrier against invaders, typically nasty little microbes (larger creatures that would invade your tissues, say, lions, are usually called "predators"). And your skin doesn't just sit there, oh, no. It's also proactive against those microbes. It produces a peptide called hBD-2 that pokes holes in microbial cell walls. Dehydration is taken care of thanks to the fact that your skin is waterproof. Water doesn't get in, but more importantly, water doesn't get out, either.

The system also helps regulate body heat. When it's hot, you sweat and the evaporating sweat carries away heat from your body. When it's cold, you retain heat by constricting blood flow to the skin (to keep heat from leaking out as quickly). When you're cold, you also get goose bumps. In hairier creatures, this would help trap

Africa is home to the shortest (the Pygmy) and tallest (the Watusi) people in the world.

heat close to the body by making hair stand up. In relatively hair-less humans, it's usually a signal to crank up the thermostat.

VENT THIS, PAL
Spleen: Make a loose fist with your left hand. Now put it midway up the left side of your abdomen. This is both the size and general location (on the internal side of the rib cage, obviously) of your spleen, which acts as one of your body's primary blood filters.

Here's how it works. Blood enters the spleen from an artery that branches right off the aorta (the artery that comes directly out of your heart). The spleen has all these various cavities designed to hold blood (the "red pulp") and areas called "white pulp," which hold those important disease-fighting elements like white blood cells.

While blood is sitting there in your spleen, it's checked over for microbial infections. If infections are found, they're ambushed and the alarm goes out to the rest of the immune system to be on the lookout. In case you've ever wondered where old blood cells go to die, the spleen's the place. There, their hemoglobin (the stuff that carries the oxygen) is broken down into iron (which is recycled) and bilirubin, a pigment that's filtered out by the liver. The spleen also traps old platelets and white blood cells. It's a very busy place, as you can tell, with lots of comings and goings.

The spleen is an important organ, but you can live without one. This is good news because the spleen is nicely situated to be poked by a broken rib, causing massive hemorrhaging (remember, it's filled with blood all the time). In a case like this, taking the spleen out is often safer than keeping it in. But don't think that a spleenless life is the same as a spleenful life. Uh-uh. People without spleens are susceptible to sepsis: bacterial infections of the blood. So be good to your spleen and it'll be good to you.

YOUR OWN INTERNAL SEWER SYSTEM
Lymphatic system: The aforementioned spleen is an integral part of the lymphatic system, which performs two important functions. It keeps your blood from leaking out of your circulatory system, and it keeps your body from keeling over from infection. It's a funny name (from *lympha*, Latin for "river water"), but don't laugh, it's better than being bloodless and infected.

So how the heck does blood get out of your circulatory system? Good question. Aside from traumatic events like cuts,

People with blue urine suffer from a hereditary condition called porphyria.

punctures, and vampire bites, blood plasma naturally leaks out of your capillaries, those teensy blood vessels that allow your body's cells to exchange oxygen and nutrients with the bloodstream. Most of it goes right back into the bloodstream, but there's always a small percentage of plasma and other material that doesn't make the return trip. It's not much, but it can add up. If it's not drained, it can lead to edema (a swelling in places you don't want swollen), which leads to tissue damage, which leads to death, which leads to you missing every appointment you have next week.

This wayward plasma drains into an extensive network of lymphatic capillaries that drain into larger lymphatics and eventually all the collected lymph (as this blood plasma is now called) is delivered back into the bloodstream through a connection in your left and right subclavian veins, which are located below your neck on either side. It's kinda complicated, isn't it?

Unlike your blood, which moves through your body thanks to pressure provided by your heart, the lymph is carried along by minute muscle contractions. If you're very still and think about it, maybe you can feel all those little muscles contracting.

Remember the second lymphatic function—disease defense? Here's how it works. Besides the aforementioned lymphatic passageways, you've got a few other lymphatic organs working overtime to help coordinate your body's blood-borne defenses (which you can think of as your very own personal SWAT team). On your team you've got B and T cells, which are known as "lymphocytes," a kind of namby-pamby name for a couple of tough guys who ferociously track down and kill any little organism in your body that is not actually part of you. The lymphocyte-developing organs include bone marrow (where B and T cells are created) and the thymus (where T cells mature).

Your lymphatic system also features lymph nodes, which are bean-shaped glands strategically placed along the system. These are the body's equivalent of a border checkpoint. Lymph moving along the system collects there and is checked for alien material. If any is found, it is (heh) "detained," at which point an alarm goes off and lymphocytes are released into your bloodstream to track down any additional offenders.

HORMONALLY YOURS
Endocrine system: Look, you have hormones. Don't make us trot out Jennifer Lopez or Brad Pitt to bring this point home. But what

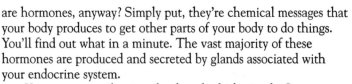

are hormones, anyway? Simply put, they're chemical messages that your body produces to get other parts of your body to do things. You'll find out what in a minute. The vast majority of these hormones are produced and secreted by glands associated with your endocrine system.

Your average endocrine gland works fairly simply. Say your body needs to do something: have a growth spurt, release an egg, or run like hell because a large, angry man is heading toward you with a chainsaw. To prime your body for said activities, the appropriate endocrine gland is activated, and it releases one of its hormones into your bloodstream. Your bloodstream dutifully carries the hormone along until it reaches a cell that "reads" the hormone's message. Before you know it, you've outgrown your pants, you're ovulating, or you're running as fast as your little feet will carry you.

Just about every system and organ in your body relies on hormones, and the endocrine glands that produce them can be found everywhere from your brain to your groin. Some of the more famous glands include the pituitary (its hormones regulate human growth), the pancreas (which produces insulin), the adrenal glands (they make adrenaline, which primes the body for action by upping heart rate, breathing, and alertness), and the testes and ovaries, both of which produce testosterone and estrogen (and other hormones) in varying amounts depending on your sex.

A MOM & POP OPERATION
So, there you have it. Your body's second string is there when you need it. And they aren't just taking up space on the bench. They're hard at work right this very minute, keeping you warm, taking out the garbage, protecting you from invasion—kind of a Mom-Dad-watchdog-friend all rolled into one.

* * * * *

IS IT TRUE THAT HUMAN BEINGS ONLY USE 10 PERCENT OF THEIR BRAINS?
Even though only about five percent of the brain's neurons are active at a given time, researchers haven't found any unused areas of the brain. Because it only weighs three pounds (1.4 kg), the human brain is too small, uses too many of the body's resources, and has too much to do for 90 percent of it to be inactive.

Blind people don't see images in their dreams, they hear and feel.

DR. BURKITT'S DISEASE

How a curious doc used his patients as his laboratory,
and found the first link between viruses and cancer.

Right after World War II, Presbyterian medical missionary
Dr. Denis Burkitt was put in charge of health care for the
entire African nation of Uganda (which was still a part
of the British Empire). After about 10 years there, the good
doctor couldn't stand it anymore—not the work, which he
loved—but the fact that an unusually high number of Ugandan
children had sores on their mouths and faces, which Dr. Burkitt
diagnosed as lymphoma, a cancer of the lymphatic system.
Why it was this particular cancer so common in Uganda and
so rare in other places?

GOING AFTER THE BIG MONEY
So the doctor got himself a research grant for the fabulous sum of
$75 and with it, he devised a questionnaire that he mailed out to
other African hospitals. He wanted to see how widespread the
disease was. His findings were astounding—and made him even
more curious: The disease was almost completely confined to the
latitude between 10°N and 10°S, on either side of the equator.

THE BIG, BIG MONEY
Next, Dr. Burkitt spent about $1,000 putting together a safari to
visit the areas where the disease was so rampant. As he went from
place to place, he created a "map" of the occurrence of the
disease. That was the clue he needed. The mapped area coincided
directly with the map of endemic malaria, a much more common
tropical disease. It turned out that the children who had
lymphoma also had malaria, which was suppressing their immune
system so that a normally inactive microbe (later called the
Epstein-Barr virus) could run rampant.

NOT ONLY THAT...
So Dr. Denis Burkitt—at the ridiculously low research cost of
$1,075—had established the first link between viruses and cancer.
And if that wasn't enough, in 1969, Dr. Burkitt—after a long
study of the health and diet of his patients—was the first to
suggest a link between fiber and colon cancer.

Type O (46%) and Type A (40%) are the two most common blood types.

THE SCIENCE OF MOVING PICTURES

In 1872, Leland Stanford offered photographer Eadweard Muybridge $25,000 to perform an experiment. Muybridge wasn't sure he could do it, but with so much money at stake, he took on the challenge.

When a horse is running or trotting, do all four hooves ever leave the ground at the same time? That was the basis of the wager that Leland Stanford, former governor of California and founder of Stanford University, made with some friends. This was a subject of much controversy in horse racing circles at the time. Most people believed that a horse always had one hoof in contact with the ground, but Stanford thought otherwise. Because a horse's legs are moving so fast, it's impossible to tell just by looking, so Stanford needed a way to slow down the movement so it could be studied.

THE CHALLENGE
In 1872, Stanford offered Eadweard Muybridge, a world-famous landscape photographer, $25,000 to find the answer. Muybridge had no idea if he could successfully set up and perform an experiment to settle the dispute, but he figured he'd give it a go.

THE EQUIPMENT
In most 19th-century cameras, a picture was taken when the photographer removed the lens cap for several seconds in order to expose the film and capture an image. The subject had to remain perfectly still during this time or the resulting photograph would be blurred. In order to capture very fast action like a galloping horse, the exposure time would have to be very short.

THE SHUTTER
Muybridge invented a fast shutter mechanism that relied on a small piece of wood with a hole drilled in it that slid past the lens. The wood was positioned so that a pin held it in place, covering the lens. When the pin was removed, gravity would cause the wood to drop and as the hole moved past the lens, the film was exposed for a fraction of a second.

THE PROCESS

The first time Muybridge tried taking a photograph as a horse ran by he didn't get much of an image at all. He tried various methods of making the shutter move faster and faster to shorten the exposure time, and as he did the quality of the image began to improve. Finally he hit upon the idea of using two pieces of wood and slipping them past each other so quickly that he could achieve an exposure time of about 1/500th of a second. That solved the problem of capturing a reasonably clear image of a horse at a gallop, but he still had to settle the bet.

THE SHOOTER

In 1874, his work was interrupted when he shot his wife's lover—not with a camera, but with a gun. Muybridge suspected that the miscreant (now a dead miscreant) was the father of a child his wife had borne earlier that year. Muybridge was imprisoned until his trial in February 1875. At the trial he was acquitted—thanks to the lawyer that Stanford had hired for him—but afterward he decided to leave the country for a while and dropped his experiments until his return to California in 1877. He then continued his work on increasing the shutter speed until he had reduced the exposure time to less than 1/2000th of a second.

THE TRIGGER

Once Muybridge was satisfied with the quality of the images, he had to figure out a way to capture several images in sequence. He decided to place several cameras in a row all pointing in the same direction and to trigger them in sequence as the horse galloped past. He attached strings to all the camera shutters and stretched them across a track, so that as the horse passed by, it would touch each string in turn, and the cameras would take their pictures one at a time and in sequence.

THE MONEY

In 1878, after years of experiments, Muybridge got what he wanted. He had a sequence of 12 images, and one of them clearly showed that all four of the horse's hooves were off the ground at the same time. It was the first successful photographic representation of a sequence of movement and it made Muybridge internationally famous. And relatively prosperous. He collected his well-earned $25,000 from Stanford.

Dry ice is used to seed clouds and produce rain.

THE NEXT STEP
In 1879 he invented the zoopraxiscope, a device with counter-rotating discs that projected the images sequentially. Now an observer could actually see the horse galloping—and the effect was truly stunning. After a public showing in San Francisco, a reporter gushed, "Nothing was wanting, but the clatter of hoofs upon the turf and the occasional breath of steam to make the spectator believe he had before him the flesh and blood steeds."

THE DIRTY PICTURES
Muybridge continued his experiments using more cameras and photographing the motions of other animals and later did extensive studies of human movement. He eventually published his photographs in a portfolio called *Animal Locomotion* (1887) and two books: *Animals in Motion* (1899) and *The Human Figure in Motion* (1901). The latter created quite a stir at the time for its use of nude male and female models.

THE CREDIT
Thomas Edison is usually credited with creating the first movies in 1889, but it was the work of Eadweard Muybridge—and a $25,000 bet—that provided the cornerstone of Edison's invention and the evolution of motion pictures.

* * * * *

WATCH THE BIRDIE

Wilbur and Orville were stuck. Someone had already invented an early version of the hang glider, but they didn't care. The brothers Wright wanted a plane they could control, a plane that would turn. After watching pigeons in flight they realized that the birds kept adjusting the positions of their wings. When they wanted to turn, they lifted the front edge of one wing while tilting the edge of the other wing down. But the Wrights still couldn't figure out how to apply this concept to their design.

Wilbur found the answer one day after he'd taken a bicycle inner tube out of a long cardboard box. He found that by twisitng the ends of the box, he could make the edges of it twist just like a bird's wings. They first tested the idea on a glider and after many, many adjustments, they got it just "Wright."

WHY CURLING ROCKS!

The science behind a sport that's "sweeping" the globe.

The game has been practiced since the 16th century, but a lot of people probably thought curling was something that only happened to hair until the 1998 Winter Olympics introduced millions to this old Scottish sport.

EVERYBODY MUST GET STONED

Some people call it shuffleboard on ice. The playing surface is a rink 46 yards (42 m) long and 14 feet (4.3 m) wide. As in shuffleboard, the goal is part of the surface. At each end of the rink lies a circular, archerylike target called a "house" and in the center of each house is a bull's-eye called the "button." (The game requires skill and a translator's dictionary.) Each team has four players who try to slide (or "curl") their team's stones onto the house and as close as possible to the center. They also try to keep their opponents' stones out of the house. A point is scored for each stone closer to the button than any belonging to the other team.

FROM HACKS TO HOGLINES

When British Olympic gold medalist Rhona Martin launches a rock down the ice, she starts from a foothold called a "hack" and glides forward in a sort of kneeling-squatting position up to a demarcation called the "hog line." At the hog line, she releases the stone, putting a bit of a spin on it. The stone slides over the ice toward the button. Meanwhile, two of Rhona's teammates rush along in front of the stone, sweeping the ice (that's right, sweeping!) with special brooms. Rhona, as the captain or "skip" of the team, directs her sweepers by yelling out instructions. A skip often admonishes the sweepers to "Hurry hard!" And they do.

ROCKS THAT ROLL

Curling stones spin either clockwise or counterclockwise as they slide toward the house. The curling motion, like a long, slow curveball, gives the sport its name. Curling stones have created something of a mystery. Fans—and scientists—have wondered exactly why a curling stone curls.

Earth's water is 97% salt water, 2% frozen water, and 1% fresh water.

ROCK(ET) SCIENCE

When curling was first played, chunks of ordinary rocks were hurled on frozen rivers. Modern curling teams use milled granite stones that are concave (indented) on the bottom. The specially designed stones are a foot in diameter and weigh about 42 pounds (19 kg). Just before the game a fine spray of water is applied to the curling rink. The water freezes immediately, creating a playing surface covered with smooth bumps like little pebbles.

The relationship between the pebbles and the concave granite is a key to curling's curves. As a stone spins over the ice, the small traveling surface of the concave granite connects with the small contact areas at the top of the ice bumps. One theory is that the contact between these two limited areas creates enough friction to melt the ice and create a thin film of water.

IS CURLING ALL WET?

Granite attracts water, and once the wet film forms, it clings to the stone. The clinging layer of water lubricates the granite and reduces friction so the stone can travel faster with less of a grip on the ice. And remember those sweepers? They're aiming at more than a Good Housekeeping Award. Their brooms are supposed to warm the ice pebbles to encourage the continued formation of the film of water, reducing the friction even further and making sure that the stone stays lubricated.

THE CURL BEHIND CURLING

The watery film not only helps the stone slide farther; it's also a clue as to why the stone curls. The spinning stone is tipped forward as it travels, which puts more pressure on the front edge, so the liquid film under the granite is concentrated at the front. In addition, if the stone spins, say, counterclockwise, a sideways vector of force will occur to the right, and the stone will also get wetter to the right. More pressure on the right and on the front puts more liquid on the right and on the front of the stone. The back and left side of the stone are drier, so they drag on the ice. It's this drag that causes the stone to curl to the left. Of course, the reverse is true. If the stone spins clockwise, the sideways vector will cause the left side to get wetter and more slippery so the stone will drag on its drier right side, and it will curl to the right. That's what puts the curl in curling.

THAT'S AMORE!

Some of the bizarre goings-on in Mother Nature's singles bar.

B irds do it, bees do it, even fishes in the sea do it. And how! Stick with us and you'll find out how really strange things can get out there. It's a jungle.

THE PLAYER

This may come as a shock, but it's not always fun to be the guy with the world's hottest love life. Just ask the antichenus, an Australian marsupial mouse. During the mating season, the male antichenus dedicates his short life to mating with as many females as possible. He goes into a sexual frenzy, skips meals, and gives everything he's got to getting breeding action for up to 12 hours with each female. By the end of mating season, the antichenus is worn out and his immune system is so vulnerable to parasites and infections that he very soon dies.

And do his ladyloves miss him? Sorry bud, not likely. It's much easier for pregnant females to get food once their exhausted lover has dropped dead and isn't around to bother them anymore.

THE RED-HOT MAMA

In nature, it's usually the males who dazzle with their sexual ornamentation, but female baboons make their way to the top of the sexual heap on their bottoms. Their big red bottoms, to be exact.

A female olive baboon's rear end sports an "ischial callosity" that swells up and turns red when she's fertile. The males compete for the chance to mate with females, and the bigger and brighter her bum, the more the males will fight over her. Researchers have discovered that this preoccupation has a survival purpose: Females with bigger and brighter behinds are more fertile and tend to have more offspring that live longer. On the downside, her large, colorful swelling makes her vulnerable to infections and parasites, not to mention the fact that it's probably tough to sit on.

THE SNAKE IN THE GRASS

Literally. And specifically, a red-sided garter snake. When these nonvenomous snakes wriggle out of hibernation in the spring, the excited males all rush to surround one female, forming what are called "mating balls." Within these mating balls, the larger males usually have the advantage at getting to the female. But not when they're dealing with a "sneaker," a real-life snake in the grass who can disguise himself as a female by producing female attractiveness pheromones. When this sneaker calls "Yoo-hoo, boys!" the other males flock to surround him in a mating ball. After the big boys wear themselves out with unsuccessful attempts at mating, the crafty little snake sneaks off to mate with a female. He's outsmarted all his brawny—but exhausted—rivals.

THE CODEPENDENT

Talk about neurotic relationships! Not even Freud could solve this couple's problems. Guess no one ever told the anglerfish that even good things like togetherness should be practiced in moderation. Of course, the anglerfish alliance is unbalanced from the beginning, since the female is over six times larger than her mate. During the mating process, the male bites the female, anchoring himself on top of her, and he stays there—for the rest of his life! Eventually the male becomes a parasite of the female as their digestive and circulatory systems merge, and they literally become one. The female finds the food while the male provides the generative organs that fertilize the female's eggs over her lifetime.

MR. MONOGAMOUS

The California mouse is a prince of a guy who shares in the work of raising his offspring with the female. If he dies, the female grieves so much that she may stop lactating and lose her ability to raise her brood. So let's hear it for this California couple—who says they don't have family values in Hollywood?

THE SHOW-OFF

During mating season the male peacock stays by himself and will fight at the drop of a hat to protect his territory from other males seeking females. He constantly screams his raucous call so the hens know where to find him. When they do, he spreads his tail feathers and struts his stuff. When a peahen has a choice among peacocks, she'll choose the one with the most eyes on his tail feathers. Once mating season is over, the male sheds his tail feathers until he needs them again.

The only prime numbers that end in 2 and 5 are 2 and 5.

MATH MNEMONICS

Even mathematicians mneed mnemonics to help them remember stuff. Here are a few of their favorites.

PREFIXES IN THE METRIC SYSTEM
Kilo, Hecta, Deca, Unit, Deci, Centi, Milli
- Kevin Had Ducked Under a Dark Creepy Monster.
- Kids Have Doodled Upside-Down Converting Metrics.
- King Hector Doesn't Usually Drink Cold Milk.

Deci, Centi, Milli, Micro, Nano, Pico, Femto, Atto
- Dairy Cows Make Milk, Not Pink Fruit, Arthur.

Tera, Giga, Mega, Milli, Micro, Nano, Pico, Femto, Atto
- To Go Metric Man Must Not Put Fools Aside.

THE SQUARE ROOT OF 2 = 1.414
- I wish I knew (the root of two).

THE ASCENDING ORDER OF ROMAN NUMERALS
L, C, D, M = 50, 100, 500, 1000
- Lucky Cows Drink Milk.
- Lucy Can't Drink Milk.

TO REMEMBER WHAT AN ISOCELES TRIANGLE IS
(sung to the tune of "Oh Christmas Tree")

Oh isosceles, oh isosceles,
  Two angles have
  Equal degrees.

Oh isosceles, oh isosceles,
  You look just like
  A Christmas tree.

TO CALCULATE THE CIRCUMFERENCE OF A CIRCLE
- If you cross a circle with a line,
  Which hits the center and runs from spine to spine,
  And the line's length is d,
  The circumference will be d times 3.14159.

Some spiders produce threads that are stronger than a steel wire of the same size.

THE VALUE OF ∏ (Pi)
(The number of letters in each word equal the numbers in question.)

3.141592653
• Now I know a super utterance to assist math.

3.1415926
• May I have a large container of coffee?

3.14159265358979323846
• Sir, I send a rhyme excelling
  In sacred truth and rigid spelling,
  Numerical sprites elucidate
  For me the lexicon's dull weight.

* * * * *

PI DAY

Do scientists know how to have fun? Listen to this: For more than 13 years, the Exploratorium, San Francisco's science museum, has been celebrating Pi Day. (You must remember from math class that pi equals 3.14159 and so on into infinity.)

Well, every March 14, (that is, 3.14), at exactly 1:59 P.M., (that is, 3.14159), the museum lets down its collective hair, and celebrates, by eating—you guessed it—pie.

Then they sing "Happy Birthday, dear Albert…" Because by some crazy cosmic coincidence, March 14 is Albert Einstein's birthday!

When the Exploratorians are done singing, they have some more pie.

Gluons, leptons, and taus are some of the strange names for particles smaller than atoms.

GIANTS AND DWARFS

*Islands have a way of producing some pretty curious creatures—
from giant tortoises to pygmy elephants.*

It all started with those finches. When Darwin toured the
Galapagos Islands in 1835, he saw 14 types of finches reminiscent of ones he'd seen in South America. But each type had a
different and very specialized beak: some heavy for crushing food,
some slender for probing for food. It dawned on Darwin that the
birds had common ancestors who had "immigrated" to the islands,
and had gradually changed into several new species, each with a
special beak that helped it harvest different food.

THE SHELL GAME
The Galapagos land tortoise, the largest tortoise in the world,
lived there, too. And like the finches, they had evolved differently. Tortoises that lived in areas with lush vegetation had domed
shells; the ones who had to reach vegetation higher off the ground
had developed what are called "saddleback" shells.

One thing that all the tortoises had in common was size—
they measured around 6 feet (1.8 m) and weighed nearly 500
pounds (230 kg). But their common mainland ancestor was much
smaller. Eventually, modern biologists got around to scratching
their heads over it. Why were the Galapagos tortoises all giants?
In fact, looking at the bigger picture, what is it about islands that
produce so many giant creatures? Unrelated to big-guy Galapagos,
giant tortoises live on the Seychelles islands in the Indian Ocean.
The world's largest lizard, the nine-foot Komodo dragon, hunts
deer on Komodo Island off the coast of Indonesia.

Even flowers become gigantic on islands. Members of the
sunflower family have grown to tree size on the Galapagos;
gardenias get to be tree-sized in Samoa; and tree ferns abound in
there, too, and in the Philippines and New Guinea.

THE WORLD'S BIGGEST COCKROACH
Madagascar is home to a giant wingless hissing cockroach that
grows up to 3.5 inches (8.9 cm) long. It once was home to a
gigantic elephant bird (it became extinct in the 17th century).

Nitrogen accounts for over 75% of Earth's atmosphere.

Those 10-foot-tall (3 m) flightless birds laid the world's largest eggs—they were 13 inches (33 cm) tall and held two gallons worth of omelette fixings!

A LITTLE PROBLEM

As biologists tackled the question of gigantism, it was made more mysterious by a bunch of dwarfs! While some creatures tended to grow huge on islands, others had shrunk. The Seychelles are home to a frog the size of an ant. There were plenty of island dwarfs to ponder, including two from the Philippines: the tamaraw, a small wild buffalo that existed nowhere but on the island of Mindoro, and a spotted deer (only 2.6 feet [80 cm] tall at the shoulder). The world's most complete skeleton of a prehistoric pygmy mammoth was found on California's Channel Islands. And a cave full of the ancient bones of pygmy elephants was found on the Greek island of Tilos. Why did some creatures became jolly green giants and others little Lilliputians? The answer lies in the isolation, limited size, and limited population of islands. When an animal arrived on an island, it had to adapt to its new environment. Like an immigrant applying for a job in a new and still foreign country, island creatures had to adjust to new conditions to survive and thrive.

HOW KOMODO GOT BIG AND DEER GOT SMALL

Since islands have fewer animals, they may present creatures with opportunities for a new ecological niche. Imagine a mainland lizard who arrives on an island and discovers that the new place is loaded with pigs and deer. There are also no big predators like wolves or lions around. The lizard species might grow large enough to become the island's main predator, which could account for the Komodo dragon's size. Islands can also encourage animals to get small. The absence of predators could cause herbivores to quickly overpopulate an island and exhaust its food resources. Smaller herbivores could get by on less food.

BACK TO THE FINCHES

Biologists now believe that the mysterious giants and dwarfs on islands have used size as an adaptation strategy. Different sizes in island animals are very much like the different types of beaks on Darwin's finches. They're a mechanism for surviving and thriving within the limited niches of an island environment. You might say, in the end, that it all comes down to "survival of the finches."

AN EMPTY MATTER

*With all the instability in the world, it's good to know that some things
are sound, like the bathroom throne. You know you're sitting on a
durable piece of porcelain, right? Well, no, not exactly.*

Scientists tell us that everything we think of as solid isn't
solid at all—it is, in fact, mostly made up of empty space, as
are the bricks that make up your home. You are actually—
mostly—living in a home made of nothing—emptiness. Long ago,
scientists divided everything into either matter or energy. Matter
is everything from your hand to a wall; energy is stuff like
lightning and fire. Then it was discovered that matter is made up
of elements or combinations of elements.

TAKE THE TOILET, FOR EXAMPLE
But atoms didn't just sit in one place, all solid and tightly packed.
Rather, they are constantly on the move. The bathroom throne,
then, is not a solid mass. It's a moving, pulsating mass of atoms,
even though we don't see any evidence of this. Here's why: Atoms
consist of a very dense central core—the nucleus—and a cloud of
electrons (negatively charged particles) that surround it. Depending on the type of atom being considered, the electron cloud has a
radius about 10,000 times as great as the nucleus. So, if the
nucleus were the size of a ping-pong ball, the electron cloud would
extend over one-fifth of a mile in diameter. Most of this distance
would, of course, be emptiness—it's a cloud, remember?

LIFT THIS CUP, STRONG GUY!
The nucleus—even though it's a very small part of the atom—
makes up most of its weight. The fact that most of the empty
space comprising objects is due to the electronic cloud is what
makes them so light. And we can certainly be grateful for that.
Imagine a teacup packed shoulder-to-shoulder with nuclei that
have been stripped of their electron clouds. How much do you
think that teacup would weigh? Would you believe 50 trillion
tons? (A million maybe you could lift.) So the next time you get
told to move a heavy box, you're getting off easy—thanks to the
emptiness of matter.

Any color can be made from three colors: magenta, cyan, and yellow.

HALF A WING IS BETTER THAN NONE

Lots of Earth's critters can fly. But how did a hit-or-miss process like natural selection come up with a working wing?

A t one time or another, bugs, reptiles, birds, and mammals all had wings. They didn't inherit wings from each other—each type developed flight independently. So the complicated anatomy that allows creatures to fly has been invented more than once in Earth's history. How the heck could that have happened?

MY, WHAT A LONG TIME AGO

Scientists generally agree that life on Earth evolved by changing just a little bit at a time over a really, really long time. We're talking geological time, great spans measured in eons, which are divided into eras—such as the Paleozoic (ancient life), Mesozoic (middle life), and Cenozoic (recent life). This much time is sometimes referred to in terms of "My ago," that is, "million years ago."

So, life first appeared on Earth 4,000 My ago, but didn't really start to get interesting until the Paleozoic era, 570 My ago. Land plants appeared more than 400 My ago, and insects either about the same time or soon after, geologically speaking. Over the following 100 million years, insects started flying. During the Mesozoic era (245–65 My ago) some reptiles (the pterosaurs) grew wings and birds appeared. Mammals were around, but they weren't flying. They were mostly hiding and trying to survive. The first bats—the only mammals with true wings—didn't appear until well after our own Cenozoic era began, 65 My ago.

IT'S ONLY NATURAL...SELECTION, THAT IS

Small changes—some useless, some harmful, some helpful—occur naturally in living things. Whenever such a random mutation gives one creature an edge over others, the change is likely to be passed along to offspring, who are likely to pass it along again, and so on. Whatever lives long enough to reproduce gets to affect the shape of things to come. Over time, the mutations add up to a

---

Laser stands for Light Amplification by Stimulated Emission of Radiation.

major modification, such as a wing. But that will only happen if every variation along the way somehow helps the creature survive.

WHAT GOOD IS HALF A WING?
So what good were any tiny changes that might eventually become wings? What kind of advantage is there to having part of a wing? Well, Oxford University zoologist Richard Dawkins—a very smart man—puts it this way. "Insects and animals sometimes have to leap from one high place to another. Sometimes they fall. The ones with the most air resistance, however slight, have the best chance of surviving a fall. The same feature would increase the distance of a jump. That means there's an advantage to tiny body flaps or webbing between limbs—in certain circumstances, they'd make the difference between life and death."

So half a wing is better than none.

FROM FLAPS TO FLAPPING
Most scientists agree that the earliest insects had gill-like structures to breathe through, but eventually developed something more like a windpipe. The bugs with flaplike gill slits could jump a bit farther than others, and over millions of years, those flaps got big enough to help control diving and gliding. Then some bugs grew more maneuverable flaps, and that led to insects with much larger, flapping wings.

IT'S A BIRD! IT'S A PLANE!
Something similar must have happened to pterosaurs, birds, and bats. Any extra skin on an individual's forelimbs could have given a little lift for long-distance jumping and gliding. Eventually the entire forelimb became a wing. (We humans had other uses for our forelimbs, so we had to invent flying machines.)

My, My, My...
There are lots of creatures around today who could be said to have just half a wing: frogs with big webbed feet, tree snakes that can flatten out their bodies, fish with extrabig fins, lizards with extendable ribs, not to mention squirrels and marsupials with extra skin between their forelimbs and hind limbs. They all glide through the air just fine.

And in, say, another 50 million years...well, who knows?

Mayans invented the symbol for the number zero.

MIRAGE: IT AIN'T JUST A CASINO IN VEGAS

What do wet, glistening highways, floating castles, and an oasis in the desert have in common? They're all typical illusions seen by travelers, sober and otherwise.

You've seen mirages in movies and cartoons: a cool oasis surrounded by palm trees that appears off in the distance, only to evaporate when the crawling, exhausted, and thirsty traveler gets there. You've seen real mirages, too: those wet, shiny patches on the road ahead that disappear as you get closer.

HEAT RISES: ALWAYS HAS, ALWAYS WILL

Mirages are caused by layers of hot and cold air, and light. Have you ever noticed waves of heat rising from the street on a hot day? The layer of air closest to the ground is hotter than the rest of the air—it isn't as dense than the air above it—that's why it rises. At the boundary of the hot and cooler air, sunlight is refracted, or bent, so you no longer see the road or desert floor; what you see is light refracted from the blue sky, which, because it's now on the ground, looks like water.

MIRROR, MIRROR ON THE ROAD

So that "wet" patch that you see on the road is actually a mirror image of the sky. Because the heat bends the light upward, your eyes see the mirage below the real image. This kind of mirage always appears below eye level, like the one that the thirsty desert crawler sees as he crests the sand dune—and thinks is going to save him. (Sorry, chum.)

NOT THE ONLY MIRAGE IN TOWN

Another kind of mirage does the opposite. It appears above the real image—the result of alternating layers of cold and warm air. In this case, the air closest to the ground is colder than the air above it. The colder temperature bends the light toward the earth, rather than away from it.

You can retain about seven unrelated facts at a time in your short-term memory.

HELLO, SAILOR

Early explorers in the Arctic Circle reported seeing tall mountains that were never found. What they were seeing was a *fata morgana*, the mirage of a mountain or a castle floating half in the air and half in the sea. The name is a literal Italian translation of "Morgan LeFay," King Arthur's mystic sister, who supposedly lived in an undersea palace. When she was in a wicked mood, she'd make the palace rise up out of the sea so she could lure innocent sailors to their deaths. That's the story that people used to tell, anyway. As if there's such a thing as an innocent sailor—especially an Italian one.

WHAT DO MEN SEE IN HER?

A fata morgana—just like Morgan herself—is two or more mirages superimposed on each other. In this case, light travels through alternating layers of cold and warm air. Valleys or coastal regions are the perfect breeding ground for a fata morgana. The light gets bent either up from the earth (in warm air) or down toward the earth (in cold air), and several reflections of ground features and sky combine to look like a half-floating mountain. Like we said, this one takes more work.

NOT JUST IN YOUR MIND

Mirages aren't just in your mind, by the way; they're real and they can even be photographed. There's a theory that mirages in the sky may also be one of the sources of reported UFO sightings. The planet Venus—as magnified and distorted by a mirage—makes a pretty believable flying saucer.

* * * * *

"Eventually, all things merge into one, and a river runs through it. The river was cut by the world's great flood and runs over rocks from the basement of time. On some of the rocks are timeless raindrops. Under the rocks are the words, and some of the words are theirs.

"I am haunted by waters."

—Norman Maclean, *A River Runs Through It*

While an alligator lives about 50 years, a crocodile lives about 100.

THE JOHNNY AWARDS

Every eon, Uncle John recognizes the contributions of our furry, slimy, or otherwise clad friends. The awards ceremony was a dressy affair: We saw lots of ermines and pearls. Congratulations to all our winners!

Uncle John's Busy Bee Award: The Busy Bee Award goes to, well, bees. Bees collect nectar from two million flowers just to make a one-pound (0.5 kg) comb of honey. The runner-up is the gopher, whose burrowing rate is equivalent to a man digging a tunnel nearly 18 inches (46 cm) in diameter and seven miles (11 km) long in a period of 10 hours.

Uncle John's Sneaky Busy Bee Award: You thought sponges just sat around doing nothing, but they're actually working hard without you noticing it. The humble sponge filters its food out of seawater, which, though it may sound easy, isn't. The sponge has to filter a ton of water to gain one ounce of body weight.

Uncle John's Bad Table Manners Award: The clear winners: toads and frogs that can eat with their eyes. When they swallow, they close their eyelids, press down with their tough eyeballs, and lower the roof of their mouth against their tongue, forcing food down into their stomach—not a pretty sight. Runner-up to the butterfly, who tastes its food with its feet!

Uncle John's Lazy Goof-Off Award: This hotly contested prize almost went to cats because on average, a cat will sleep for 16 hours a day. But the award really belongs to desert snails, who've been known to doze for three years at a time! (Naturally, the lazy goof-offs couldn't make it to the ceremony.)

Uncle John's Survival Award: The winners are cockroaches, who can lose their heads and live for a week…till they starve to death.

And now, (drum roll) at last, our most prestigious award, the one you've all been waiting for…

Uncle John's Bathroom Achievement Award
The baboon wins it hands down. Seeds of the African baobab tree sprout more easily after they've been eaten by a baboon. The acid in the animal's digestive juices erodes the seed's tough shell. After it passes through a baboon's digestive tract and the seed emerges in baboon dung, it not only absorbs water more easily, it comes equipped with its own fertilizer.

What do cats and beavers have in common?

SHARKS WITH LIGHTS

Built-in lights, field detectors, flotation devices:
Sharks have mastered the evolutionary tricks of a killing trade.

Hit men from the Mob have nothing on sharks. Over the past 400 million years, sharks have evolved into nature's perfect predators. They can attack silently and with great bursts of speed. Their jaws can snap a sea lion in half, and their enormous gullet can swallow both pieces whole.

THEY'RE EVERYWHERE!

If limb-crunching, man-eating sharks haunt your nightmares, you won't enjoy knowing that there are nearly 400 species, ranging from about six inches to 50 feet long (15 cm to 50 m), inhabiting every oceanic corner of the globe. The good news is that most of them don't have the least interest in you. Some, like the polka-dotted whale shark (weighing in at 13 tons), are perfectly happy with plankton and schools of small fish. The most common shark, the dogfish, lives mainly on fish, crabs, octopus, and squid. In fact, instead of eating people, the reverse is true. These sharks, among others, actually appear on our dinner tables.

ARMORED AND DANGEROUS

All the same, sharks must be respected as dangerous predators with evolution's mean streak on their side. The shark's torpedo-shaped body can shoot through the water at speeds of over 30 mph (80 kph). Their skeletons are made of lightweight cartilage rather than bone, which gives them great flexibility in battle. Even the shark's liver helps it catch prey. Rich in oils and lighter than water, the liver works like a flotation device to keep a shark buoyant, cruising along easily while it hunts for food.

Both of their offspring are called kittens.

JAWS

Then there are those "jaws." The biting strength of some sharks is a crushing 6.5 tons per square inch. The great white slashes at its victims with over 3,000 teeth. (Most sharks have at least four parallel rows of teeth—if one tooth breaks or is knocked out, another tooth moves forward to replace it.) And a shark's teeth aren't all in its mouth. Its skin is completely covered with thousands of tiny teeth called placoid scales. These sharp, pointy scales are covered with enamel, just like the teeth, and make shark skin so abrasive that it becomes a weapon. A shark can tear at its prey just by brushing against it. Scared yet? There's more.

SENSING THEIR SUPPER

You can swim from hungry sharks, but you can't hide. Their eyes have what's called a "tapetum," a reflecting layer behind the retina that enhances vision. Sharks' eyes are so sensitive to individual flickers of light that they can pick up the slightest movement. Lantern sharks, which live in dark water 6,000 feet (1,800 m) deep, have phosphorescent lights embedded on their bellies to help them see in the dark. But if a shark decides to kill, it doesn't have to rely on sight alone. Sound travels nearly five times faster in water than in air, and a shark can pick up the sounds of prey from a distance of 3,000 feet (900 m) away. They're primed to hear low-frequency sounds, like the sound of contracting muscle tissue in an injured, struggling fish—or human.

A shark's sense of touch is enhanced by a strip of sensory cells along each side of its body that can feel the vibrations of prey moving through the water. And if by some chance a shark doesn't see or hear or feel its prey, the hunt isn't over. Its sense of smell is so acute that some sharks can smell one drop of blood diluted in one million drops of seawater! Yikes!

THE SIXTH SENSE

If five powerful senses aren't enough, sharks have an astounding sixth sense. All animals, including human beings, emit electrical signals, which a shark picks up with a special system of gel-filled pores around the head and mouth. In dark, deep water or sandy shallows, electrical detectors allow a hunting shark to position its head and mouth, then close in on a victim that it can't even see.

What do cows and elephants have in common?

LIGHTNING STRIKES VS. SHARK ATTACKS

With all that deadly equipment, it's not surprising that sharks sometimes kill humans. But shark attacks on humans are rare. Why? Probably because we're bony and taste bad. Sharks swim near bathers every day without bothering them. And sometimes people survive because a shark bites them, then abandons them— or even spits them out!

SWIMMING WITH SHARKS

In the 1970s, the movie *Jaws* scared the world with its story of a great white shark devouring swimmers and boaters on the Atlantic coast. But the great white and other large sharks aren't mindless demons with an overwhelming desire for human flesh—they happen to feed in the shallows where humans like to swim. Researchers now believe that attacks occur when a shark, in murky water, mistakes a swimmer for a school of fish or a threatening enemy. A diver in a wetsuit can resemble the great white shark's favorite meal: a tasty seal or sea lion.

SHARK KILLS GO OVERBOARD

Peter Benchley, author of *Jaws*, says that if he rewrote the story today, the great white shark would be a victim, not a villain. Sharks existed before the first dinosaurs appeared, but in the past two decades—partly because they're so terrifying—humans have slaughtered millions of sharks. Now, some species (including the great white) are in danger of extinction. When sharks disappear, other sea life does, too. Lobsters, for example, become endangered when there aren't enough sharks to control the lobster-eating octopus population. Benchley and other naturalists are fighting to save these magnificent underwater killers and warning that the world will suffer if the shark can't do its lethal job.

* * * * *

BABY TEETH

Sharks can be dangerous even before they're born! While examining a pregnant sand tiger shark, a scientist was bitten by the shark's embryo.

Both of their offspring are called calves.

I JUST WON THE NOBEL PRIZE: HAVE A CIGAR!

How tobacco helped create 20th-century science.

People don't know that tobacco isn't just about smooth flavor and lung cancer: It's a scientific workhorse—as common in some laboratories as microscopes and Bunsen burners.

I'D WALK A MILE FOR A VIRUS
In the 19th century, nobody knew anything about viruses. Bacteria they knew, but viruses were too small to be seen with the microscopes of the day. Viruses were discovered because scientists decided to study a disease that attacked tobacco.

HEY, VLADIMIR, COME AND LOOK AT THIS THING!
Tobacco was an oh-so-valuable crop, but it was prone to a disease called mosaic (because the light and dark mottling it produced made the leaf look like a mosaic). After years of research, some Russian and Dutch scientists theorized that the disease was caused by—eureka!—an organism smaller than a bacterium, which they called a virus.

THE VIRUS BANDWAGON
Tobacco mosaic virus (TMV) soon became the object of intense scientific study. In fact, scientists learned most of what they know about viruses from TMV. In the 1930s, Wendell Stanley crystallized TMV so that its structure could be observed; this was the first time a virus could be studied in any detail (and he won a Nobel Prize in Chemistry for it).

When the team of Bawden and Pirie studied TMV, they discovered that the genetic material in all living things was made of deoxyribonucleic acid (DNA). This was in the middle of the 20th century and pretty amazing and controversial. After all, you can't understand genes and therefore the nature of life itself, if you don't know about DNA. (But they didn't win a Nobel Prize for it, not even one to share between the two of them.)

A turkey gobbles, a tiger growls, and a monkey gibbers.

HOW A VIRUS SPENDS HIS DAY

All these studies on TMV helped to show that viruses were very simple organisms, nothing but little chunks of DNA (or RNA, ribonucleic acid, DNA's partner in genetic activity) tucked inside a protein coat. Viruses are like tiny little criminals. They spend every second of their day attacking a host cell, hijacking that cell's biological mechanisms and forcing it to create more copies of the virus. Then the copies go off to find new victims. Since viruses are almost nothing but DNA or RNA, scientists learned a lot about them from studying viruses. All later breakthroughs in molecular biology and genetic engineering have roots in the study of tobacco mosaic virus.

A VIRUS JOINS THE MARCH OF DIMES

And not only that. After World War II, the National Foundation for Infantile Paralysis (now known as the March of Dimes) was searching for a polio vaccine, but they needed to know a lot more about viruses in general. They chose TMV as one of their model systems because it was the most-studied virus available. That work helped to develop the polio vaccine.

In the process, so much was learned about the biology of the tobacco plant that it became a common model system for scientists to use in their labs, like a green version of the lab rat or fruit fly—even if the research had nothing to do with agriculture or plants. But of course, the primary reason for tobacco being studied in the first place was that, as a crop, it was worth a ton of money.

TOBACCO HAS COME A LONG WAY, BABY!

Even today, the tobacco plant continues its work as a lab rat. In a nice bit of irony, genetically modified tobacco cells are being used as biofactories to produce proteins that reduce the risk of tissue rejection in organ transplants, neutralize soil pollutants, and—get this—fight cancer.

* * * * *

"A virus is a Latin word translated by doctors
to mean 'Your guess is as good as mine.' "
—Anonymous

Blackbirds live on average 12 years, canaries average 24, but the crow can live to age 100.

GOT GAS? PART II

In which various doctors and charlatans find
amusing ways to use laughing gas.

After Joseph Priestley discovered nitrous oxide in 1772, it hung around for 28 years doing nothing until it drew the attention of Humphry Davy of the Medical Pneumatic Institute in England, where various ailments were treated using newly discovered gases. Davy gave his patients a few snorts of nitrous oxide and they seemed to enjoy it. That's where it got the name "laughing gas." The idea of gas-treated cures proved a failure, but nitrous oxide lived on.

A MAN AHEAD OF HIS TIME

Davy wrote about the possibility of using it as an anesthetic in 1800, but surgery and tooth extractions continued without painkillers for another 45 years. Doctors were concerned about its side effects: slower pulse, attacks of giddiness, not to mention occasional scary lapses into unconsciousness.

COME ONE, COME ALL!

Laughing gas's next incarnation was as a carnival amusement. Nineteenth century thrill-seekers paid for one minute with "fun gas." Gardner Quincy Colton, a medical school dropout, ran one of these fun-gas shows until he realized there was more money in anesthetics. In 1864, he established a chain of "painless" dental clinics. Dentists still use laughing gas as a mild sedative; anesthesiologists use it in small amounts with other gases for general anesthesia. It's important in heart surgery, too, specifically in the "balloon" procedure, which opens clogged arteries. Balloons are filled with laughing gas, which, when it cools to 14°F (10°C), freezes the plaque, which then breaks into tiny pieces to be flushed away by the body. Besides its medical uses, laughing gas is:

- an oxidant in semiconductor manufacturing;
- an ingredient in the chemical that inflates airbags;
- a component in certain rocket fuels;
- a power booster for race car engines;
- a propellant for canned whipped cream.

There are 85 calories in an apple but 325 in a slice of apple pie.

GRAB YOUR SUNSCREEN!

That crazy person on the street corner is onto something:
The end really is coming, and it's coming from above—
way above. Here's how it'll go down.

It's no lie. This planet is doomed. Even if we avoid annihilating ourselves in a war, defeat drug-resistant superbugs, cool down the global warming, and evade divinely ordained apocalypses, we're still slated for the universe's recycling bin. And the thing that's going to do us all in is the thing we'd least expect: the Sun.

BUT THE SUN IS SO WARM AND FRIENDLY!
You're familiar with the Sun—big glowing ball of gas, 93 million miles (150 million km) away, responsible for the creation of the solar system, and all that. For the last few billion years, the Sun's been pretty good to Earth, providing our little planet with all the energy it needs.

FUN IN THE SUN
The Sun is also ruled by its own internal nature, and its nature is nuclear fusion. It produces energy when hydrogen in its stellar core is smashed together, fusing to create helium and releasing incredible amounts of energy that eventually finds its way into space. Every second of every day, 600 million tons of hydrogen are turned into helium and energy—and this has been going on for a good five billion years. If you do the math, you'll realize that's a heck of a lot of hydrogen.

UH-OH!
The problem is, the Sun doesn't contain an infinite amount of hydrogen. Oh sure, it's got a lot—so much, in fact, that even with all that extravagant hydrogen burning over the last few billion years, the Sun has only burned through about half of its supply. But in about five billion years or so, our pal the Sun is finally going to run out of hydrogen to burn. And that's when the trouble starts.

The Great Gippsland earthworm of Australia can grow over four yards long.

YOU THINK IT'S EASY BEING A STAR?

Mind you, it's not just the Sun. All stars burn hydrogen; all stars eventually run out of it. What happens then depends on how big the star is. When really big stars—the ones that are bigger than 10 or 15 of our Suns—go through all their hydrogen, they take all the helium they created and start burning that. That works for a while, but not as long as burning hydrogen, because helium slams together to make carbon. Helium is gone? Start burning carbon and oxygen, then neon and magnesium, silicon and sulfur—each heavier material burning for a progressively shorter period, until what's left at the star's core is iron. As you might have guessed, iron is a truly lousy nuclear fuel. So, nuclear fusion stops dead. The star's mass collapses in on itself and then explodes as a supernova. If there was a solar system around that star, it's officially dead meat now, since anything that's not vaporized in the supernova blast is left to orbit the black hole created by the gravitational pressure of the star's immense mass imploding in on itself.

The good news is that the Sun won't go kerplooey as a supernova and collapse into a black hole that sucks the Earth screaming into its infinitely gaping gravitational maw. The Sun simply isn't massive enough for that fate. As stars go, it's a lightweight; some astronomers (not sensitive ones) classify the Sun as a yellow dwarf. Rest assured, however, that whatever happens to the Sun will be bad enough for anyone still lounging about on Earth.

BIGGER AND REDDER

Here's what will happen. Once the Sun uses up all its hydrogen, it will begin to burn helium, just like any star. When this happens, the Sun's core will contract, shrinking to provide the pressure needed to start helium fusion. As the core shrinks, the outer layer will expand and cool. The Sun's surface temperature, now at about 11,000°F (6,000°C), will dip to 6,500°F (3,600°C) or so—not frosty, but a lot cooler. With the dropping surface temperature and expanding size will come a new color and a new designation. The yellow dwarf will now be a red giant.

FEED ME!

"Red giant" is not just a cute phrase—the Sun really will expand tremendously and in the process, start to kill off its children, the planets. Mercury, the closest planet to the Sun at 36 million miles

(58 million km): an appetizer. The Sun's rapidly expanding surface will swallow sad little Mercury and won't even take time to chew. Venus, currently stationed at 67 million miles (107 million km) out, likewise will be swamped by the engorged star, which will vaporize Earth's twin without so much as a twinge of conscience.

SIX OF ONE...

From here on out, two things could happen. If the Sun continues to grow, it will simply swallow Earth, like it did Mercury and Venus. Of course, that's the end for Earth; it's very hard to survive as a planet inside the seething surface of an actual star. The other option is that the Sun stops expanding short of Earth's orbit. But really, how much better is that? Instead of being vaporized, Earth is blasted mercilessly with immense doses of solar energy that the Sun, now obscenely overinflated in the daytime sky, hurls at our tiny, defenseless planet. Oceans boil away, the atmosphere is blasted off, and the Earth, naked and bathed in searing radiation, is basically nothing more than a hot rock. Anyone still on Earth is advised to wear sunscreen—SPF 15 billion.

IT'S NOT OVER YET

After the Sun burns away all its helium, the end is near. The last gasps of helium burning strip away the Sun's outer layers, creating a planetary nebula as the shells of gas expand through the solar system—a nice spectacle for observers many light-years away, but not so good for anyone still in the neighborhood. The Sun's core then contracts once more into a white dwarf, a sphere of carbon a few thousand miles in diameter that no longer sustains nuclear fusion, since there's not enough mass to trigger carbon burning. Think of it as an immense charcoal briquette. Still, there's enough residual heat in this briquette to keep it warm for billions of years.

FINIS, FINALLY

Eventually, even that heat bleeds away, and what's left is a cold, black cinder floating in space where a living solar system used to be. There's some speculation that this stellar cinder might actually contain diamonds (after all, what are diamonds but highly compressed carbon?). But don't get too excited. Even if it turns out to be true, there'd be no place on Earth to spend the riches. There'd be no Earth there at all.

Because they have green thumbs.

VACATIONLAND U.S.A.

The top 10 natural tourist attractions in America, according to UNEP-WCMC, a highly unwieldy acronym that stands for United Nations Environment Programme World Conservation Monitoring Centre.

1. The Great Smoky Mountains National Park
The Smokies are #1. No showy geysers—just 800 square miles of perfect serenity in North Carolina and Tennessee, and 800 miles of hiking trails in the oldest mountain range in America. Don't wander too far off the trail, though. You saw *Deliverance*.

2. Grand Canyon National Park
A river runs through it. And that's why it's there. The Colorado River has been eroding the canyon for millions of years, and the spectacular result is 277 miles long, up to 18 miles wide, and more than a mile deep. But it's not in Colorado; it's in northern Arizona. Tip: Get there just before dawn.

3. Yosemite National Park
Mother Nature's best stuff—meadows, forests, mountains, water-falls—on display in California's Sierra-Nevada. Abraham Lincoln signed the bill making Yosemite Valley an "inalienable public trust" in 1864—the first time any government in the universe set aside scenic lands to protect them and make them available for all of the people, all of the time.

4. Olympic National Park
Three pristine parks for the price of one: glacier-capped moun-tains, 57 miles of wild Pacific coast, and a lush green rainforest with old-growth trees. The wettest spot in the continental US (bring your raincoat) and home of America's own Mount Olym-pus, the park's highest point, and of the gorgeous gods of nature.

5. Yellowstone National Park
The oldest national park in the universe (established 1872) and the largest in the lower 48 states, it measures 3,472 square miles. That famous geyser, Old Faithful, is the star: It goes off every 70 minutes on average. The park is home to lots of wolves and grizzly bears. Don't wander off the trail.

6. Waterton-Glacier International Peace Park

What began as two national parks are now one that straddles the border between Montana and Alberta, Canada. The glaciers that formed the landscape are long gone, but 50 smaller glaciers remain, 37 of which are big enough to have their own names. The biggest, Grinnell, covers 300 acres and its ice is 400 feet thick; it's named for conservationist George Bird Grinnell.

7. Mammoth Cave National Park

It took Mother Nature over 250 million years to form Mammoth Cave and thousands of years for humans to explore and map it. Its grand total of 336 miles of passageways make Mammoth the world's longest-known cave system. In south central Kentucky, it offers a wide variety of tours, even a wheelchair-accessible one.

8. Hawaii Volcanoes National Park

Mount Kilauea—the most active volcano in the whole world—is called the "drive-in volcano" because it's so accessible. Meanwhile, its neighbor, Mauna Loa, is the world's most massive volcano, which doesn't get it as much attention as being active.

9. Everglades National Park

You thought it was just a big swamp. Yes, if you want to call a freshwater river that's 100 miles long, 50 miles wide, and a few inches deep a swamp. It's more demanding on the visitor than most national parks. You need a boat for one thing. The park supports a huge variety of wildlife because it straddles two zones: subtropics and temperate. It's the only place in the world where alligators and crocodiles exist side-by-side. (As if they weren't already hard enough to tell apart.)

10. Carlsbad Caverns National Park

Carlsbad, in the Guadalupe Mountains of New Mexico, is only one of 80 caves in the park. The most attractive thing about the caverns is that stalactites meet stalagmites in the middle where they form massive pillars, so you don't have to remember which is which. And the bats. Hundreds of thousands of them take off every night at sunset during the warm months. You can be there to watch them. (But we'd wear a hat. Maybe a hood. Maybe full-body armor.)

One of the first known maps was drawn by the Greek traveler Hecataeus around 510 B.C.

VACATIONLAND, THE WORLD

The top 10 natural tourist attractions outside of America, according to the EPWCMC (see Vacationland USA for explanation).

1. Canadian Rocky Mountains.
Seven preserves in the Rockies: 4 national parks—Banff, Jasper, Yoho, and Kootenay—in Alberta, and 3 "provincial" parks in British Columbia—enough room to get seriously lost in. Don't make the forest rangers have to go in after you. Keep to the trails.

2. Wet Tropics
It takes up more than two million acres along the northeast coast of Queensland, Australia. The original owners, 16 aboriginal groups, play an important role in preserving the exotic flora and fauna: tree-kangaroos, flying foxes (bats, really), cassowaries (huge endangered flightless birds), feral pigs, wallabies, platypuses, and crocodiles. Leave your own pets at home. It's the law.

3. Great Barrier Reef
More tourists for Australia. The world's largest coral reef—over 1,250 miles long—isn't a single reef at all; it's made of over 2,900 individual reefs very close to each other. Tourists are cautioned not to walk on the reefs or snap off any coral for a souvenir.

4. Central Eastern Rainforest Reserves of Australia
It must get a little crowded around tourist season, hey, matey? More rainforests! As if there weren't enough in the Wet Tropics. Here there are not one, not two, but five different types of rain-forests: subtropical, littoral, warm temperate, cool temperate, and dry. (Add to your oxymoron list right next to jumbo shrimp.)

5. Pyrénées—Mont Perdu
France and Spain are the co-owners here. "Perdu" means "lost" in French, and hard to get to in any language. The mountain is the centerpiece of the Spanish Parque National de Ordesa y Monte Perdido, established in 1918 with a measly eight square miles. The

---

A peanut is not a nut; it is a legume, more pea than nut.

park has grown to over 60 square miles. (Hey, there isn't that much room left in Europe; they're lucky they have any set-aside land at all!)

6. Iguazu/Iguacu
Two spellings—Spanish and Portuguese— because the park is partly in Argentina (with the Z) and Brazil (which has its own Z). However you spell it, Iguazu has waterfalls out the Iguazu: 275 of them side by side; so close to each other they look like one (2.5 mile long) spectacular waterfall. You'll never go back to Niagara.

7. Tongariro
Move over Australia; and make room for those little islands to the right and down a little—specifically New Zealand's North Island, where Mount Tongariro and its neighboring volcanoes started upchucking lava over 260,000 years ago. The volcanoes left the park's terrain looking so alien that movie director Peter Jackson found it the perfect setting for his *Lord of the Rings*.

8. Te Wahipounamu
New Zealand scores again (and wins the wackiest name award.) The name means "the place of greenstone," the Maoris' most precious stone, used for tools, weapons, ornaments, everything. To travelers, it means fjords, rocky coasts, towering cliffs, lakes, and waterfalls. The park is home to the rare and endangered takahe, another one of those hapless, large flightless birds.

9. Lake Baikal
This time Siberia scores. What? You don't think of Siberia as a tourist attraction? Well, it's in southern Siberia. Does that make a difference? The largest freshwater lake in the world is so big that if drained, it would take all the Great Lakes to refill it. The lake freezes in the winter, but what do you care? You won't be there.

10. Tasmanian Wilderness
Back to Australia, this time to the island of Tasmania, 20 percent of which is designated wilderness, nearly 3.5 million acres of rugged mountains, caves, moorlands, forests (both rain and other-wise). Best thing? It's home to the legendary Tasmanian devil, a fierce, nocturnal marsupial that, with its sharp little teeth completely devours its prey: bones, fur, and all.

DEFINITELY DUNG

What do Uncle John and Cleopatra have in common? Their favorite bug.

Dung beetles come in all sizes, up to 6 inches (15 cm) long. Some even fly, the better to zero in on fresh droppings. They're tough, stubborn, and ingenious—and their diligence should never be underestimated.

BUGS WITH A HISTORY

Don't look down your nose at them, either. Dung beetles (a.k.a. scarabs) were revered in ancient Egypt as symbols of regeneration: Scarab-shaped jewelry was worn by—and entombed with—the pharaohs; Roman soldiers wore scarab rings; and the ancient Greek dramatist, Aristophanes, in his play *The Birds*, has his hero fly to Mount Olympus on the back of a giant dung beetle.

PICKY, PICKY

It seems like there's a dung beetle for every kind of dung. Among the 7,000 species, there's one that collects monkey dung from high up in the trees of a jungle, another that will only go for sloth dung, and so on.

Australian cattle ranchers got the picky-picky message. Their native dung beetles preferred native dung—from kangaroos, wallabies, and even those rabbits. Cow patties just didn't cut it. Considering the average cow contributes seven tons of patties to the pasture every year, the Aussies didn't need calculators to figure out they'd soon have piles of dung, but no pastures.

A quick call to England solved the problem: Send us some dung beetles that prefer cow offerings. Thanks to those beetle imports, beef is now a major Aussie export.

A CLASSY DAME

But the dung beetles that get the starring roles in beetle flicks on the Discovery Channel are the rollers. The female dung beetle rides across the African veldt on top of a ball of dung that's sometimes 50 times larger than her mate, who pushes it along like a humble servant. Audiences love this. They cheer the hero beetle as he rolls it along, especially when the love of his life is perched atop. And she isn't as insouciant as she seems. She's partly there to defend against interlopers, and trust us, she's quite capable of giving them hell when they need it.

IT MAKES SCENTS

It can be as subtle as a bowl of potpourri or as overpowering
as that woman standing next to you in the elevator.
Welcome to the world of fragrance.

When we smell something, what we're smelling are the molecules the substance is giving off as it evaporates. The stronger the smell, the more volatile—faster-evaporating—it is. When we inhale, we pull those molecules into our noses, where they pass over our olfactory glands. Tiny hairs in these glands—called cilia—collect the molecules and transmit them to the neurons they're attached to. The neurons interpret them as a smell—the dirty stench of an unwashed dog or the fragrant scent of a fresh rose. Scientists believe that humans can distinguish as many as 10,000 different smells. We'd like to concentrate on the nicer smells.

HOW TO TRAP A SMELL
How do perfumers trap something as elusive and transitory as a smell? The odor comes from what are known as "essential oils"; what we smell is actually the oil evaporating. Essential oils can come from flowers (jasmine, rose), spices (cinnamon, nutmeg), woods (sandalwood, cedar), or mosses (usually oak moss). There are hundreds of potential ingredients.

AT THE PERFUME FACTORY
But how do you get the oil out of the plant? The most common way is to distill—or evaporate—them out with steam. But heat can change the smell of more delicate flowers. So perfumers use solvents instead of water because they boil at a lower temperature.

Then there's something called "enfleurage," which is when you put flower petals on greasy sheets of glass and let the grease absorb the oils. Enfleurage isn't used much anymore because it is very time-intensive. Finally, you can use brute force and squeeze—or "express"—the oils out with sponges and presses.

MUSICAL SMELLS
The smell of perfume changes the longer you have it on because most perfumes are made from a blend of essential oils that evapo-

rate at different rates. These different smells are called "notes." The top note has the strongest smell (this is the one that entices you to buy); it also evaporates the fastest. When the top note oils have evaporated, you can smell the middle note oils. There are usually more middle note oils than any of the others. The bottom note oils are the longest-lasting: the faint smell that still lingers by the time you're ready to shower again.

HOW TO TRAP A SMELL II

But if something like perfume works because it evaporates, an immediate problem is how to prevent it from evaporating too quickly; something is needed to help control the rate of evaporation. Enter what are called "fixatives," which, by the way, also add to the scent. A lot of fixatives come from the musk glands of various animals—musk deer, muskrat, civet cat, whales, and beavers. Other fixatives come from mosses, resins, and aromatic chemicals.

PUT IT ALL TOGETHER

Then, since the smell of essential oils and fixatives are so strong, they have to be diluted in something—alcohol. The professionals use ethyl alcohol, but amateur perfume-making guides call for alcohol in the form of vodka. The oils and fixatives dissolve in it, but their scent remains.

* * * * *

THAT FISHY SMELL

Young salmon live in freshwater streams for a while, then head downstream. Along the way, their bodies adapt for saltwater life, even though none of them has ever seen the ocean. They also change their striped brown color—suitable for hiding in a stream—for silvery ocean camouflage.

Years later, most of them return to the very place where they were hatched. Once they get into the right neighborhood they apparently find the home stream by smell. Fish can smell? Well, when researchers stuffed cotton balls up the noses of some Northwest Pacific salmon, those fish got lost. Fish have nostrils? Yes. In fact, some scientists believe that the salmon's sense of smell is much, much, better than a dog's.

The average elephant produces 50 pounds of dung a day.

POOL SHARKS

*How Olympic swimmers are beating the clock with a little help
from high-tech science and low-tech fish*

Freestyle competitive swimming seems like the simplest of
sports, but at the world-class level, the clock is king, and
shaving seconds (or hundredths of a second) off the prevail-
ing record has become a science.

BEAT THE CLOCK
Swimmers like Australia's Ian "Thorpedo" Thorpe have to master
a lot of components to bring in those gold medals. Among them:

• Reaction speed—ability to be quick off the mark at the start

• Acceleration—ability to reach maximum speed in the shortest
possible time

• Maximum speed—peak swimming speed

• Speed-endurance—speed that swimmers can sustain for long-
distance races.

SWIMMING IS SUCH A DRAG
To further complicate the situation, physics dictates that despite
his super abilities, Thorpedo has to overcome the problem of drag
when he tries to go faster. Drag is caused by the friction and pressure created by the water, which resists an object's movement
(even when that object is as powerful a swimmer as Thorpe).

There's frontal drag when Thorpe swims and has to move
water out of his way, and skin drag when water flows across the
surface of his body (creating a turbulent wake that increases drag).
Here's an example of the power of drag. Swimmers shave off
surface hair because smooth skin creates less skin drag than hairy
skin. This helps them gain about an extra second per 100 meters.

For 200 million years humans have been accustomed to
moving through air. Water is nearly 800 times denser than air and
55 times more viscous (resistant to flow) than air. The world's best
swimmers have to struggle to go faster than four miles an hour!

SIZE MATTERS
Genetics plays a big part in making great swimmers. A swimmer

The smallest spider, the comb-footed spider, is smaller than a pin's head.

with the right stuff has a tall, lean body. Most elite male swimmers
are over six feet (like Olympic gold medal winner Alex Popov at
6'7"). Long bodies give swimmers a longer reach for a powerful
stroke, and being lean helps a swimmer cut through the water in
as streamlined a fashion as possible.

YA GOTTA HAVE HEART
Superswimmers also have "big hearts." Studies show that the best
swimmers have large heart muscles. Some long-distance swimmers
have cardiovascular systems that deliver twice as much oxygen to
muscle cells as the average young person who's reasonably fit.

TECHNIQUE MATTERS
It takes more than a "genetically correct" and well-conditioned
body to bring home gold. Elite swimmers use constantly evolving
technology. Videos, computer analysis, stroke digitalization,
and physiological testing equipment are as much a part of world-
class competitive swimming as the splash of water and the smell
of chlorine.

HIGH-TECH IS ALL WET
If you don't believe that great swimmers and their patrons invest
in serious science, you've probably never heard of a flume, which
is a kind of water treadmill that coaches and swim scientists use to
zero in on the strengths and weaknesses of competitive swimmers.
Put a great swimmer like the U.S.'s Brooke Bennett in a flume and
you can tape her winning form with stationary videocams above
and below the water level. Stroke digitalization uses computers to
identify points on the joints of her shoulder, elbow, wrist, and
hand; it tracks these points through a stroke cycle so that even the
slightest need for adjustment becomes obvious. And all the while,
testing equipment is measuring Bennett's heart rate, oxygen levels,
energy levels, and so on. Talk about fine-tuning.

FROM FLUMES TO FLIPPER
Athletes are also turning to scientists for research on the biome-
chanics of some of the world's other great competitive swimmers—dolphins and sharks. Even air-breathing mammals like
dolphins can leave our best swimmers rocking in their wake. The
best human swimmers expend tremendous energy to reach four
mph (6.4 kph), but a dolphin can cruise by at 20 mph (30 kph)

without breaking a sweat, so to speak. Dolphins try to avoid the surface where "wave drag" slows them down. When they're migrating, dolphins swim underwater and lift themselves up out of the water when they need to breathe. Some competitive swimmers are making use of dolphin wisdom: They'll glide faster in a turn if they go deeper.

SWIMMING WITH SHARKS

Here's what you get when technology meets biomimicry. Sharks have denticles on their skin (scales that are actually tiny teeth all facing toward the tail) that direct the flow of water over a shark's body, creating a film that reduces drag. A British shark expert helped Speedo design a bodysuit for swimmers called the Fastskin. Made of a ridged material that mimics sharkskin, the suit is said to reduce drag by three percent. Does the Fastskin work? Ask Michael Klim and Grant Hackett, who won Olympic gold wearing Fastskin bodysuits at the 2000 Sydney games.

SWIM LIKE A FISH

Some fast-swimming fish have fins that can be tucked away in special grooves to make them more streamlined when they need to move fast. Now some swimmers are wearing (and swearing by) special, slithery bodysuits that compress their muscles and make their bodies more streamlined.

And just in case you were thinking of taking up the sport, the experts will tell you that what you wear will not replace training and preparation. Technology aside, it's the engine in the car that determines how fast it'll go.

* * * * *

THE FISH OLYMPICS

The 100 meter Olympic swimming freestyle record is about 48 seconds, a snail's pace to many of the ocean's regular inhabitants. The fastest fish in the ocean—a sailfish—can move as fast as 67 mph (100 kph), so it could complete the 100-meter human race in about 3.5 seconds.

Aluminum was once considered a precious metal and was used to craft jewelry.

THIS MITE SURPRISE YOU

After a long, busy day, you deserve better than this.

You drag yourself to bed for some well-deserved rest. As you burrow under the covers and slowly drift off to sleep, a massive army of tiny bugs begins to munch on your skin. Take heart, you're not being eaten alive. The millions of microscopic eight-legged members of the spider family in bed with you are gorging on your dead, decomposing skin scales.

Scientists call them *Dermatophagoides pteronyssinus*. We prefer to use the common folk's term: house dust mites. They were officially discovered in 1964 and infest homes all over the world. They need a humidity of from 70 to 80 percent and temperatures of 75 to 80°F (24 to 27°C) to thrive.

QUIT HOGGING THE COVERS!

You bring a brand new mattress home and by the time it's four months old, you've got something like 200 million or more dust mites sharing it with you. They also infest pillows, stuffed animals, and upholstery—any fabric, in fact, including clothing. Just because you've got them doesn't mean you're a crummy housekeeper. You can't get rid of them permanently, no matter how hard you try. Look on the bright side At least they don't transmit human diseases.

THE OFFICIAL POOP

Their droppings are another matter. They're the main cause of a lot of allergies, including asthma. Dust mite feces are the right size to be breathed into the nose and to penetrate the eye membranes. Kind of makes you wonder how much dust mite poop you breathe in each time you walk into the house, pull on a shirt, or toss in bed. Let's try not to think about it.

A-HUNTING WE WILL GO

At just one-quarter to one-third millimeter in size, dust mites are almost invisible to the naked eye. If you really want to see them without a microscope, try this. Gather a pile of dust on a dark background in a warm and humid environment. If you stare at the dust long enough, sometimes you'll see the occasional white dot moving. Your eyes aren't playing tricks on you. What you are seeing is a dust mite. Probably a female since they tend to be larger, hardier, and travel solo. The males are smaller with weaker shells, and they usually cluster together to preserve water.

THEY CAN'T SEE YOU EITHER
A dust mite has no eyes, ears, or nose; just a tiny, hungry mouth that's capable of eating but not drinking. Dust mites absorb water from the air. If the humidity falls below 50 percent, a mite will dry out and die. That's why people with allergies are more comfortable in places like the Arizona desert.

A MICROSCOPIC DONNER PARTY?
Researchers have yet to find out what happens to the bodies of dust mites after they go to The Great Futon in the Sky. It might be that the carcasses decompose (dust mite body particles have also been proven to cause allergies.) Another possibility is that dust mites are cannibals and eat their own species. Scientists have discovered that besides skin scales, dust mites eat insect bodies or fragments, fungi and molds, pollen grains, and bacteria.

DUST TO DUST
If conditions are perfect, a house dust mite will live for 90 days—no longer. A dust mite grows up fast. He whisks through the "teenage" (tritonymph) stage in about two days (during which time, of course, he gets his driver's license). Within 24 hours of reaching the adult stage, at about nine days old, he mates. The female lays between 40 to 100 eggs—one to three a day—during her lifetime. It only takes about ten days after mating to the birth of her first eggs.

So, next time you snuggle under the covers, try not to remember this: **YOU ARE NOT ALONE.**

If you are itching for more , check out
"I've Got You Under My Skin" on page 277.

* * * * *

TOM SWIFTIES FOR SCIENTISTS

"I wish I'd invented the telegraph," Tom said remorsefully.
"This old pipe is rusty," Tom said ironically.
"That darn scale keeps forming inside this kettle,"
Tom said recalcitrantly.

As many as 275 bacteria colonies are exchanged during a kiss.

WHAT MAKES A PERFECT STORM?

Maybe you've seen the movie, but do you know what makes a perfect storm? And will we predict the next one in time?

Some people called it the meteorological event of the century. In late October of 1991, a superstorm slammed the Atlantic coast, causing flooding in the Dominican Republic and a hurricane as far north as Nova Scotia. Waves of over 30 feet swamped the Atlantic shore. That same week six fishermen from Gloucester, Massachusetts, went out for swordfish and never came back. Their ship was the *Andrea Gail*, a 72-foot-long, steel-hulled fishing boat.

The bravery and skill of the drowned Gloucester fishermen inspired journalist Sebastian Junger to write their story. To Junger's surprise, his book *The Perfect Storm* became a best-seller. It also served as the basis for a Hollywood blockbuster that made the plight of the *Andrea Gail* world famous.

THE PERFECT TITLE
Before the book came out, the storm was generally known as the Halloween storm (because it arrived in the last days of October). But when Junger was researching the story, he talked to a retired National Weather Service forecaster who explained that the combination of the three weather systems that collided that fateful week in 1991 was "perfect" for creating devastating weather. From this, Junger coined the term "the perfect storm."

NASTY NOR'EASTERS
When the storm began on October 26, it didn't seem remarkable. It was a typical northeaster or "nor'easter" as native New Englanders call them. Nor'easters commonly form off the coast of New England in late fall as cold air masses from Canada move south where they often meet a warmer air mass that still holds some summer heat. When the two air currents clash over the North Atlantic, the contrast in temperatures creates wind and/or storms that begin with strong winds from the east or northeast (hence

the name); they whirl in a counter-clockwise cyclone pattern, pull moist air in from the ocean, and bring rain and snow.

HEAVY WEATHER

That October, as waves and tides hit record highs, hundreds of homes and business along the coast were knocked off their foundations or pulled into the sea. In the Atlantic, a weather buoy east of Long Island reported 40 to 80 foot (12 to 24 m) waves. A 101-foot (31 m) wave was recorded by a weather buoy near Nova Scotia. In addition to the lost crew of the Andrea Gail, a rescue airman was drowned when he was forced to bail out of his helicopter. Other fatalities included two men capsized in a boat, a man blown off a bridge, and a fisherman swept off the rocks by swollen surf.

TROUBLE COMES IN THREES

The perfect storm was a triple whammy. As a Great Lakes storm system moved east, an icy Canadian cold front moved south. Meanwhile, Hurricane Grace, born in the tropics around the Bahamas, was headed to the southeastern U.S., when she took a freakish turn to the North Atlantic. As the high-pressure Great Lakes storm hit the low-pressure Canadian cold front, the result was a powerful nor'easter, but the addition of Grace (which may have been pulled in by the cyclone winds of the nor'easter) put a match to dynamite. The hurricane and nor'easter merged into a huge, monstrous hybrid.

KILLER WIND

Meteorologists use the Beaufort scale to measure wind. A wind of force 9 on the scale signals a 47 to 54 mph (76 to 87 kph) wind that's classified as a "severe gale." At sea the gale causes dangerously high waves; on land it can blow the shingles off roofs. A force 11 wind is rarely seen on land. That's a good thing, because force 11 winds have been known to topple trees and—forget about shingles—they can blow entire roofs off.

Only a few times in a century does the coast see winds at the highest Beaufort scale rating of 12. The perfect storm recorded winds at force 12—classified as "hurricane force"—that is, over 73 mph (117 kph). Those winds can whip up 80-foot (24 m) waves and turn the sea white with driving spray. On land, two simple words describe their effect: violence and destruction.

The costliest hurricane occurred in 1992; Andrew cost in excess of 25 billion dollars.

THE DEATH OF THE *ANDREA GAIL*

On the evening of October 28, as the storm was building, Captain Billy Tynes radioed from the *Andrea Gail* to tell other swordfish boats that a storm was coming. Tynes reported that the winds were so powerful that they'd blown some equipment off the deck of his ship—even though the equipment in question had been bolted down with steel bolts. As he signed off, Tynes couldn't know that his boat was heading into a meteorological nightmare.

It's said that Tynes and his crew met waves over 100 feet (30 m) high and winds over 120 mph (193 kph). We'll never know for sure, because his radio message was the last heard from him. But could Tynes have been warned in time to take a different route? Could the crew of the *Andrea Gail* have been saved?

PREDICTING PERFECTION

Meteorologists at the U.S. National Weather Service knew that when the three weather systems collided, there would be unprecedented trouble at sea; they predicted waves from 50 to 100 feet (15 to 30 m). They sent out immediate marine warnings, but by the time they saw the data and realized how devastating the storm would really be, it was too late to get every boat back in time.

DOWN TO THE SEA IN SHIPS

Today, almost 85 percent of forecasting information comes from satellites. Satellite photos can track warm and cold air masses, show meteorologists where air systems are likely to meet, and tip them off to the first stages of storm development, which helps the weather bureau predict storms earlier and more accurately. As people continue to sail and fish the waters of the North Atlantic, the men and women in the weather service work to save them from the next "perfect storm."

* * * * *

Rule: You'll drown in deep water if you don't know how to swim.
Rule Breaker: Except in the Dead Sea. Even nonswimmers find it hard to drown in the Dead Sea. The salty water is so buoyant that it's tough to even get your body well below the surface.

Lindbergh was only 25 when he made the first solo transatlantic flight in 1927.

WHY THERE'S SO MUCH SAND IN THE SAHARA

Or…who ate the cedars of Lebanon?

In the vast Sahara, seas of sand ripple for miles. They rise up in wavelike dunes that can crest at over a thousand feet. With temperatures that have been known to reach 136°F (58°C), the desolate Sahara covers most of North Africa and over a third of the African continent. It's the world's largest desert, home to over three million square miles of dust, stone, and sand.

PARADISE LOST

In the sweltering Sahara, a cool vision of waving grass and shining lakes can seem like a mirage (or the first signs of heat exhaustion), but it's a glimpse into the Earth's astounding past. Hard to believe, but this hostile ocean of sand was once an earthly Eden. Fish swam in ancient lakes; giraffes, elephants, and gazelles roamed grassy savannas; and hippos wallowed in ponds and mud.

And people had a great time, too. Prehistoric rock paintings show ancient Saharans feasting and drinking and—it's true!—swimming. They had steady jobs, first as fishermen and hunters, later as shepherds, cattlemen, and farmers. That was in the old days, around 5,500 years ago. But 2,000 or so years later (just a wink of the geological eye), the lakes had dried up, the vegetation and animals were gone, and farmers were forced to leave a land where nothing could grow. So what happened?

TRUE GRIT

Over thousands of years, as rainfall lessened and temperatures rose, what little rain there was eroded the soil and dissolved it, releasing grains of silica sand. Wind slammed sand into rocks, wearing those rocks away, which created more sand. Hot days and freezing nights subjected rock outcroppings to extreme temperature changes. This daily expansion and contraction eventually shattered mineral crystals in the rocks so that the cliffs broke into boulders, boulders shattered into pebbles, and pebbles crumbled into sand.

Americans toss out 25 million plastic drink bottles every hour.

But what caused the climate to change in the first place? Why did drought transform the Sahara from a wet wonderland to a desert badland? Explanations involve everything from the tilt of the Earth to the appetite of the humble goat.

A VENUS AND JUPITER SANDWICH

Up in space and completely unaware of giraffes, hippos, or swimming Saharans, Jupiter's gravity combined with Venus's gravity to influence the tilt of the Earth's axis. Nine thousand years ago, when the Sahara was blooming, Jupiter and Venus kept the Earth's tilt at 24.14 degrees, compared to the 23.45 degrees it is today. The perihelion (when the Earth is closest to the Sun) occurred at the end of July—now it occurs in early January. This means that a very long time ago, the Northern Hemisphere basked in much more summer sunlight, and the summers in Africa were hotter.

Hotter? So what's the problem? Well, ironically, hot summers meant water for North Africa and lots of it. When the African landmass is much hotter than the Atlantic Ocean, the temperature contrast increases the number of summer monsoons that rain on the Sahara. As the Earth incrementally wobbled into its current axis, the summers grew cooler, the African monsoons grew weaker, and the cool, moist Sahara became hot, dry, and eventually sandy.

NUDE LANDS ARE BAD LANDS

As rainfall decreased, plants died. The death of vegetation in turn increased the drought. Plants hold moisture in the soil and summer sun evaporates the moisture into the atmosphere, where it's converted to rain. Barren land with no plants or trees holds less moisture, so the surrounding atmosphere produces less rain. Plants absorb sunlight, whereas bare land and bright sandy deserts reflect the sun's heat, which leads to fewer clouds and less rain.

This drought cycle picked up momentum until finally the desert took over fertile ground. And remember the rock paintings showing the farmers, shepherds, and cattle drivers? It may be that those folks helped the drought cycle along, turning their heavenly little Eden into the hot hell of the Sahara.

WHO'S TO BLAME?

Some scientists believe that ancient man was the victim of the climate change, but others think he was responsible for it and that

Leonardo da Vinci conceived the idea for contact lenses in 1508.

poor farming practices, as well as overgrazing and deforestation, contributed to drought, barren land, and the eventual creation of deserts. In fact, a famous scientific study suggests that deforestation along the southern coast of West Africa could cause a complete collapse of the Sahara's dwindling monsoon system.

BETTER GET YOUR GOAT

Even in ancient times the loss of forests were a problem. A famous example involved the great cedars of Lebanon, which were nearly decimated not just by lumbermen but also by herds of goats that chomped on the bark and devoured young saplings. And guess what? Even today, widespread exploitation of those same cedars—goats or not—has contributed to increasing deforestation, which leads to soil erosion, which leads to sand...and lots of it.

SAND MARCHES ON

Today, there's controversy over whether human activity is causing the Sahara's size to increase. Critics of the idea argue that satellite photos show the desert fluctuating in size, but not steadily growing larger. Nevertheless, people living on the edge of the great desert, in places like Niger, Chad, and Mali, complain that the Sahara has steadily encroached on their precious farmland.

THE GREENING OF THE SAHARA

What about turning back the clock? Can more rain and rivers and even lakes return to the Sahara? Can we help nature re-create an Eden in North Africa? Scientists believe that replanting trees and vegetation, as well as conserving groundwater and runoff, could reverse the desert's drought cycle. Some theorists even propose that global warming (if it increases the heat of the African land in summer) will eventually increase the amount of monsoons. With the help of humans, the desert just might bloom again, but since a reversed drought cycle could take a couple of centuries to work, don't hop off your camel just yet.

* * * * *

"To see a World in a Grain of Sand
And a Heaven in a wild Flower,
Hold Infinity in the palm of your hand
And Eternity in an hour."
—William Blake,
"Auguries of Innocence," 1810

The jugular vein is actually an artery.

CONTINENTAL DRIFT: PART II

In Part I, we found out what the Earth used to look like.
Here's a look at what awaits:
a guide to the future of the continents.

We know how it is. You're sitting out on your front lawn in Ohio or Oklahoma, where the nearest "beach" is an overchlorinated swim park, and you're thinking to yourself: "Sure, it's not beachfront property now. But in 20 million years, once California has sunk under the waves, this is going to be right on the water." No, you won't be around to see it, and whatever descendants you have will have evolved into creepy little extraterrestrial thingies that probably can't even dog paddle. But that's not the point. The point is, 20 million years from now, something genetically related to you is going to have a clambake on whatever remains of your property.

FUTURAMA

Well, maybe. But probably not. We've seen the geological models of the continents of the future and we've got two pieces of bad news. First: California never actually sinks into the Pacific. Second: Ohio, Oklahoma, and nearly every other inland part of the U.S. pretty much stays inland for at least the next 250 million years. To understand why, we need to do a quick review of the science of plate tectonics.

MORE PLATE TECTONICS

Remember the setup? The surface of Earth was once covered with one giant continent called "Pangaea." It started coming apart about 200 million years ago and eventually formed the continents we know and love today. And the continents are made up of "plates" that jostle around. Like the way ice floats on water, they float on denser, partially molten rock.

The plates the continents rest on grow and shrink over time, as the plates move against (and over and under) each other. When continents knock up against each other—as sometimes happens, one doesn't slide under the other—they just ram each other head-on, and what you get are huge crumple zones at the point of impact—otherwise known as "mountain ranges." The Himalayas are one of those crumple zones, from when India rammed into Asia 50 million years ago.

THE SHAPE OF THINGS TO COME
Today the continents are about as evenly spaced as they're ever going to get. From here on out, if current plate motions hold and geologists have guessed correctly, all the continents are eventually going to slam back into each other again.

Among the first of these big slams will be Africa driving into Southern Europe. If you're planning a Mediterranean vacation, take it now. In 50 million years, the Mediterranean Sea will be a distant memory, replaced by an immense mountain range stretching from Spain to Turkey.

Africa likewise jams into the Arabian Peninsula, squishing it into Eastern Asia on the other side. All of the African/European/Asian megacontinent (Aferasia?) also twists north and clockwise; the equator, which currently runs through Kenya and Uganda, will run through Zimbabwe, rather substantially south. Meanwhile, the British Isles get launched toward the Arctic Circle. If you thought it was cold and depressing there now, well, just you wait.

NORTH NORTH HOLLYWOOD
Also heading north: California. California doesn't fall into the sea (get over it), but plate movements send the Golden State up the Pacific coastline so that in 50 million years, residents of Malibu will be able to look out of their windows and wave to the folks in Anchorage. Fortunately for the Anchorage folks, the land bridge between Siberia and Alaska will be open for business again, so they'll have an escape route. Otherwise, North America will pretty much look the same.

KOALAS IN SWEATERS
Fast-forward another 100 million years, and Australia, the land down under, really starts living up to the name as it whacks into Antarctica. Koalas everywhere reach for their sweaters.

The Atlantic and Indian Oceans will shrink as the continents pull closer together, and as the plate holding the Atlantic gets pushed under North America, the U.S. eastern seaboard gets pushed up. New York, Washington, and Boston, if still existing, will rival Denver as mile-high cities. The Midwest remains beachless.

NEVERGLADES NATIONAL PARK

Another 100 million years after that (250 million years from today), the Americas, Africa, Europe, and Asia will finally be smooshed together in a huge supercontinent (Amafeura?), with only the mashed-up remains of Australia and Antarctica standing apart as a second, much smaller landmass. The Atlantic Ocean is now part of the mainland, as are the Caribbean and the Gulf of Mexico. All you landlubbers who yearned for beachfront views get the satisfaction of knowing that Florida becomes a Plains state.

NORTH NORTH AFRICA

- Africa will be well north of much of North America; any New Yorkers still hanging around will be living at the same latitude as residents of Namibia.
- South America will turn 90 degrees counter-clockwise as it hugs what used to be the southern tip of Africa.
- Tierra del Fuego will be joined at the feet with the remnants of Southeast Asia.
- Where the Americas meet up with Africa will be a mountain range that makes the Himalayas look like mud piles.
- What's left of the Indian Ocean will be transformed into the biggest lake ever. You could walk from Alaska to China without needing to cross a body of water larger than a river. Or your descendants could, provided they still actually walk.

Hey, it's evolution. You never know.

* * * * *

YOU WOULD THINK...

If the ocean floors spread and opened when their plates moved, the water would disappear into the holes.

It would if it could. What stops it is the tremendous pressure of the molten rock that spews through these rifts. That force won't let even a single drop of water escape into the center of the Earth.

Herbert Spencer, not Darwin, came up with the phrase "survival of the fittest."

GO GET BENT

There's a reason scuba divers have to be trained before they strap on an oxygen tank and dive—the human body is vulnerable to a particularly nasty problem known as "the bends." Here's the science behind the malady.

B efore the advent of scuba (self-contained underwater breathing apparatus) gear, the skill of underwater divers depended on one thing: how long they could hold their breaths. Later divers depended on snorkel-like devices, or diving bells or helmets that piped in air from above the surface. Thanks to 19th century work with compressed air, deep-sea divers can now stay underwater for much longer periods. But staying underwater isn't really their main worry—coming up to the surface is.

DEEP THOUGHTS
Ascending from the depths puts divers at risk of decompression sickness, or "the bends," caused by rising too rapidly to the surface. Medical awareness of the problem developed alongside diving technology. The first underwater breathing systems, the ones that used air from the surface, didn't permit the long, deep dives that cause the bends.

ALL BENT OUT OF SHAPE
When an English engineer perfected a system of working on the sea floor in upside-down pressurized containers called caissons, awareness of the mysterious illness called "caisson disease" began to spread. Workers who did underwater exploration and construction in caissons complained of "cold and rheumatism," joint pain, and breathing problems. In the throes of the malady, they had a characteristic, bent-over gait, hence the nickname, "the bends."

BAD BENDS IN BROOKLYN
The bends apparently killed 14 workers on the St. Louis Bridge project in the early 1870s and caused paralysis in 30 others, while at least three men were killed by the bends while working on the Brooklyn Bridge in New York in the last half of that same decade.

The builder of the St. Louis Bridge, James Eads, hired a doctor to work on the mysterious caisson sickness there. By the time the Brooklyn Bridge problems began, the doctor had already

The screwdriver was invented in 1550 and is attributed to gunsmiths and armorers.

had some success using slow decompression to treat symptoms. But because of an argument with Brooklyn Bridge chief engineer Washington Roebling, Eads never told him of the discovery. Roebling himself paid dearly for that falling out. An attack of the bends left him partially paralyzed, partly blind, deaf, and mute.

CAN YOU TAKE THE PRESSURE?

On dry land, the air around us has a pressure of about 14.7 pounds per square inch (PSI), also known as 1 atmosphere (the baseline, if you will). Water is much heavier than air, so it exerts much more pressure on the body. At a depth of 33 feet (10 m), it's twice what it is on land. If you hold your breath and dive down to 33 feet (10 m), the pressure is so strong that your lungs will actually contract to withstand the pressure.

When divers breathe from a scuba tank, the air from the tank has to have the same pressure as the water pressure around the diver or it won't come out of the tank. A diver at a depth of 33 feet (10 m) is breathing air with twice the pressure of surface air; at 66 feet (20 m) it's three times the pressure, and so on.

LIKE A PEPSI?

When the gases in that compressed air meet the water, they dissolve. When you look at a bottle of soda, you can't see any bubbles because the water in carbonated drinks has been exposed to high-pressure carbon dioxide gas that has dissolved into the water. Maintaining that mix requires a steady pressure, which is why soda comes in sealed cans or bottles with tight-fitting lids. When you open the soda, you release the pressure. The gas is released from the water and bubbles rise quickly to the surface.

A diver is something like the soda in that can or bottle. As a diver stays underwater breathing compressed air, some of the nitrogen in that air dissolves in the water contained in his or her body. The deeper the diver goes, and the longer he or she stays underwater, the greater the amount of nitrogen in the blood.

KILLER BUBBLES

If the diver comes back to the surface carefully, the nitrogen dissolves slowly and safely. But if the diver releases the pressure by coming up to the surface too quickly, the gas is released from the water and large nitrogen bubbles can form in the body—just like that can of soda.

One out of every 2,000 infants is born with a tooth.

Unlike the harmless bubbles in a bottle of soda, nitrogen bubbles can kill a scuba diver. The bubbles can form in lots of places: in the joints, bones, and muscles (which can cause intense pain); in the blood (which can block circulation and even kill tissue); in the brain (causing unconsciousness, dizziness, convulsions, even blindness and paralysis); or in the spinal cord (causing paralysis).

FOLLOW THE BUBBLES

Trained divers are taught to resurface slowly; they've been cautioned to "follow the bubbles," or to rise in the water more slowly than the bubbles caused by their own exhalations. If a diver ignores these precautions or if something goes wrong, the unlucky diver is put in a decompression chamber and placed under high pressure to allow the nitrogen bubbles to redissolve in the blood and tissues. The chamber's pressure is then slowly reduced to allow the dissolved nitrogen to be released slowly.

TAKING A DIVE

But most of you don't have to worry, even if you dive at "recreational depths" of less than about 100 feet (30.5 m). You could drown, of course, or get eaten by a shark, but as long as you ascend at the proper rate of speed, you'll live to tell your grandchildren how you almost drowned and fought off those killer bubbles.

* * * * *

OLD FUDDY-DUDDY FISH

Because fish keep growing all their lives, the question of fish immortality was a topic of serious scientific debate until the 1930s. We now know that fish do, in fact, age, and even become geriatric—with curvature of the spine, failing eyesight, and the general slowing down that comes with old age.

So how old do fish get?
The Shortraker Rockfish is the champ at 157 years old.

Mount Everest is so cold that the temperature can drop to –40°F.

THE CREATURE WITH TWO BRAINS

No, it's not some sci-fi monster—it's you!
Come on along and meet brain number two.

Remember the last time you had a really good scare. Did you suddenly lose your appetite? Did your stomach tie up in knots? Did you feel a pressing need to visit the bathroom?

If you've ever reacted in any of these ways to fear, then you've probably noticed something a little puzzling—a good fright always seem to hit you in the gut. Loss of appetite, digestive cramps, diarrhea—all problems of the stomach. And do you know why?

Because you've got a second brain and it's in your stomach.

IN MY STOMACH?

Yep, that's right—your second brain is in your tum-tum. It's called the enteric nervous system, and scientists have only known about it for 30 or so years. They compare it to a microcomputer with the better-known brain in your head being the mainframe. So, what does this second brain have to do with us getting butterflies in our stomachs when we walk into a job interview or when an airplane ride starts getting a little too bumpy?

CODE RED!

A lot of your gut brain's time is taken up with controlling and directing the digestion and absorption of that cheeseburger you had for lunch. But all the same, it's ready for emergencies at a moment's notice. The brain in your stomach is connected to the one in your head through what's called the vagus nerve. And when danger approaches, the head brain sends a rapid-fire signal via the vagus to the stomach brain.

How the stomach reacts is a matter of individual genetic programming. For some people, their stomach will tightly constrict, producing an uncomfortable cramp. Others will get an instant case of the runs. And the really unfortunate ones will be sent rushing to the nearest toilet to vomit.

So, what good does this do when you're in a state of panic?

In experiments, octopuses learned to unscrew jars to get to the food inside.

FIGHT OR FLIGHT

Back in the bad old days when that stomach cramp was due to the presence of a large and hungry carnivore, your ancestors had a simple choice—fight or flight. And no matter which option they chose, doing it on an empty stomach was going to be a whole lot easier. So the enteric nervous system directed the stomach to empty its digestive system one way or another. That's how scientists explain why we get all those yucky feelings in our guts when we get scared. But the enteric nervous system does more to keep us safe than just getting rid of food.

IMMUNE BOOSTERS

It turns out that a danger signal from the brain (the one in your skull) causes your immune system to kick in. The brain is telling so-called mast cells in the lining of the small intestine and/or colon to release chemicals that trigger an inflammatory response inside the small intestine. this attracts immune cells from the bloodstream into the area, which readies the body for trauma that might introduce dirty—and infectious—material into the colon.

Protecting the midsection is serious business, since the contents of the digestive tract are swarming with bacteria that can be deadly if they escape. If the body is prepared by the presence of large numbers of inflammatory cells called neutrophils, it has a better chance of controlling any infection arising from an injury. This is a very ancient—even primordial—bodily response.

THE DOWN SIDE

For all the good it does, this inflammatory response can sometimes get out of whack—that's what gives us problems like irritable bowel syndrome (a spasmodic condition that plagues its victims with diarrhea, gas, and constipation) and ulcerative colitis (a nasty inflammatory disease of the colon).

The enteric system can explain other problems that are sometimes considered psychological in origin, like difficulty swallowing, ulcers, or chronic abdominal pain. They're all stress responses in action, stress being a form of fear.

To your ancestor it might have been a saber-toothed tiger closing in; to you or the guy next door, it might be a letter from the IRS.

A chest X-ray has from 90,000 to 130,000 electron volts.

WHAM, YAM, THANK YOU MA'AM

*The contraceptive known as the Pill
started out as one of those unplanned births.*

The desire to control female fertility by chemical means is not a 20th century phenomenon. Women first began taking substances by mouth to prevent pregnancy as far back as 4,000 years ago. Chinese women drank mercury, the Greeks consumed diluted copper ore, the Italians sipped a tea of willow leaves with mule's hoof, and Native Americans in Canada downed alcohol brewed with dried beaver testicles. And if they lived through it, there were still no guarantees.

Oh, no. A pill would be better. But it was a long way off. It wasn't until the 20th century that scientists started—slowly and circuitously—assembling the ingredients.

THE FIRST STEP
In the 1920s, an Austrian endocrinologist asked himself a very simple question: "Why doesn't a pregnant woman get pregnant again during a pregnancy?" He pinpointed the female sex hormone progesterone, which is produced naturally when a woman is pregnant and which prevents her from ovulating.

THE SIDE STEP
Twenty years later, in completely unrelated research, Russell Marker, an American chemist, discovered diosgenin (a steroid that can be transformed into progesterone) in a yam root in the mountains of Veracruz, Mexico. But Marker was looking for ways to use the yam's steroid to make a synthetic form of cortisone.

To this end, Marker launched the Mexican chemical firm Syntex—and a few years later, hired the brilliant Carl Djerassi (who was instrumental in the creation of the first antihistamine). Djerassi managed to find a way of using the yam's steroid to make synthetic cortisone. Success for Syntex! But still, no pill.

GETTING CLOSER
Competing U.S. companies with much bigger budgets were stunned by the discovery. In addition to synthetic cortisone, Syntex soon became the largest producer of synthetic

---

The kite is the earliest form of flying machine.

progesterone, which was also used to treat menstrual disorders. But the hormone could be administered only by injection, which made it an expensive and not always practical treatment. (Natural progesterone couldn't be given orally because it's destroyed in the digestive system when ingested in its natural form.) An orally delivered version would avoid all these problems. Back to the drawing board.

HE HAD NO CONCEPTION
In 1951, Djerassi and a graduate student eventually converted a version of synthetic progesterone into norethindrone, which could be taken orally. But even at this stage Djerassi didn't dream of using the drug to prevent pregnancy.

FINALLY!
It wasn't until five years later that Massachusetts research scientist Gregory Pincus began testing birth control pills using a substance nearly identical to norethindrone.

And it wasn't until 1960—nearly ten years after the discovery—that the U.S. Food and Drug Administration finally approved the Pill for public use.

The Pill brought revolutionary changes to the lives of women worldwide. For the first time in history, women had complete control over their own fertility just by swallowing a tiny little pill.

* * * * *

DID YOU HEAR THAT?
In 1965, radio astronomers Arno Penzias and Robert Wilson were tuning a powerful horn antenna used for sending and receiving microwave signals, but low-level static kept disrupting reception. They checked all their equipment, but they couldn't find any malfunction. They tried pointing the antenna in different directions, but the noise persisted. They didn't know it at the time, but they'd stumbled onto something huge: the most conclusive evidence to date supporting the Big Bang Theory, the idea that the universe was formed from a tiny explosion millions of years ago. The theory had first been proposed in the 1920s by George Lemaitre and Edwin Hubble—who, even before he invented his famous telescope, observed that galaxies could be measured moving away from our own, that is, still reacting to the effects of the ancient explosion. Penzias and Wilson were hearing the faint echo of the Big Bang. For their accidental discovery, Penzias and Wilson were awarded the Nobel Prize in Physics in 1978.

Invertebrates comprise 95% of all animal species.

THE STRANGE TALE OF PHINEAS GAGE

A gruesome accident and its strange aftermath: the birth of the lobotomy.

E ven if you're not a neurologist or a psychotherapist, you may have heard of Phineas Gage. When a guy survives being impaled with a three-foot iron rod in the skull, he tends to gain a certain notoriety. What makes Gage's case interesting isn't the fact that he survived, it's how he changed after his accident.

A HOLE IN ONE
Phineas Gage considered himself a lucky man. At the age of 25, he had a responsible, well-paid job as construction foreman for the Rutland and Burlington Railroad in Vermont. On September 13, 1848, as Gage was packing a load of explosives into the ground, the charge exploded without warning. The iron rod he was using to tamp the explosives into the earth flew into the air with the force and speed of a rocket, hitting Phineas Gage directly in the head. The 3'7" rod (109 cm), which weighed 13 pounds (6 kg), entered his left cheek, careened straight through his skull and brain, and emerged out of the top of his head like a yard-long bullet.

SURVIVOR
They loaded him into an ox cart and took him—still conscious— to a hotel where some local doctors treated him. They never expected him to live; he was bleeding horribly and blind in his left eye. Yet, Gage was still able to walk, talk, even to work. He returned home just ten weeks after his accident. However, Gage wasn't unscathed, not by any means. The iron bar that had practi- cally destroyed the front left lobe of his brain had irrevocably changed his personality.

I FEEL LIKE A NEW MAN
A few months after the accident he was feeling well enough to return to work, but his old boss wouldn't hire him back at the same position because—even though Gage was almost back to

normal physically, emotionally, and mentally—he was a changed man. Before his accident he'd been efficient, capable, kind, and polite; now he was foul-mouthed, rude, and easily annoyed.

A FREAK, ALIVE OR DEAD
Gage never worked as a foreman again. He drove coaches and cared for horses in New Hampshire and in Chile. He exhibited himself (and the rod) as a curiosity at P. T. Barnum's Museum in New York. All in all, he lived 13 years after his dreadful accident and died in 1860 after a series of epileptic seizures.

Gage's skull (and the rod) are now on display at Harvard Medical School, where they've been studied intensively over the years by neuroscientists.

FIRST THE GOOD STUFF
Gage's abrupt personality changes clued neurologists in to the fact that certain portions of the brain corresponded with personality functions. And in fact, Gage's case made the very first brain tumor removal operation possible in 1885. After studying what had happened to Gage, the operating physician concluded that lesions or tumors located in the frontal lobes of the brain didn't affect the brain's ability to take in sense information. Nor did they have an impact on physical movement or speech. However, such localized lesions or tumors did produce highly characteristic and unusual personality changes like Gage's.

In 1894, that same surgeon removed a tumor from a patient's left frontal lobe. The patient had complained his thinking was becoming increasingly slow and dull. Seeing the similarities between this patient's mental faculties and Gage's, the doctor successfully removed the tumor that lay, just as he expected, in the left frontal lobes of the brain.

THE BIRTH OF THE LOBOTOMY
Gage's case put scientists on alert. Now they knew that certain areas of the brain were responsible for certain functions. In 1890, after a German scientist discovered that dogs were tamer and calmer after their temporal lobe was removed, the attending doctor at a Swiss insane asylum began to perform lobotomies on his patients—six in 1892. The patients who had been hard to handle, restless, and even violent, seemed much calmer after their surgeries. Lobotomies fell out of favor for a time, but were revived

in the 1930s. Suddenly, a sort of lobotomy frenzy overtook the American psychiatric world.

THE ICE PICK TRICK

Along came enterprising physician and neurologist Walter Freeman, a.k.a. the Lobotomy King, who performed over 3,000 lobotomies from the 1930s to the 1960s. Impatient with the slowness of other brain surgery methods, Freeman even created the superquick ice pick lobotomy. Instead of surgically opening a hole in the patient's head, he put his patients under local anesthesia and plunged an ice pick through the skull and into the brain. Once in, Freeman would swing the ice pick swiftly back and forth, severing the prefrontal lobe. An ice pick lobotomy took only a few minutes. The lobotomy-happy Freeman would set up production lines at mental hospitals, operating on as many as ten patients in a single afternoon.

EVERYBODY'S DOING IT

Lobotomies were the psychiatric cure-all of choice in the 1940s and 1950s. They were used not just on uncontrollable patients, but homosexuals, political radicals, "troublesome" personalities, and other so-called undesirables who veered from established norms. Even amateur surgeons got into the act; they performed hundreds of lobotomies without first performing psychiatric evaluations. Joseph Kennedy ordered a lobotomy on his "difficult" daughter Rosemary in 1941 without consulting anyone else in the family. Playwright Tennessee Williams was devastated to find in 1937 that his schizophrenic sister Rose Williams had been lobotomized, altering her personality utterly and permanently. The movie, *Frances*, is the true story of fiercely independent actress Frances Farmer (as played by Jessica Lange), who, after her lobotomy, is a tragic picture of blandness.

LOBOTOMY TODAY?

Lobotomies are now outlawed in most countries, although they're still occasionally performed to control violent behavior in Japan, Australia, Sweden, and India.

Even though Phineas Gage needed that 1848 accident like a, well, like a hole in the head, his case revolutionized brain surgery—in good ways and bad.

The most yolks ever found in one chicken egg was nine.

SCIENTIFICALLY SPEAKING

Science as seen on screens both big and small...

"I don't know if I was interested so much in the science as I was in the slime that goes along with it. Snakes and frogs. When I saw how slimy the human brain was, I knew that's what I wanted to do for the rest of my life."

—Dr. Michael Hfuhruhurr,
as played by Steve Martin
The Man With Two Brains

"That's how science works. You ask an impertinent question and get a pertinent answer."

—Agent Mulder, as played
by David Duchovny
The X-Files

"We're now a quarter of an inch tall, and sixty-four feet from the house. That's an equivalent of 3.2 miles. That's a long way. Even for a man of science."

—Nick, as played
by Rick Moranis
Honey, I Shrink the Kids

"Back off, man. I'm a scientist."

—Dr. Peter Venkman,
as played by Bill Murray
Ghostbusters

"Nothing shocks me. I'm a scientist."

—Indiana Jones, as played
by Harrison Ford
*Indiana Jones and
the Temple of Doom*

"Well, once again, my friend, we find that science is a two-headed beast. One head is nice, it gives us aspirin and other modern conveniences.... But the other head of science is bad! Oh, beware the other head of science, Arthur! It bites!"

–The Tick, as played by
Townsend Coleman
The Tick

ASK UNCLE JOHN:
SCIENTIFIC CONCEPTS

Uncle John Einstein tackles some toughies.

Dear Uncle John:
*What's the difference between nuclear fission and
fusion? Isn't one nuclear explosion as good as the next?*

Well, leaving aside the question of what constitutes "good" here—
the fact of the matter is that you don't want to be near either a
fission or fusion reaction because your tender little body would
vaporize in a flash—nuclear fission and nuclear fusion are two
entirely different nuclear processes. One creates energy by splitting
atoms, while the other creates energy by bringing atoms together.

Nuclear fission is the process we're more familiar with. The
idea is to split apart a large, heavy atom (uranium and plutonium
are favorites) into two smaller atoms. The newly divided atoms are
almost, but not quite, the same weight as the uranium or plutonium atom was to begin with. But some of the mass of the original
atom gets turned into energy (using Einstein's famous $E=MC^2$
equation), and that's what gives the fission reaction such a
tremendous kick, and which will also turn you into a crispy critter
if you get too close. So don't. The energy released can also induce
other nearby heavy atoms to split, causing a chain reaction.

Nuclear fission is used primarily for two things: nuclear power
plants and nuclear bombs. In nuclear power plants, the nuclear
fission process is carefully inhibited and monitored to make sure
that it will create enough energy to make power, but not so much
to induce a meltdown. Nuclear bombs, on the other hand, are
allowed to go off full force. The major problem with nuclear
fission in a power plant is that keeping the fission reaction
controlled is no small task, and that the end result of nuclear
fission is radioactive nuclear waste, which has to go someplace.
The major problem with nuclear bombs, of course, is that they
can turn your hometown into a mushroom cloud.

Fission turns heavier elements into lighter ones, whereas nuclear fusion, on the other hand, takes lighter elements and turns them into heavier ones. This is the reaction going on in the heart of the Sun, where atoms of hydrogen, the lightest element, are rammed together under intense pressure and temperatures to create helium, the next lightest element. In the resulting fusion, a little bit of mass is turned into energy, just like in fission. Do it enough and you've got a source of energy (the Sun) that ultimately keeps all of us alive.

Humans would love to be able to make nuclear reactors that use fusion. Unlike fission, fusion can be created using just water as a hydrogen source—and it doesn't create any dangerously radioactive by-products. It would create cheap, plentiful power for all. Unfortunately, progress toward a workable fusion reactor has been very slow. Many scientists optimistically predict fusion reactions within the next 50 years or so, but it's also worth noting that they've been saying fusion is 50 years away for the last 50 years. In other words, don't hold your breath.

Dear Uncle John:
What are greenhouse gases, anyway, and how will they affect my beach house?

Greenhouse gases are gases in our atmosphere that trap heat. It starts with sunlight, which hits the Earth's surface and is turned into heat. Some of that heat radiates back into the lower atmosphere, where greenhouse gases trap it and hold it in the atmosphere for a longer period of time than it would be in the atmosphere otherwise. Greenhouse gases are definitely not all bad—if it weren't for a certain amount of them in the air, the temperature would be a lot colder here on Earth, say, about −100°F (−38°C). But the worry is that too many greenhouse gases will trap too much heat, melting polar ice caps, flooding low-lying coastal areas, and making a mess of weather patterns.

There are several gases that are considered "greenhouse gases." The one we hear about the most is carbon dioxide, which occurs naturally but is also a side effect of human industry. Water vapor is also a greenhouse gas, as is methane—much of which comes from cows (they release it when they burp. No, really). Some people like to say that cows generate more greenhouse gases than human industry does; which may or may not be true, but it's also true that the reason there are so many cows to produce so much methane is because we humans do love our hamburgers and milk.

Most scientists now agree that humans directly and indirectly have caused many more greenhouse gases to be dumped into the atmosphere, and that it's having an effect on the climate. What's not settled is how much an effect it will ultimately have, and how much of the Earth's current warming trend can be blamed on humans. After all, the Earth has been notably warmer and cooler in the past than it is today, and it did it without human intervention. In the meantime, however, if you've got beachfront property, invest in sandbags and stilts. Hey, you never know.

Hey Uncle John:
Is it true that the orbits of the planets fit into an ancient formula that predicted the positions of planets the ancients couldn't even see?

No, but for a long time it sure looked like the answer was "yes." The formula in question is something called "Bode's Law," which was popularized in the 1770s (so it's not ancient, just old). It worked like this: Starting with zero, add three and then double the result for each successive number (so: 0, 3, 6, 12, 24, and so on). Add four to each number (4, 7, 10, 16...) and then divide each number by ten (.4, .7, 1, 1.6...) The numbers you get correspond, roughly, to the distance that each planet in our solar system was from the Sun in Astronomical Units (one AU = about 93 million miles). This pattern worked for every planet then known—and the one Bode's Law number that didn't have a planet associated with it (2.8 AU) is where the asteroid belt is.

The problem with Bode's "Law" is that using the law, the eighth planet in the solar system should be at about 38.8 AU, and it's not. Neptune, the eighth planet, orbits at roughly 30 AU from the Sun. Oddly enough, Pluto's average distance from the Sun is about 39 AU, but it's the ninth planet from the Sun, not the eighth (excepting the brief period of time in which Pluto's highly eccentric orbit actually brings it closer to the Sun than Neptune, making it the eighth planet for about 20 years every 248 years. But that still doesn't explain the presence of Neptune). So, out with this "law." It's coincidence, not science.

If a flock loses its rooster, a hen may step in, stop laying eggs, and begin to crow.

KRISTIAN'S CANNON

In which yet another scientist makes a startling discovery by accident.

EAT YOUR HEART OUT, RONNIE!
A good 80 years before President Ronald Reagan's proposed American Strategic Defense Initiative—the so-called Star Wars missile defense system—an obscure but visionary Norwegian physicist by the name of Kristian Birkeland built and successfully tested a prototype Star Wars weapon. Not only that, he made his discovery pretty much by accident.

HE SAW THE LIGHT
What Birkeland was actually searching for was a solution to one of the great unsolved mysteries of the natural world—the Northern Lights—or aurora borealis. Throughout the ages, the lights were believed to be messengers of the gods, signs of apocalypse, or even the souls of the dead. In the early 1600s, Galileo first distinguished the lights from other phenomena in the sky by calling them the boreale aurora, or "northern dawn."

NORWEGIAN NIGHTMARE
To study the Northern Lights firsthand, Birkeland mounted an expedition to the Arctic coast of Norway at the end of 1899. Unfortunately, these expeditions were not only potentially danger-ous, but also very expensive, a situation aggravated by Birkeland's cavalier disregard for things like budgets. To finance his expedi-tions and pay off his mounting debts, Birkeland began to think about inventions that he could sell to industry. After sitting on a government committee that was examining ways to advance the hydroelectric system in Norway, a private hydroelectric firm hired him as a consultant. Here was Birkeland's opportunity.

WHAT A BLAST!
After spending countless hours bending over circuits and switches and observing the firm's engineers at work, Birkeland eventually noticed that the major difficulty the engineers were experiencing was breaking the electric current at the plant once it was flow-ing—switching the power on and off. If Birkeland could design and patent a switch that would work, he just might be able to earn the funds he needed to finance his expedition.

The dwarf shark is no bigger than your hand, but the whale shark is as big as a bus.

By late autumn 1902, Birkeland had ironed out the kinks in his new circuit-breaker switches and was ready for a test demonstration. When everything was ready, Birkeland pulled on a metal switch that should have broken the current. Instead, a huge arc of electricity jumped from the circuit to the metal switch in Birkeland's hand, throwing him clear across the engine room, blowing all the fuses, and setting the entire power station on fire. As the plant managers and engineers ran for their lives, Birkeland sat on the floor laughing till his sides hurt.

HE HAD A COUPLE OF SCREWS LOOSE

But he wasn't crazy. During the course of his experiments, he'd been tinkering with an experimental switch that used a solenoid (a large coil of metal connected to an electric circuit). This time, during his supposedly disastrous demonstration, he noticed that when he switched on the power, two metal screws were sucked into the solenoid with great force. When he reversed the current, they were violently ejected. He knew that he had invented the first device—which he dubbed "Birkeland's Electromagnetic Cannon"—capable of launching a projectile using the power of electricity. Finally, he built a successful prototype of his weapon. It was about 13 feet (4 m) long, fired 22-pound (10 kg) projectiles, and had a potential range of 60 miles (96.5 km)!

UNHAPPY ENDING

Despite the successes of some earlier tests, not to mention the interest of several nations (Britain, France, and Germany), no country's armed forces ever adopted his electromagnetic cannon. It took nearly a century for anyone to adapt and extend the technology to make "railguns" (electromagnetic mass accelerators) for the American Strategic Defense Initiative, a.k.a. Star Wars.

In the end, Birkeland's obsession with the workings of the cosmos cost him his health, his happiness, and ultimately his sanity. He wound up alone and stranded in Egypt by World War I, relying more and more on alcohol and drugs to combat his insomnia, a treatment that only served to fuel his growing paranoia. (He believed that spies from Britain were everywhere, trying to steal his secrets.) Birkeland died in Japan in 1917, at age 50, under suspicious circumstances. It was rumored at the time that British spies might indeed have been involved.

VCRs use magnets to play both sound and pictures.

THE COSMIC SPEED LIMIT

Here's a riddle. You can't touch it, but you can feel it. You can't see it but you're blind without it. It travels faster than anything, yet it never has to speed up or slow down. What is it?

It's light, silly. And here we plumb the depths of one of the great riddles of science: the speed of light. Hang on to your hat. And give your head a good shake—you'll need all the noodle power you can get.

SURFING THE COSMOS
How fast is light? So fast that if it were to get any faster, you'd be able to see it before it even existed. Sound impossible? That's why we call it the ultimate speed limit.

In the depths of space, light barrels along at 186,000 miles per second (299,792,458 meters per second) or 700 million mph (1,126 million kph). A light-year is the distance it takes for light to travel in a year. But how far is that?

Well, for one thing, our solar system isn't even one light-year across. And even the short distances across our solar system seem vast to us. It took days for us to reach the moon. Neil Armstrong called it "one giant leap," but actually it was more like a tiptoe in cosmic terms.

A COSMIC TIME MACHINE
In order to appreciate how far away a light-year is, go outside on a clear night and look up. Did you know that when you look at the stars, you're looking back in time? That's right, the world's first time machine, right in your backyard. The light you see from the stars doesn't show how the stars look now, but how they looked when the light you see first emitted from the star. It actually took years for that light to get to us. For all you know, that star could be long gone now.

TWINKLE, TWINKLE, LITTLE...STAR?
Need an example? So did we. Nature has kindly provided us with one. In 1987, a star exploded. However, it didn't actually happen in 1987. The only thing that happened in 1987 is that the light from the explosion finally reached us. The explosion actually

---

Videotape is made up of millions of magnetic particles glued to the tape.

happened about 190,000 years ago. It took that long for the light of the explosion to reach us. What does it look like now? You'll have to wait 190,000 years to find out.

OUT THERE
The farthest objects we've ever seen are about 18 billion light-years away. So, like the star, the objects that we see out there probably aren't even there anymore.

CLOCKING LIGHT
How did anybody figure out the speed of light anyway? Galileo first tried to measure the speed of light by covering and uncovering lanterns with a couple of his friends. He sent one of them to a far-off hill, who agreed to cover his lantern when he saw Galileo uncover his. A third buddy stood between them and tried to time the delay between the coverings and uncoverings. As you might expect, the only useful thing they concluded from this experiment is that light travels really, really fast.

HOW FAST IS FAST?
We may laugh now, but Galileo was onto something. Later, a French scientist named Louis Fizeau came up with the idea of spinning a wheel and shining a lantern through the wheel at a mirror far away. He kept spinning the wheel faster until it spun fast enough so that he could no longer see the light returning through the tines of the wheel. Because he knew how fast the wheel was spinning and how far away the mirror was, he was able to come up with a reasonable approximation of how fast the speed of light was.

HOW FAR IS FAR?
But "reasonable approximations" are never good enough for us. Over the years, various scientists got the measurements so exact that they ran into a problem. No unit of measurement was precise enough to measure it with. Long story short, after much back and forth, in the early 1980s an international standards committee decided to change the definition of the length of a meter to reflect this problem: A meter is now "the length of the path traveled by light in vacuum during a time interval of 1/299,792,458 of a second." (And they make fun of our inches and feet?)

THE DEEP STUFF

The speed of light always stays the same, no matter how fast you're moving. If you were to shine a flashlight from a point on the ground, the rays of light would move at the same speed as the light from a flashlight held by a pilot in a supersonic jet. The light doesn't get any extra velocity from the jet. It doesn't matter if it's heading toward you or away from you—the speed stays the same.

What's more, light never has to speed up or slow down. When light emits from a luminous object, it emits at the speed of light, instantaneously traveling at 299,792,458 meters per second.

"SULU, BRING US TO WARP FACTOR TWO"

We like speed. If we didn't like it so much, cops wouldn't spend so much time by the side of the road writing tickets. Just as we often break the speed limit on highways, scientists have tried to break the so-called light barrier ever since they knew it existed.

GOT A ROCKET IN MY POCKET

There have even been proposals for a sort of warp drive, using something called "warp bubbles." On paper it looks good. Calculations show it may be possible to actually warp the fabric of space around a starship, allowing it to travel faster than light while at the same time protecting it from the stresses of traveling at such speeds. But in real life it isn't yet feasible, since the ship would have to be microscopically small (if the exterior of the bubble were bigger, more energy would be needed to form it than exists in the entire universe).

WAS EINSTEIN WRONG?

If one scientist says it can't be done, then you can bet next week's paycheck that another scientist will try to prove him wrong—nevermind that the scientist in question was Einstein. Even if scientists never break the light barrier, they are sure to invent and discover all sorts of useful stuff trying to do so, making it well worth their while for the rest of us.

* * * * *

"The night
Shows stars and women in a better light."
—Byron, *Don Juan*, 1824

Early vacuum cleaners used gasoline instead of electricity.

SURF'S UP!

If you see one coming, it's too late to run.

Tsunamis are completely unlike other ocean waves and don't usually even look like waves when they hit shore. They're sometimes called "tidal waves," but they really have nothing to do with the tides, or the gravitational pull of the moon, or wind blowing over the ocean's surface.

CATCH THE WAVE

Tsunamis are killer waves generated by high magnitude earthquakes under the sea floor, underwater landslides, or undersea volcanic eruptions. When the ocean floor heaves upward in an earthquake, huge volumes of water are suddenly thrust up with it and begin to roll away from the epicenter of the quake in concentric circles—like a ripple on a lake after you throw a stone into it, only much, much bigger. Way bigger.

MOVING RIGHT ALONG

In the deep ocean, near its source, the tsunami isn't dangerous. It is only two to three feet (61 to 91 cm) high and moving so fast—as much as 670 mph (1,078 kph)—that it passes under ships at sea unnoticed. As it moves into more shallow water near land, it slows down and the faster-moving water behind the front of the wave starts to pile up. Are you getting the picture? (Run for your lives!)

ON THE WAVY TRAIN

That two- to three-foot roll at sea is now maybe hundreds of feet high, still moving but slower, at 45 mph (72 kph) or so. Most tsunamis aren't large, steep-faced waves that break on shore. Most loom out of the sea as a gigantic advancing tide without a breaking wave face. Like a ripple, only gigantic. Tsunamis come in waves (pun absolutely intended). They roll in in groups of five to nine in a tsunami "wave train."

THE RING OF FIRE

Most tsunamis are born in the Pacific Ocean's infamous "Ring of Fire," although they've occurred in the Mediterranean and Caribbean Seas and the Atlantic Ocean, too. What makes the Pacific so special? The Pacific ring accounts for 80 percent of the

world's earthquakes and 2,200 of the 2,500 known volcanic eruptions in recorded history. Japan and Hawaii are particularly
vulnerable to a tsunami, which is Japanese for "harbor wave."
Hawaii has been hit by 41 tsunamis since 1819. Some tsunamis
travel thousands of miles before wreaking their destruction. In
1960, earthquakes in Chile produced tsunamis that struck Japan
by covering over 10,000 miles (16,093 km) in 22 hours.

THE KILLER WAVE
The death toll from tsunamis illustrates why these waves are truly
killers. Krakatoa's eruption in Indonesia in 1883 caused a tsunami
that drowned 36,000 people. In 1976 in the Philippines, 8,000
souls were lost to a tsunami. Ninety percent of the deaths in the
Alaska earthquake of 1964 were due to the tsunami it generated.

THE FIFTH WAVE
A 13-foot (4 m) wave hit Crescent City, California, in 1964,
about four hours after the Alaskan earthquake that started it. That
lead-time gave the town time to evacuate. The second wave was
smaller, so some residents thought it was over and returned to
clean up the damage. Five of them were drowned by the third
wave. After the fourth wave came and went, more folks returned.
But what they hadn't banked on was that it was now high tide. So
the fifth wave—at 20 feet (6 m) high—claimed the lives of 12
more people. Computer models for the coasts of California,
Oregon, and Washington show expected tsunami wave heights
from an earthquake on one of these subduction zones could reach
30 to 70 feet (9 to 21 m).

BIG WET ONE
America's West Coast has enough to worry about from a monster
quake on the San Andreas Fault, but here's another worry. Scientists say that the Alaska-Aleutian subduction zone (the sinking of
one crustal plate under another as they collide) could produce a
monster tsunami. The probability of a 7.4 or greater quake in that
region before 2008 is estimated to be 84 percent. Another worrisome area, the Cascadia subduction zone, ranges in a line from
British Columbia to northern California and has a 35 percent
chance of going off before 2045. A tsunami from an earthquake on
that fault line could arrive on shore in 15 minutes. Maybe you
should forget about that dream beach house.

Molds are living things that exist by eating dead plants or animals.

FOOD TERRORS PART II
WASTE NOT, WANT NOT

Fertilizers are supposed to make things grow—not kill them, right?

A **FERTILIZER THAT KILLS THINGS**
It's a nail-biter of a toxic drama that begins in the cow town of Quincy, Washington, in 1991. Mayor Patty Martin overheard some farmers in the area wondering why their wheat and corn crops were doing so poorly, and why cows were getting sick and dying. After some investigation, they discovered some horrifying facts.

ENVIRONMENTAL PROTECTION, HUH?
Because of the stringent environmental protection laws enacted in the 1970s, industrial waste producers couldn't just let their waste go down the toilet, or throw it in the river, or put it wherever else they felt like putting it. But they had to get rid of it somehow. Landfill space was the most obvious, but expensive. So waste producers started selling their wastes to fertilizer producers. The practice spread untold amounts of toxic chemicals (such as sulfuric acid and heavy metals on food-producing land—yum!). Dangerous you say? Very probably. And all perfectly legal.

THE SEWAGE STORY
This is what the Quincy farmers found out when they raised a ruckus—both at the state level and with the EPA. Though fertilizers made of "biosolids" (that's sewage to you and me), are strictly regulated for their heavy metal content, there are no federal controls on fertilizer made from recycled industrial wastes.

FERTILIZER THAT'LL MAKE YOUR PLANTS GLOW
Yeah, but the ingredients are listed right on the package, you say. Nope. Current laws in the vast majority of states don't require toxic materials to be listed among fertilizer ingredients. In fact, most fertilizer packages don't list all their ingredients—just the percentage of beneficial ingredients like nitrogen, potassium, and

---

There are over 70,000 types of fungus.

phosphate. Consumers and farmers who buy infested fertilizer and dump it on what will become our food don't have the slightest idea what they're using.

RICE? NOT SO NICE
No study has scientifically documented that fertilizers made with hazardous wastes have done any harm to humans or animals, but a widely quoted Japanese study showed that rice farmers had become ill after a fertilizer containing cadmium (listed by OSHA as an extremely toxic metal) was used on their crops. The cadmium also appeared in the rice itself.

STEEL YOURSELF FOR THE STATISTICS
From 1990 to 1995, 606 companies in 44 of the 50 states sent more than 270 million pounds (122 million kg) of toxic wastes to farms and fertilizer companies. To put that number in perspective, during the same time period, 500 billion pounds (227 billion kg) of fertilizer were sold in the U.S. The steel industry was the largest contributor, at more than 80 million pounds (36 million kg) of steel wastes. Electronics manufacturers and chemical companies also contributed hefty shares of the total. In the United States, only New Jersey and Massachusetts require reporting of where the wastes ultimately end up.

WHAT YOU DON'T KNOW CAN HURT YOU
And because they're not required to notify farmers what's in their fertilizer, some fertilizer producers have sold fertilizers with a higher lead content than that in lead-based paint, not to mention more arsenic than you'll find in a lot of hazardous waste dumps.

In 1997 a lot of fertilizer makers agreed to limit the amount of toxic wastes in fertilizer, and to label products more accurately. Since then, states like California and Georgia have passed laws requiring better labeling. These and other states are slowly starting to set limits on potentially dangerous chemicals in fertilizer. But until better controls (and better labels) are placed on fertilizer products, let's hope that farmers are thinking twice, maybe even three times, about what's going onto their crops. And, hey, all you backyard tomato-growers! You be careful out there, too.

ASK UNCLE JOHN: VENOMOUS CREATURES

Not all venom is created equal.

Dear Uncle John:
We all know that rattlesnakes are nasty customers, not to be trifled with, but what, exactly, does their venom do to you? I know it's painful, but I want details.

Well, then, details you shall have. There are several different species of rattlesnake all across North America and in every U.S. state except for Alaska, Hawaii and, oddly enough, Delaware. (The state of Arizona has 11 different species, which makes up for those other three states.) The toxicity of the venom in these various species ranges from the "merely" dangerous to actually life-threatening, the most toxic venom coming from the Mojave rattlesnake, which can take out a full-grown human with one good swipe of the fangs.

The primary feature of all rattlesnake venoms are hemotoxins, which are poisons that attack blood and tissues—what these do, more or less, is melt blood cell and tissue walls, turning the bite area into a nasty, toxic blood pudding. Hemotoxin will damage tissue, cause a great deal of pain, swelling, edema, redness, blood clotting, and nausea; necrosis (tissue death) is not uncommon; and in severe bites to hands or feet, people have been known to lose fingers and toes.

What makes Mojave rattlesnake venom even more dangerous is that in addition to the usual hemotoxin cocktail, Mojave rattlesnake venom also features a heaping helping of neurotoxins (up to ten times more than other rattlesnake venoms), which help to paralyze the nervous system—this leads to immobility, heart failure, and suffocation, which often leads to death.

And if that's not bad enough, there's some anecdotal evidence that rattlesnake venoms in general are getting more toxic, although there's no clear-cut reason for this. The good news is that rattlesnakes by nature aren't looking to bite humans; they're typically retiring creatures, and humans are a little big to be a food source anyway. By and large, if you leave that rattlesnake alone, it'll leave you alone. If you go out of your way to taunt a rattlesnake, well, you just better hope it's not a Mojave rattler.

Dear Uncle John:
Pound for pound, what's the most venomous creature?

You mean, to humans? It's hard to say, since we don't keep labs full of humans, to whom we apply varying levels of animal venoms to see which humans survive and which keel over dead. But we *do* keep labs full of mice, and we *do* inject those little critters with animal venoms, just to see what'll happen. You animals' rights types will want to turn away here, because what the researchers are looking for is an amount of venom that will kill 50 percent of the subjects within 24 hours. That number is called "LD50"—for "lethal dose 50." The lower the amount of venom that produces an LD50 value, the more toxic that venom is.

By this method, several candidates present themselves for the award of "Most Venomous Creature." Among the insects, the winner is the harvester ant—it takes just .12 milligrams of the harvester ant venom to kill off half the mice in a kilogram. There are about 50 mice to a kilogram (23 or 24 mice to a pound), so that's 25 dead mice in the metric system. That just about equals the LD50 value of the venom of the reef stonefish, the most toxic fish. Among spiders, it's the Sydney funnel web spider, whose venom includes the toxin Robustoxin, with an LD50 of .16 milligrams per kilogram. All of these, however, bow down to the toxicity of the most venomous snake, the inland taipan of Australia, whose LD50 value is .01 milligrams per kilogram. If you think *that's* toxic, consider that the LD50 for the bacteria that produces botulism is 0.001 milligrams per kilogram. Think about that at your next botox party.

Dear Uncle John:
The killer bees are coming! Should I arm myself?

Only if you have very tiny guns. The "killer bees" we've heard so much about are Africanized honey bees, which differ from the domesticated honey bee in that they haven't been bred for

A rhino's horn is made of compacted hair.

generations to: a) make lots of honey, and b) not to be twitchy and haul off and sting people and animals they see as threats to their hive. As a result, Africanized bees are more aggressive than your average bee, which means that they'll go after perceived threats faster, and at a greater distance from their hive. And, of course, they'll sting more often. They also produce far less honey, which is the most immediate concern for beekeepers, who are concerned that Africanized bees will take over their more docile colonies and turn them into hives of ill-tempered slacker bees.

But Africanized honey bees don't swarm from neighborhood to neighborhood, picking fights with the local citizenry, stinging people just for looking at them funny. The "killer" aspect is exaggerated, and so far their spread has been confined to the southern portions of the U.S. If you think you've stumbled on a hive of killer bees, just cover your head (a primary target for stings) and run to shelter. Your average killer bee is testy but not especially fast, so if you're in reasonable shape, you should be able to outrun them. If a hive suddenly sets up shop near your home, don't be a hero and try to take them on with a bat and a can of Raid. Have a pro come and take care of the eradication effort.

Dear Uncle John:
There are venomous reptiles, fish, insects, and arachnids. Are there any venomous mammals?

You bet there are. The most prominent of these venomous mammals is the duck-billed platypus, that nutty, thrown together, barely-a-mammal thing that lives in Australia. The female platypus is venom-free, but the male has spurs on the inside of its hind feet that hold venom; the spurs are used during combat with other male platypi to see which will get to mate, and for self-defense. The venom is reportedly excruciatingly painful and can cause short-term paralysis in humans, so the moral to this story: Don't mess with the platypus. He's packin' heat.

* * * * *

"It is inexcusable for scientists to torture animals; let them make their experiments on journalists and politicians."
—Henrik Ibsen

You cannot catch a cold by getting cold; only germs can make you sick.

HOW BIG?

Sizing up whales.

The blue whale's heart is the size of a Volkswagen New Beetle and pumps ten tons of blood through its massive body; its largest blood vessel, the aorta, is so wide a person could crawl through it. Its tongue weighs more than an elephant.

A WHALE OF A TALE

Big blue is the largest animal on earth—at as much as 115 feet (35 m) long and 150 tons. The largest dinosaurs were smaller than the blue whale. The blues eat four to eight tons of krill (a shrimp-like crustacean) every day during the summer months. To process that much food, the whale uses its three stomachs and stores the excess energy in its two-foot-thick layer of blubber.

BABY BLUES

Whales are the only mammals that reproduce at sea. The babies are born tail first so they're ready to swim to the surface for that first breath of air. Baby blues measure 23 feet (7 m) long and weigh roughly 30 tons at birth. As mammals, whale calves drink mother's milk, and do they ever drink. A baby blue whale is the fastest-growing organism on earth, putting on a staggering 220 pounds (100 kg)—one whole fairly large person,—per day in its first weeks of life. To feed such a hungry calf, the female blue whale produces 1,100 pounds (499 kg) of milk every day.

IF THE KILLER WHALES DON'T GET YOU

They used to be hunted for their oil, their meat, and their bones, which were used in corsets, buggy whips, and umbrella ribs. Hunting blue whales is illegal in the U.S. now. It's hard to tell how long whales live because they haven't any teeth (which is how age is estimated in other mammals), but it's believed they live to the ripe old age of 50. So all they have to worry about are packs of killer whales, polluted waters, or being hit by a *really* big boat.

Twenty-five million gallons of water can fall during a 20-minute thunderstorm.

WINNIE THE POOH THEY AIN'T

Bear with us here. Smokey, Yogi, Gentle Ben, and Pooh have had
their ten minutes of fame. Take ten now for the biggest bear
of all, the bright white polar bear.

It's hard to love a polar bear. In the movies they beat up on sled dogs. In real life, when they see a seal—one of those adorable bewhiskered creatures with soft eyes and the amazing ability to balance beach balls on their noses while clapping their flippers—they have them for lunch. There has to be *something* to love about them. Let's get up close (but not too close!) and personal.

OPEN 24 HOURS
In the far reaches of Canada's frozen north, on the shore of Hudson Bay, at a place called Churchill, Manitoba, the main tourist attraction isn't the aurora borealis, it's the local landfill, a typical small-town garbage dump. Churchill's main drag is dotted with signs that read: YIELD TO POLAR BEARS. The dump, as it turns out, is to polar bears what picnic baskets are to Yogi and honey pots are to Pooh.

SMARTER THAN THE AVERAGE BEAR
Who can fault a hungry polar bear with a choice between swimming 20 miles (32 km) in freezing cold water looking for a seal or walking a mile or so to the dump for an all-you-can-eat buffet? Polar bears are not stupid. (In fact, some researchers think they're at least as smart as apes.) But they're still hunters at heart. Every October and November, polar bears from miles around congregate at Churchill to wait for the ice. Garbage is okay as an appetizer, but the seals out on that ice are the main dish, and the bears can't catch them in open water—they need winter ice for hunting.

A volcano never has fire in it, only heat.

THAT'S AGLU, NOT IGLOO

On the ice, the bear's the boss. Seals, as talented as they are, haven't yet learned how to snorkel; they have to come up for air every ten minutes or so. The seals carve holes known as aglus through the ice—often up to 15 of them for one seal—and keep them open over the winter. The seal not only has sharp teeth for chowing down on fish—bones and all—it also has sharp claws on its front flippers that can hack through ice as much as six feet (1.8 m) thick. But seals are no match for a wily, patient omnivore that can weigh 1500 pounds (680 kg) plus and who knows an aglu when it sees one.

AQUABEARS ON ICE

The polar bear is not called *ursus maritimus* for nothing—that's "sea bear" in Latin. The polar bear can boogie along in the water at six miles an hour, helped along by his partially webbed forepaws that work like oversized paddles.

The polar bear doesn't run from aglu to aglu every time a black nose and whiskers pop up; he picks one aglu and settles down to wait. Eventually—and it may take days—up pops the seal. One swipe of the bear's 12-inch-wide paw and that seal's out of the aglu and served up on a platter of ice.

COLD COMFORT

Shades of Gore-Tex! How does the bear bear it—sitting in one spot for days? Even NASA wanted to know. They found that polar bears experience almost no heat loss. Infrared images of Mr. Bear show only the puff of his condensing breath. That means a lot of fat (a three-to-five inch [8 to 13 cm] layer) and on top of that more layers of hollow-core hair—like an elaborate wet suit without the wet. The hollow core and fat also add to the bear's buoyancy, important for a marine mammal that sometimes has to swim 60 miles (97 km) without a rest.

THE BEAR NECESSITIES

Even though they dine on cutesy-pie seals or filthy garbage, they aren't such bad guys after all. You've got to admire them for their patience. And how they manage to survive the frozen north in style: White-on-white is *so* in this year.

MY, WHAT A BIG GIRL YOU ARE!

Over the last century, the average age for the onset of puberty in American girls has dropped to an almost weird ten years old. What's making American girls grow up so quickly?

In 1999, America's only medical group specializing in early puberty, the Lawson Wilkins Pediatric Endocrine Society, lowered its estimate for the average age of the start of puberty in American girls: 9 years old for African Americans and 10 for European-American girls. Previously, the average age for the onset of puberty—characterized by budding breasts and the appearance of pubic hair—was thought to be 11. The onset of menstruation in American girls has fallen from 16 to 12 in the last century.

YOUNG AMERICANS
The age drop can have far-reaching consequences. When girls mature earlier, they stop maturing earlier, too; they may never reach their full height, or their internal organs may fail to develop properly. They also face social problems and uncontrollable mood swings. They're only kids, after all.

THE PUBERTY PUZZLE
Scientists bicker over what's caused the age drop, but one thing seems clear—the age shift seems to be largely an American phenomenon. Girls in developed countries like Europe or Japan are maturing at a slightly younger age than they did a few decades ago, but girls in less-developed countries, like sub-Saharan Africa, typically mature around age 12 to 13. This sets up a real paradox: African American girls typically mature earlier than European-American girls. But these African American girls mature much earlier than African girls, typically starting puberty three to four years earlier.

Just what is causing American girls to sprout so early? And why is there a difference between the maturation rates of African American and European-American girls?

Quinine, used to cure malaria, comes from the leaves of the cinchona plant.

YOU ARE WHAT YOU EAT

America's protein-, vitamin-, and calorie-rich diets have made us one of the healthiest, hardiest people in history. We don't have to worry about deficiency diseases like scurvy or goiter, but our diets have other unexpected consequences—one may be early puberty.

I'LL HAVE THE HORMONE BURGER

Americans tend to eat far more meat than people in other societies, particularly meat that's grown on factory farms that use hormones to boost quick growth. A lot of the hormone compounds contain estrogen or something like it. Since estrogen is the main hormone responsible for ushering in puberty, there could be a link. There's no proving it yet, but we already know that these hormones appear in meat and milk products consumed by humans. Kind of makes you think twice about that burger topped with cheese made from milk that came from a hormone-fed cow, huh?

HOW ABOUT THE ALTERNATIVE BURGER?

Don't make it a soy burger. Soy—that staple of vegetarian cuisine—contains an estrogen-like compound. About 25 percent of American bottle-fed babies drink soy-based infant formula, and sales of soy products are up about 250 percent over 1980s levels.

AND WASH IT DOWN WITH SOME PCB?

Some researchers believe that premature development may result from environmental toxins like PCBs, the long-lived chemicals that were once used in the electric power industry. These chemicals seem to bind to estrogen receptors in a way scientists don't yet understand. Even though they're banned, PCBs have a shockingly long life and still linger in animal products and water sources.

DDT'S ANNOYING COUSIN

Then there are other lingering toxic substances, like DDT. Sure, it was banned in the U.S. in 1972, but its legacy is still with us in the form of a substance known as DDE, which contains compounds that may mimic some of the hormones that play a key role in the development of the reproductive system.

Robert Ludlow was the tallest recorded man at 8 ft. 11.1 in. (272 cm).

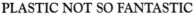

PLASTIC NOT SO FANTASTIC
Our heavy use of plastics may also play a role—plastics often contain estrogen compounds that are leached out into food stored in plastic containers, particularly when the containers are heated in a microwave. That plastic container might be doing a little more than just keeping your sandwich fresh.

TOO MANY BURGERS
Another theory revolves around the significant, uh, growth of American children. Today's crop of kids is significantly fatter than their parents, with around one in eight kids from ages five to eight considered officially obese, about double what the number was in the 1980s. Statistically, African American girls are even more likely than European-American girls to be obese.

Very overweight girls tend to mature earlier than very thin ones. Fat cells produce a protein called leptin that helps usher in puberty. Overweight girls also have more circulating insulin in their blood, which appears to stimulate the production of sex hormones in the ovaries and adrenal glands.

CLEAN HAIR = EARLY PUBERTY?
Scientists are also starting to take a look at what we put on our bodies as well as what we ingest. And African American girls may be getting a puberty boost from their shampoos. Nearly half of African Americans use hair shampoos or conditioners containing female hormones like estradiol (the most potent of the naturally occurring estrogens), and most also use these products on their children—this according to the Child Health Institute in Seattle. These hormones could be absorbed through the scalp and hit the bloodstream, causing early sexual development to kick in.

BOYS WILL BE GIRLS
No clinical studies have conclusively proven any of these theories, but that doesn't mean that each doesn't play a role. In fact, with so many sources of increased estrogen in our air, water, and food, it seems amazing that puberty doesn't occur much earlier.

And we haven't forgotten you boys—you eat burgers, too, and have been known to occasionally wash your hair. Some of you, in fact, have grown breasts when exposed to strong doses of estrogen. Who knows what other mischief all that hidden estrogen is up to?

Stupidest dinosaur? The stegosaurus had an elephant-sized body and a walnut-sized brain.

THE TOILET TREATMENT

What's this—a medicine cabinet in the toilet bowl? No, Uncle John hasn't flipped his lid. Urine as medicine may sound disgusting, but it could be mankind's answer to a whole host of health problems. Besides, it's a whole lot cheaper than the stuff they sell at the drugstore.

THE NUMBER ONE WAY TO STAY HEALTHY
Urine medicine may sound like some kind of wacky New Age therapy, but it's been around for nearly as long as we've been producing the stuff. The ancients were all very much in tune with the cycles of nature; they believed that the urine cycle was meant to be unbroken, that reingesting urine was the best way to stay healthy. Here's how some of our forebears fiddled with their piddle:

India—The *Vedas* (sacred Hindu writings) call urine "the nectar of the gods" and the "fountain of youth." This starts a wee drinking craze, which has persisted in the East to this day.

Rome—Urine is so important to the ancient empire that the emperor places a tax on its commercial sale. Ulcer and cancer sufferers are convinced that ingesting urine will cure them of their ills. Taking showers in urine are also a popular body treatment.

China—Urine is seen as the perfect vehicle for the delivery of medicinal herbs to the body. It's believed that mixing medicine with a patient's urine can more than double the effect of any herb. The potion is then either gulped down or applied externally to open wounds.

Egypt—Urine is drunk down, rubbed on, bathed in, and stared at (as in urine analysis) to overcome illness. A popular test for pregnancy is to moisten barley seeds daily with the urine of the woman. If the seed germinates, she's pregnant.

MIDDLE-AGE PIDDLE
Germany—The urine of a young man is a valued eye curative when boiled lightly with honey.

England—After a night of overindulgence, those in the know prevent the shakes by rubbing their warm urine directly onto their hands and legs immediately after producing it. Gargling urine with saffron is also seen as the best way to ward off throat inflammation during winter.

France—Drinking your own morning urine on an empty stomach helps relieve the symptoms of dropsy (an accumulation of fluid that causes the body to swell) and jaundice (a yellowing of the skin caused by anything from cirrhosis to malaria).

A WEE REVIVAL
As 19th century medicine became more sophisticated, urine treatment fell out of favor among the "enlightened" physicians of the Western world. However, today, some members of the alternative medicine community remain convinced that the cure of a whole host of ailments lies at the bottom of the toilet bowl.

A FEW WEE TRUTHS
Before you write off the urine gulping–fraternity completely, consider a few little-known piddle facts:

- Despite what many people think, urine is NOT a toxic waste product.

- Ninety-five percent of urine is water, 2.5 percent is urea (the chief solid component in urine), and the remaining 2.5 percent is a mixture of enzymes, minerals, salt and hormones.

- Although urea can be poisonous in very large amounts, the small portions present in urine actually purify the body, clear up excess mucus, and replenish the skin (that's why it's a main ingredient in women's cosmetics).

- Urine is completely sterile and has an antiseptic effect.

- Urine contains antibodies that, when reingested, can help the body fight off illness.

  So, are you ready to take a sip?
  Thought not.
  Okay, then—you can go ahead and flush.

WHO STOLE SATURN'S RINGS?

Sky watchers were startled, to say the least,
when Saturn's rings suddenly disappeared.

In 1610, the astronomer Galileo Galilei saw an astounding sight through his telescope. What he'd seen were the rings of Saturn. But since his primitive telescope showed the rings as blurry blobs of light, he decided that Saturn had a moon on either side of it. The astronomer kept his findings a secret (probably planning to publish them), but in 1612 he looked again, only to find that his important discovery had vanished!

SO WHO STOLE SATURN'S RINGS?

Saturn was still there, but her "moons" (that's rings, to you) were gone! Just like that! Eventually he saw them again, but he died without knowing how they disappeared in the first place. Over the centuries, other sky watchers encountered the same mystery.

NOW YOU SEE IT, NOW YOU DON'T

Now we know that Saturn's rings, which look like solid disks, are actually orbiting chunks of ice and rock. The particles vary in size from boulders to snowflakes to micrometer-sized dust. It's the predominance of ice (which reflects sunlight) that makes the rings brightly visible. But every 15 years or so, they seem to disappear.

LOSING IT

The layer of debris that forms Saturn's rings is wide and shallow— 185,000 miles (297,729 km) wide but only a little more than a half-mile thick. What happened back in 1612 was that Earth's orbit crossed the plane of Saturn's rings. This meant that the Earth was positioned so that astronomers could only view the rings edge-on. Saturn's rings are so skinny that with primitive telescopes their edge is about as easy to see as the edge of a razor blade in the dark, which made them invisible! This "ring plane crossing" happens every 15 years, and even with modern, powerful telescopes, the rings can barely be seen.

WANT TO JOIN THE FUN?

So, hey, all you nonastronomers out there! If you're interested in not seeing Saturn's rings, the next ring plane crossing will be on September 4, 2009.

The quahog clam is the longest-living sea creature: aged 150 years.

CIRCUS MINIMUS

Fleas are more than just carriers of bubonic plague...
they're also the star performers in the tiniest show on earth!

Flea circuses are not an urban legend—they're absolutely real and they've been entertaining incredulous audiences for more than 300 years. A mere century ago, parlors in Victorian England swarmed with them, while in America, folks itched to see them at county fairs. Nowadays, you still won't find them on every street corner—or even on every scruffy dog that walks by. But they're there, if you look hard enough.

WHY FLEAS?
Fleas have certain talents that set them apart from other insects. They're strong—they can pull objects that are 160,000 times their own weight, the equivalent of a human pulling 24 million pounds (10.8 million kg). They can jump 150 times their own height and what's more, they can do it 30,000 times without stopping.

TRICKS OF THE TRADE
Trainers use positive reinforcement for the desired behavior—blood is their favorite, but they also like the vibrations given off by a tuning fork. Heat, in the form of the flea trainer's breath, attracts them. The carbon dioxide given off in a breath tells the flea there's a warm body nearby and, therefore, food. They'll move toward the warmth. To get a flea to move in the opposite direction, the trainer uses light, which fleas don't like. It gives them a good incentive to pull that 24-million-pound locomotive or circus wagon in the opposite direction.

SO THE ACT HAS A FEW BUGS IN IT...
Flea circuses pretty much follow the typical big-top circus format: trapeze artists who work without a net, tightrope walkers who balance on the high-wire on top of tiny chairs, and the flea version of human cannonballs shot out of itty-bitty cannons through flaming hoops. Not to mention feats of great strength like lifting cotton balls hundreds of times their size.

IT'S A FLEA COUNTRY
The next time the circus comes to town, bring your high-powered magnifying glass so you can enjoy all the thrill and chills of—ladies and gentlemen—the tiniest show on earth! (Not recommended for the near-sighted or the chronically itchy.)

Record domestic litters include 19 cats and 23 dogs.

HOW TO MAKE A BLACK HOLE

Really, it couldn't be simpler. All you need is hydrogen—and a lot of time.

Hey, kids! Bored on a rainy day? Played all your video games, watched all the TV you can stand, and yearn for something new? Are your parents wondering if you'll ever do something productive with your life? We've got a fun—and educational—way to take care of all three problems in one fell swoop. Get some of your friends together and make a black hole!

TROUBLE, SHMOUBLE

"Now, wait," we hear you say. "Isn't a black hole a singularity in the time-space continuum where gravity is so strong that noth-ing—not even light—can escape? Aren't those a little dangerous? I could get in trouble!" Well, we won't lie. Black holes *can* be quite dangerous to nearby matter, including people, pets, planets, and stars, if they aren't watched carefully. However, with proper safety precautions, like goggles and a good understanding of basic physics, you should be able to make one pretty easily.

As for getting in trouble—hardly! Black holes are theorized to be quite common; there may even be one in the center of our own galaxy. And certainly, there's no federal, state, or local law against creating one on your own. In other words, not only is creating a black hole fun, it is in fact entirely legal. So let's get started!

ONE INGREDIENT: THAT'S HOW EASY IT IS!

The best thing about creating a black hole is how simple it is. You only need one ingredient: hydrogen. That's it. You do need a lot of it, though. How much? Let's say, enough to create a star that's about 50 times as massive as our own Sun (which is itself 333,000 times as massive as the planet Earth). Yes, that's a lot of hydrogen to get. The good news here is that hydrogen is the most abundant element in the universe, comprising just about 75 percent of everything, everywhere. In other words, it's really cheap.

STEP TWO

Once you've collected your hydrogen into one place, you need to compress it so that it falls onto itself gravitationally and becomes a

---

With jaws shut, a crocodile's fourth tooth protrudes but all of an alligator's teeth are hidden.

new star. A shock wave from an exploding supernova should do very nicely—that's probably what did the trick for our own star, the Sun. Once the hydrogen starts falling in on itself, it'll eventually become so compressed and pressurized that nuclear fusion will begin in the center of the collapsing ball of hydrogen, and the resulting energy of the fusion—hydrogen turning into helium—will stabilize the hydrogen to keep it from collapsing further. Congratulations, you're the parent of a bouncing baby star!

A WATCHED STAR NEVER BURNS
Remember, we're not here to make a star, but a black hole. A star is a good start, but it's only halfway there. What we need to do now is wait for the star to burn through all its hydrogen fuel. In a smaller star, like our Sun, this could take billions of years, and really, who has time for that? The good news is that the larger the star, the quicker it burns through its fuel—and really big stars, like the one we've created, burn through their hydrogen in just 100,000 years. That's still a fair amount of time, so bring a few good magazines or some puzzles with you while you wait.

AWWWW...STAR FALL DOWN AND GO BOOM
After your star burns all its hydrogen, it'll start burning the helium that was the end product of the hydrogen fusion—that'll take far less time. After it's done burning the helium, your star will start burning the progressively heavier elements it creates in its fusion core, in progressively shorter and shorter cycles until finally (whew!) the only thing left in the stellar core is iron, which can't be used as nuclear fuel. Bad news for the star.

CAREFUL, THERE!
Here you might want to step back just a little, because when your star reaches the iron-core stage of its life, what it does next is explode in a cosmos-wrenching blast known as a supernova, in which a star rips itself apart, flinging its mass into the inky darkness with such violence that in this one final explosion, a single supernova star can outshine the hundreds of millions of other stars in the galaxy. That's going out with a bang!

ONE SINGULAR SENSATION
This is where all your hard work and diligence pays off. What's left of your star is a corpse—a stellar core of degenerate nuclear material that, while far smaller than the original star, is still pretty substantial: more than three solar masses (or a million times the

weight of the Earth). This material can no longer create fusion to prop itself up against its own gravitational pull, so the material is squeezed by gravity and ultimately collapses into a singularity—a dimensionless point in space with an infinite gravitational pull.

YOUR VERY OWN BLACK HOLE

Although the black hole itself has no meaningful dimensions, there is a sphere that surrounds it: the "event horizon." The event horizon marks the point at which the black hole's gravitational pull is so strong that even light is sucked into it (that's why black holes are black, after all). So while you admire your black hole, be sure that you admire it from afar. And don't worry about rushing your friends over to admire your handiwork—a black hole of the size you've just created will be there for trillions of years.

There you have it, your very own black hole. That sure beats TV, doesn't it?

* * * * *

MNIFTY MNEMONICS

The Satellites of Jupiter: Io, Europa, Ganymede, Callisto
• I Expect God Cries.   • I Eat Green Cheese.
• I Eat Good Cake.   • I Embarrass Good Christians.

The Satellites of Saturn: Mimas, Enceladus, Tethys, Dione, Rhea, Titan, Hyperion, Iapetus, Phoebe

• Miriam's Enchiladas Taste Divine Recently. Tell Her I'm Proud.

This one lends itself to a variation that actually makes a sentence itself (sort of):

• MET DR THIP

The Satellites of Uranus: Miranda, Ariel, Umbriel, Titania, Oberon
• Mispronunciations Afflict Uranus Too Often.
• My Angel Uriel Takes Opium.

The Satellites of Neptune: Naiad, Thalassa, Despina, Galatea, Larissa, Proteus, Triton, Nereid.
• Neptune's Tiny Dancing Girls Look Pretty To-Night.

The pill bug is one of the few crustaceans that live on land.

VOLTS, WATTS, AND BAKELITE

Our lives are full of things with unlikely names. Just who were these guys who are immortalized in electricity, motor fuel, plastic, and temperatures?

THANKS SIGNOR VOLTA
Travel abroad with a hair dryer and you'll find it won't work properly even though you're equipped with one of those adaptor plugs with differently shaped metal arms sprouting in all directions. That's because voltage varies. The strength of electromotive force from a socket in a U.S. hotel room is half as strong as that which most European countries allow. Result? You probably have to use your hairdryer on a lower setting in London than in New York. And your hair will dry faster. But, alas a Frenchman using a Parisian-made hairdryer in Miami will have to turn the pesky thing up higher than usual and allow more time.

A volt is a unit of electrical potential difference and electro-motive force equal to the difference of potential between two points. So it's handy to be able to measure it. Enter Alessandro Volta, a native of sunny Italy from 1745–1827. Volta was a physi-cist who invented the battery and gave his name to volts. He called his battery "the voltaic pile," a name which did not stick, although his battery design is used today virtually unchanged.

SO WHAT ABOUT WATTS?
A watt is a unit of power equal to the expenditure of one joule of energy in one second, or to the electrical power required for one amp of current to flow across a potential difference of one volt. So Watt? His given name was James and he was a Scottish engineer. He effectively invented the steam engine, which powered Britain's century-long Industrial Revolution. He lived from 1736 to 1819, half a generation before Volta.

AMPS AND JOULES
And, still on electricity, who were Ampere and Joule? Andrè Marie Ampere (1775–1836) was the father of the amp, his rather

elegant French name ignominiously reduced to three letters and sometimes to the single letter A. An ampere or amp is a unit measuring the flow of electricity. The formula for calculating it came to Ampere, a mathematician, as he sat watching a public demonstration of another scientist's discovery—a wire connected to one of Volta's batteries could send a compass needle whizzing.

Joule, Gallic though he sounds, was a dour Brit born only the year before Watt's death. James Prescott Joule (1818–1889) determined precisely how much energy you need to create one unit of heat. His name remains the bane of dieters' lives. Joules are the metric answer to calories and get sternly listed on food packaging.

TEMPERATURE—TWO VERSIONS
Whether you switch on the air conditioning because it's 90° or 30° in the shade depends on where you live. Most Americans still cheerfully use Fahrenheit, a system invented by a German physicist, Gabriel Daniel Fahrenheit (1686–1736). He set the freezing point of water at 32° and its boiling point at 212°. Not long after, in 1742, came a centigrade version from Swedish astronomer Anders Celsius who—boringly but logically—had his water freezing at 0° and boiling at 100°. In most of the world outside the U.S.—and also in most laboratories and other scientific hangouts—Celsius has eclipsed Fahrenheit.

PLASTIC PHONES
Leo Baekaland (1863–1944) was a Belgian-born American scientist who invented a form of plastic that doesn't melt when you heat it. He did it by combining phenol with formaldehyde and called it "bakelite." Modern plastics owe a lot to his work. Think of Baekaland when you pick up a phone or radio.

THE DROWNING OF DIESEL
Rudolph Diesel (1858–1913) invented the first combustion ignition engine. It was twice as efficient as the old steam engines pioneered by Watt and company. It was also cheap to build and it could run on less expensive fuels. Sadly its inventor didn't live to see his engine take the world by storm. He disappeared from a ferry between Antwerp, Belgium, and Harwich, Britain, but there were no diesel-belching freightliners abroad in those days. One presumes poor Herr Diesel fell overboard and drowned.

FOOTBALL GETS (PHYSICS)AL

Jocks and nerds unite! There's science in the crash and smash of football.

So you think you know football. You've got a favorite team, you analyze the plays, predict the point spread, and maybe pick up a few bucks in the office betting pool. What else is there to know? How about physics and aerodynamics for a start?

THE KICK-OFF
Science is everywhere you look when a bunch of massive guys struggle over that little prolate spheroid (that's a football, pal).

Remember Sir Isaac Newton, the guy from the 17th century who discovered the force of gravity when an apple fell on his head? (Maybe he should have been wearing a helmet.) Anyway, if Sir Isaac could watch the Rams and the Ravens square off on the gridiron, he'd see plenty of evidence to support the scientific laws of motion he formulated way back when.

NERDY NEWTON'S FOOTBALL LAWS
When 335-pound defensive tackle Sam Adams of the Baltimore Ravens collides with a smaller opponent who goes flying through the air, the play is just another demonstration of Newton's Third Law of Motion: For every action, there is an equal and opposite reaction. Adams feels the force of collision, too, because—as Newton could have told him—the force of the impact between two colliding forces will be equally distributed.

Then there are the Newtonian laws that apply to the kicking of a football. When, say, St. Louis Rams field goal kicker, Jim Wilkins, thwacks a ball through the uprights, he's demonstrating Newton's second law: $F = MA$, that is, force equals mass times acceleration. Since all footballs are the same mass, the harder Wilkins' kicks it, the more acceleration the ball will have and the farther it will go.

GETTING THE SACK
Physics—as a study of motion and its causes—is perfectly suited to tackle football. To translate another concept of physics into foot-

ballese—the ability of velocity and mass to move a stationary object—our stationary object will be a 198-pound (90 kg) quarterback who's stopped to throw a pass. Coming up on him is our example of velocity and mass, a sacking expert, say, like 285-pound (129 kg) defensive tackle, Le'Roi Glover. When Glover blindsides a quarterback at about 20 mph (32 kph), the laws of physics predict that Glover will have enough mass and velocity to make that quarterback eat AstroTurf. And let us not forget the very important element of momentum (mass times velocity), which is pretty self-explanatory. You're big, you go fast, you've got momentum. See how it works?

COACHING PHYSICS

When football coaches teach tackling, they're also teaching physics. When they tell linemen to stay low during a tackle, it's not just good advice. It lowers a player's center of gravity, which makes it more likely that if he's tackled, it'll be near his "center of mass"—the spot where it's hardest to rotate a player on contact.

PHYSICS AT WORK

Then there's the "work" of football, but not the nine-to-five kind of work. In physics, work is the transfer of energy as measured by force times distance. University of Nebraska physics professor, Tim Gay, gives short physics lessons to the crowd during halftime at Cornhusker games. According to his lesson on work, during the first plays, both football teams do enough combined work to lift a pickup truck about 10 yards (9 m)—the length of a first down—straight up in the air.

PUTTING A SPIN ON IT

Remember that part about a football being a prolate spheroid? Put another way, unlike soccer or basketballs, footballs are oblong, and that shape makes it unstable in flight—the ball tends to wobble. In a well-thrown pass, the football flies with one end facing its target and is given a rotation that spins around the ball's long axis (the lengthwise one). The combination of aim and rotation combats the wobble, wind resistance, and gravity to give the pass "angular momentum." The faster the rotation and velocity of the ball, the farther the ball will go. In a good punting kick, the kicker uses his instep to give the ball a similar spin. But in a good field goal kick, the ball is given a spin around its shorter, crosswise axis and the ball rotates end over end to get that angular momentum.

A chameleon's tongue is twice as long as its body.

AERODYNAMICS THROWS A CURVE

An aerospace engineer who's been studying footballs in flight found that at the end of a long pass, the spiraling of the ball ultimately makes it curve a couple of yards from its intended target. When a right-handed quarterback puts a spin on a long pass, the ball will curve right; a lefty's pass ends with a drift to the left. Experiments showed the curving tendency was consistent—but conversations with quarterbacks revealed that most of them were unaware of it. Once they find out, though, their wide receivers may never have to step out of bounds to catch the ball again.

NAILING DOWN THE PAIN

A *Los Angeles Times* survey found that 78 percent of retired NFL players reported physical disabilities. Physicists are working in this arena. They note that spreading out the force of impact will help a player avoid injury. To demonstrate the principle of distribution of force, scientists compare the damage of football collisions to lying on a bed of nails. Lying on all the nails at once distributes a person's weight over all of them. The experience doesn't hurt as much as the concentrated pressure from a few nails would.

DEEP IMPACT

Strong muscles help, too. When a player is tackled, the force of impact can push his joints beyond the normal range of motion, resulting in sprains or breaks. Strong muscles will stabilize and protect those bones and joints, so that impact is less likely to force them beyond their normal range of motion. Professor Gay is also working with fitness coaches to help athletes build muscles that will help prevent injury.

SPREADING THE PAIN

Helmets and pads are designed to absorb the energy of collisions and to dilute and spread out the force of impact. Dropping a cantaloupe from ten feet (3 m) will make a mess, but if the melon is secured inside a football helmet and dropped from that height it'll be bruised, but still in one piece. That's because helmets distribute the impact over a larger area. If physicists have their way, helmets and other safety equipment will become more efficient at spreading impact to protect players. Maybe the next time you get an urge to pick on a guy with taped-up glasses, think about this. That geek might be working on a way to save your butt.

YOU'RE PRICELESS

When the numbers add up, you own a lot. Discover some fascinating numbers and facts about your body.

Wish you were a millionaire? You may be richer than you think. It started with the more than 26 billion cells you owned from the time you were a newborn baby. With hard work and healthy investment procedures here's what you now own:

- 1.3 to 1.6 gallons (5 to 6 liters) of blood
- 206 bones
- Over 650 muscles, from the tiny muscles that move your eyes to your largest muscle, the gluteus maximus (that big muscle you sit on)
- 10,000 taste buds in your tongue, palate, and cheeks
- You have so many arteries, capillaries, and veins that if you laid them end to end, they'd stretch for about 100,000 miles (160,900 km)—enough to wrap around the world four times
- 1 million tubes in your kidneys, which add up to a hefty 40 miles (64 km)
- About 13.5 million neurons in your spinal cord
- 19 million cells in each square inch of your skin
- About 40 million olfactory receptor cells to help you smell
- 6,000 million, million, million hemoglobin molecules in your bloodstream
- If you're "just average," you have about 75 to 100 trillion (100,000,000,000,000) cells.

YOU'RE A HARD WORKER
If you think you deserve your wealth, you're right. You work hard and you're anything but lazy. Even when you lie on the couch watching scary movies, every hair on your head has a tiny muscle ready to make your hair stand on end!

- Your mouth produces about a quart of saliva each day.

- Your digestive system works 12–15 hours to digest a meal.

- Your liver performs at least 561 known functions to keep you alive, including removing bacteria from the bloodstream, regulating blood clotting, producing bile to digest foods, and storing vitamins and minerals.

- Your heart pumps 8,000 gallons (30,283 liters) of blood every day.

- The 250,000 sweat glands in each of your feet are busy giving off almost a cup of moisture every day.

- Your heart beats about 2.5 billion times in your lifetime.

- Tired yet? There's more. You turn in your sleep at night more than 820,000 times in your lifetime.

YOU'RE A FAST WORKER
Okay, so you work 24 hours a day, but it's not because you're slow. In fact, you're a regular whiz kid. Here's how we know that you're a fast worker:

- It takes one second for your body to lose the 3 million red blood cells. It takes that same second for your bone marrow to produce enough new cells to replenish your system.

- In one minute your heart pumps blood to the lungs and back to the heart again.

- Your body pushes food through your small intestine, which is more than 20 feet long, in just four hours.

- When you cough, the air rushing out of your lungs hits speeds of 75 to 100 mph (121 to 161 km).

- When you sneeze—if you sneeze as fast as the fastest sneeze ever recorded—it will clock in at just over 100 mph (161 km).

CHECK OUT WHAT'S IN YOUR GENES
Like any hard-working trillionaire, there are unique secrets to your wealth, many of which are stored in your genetic code:

- If unwound and tied together, the strands of DNA in one of your cells would stretch almost 80 inches (203 cm)—though it would only be 50 trillionths of an inch wide.

Maybe ostriches should put their heads in the sand; their eyes are bigger than their brains.

- If written out, your genetic code would fill the pages of 200 New York City telephone books (at 1,000 pages each).

- If all the DNA in your body were put end to end, it would reach to the sun and back again over 600 times.

- The entire DNA in one nucleus of one human cell adds up to over 2,500,000,000 nucleotides.

YOU HIRE GOOD HELP

Like all busy workers, you need help to manage your wealth and work. Fortunately you have a good manager: your brain. It controls your body by sending messages through the nervous system. And let's face it—it'd be tough to manage without one. A few of the brain's major features:

- The brain consumes 20 percent of the blood's oxygen supply.

- It uses up 20 to 30 percent of your daily caloric intake.

- About 85 percent of your brain is water.

- Cholesterol makes up 15 percent of the brain's dry weight.

- The brain weighs about 3 pounds (1.4 kg) or about 2 percent of body weight. (That may not seem like much, but the stegosaurus' brain made up only 0.004 percent of its body weight. Maybe that's why you don't see a lot of them around anymore.)

- Your brainy brain contains 100 billion neurons and trillions of glia (support) cells.

- It's estimated that there are 1,000 trillion connections in the brain.

- Your brain controls the muscles in your body by sending messages through the somatic nervous system at the rate of 240 mph (386 kph).

- The neurons of your cerebral cortex would reach over 250,000 miles (402,336 km) if placed end to end.

So enjoy your day. Hey, it must be fun to be one of the lucky people who's worth over a million.

The loudest animal sound is produced by the blue whale—a 188 decibel whistle.

HOW TO MAKE FUEL

Here's the recipe. The ingredients are available everywhere.

Collect some animal carcasses, pond scum, and dead vegetation. Combine them and pack it all into the muck at the bottom of a swamp. Allow the mixture to decompose. Repeat. And repeat. And repeat. Apply heat and pressure. Keep adding more dead stuff. Increase the heat and pressure for a few million years. Drill.

Yield: thousands of servings of oil. Season to taste.

OLD DEAD STUFF

That's right. The expensive liquid you use to power your car is literally made from old dead stuff. So is the gas you heat your home with. And the coal that powers power plants. After all, they don't call them "fossil fuels" for nothing.

MAJOR MELTDOWN

If you were to break us down into our constituent molecules, you won't have much left other than a bit of carbon swimming in a puddle of hydrogen oxide (water). Carbon makes up a lot of other stuff as well. But fossil fuels aren't just made from carbon; there's one more ingredient.

THE STUFF OF STARS

Hydrogen is almost everywhere. It only has one atom, and since it powers the sun, you can imagine how volatile it is. By itself, it's very valuable as a fuel source, but with one very serious drawback. Remember the *Hindenburg*? Very explosive

But take some hydrogen atoms and some carbon atoms, put them together, and—voila!— hydrocarbons! That's what fossil fuels are known as.

"OIL, THAT IS..."

Back to the prehistoric swamp. As the remains of various microorganisms, small critters, and fish rotted at the bottom of the swamp, more of the same continued to drift down. Like what happens when you forget to add chlorine to your pool. Leave the pool alone long enough, and it will eventually completely fill in. The same thing happened to the prehistoric swamps. The gunk at the bottom got buried under tons and tons of more and more gunk.

Dr. Alphonse Rockwell, a dentist, was the inventor of the electric chair.

THE GIANT PRESSURE-COOKER

Under this immense weight, pressure started to build. Since pressure causes heat, things eventually started cooking. The gunk cooked for millions of years, as if it was in a giant oven. Eventually, it distilled into oil. That's right, distilled—just like beer and whiskey is made. Once the gunk was in liquid form, all that pressure pushed the oil into cracks in the Earth's crust, conveniently creeping into places where we could—eons later—reach it by drilling. Some oil wells have enough pressure in them that oil will spurt out of them for years.

IT'S A GAS

Cook the oil for even longer at even hotter temperatures, and it eventually becomes the holy grail of petroleum products: natural gas—clean burning, odorless, and efficient. It powers your furnace and your Bunsen burner, not to mention your kitchen stove and your fake fireplace.

MINER MISHAPS

Coal was formed by much the same process as oil, except it's made from dead plants, not animals. Coal forms first into peat, then soft coals, and finally hard coals. (Remember bituminous and anthracite from school? They're soft and hard, respectively.) Anyway, the harder the coal, the hotter it burns.

Coal is cheap, but it's dirty. So dirty that it's difficult to mine without giving those poor miners a lot of nasty lung problems. Coal is dirty to burn, too. After all, it's essentially a rock that burns. It's laced with impurities like sulfur, minerals and just plain common dirt. You don't want that coming up through your heating vents.

The coal industry has made efforts to clean up every aspect of coal—from mining it (using automated equipment these days) to washing it (with water), to burning it (they "scrub" the smoke with a water and limestone mixture that eliminates up to 98 percent of the sulfur dioxide).

YOU CAN'T HAVE EVERYTHING

But that's the way the story goes with hydrocarbons. You can either have dirty but cheap, or clean but expensive (or dangerous). So the search for the perfect fuel goes on.

BARRY BONDS KICKS ASH

In the 1930s, Rip Collins, who played for the St. Louis Cardinals, fenced his yard with broken ash bats. Thanks to Barry Bonds and Sam Holman, those days may be gone for good.

On Friday, October 4, 2001, Barry Bonds of the San Francisco Giants slammed his second home run of the night, and his 71st homer of the season. As Bonds sent the ball flying into the bleachers, he made history. He'd just set a new record for the most home runs in one season, and there were cheers everywhere—especially in Ottawa, Canada.

THE CANADIAN CONNECTION
The next Sunday, at a game in Los Angeles, the slugger/outfielder finished the year with two more home runs. Baseball fans celebrated Bond's season of 73 home runs as one of the best ever.

In Ottawa, they also celebrated the victory of the Rideau Crusher, named after Ottawa's famous Rideau Canal. (The canal was a famous feat of engineering that tamed a wilderness of lakes and rivers and launched a great waterway way back in 1832.) The Rideau Crusher was another Canadian feat of engineering—a baseball bat that just might tame the sport's great pitchers and create a new era of record-breaking super-sluggers.

BONDS BRANCHES OUT
Barry Bonds had a single-season slugging average of .863 to beat the .847 that Babe Ruth set in 1920. He demolished another Ruth record by walking 177 times. What a lot of fans don't know is that while Bonds was crushing the Babe's records, he was swinging the Rideau Crusher.

The Crusher was designed, manufactured, and carefully crafted from rock maple by Sam Holman in Ottawa, Canada. Holman's maple baseball bat is a five-year-old upstart in a conservative sport where nearly all the major league bats are made of white ash. The Babe may have swung a heavy hickory bat, but white ash bats—including the preferred Louisville Slugger—have dominated baseball's home plate since the 1930s.

The first E-mail was sent in 1971.

BARKING UP THE WRONG TREE?

Sam Holman was sitting in a local pub, listening to his friend, Bill MacKenzie (a Colorado baseball scout) complain about the number of bats that were broken in the major leagues every season. MacKenzie challenged Sam—a carpenter—to do something about it. To his surprise, Sam Holman found himself taking up the challenge. He studied baseball physics and called on his carpentry experience to invent a long-lasting bat that could take plenty of punishment. Holman realized that no one had considered one of nature's strongest woods, maple.

BAT MAN

The sugar maple, also called rock maple, is a deciduous (as opposed to an evergreen) tree that grows in the northeastern United States and southeastern Canada. Its leaves turn brilliant red or yellow in the fall. Not only is it the official tree of Canada, it takes up a lot of space on the Canadian national flag.

Maple syrup fans know the tree mainly for its sap, but those in the know appreciate it for its dense wood, one of the hardest in the world. Maple timber is used in everything from bridges and bowling lanes to Stradivarius violins.

So Sam carved the first "Sam Bat" from a piece of maple he had at home, left over from a stair rail project. His local team, the Ottawa Lynx, tried one out for a month, and after continued use, the Sam Bat was still in one piece. Since ash bats often broke within a week, Sam figured maple was a keeper.

GOING OUT ON A MAPLE LIMB

In 1997, Joe Carter of the Toronto Blue Jays tried out a Sam Bat at practice—and hit a homer on his first try. Carter sneaked the bat, (which hadn't been approved for the major leagues) into a ball game with the Milwaukee Brewers. And homered again.

Other hitters tried the Crusher, and the bat started smacking out good press. Heavy hitter Alex Gonzalez of the Mariners liked the bat's longevity. *Sports Illustrated* quoted Karim Garcia of the Tigers proclaiming, "You can't break the Sam." Royce Clayton of the Rangers called his Crusher "my sweet potato pie" and predicted, "Soon everyone will be using the Sam."

The only continent with no trees is Antarctica.

SWINGERS

Every year, the Hillerich & Bradsby Company awards a silver copy of their famous Louisville Slugger (made from the best northern white ash) to the leagues' best hitters. Ironically, many of the recent winners of the Silver Slugger Awards—like Edgar Renteria of the Cardinals, Troy Glaus of the Angels, Vladimir Guerrero of the Expos, and Albert Pujols of the Cardinals—were wielding maple Sam Bats!

But it was Barry Bonds who put maple on the map. When he took up the Crusher, his home run average, which had been sliding, improved immediately. When he started breaking records that had endured over 80 years, some nosy scientists started to wonder if Sam Holman's maple bats were a factor in Bond's success.

GOOD VIBRATIONS

The University of California Forestry Laboratory compared the properties of white ash and sugar maple. Ash is what's called a "ring porous" hardwood tree; the vessels carrying its nutrients are found in the early growth rings. Sugar maple is a "diffuse porous" hardwood tree; the vessels are diffuse and found all throughout the growth rings. This makes maple harder, stronger, and stiffer than ash, which probably gives sluggers the extra oomph to smash those balls over the fence.

SWEET SPOT FOR SUGAR MAPLE

Then there's sugar maple's "sweet spot." When a bat connects with a ball, the bat vibrates like a plucked guitar string—except at the sweet spot, which is located about six inches (15 cm) from the end of the bat. The sweet spot has the fewest vibrations, and with less energy used up in vibrations, more power goes into the ball to send it flying farther. Sam Holman is sure that his maple bats have a longer sweet spot than ash, giving sluggers another advantage.

SCIENTISTS HAVE THEIR SAY

Not all scientists agree that a stronger bat is responsible for the new records in baseball. Some say it's the talent of the hitter that really controls the game's "vibes." The start of a swing bends a bat backward, so it could just be that great hitters time their swing so perfectly that the bat snaps forward just as it smacks the ball, providing the extra force necessary for a home run.

Women blink more than men and most humans blink 6.2 million times a year.

THE BATTERS' REBUTTAL
But hitters like Jose Canseco of the Tampa Bay Devil Rays swear that a ball sails farther much faster off a Sam bat. Others, like home-run maven Bonds, are simply pleased with a maple bat's strength and long life: It allows him to get comfortable with a favorite stick both in practice and in the game.

MAPLE CAN, ASH CAN, AND ALUMINUM CAN
Players have definitely taken a fancy to it, but maple still has a way to go before it replaces ash. During Bonds's great year, Holman made plans to open a new factory and produce more than 300 bats a day. Hillerich & Bradsby Company turns out up to five times that number of ash bats daily, and sell over a million of them a year.

And let us not forget maple's third competitor—aluminum. Most high school and college players cut their teeth on and establish their batting averages with aluminum bats. A good pro hitter wants a heavy wooden bat; he can aim at a pitch as soon as it leaves the pitcher's hand, and slam a ball farther. But amateurs like lightweight aluminum bats because they move so fast that they give an inexperienced player an extra few split-seconds to judge a pitch, decide how to hit a ball, and even adjust their swing.

In fact, aluminum bats are considered a boon to major league baseball—and to conservationists. Metal bats have drastically lessened the amount of ash and maple timber needed to supply the boys of summer. Without aluminum, wood for both maple and ash bats would be in much shorter supply.

A CRUSH ON MAPLE
Back in the majors, wood is still king, and Sam Holman is busy with new innovations. Now that he's helped Barry Bonds, one of only four players to hit 600 home runs in his career, "kick ash" out of its solitary dominance over pro baseball, Holman is working on a switch to thin-barreled bats. He says that aerodynamics favors a narrower cylinder bat because it will travel faster through the air. And he's already fashioned a prototype for Expos slugger Vladmir Guerrero. Of course, since many batters believe that a big-barreled bat hits farther because it increases the area of a bat's sweet spot, Holman is going up against baseball tradition with his new idea.

But hey, he's done that before.

A goldfish kept in the dark will eventually turn white.

JAILHOUSE PINK

Color sends out waves that stimulate chemicals in the brain.
If you don't believe us, listen to what happened when experimenters
painted the jail cells of violent criminals a nice, pretty pink.

D r. Alexander Schauss got interested in the physiological
effects of color in the 1960s—hey, didn't everybody?—
while a grad student at the University of New Mexico. He
based his work on the fact that color stimulates the pituitary and
pineal glands, which in turn affects a variety of physiological
processes that alter moods and increase or decrease brain activity.

PINK FREUD
Over the next few years, in a series of experiments, Dr. Schauss
arrived at his own theory: that pink—a very particular shade of
pink to be exact—had a calming effect on the nervous system. It
slowed heart rate, pulse, and respiration, resulting in a feeling of
well being. To prove his theory, the doctor needed access to a
large number of agitated subjects in a controlled environment.
Hmmm. How about a prison? What better subjects than newly
arrived—just arrested and thrown into the clink—prisoners?

JUST WHAT THE DOCTOR ORDERED
In 1979, Schauss approached the brass at the U.S. Naval Correc-
tional Center in Seattle. He knew that if the color he wanted to
test had been a deep macho green or navy blue, he'd have a better
chance of getting the Navy's cooperation. To his surprise, when he
said "pink," they said, "What shade?" Not only were Commander
Miller and Chief Warrant Officer Baker willing, they even mixed
the paint and applied it to the walls and ceiling of a holding cell.
  The results were amazing. After 10–15 minutes in the pink
holding cell, new arrivals who'd been tossed in there kicking,
screaming, cursing—even rip-roaring drunk—were calm. And, the
effects lasted for 30 minutes after the prisoners were taken out of
the cell. The center continued the experiment for the next 156
days and the results were consistent. In his paper on the subject,
Dr. Schauss named the color "Baker-Miller pink" in honor of the

The most common dream is of falling, followed by being chased or attacked.

cooperative Navy CWO and commander. It's also been called "drunk tank" pink, Pepto-Bismol pink, and bubble-gum pink.

THE PEPTO-BISMOL EFFECT?

A close approximation of the color can be had from the paint store (Benjamin Moore #1328), but if you're thinking that Baker-Miller pink might be just the thing for your teenager's room—don't. In later experiments, the prisoners who were left in the pink room for as long as two hours seemed to overdose on Baker-Miller pink, becoming very disturbed and/or severely depressed.

The good news is that during another U.S. Navy experiment it was found that Baker-Miller pink also worked as an appetite suppressant. According to experts you can get the same results just by looking at a piece of pink paper for a few minutes at a time.

PROUD TO WEAR PINK

Other facilities duplicated the experiment, most with success. Baker-Miller pink rooms are still used by various centers across the United States. So the next time you're "detained" and thrown in the pink clink, just sit back and enjoy it. Ommmmmm.

COLOR YOUR WORLD

If pink isn't your thing, find your perfect color on the following list. Here's what researchers say are the effects of the other colors.

- Blue is calming, lowers blood pressure, and decreases respiration.
- Green is soothing and mentally and physically relaxing. It helps relieve depression, anxiety, and nervousness.
- Violet suppresses appetite, provides a peaceful environment, and is supposedly good for migraine headaches.
- Yellow energizes, relieves depression, improves memory, and stimulates appetite.
- Orange energizes and stimulates the appetite and digestive system.
- Red stimulates brain wave activity, relieves depression, and increases heart rate, respiration, and blood pressure.
- Black is a "power" color and a source of self-confidence and strength. Like pink, it also suppresses the appetite.

Humans can see over 10 million colors and smell over 50 thousand aromas.

THE STRAIGHT POOP

*Uncle John flushes out the value of a natural,
plentiful, and extremely useful substance.*

As the saying goes, manure happens. It's a good thing, too.
From animal dung in beer to bat guano in gunpowder...
What? You didn't know? Oh, yeah. In some cultures, poop
is on a par with manna from heaven. And now some modern
scientists think it could help save the world!

THE SCOOP ON POOP
Animal and human waste is usually about three-fourths water,
though that amount depends on the animal and its health. A
third of what's left is dead bacteria from the bacteria in the intestines that digest food, another third is the fiber that passes
through the stomach undigested, and the last third is a mixture of
fat, inorganic salts, protein, live bacteria, and mucus from the
lining of the intestine. Can such unappetizing ingredients produce
something valuable? Let's ask the ancients.

DAFT BEER
On the Orkney Islands off the coast of Scotland, historians discovered a 5,000-year-old brewery. If you like to kick back with a six-
pack, you're not so different from the dudes of the Neolithic Age
who fermented beer in a kiln made from animal dung and reeds.
There's one small difference. When scholars brewed a batch of the
ancient ale, drank it, and pronounced it delicious, they learned
that its distinctive flavor came from cow dung! You might say
those Stone Age Scots produced the world's most poopular beer.

THIS IS SOME SERIOUS GUANO
Peruvian Incas gathered seabird droppings, or guano, so farmers
could use it as fertilizer for crops like corn and potatoes. The
guano was so important to their civilization that seabird rookeries
were protected from disruption on pain of death.

A LAW PASSED BY THE MANURITY
The Incas weren't the only ones with laws about guano. In 1856,
to help guarantee a supply of valuable bird and bat manure, the
U.S. Congress passed an act permitting American citizens to take

"peaceable" possession of any unclaimed island containing guano. Guano turned out to be an even more useful for war. During the Civil War, the Confederacy used gunpowder containing saltpeter made from water, ashes, and bat guano.

DUNG WILL KEEP US TOGETHER
You can hold your nose at the idea, but in India and parts of Asia, Africa, and the Middle East, people use dung to build their houses. The practice has its advantages. For instance, in January 2001, an earthquake devastated the Indian state of Gujarat, leaving nearly 20,000 people dead and over 600,000 homeless. But Gujarat's tribespeople, who live in colorful painted huts known as *bhungas*, were relatively unaffected by the trembler. That's because bhungas are built of twig-lattice frames plastered with dung and mud. Even though the 2001 earthquake was one of the worst in India's recorded history, the dung-mud huts swayed, but they held together and their inhabitants remained safe.

THAT'S WHY THEY CALL THEM CAMELS?
Camel dung, dried into bits of charcoal, has fired up many a hookah and provided a relaxing smoke. And there's a tobacco produced in Syria that was once cured over a fire of camel dung.

POOP POWER
When manure is properly stored in warm, airtight containers called methane digesters, its own bacteria form both a biogas that can be used for fuel and a composted manure that has few pollutants and is good for the soil. In Hainan Province, China, pig manure produces the methane that powers village streetlights. In India, cow dung and even human waste are converted to biogas, which powers electric generators, lights, and kitchen stoves.

An energy crisis in the United States has generated new interest in methane generators. In 2001, a farm in Wisconsin began using methane to produce electricity for 225 homes. Not to be outdone, Britain has built a dung-fired power station that will operate in North Devon, England, and produce electricity from farm-animal waste.

IS DETROIT TOO CHICKEN TO GO CHICKEN?
None of this would have surprised Harold Bate. In the early 1970s, the British inventor not only devised a generator that

Pumice is the only rock that floats.

produced electricity from his septic tank, he also created the Bate Auto Gas Converter, a contraption attached to his truck's carburetor that helped Harold's 18-year-old truck roar down the road on methane. Bate's fuel cost the equivalent of three cents a gallon and produced much less pollution than petroleum.

Unfortunately, chicken-powered Cadillacs didn't catch on in Detroit. But West Virginia University scientists have developed a working blend of liquefied chicken manure and diesel fuel that could someday put a chicken in your tank.

YOU DO HAVE TO BE A ROCKET SCIENTIST

Is the stinky stuff ready for the space age? It's not powering rockets yet, but in California the space-age company Aerojet has found an interesting use for it. Aerojet has badly polluted its own rocket-testing sites with chemicals from solid rocket propellant that's even leaked into the groundwater. Since the 1980s, the company has spent millions on decontamination, and projected that it could take billions more to complete the job.

Luckily the company's rocket scientists remembered that Ph.D. could also stand for "piled high and deep." Now, at the beginning of the rainy season, workers shovel manure into the polluted soil. It feeds soil microbes that, when deprived of oxygen, break down pollutants and detoxify the ground—without the help of millions of dollars worth of technology.

THE TECHNO-POOP OF THE FUTURE

If 21st-century scientists have their way, manure will not only fuel power plants and car engines, its carbohydrates will also be used to make chemicals for plastics, animal feed, and (hey, we don't make the news, we only report it) cosmetics. Manure could help save the Earth's environment—and that's no B.S.

* * * * *

"Familiar things happen, and mankind does not bother about them, it requires a very unusual mind to undertake the analysis of the obvious."
—Whitehead, *Science and the Modern World*, 1925

IT TAKES GUTS TO BE AN ELEPHANT

A voyage through the digestive system of the world's largest vegetarian.

Ever wondered why a lion can snatch a gazelle, gobble it down, and then snooze in the sun for the rest of the day, while an elephant has to stand all day long, chomping at leaves and twigs, and never seems to get any sleep at all?

The simple answer is that the lion can get her meal business out of the way fast because lion food—flesh, that is—is concentrated, high in protein, and nutritious. So a little goes a long way. On the other hand, plant-eaters like elephants have to keep at it all the time because there's not much concentrated nutrition in a leaf. Vegetarians have to consume megaquantities to extract enough calories to sustain themselves. The poor pachyderm must wonder sometimes whether he lives to eat or eats to live.

OVER THE TEETH AND THROUGH THE GUMS

Plant-crunchers need good teeth, too. In addition to his largely decorative, occasionally combative, tusks, Mr. Dumbo has a set of massive molars at the back of his mouth. Like everything else in an elephant, these grinders are large. They have flat, pulverizing surfaces, which—unlike your teeth—don't have to last all their lives. An elephant teethes continuously. As one set of pearly whites wear down, it's replaced (every few years) by new ones that erupt at the back of the mouth and move forward along the jaw like cable cars clicking into position.

THE IMPORTANCE OF A WOOD DIET

Those teeth are efficient plant-pulpers, but most of an elephant's meals, including the meals he eats between meals, are very woody. And that means cellulose, from which the cell walls of plants are built. Since evolution has carelessly not bothered to equip any mammal with a digestive juice that can touch cellulose, the elephant has had to develop other strategies.

Cats walk on their claws, not on their paws.

LOOK OUT STOMACH, HERE IT COMES

Chewing mashes up the cellulose and helps to release the nutrients in it, but the elephant still needs a massive stomach full of friendly bacteria to break it down chemically. That's why anything an elephant eats has to sit stewing for two and a half days in the digestive juices and bacterial soup in its huge stomach.

WHY ELEPHANTS ARE SO BIG

How would he manage if he didn't have room for such a capacious stomach? He wouldn't. An elephant has solved his digestive difficulties by becoming a giant. This woody meal system wouldn't work in a creature with smaller-scale organs. It isn't a case of the elephant eating like this because he's big. His size is the evolutionary solution, not the problem.

DUMBO DROPPINGS

In spite of his in-house chemical processing facility, an elephant's dung is still very coarse. Gardeners who live near zoos that are generous with their by-products think elephant dung is the ultimate fertilizer. It's full of virtually untouched twigs, fibers, and seeds. The seeds have thick rinds so they can withstand the considerable strength of elephantine digestive juices, and some of them, in fact, can't start germinating at all unless the rinds have been loosened by a few days inside an elephant.

* * * * *

DON'T CALL HIM A WEAKLING

Do you believe that only wimps or weaklings cry? Hey, no one calls elephants weaklings—they can grow as tall as 11 feet (3.4 m) and can weigh up to 15,000 pounds (6,804 kg)—but apart from humans, the only land mammal that cries is the elephant.

PINK ELEPHANTS

Not the kind that you see when you're drunk—these are real elephants. In some regions of India where the soil is red, elephants roll on the ground and spray dust over their bodies to protect themselves against insects. The red dust clings to the pachyderms and gives their bodies a pretty pink tinge.

EYE SEE

The eyes in your head are different than the ones on, say, an octopus or a fruit fly—so different, in fact, that they're not related at all from an evolutionary point of view.

Take your eye. No, no, don't actually take it. That would hurt. Rather, consider it. A marvel of engineering, it not only allows you to register the presence of light, but also, thanks to an intricate system involving lenses, stereo inputs, and a crack interpretive computer (your brain), your eye allows you to differentiate objects in 3-D and in living color. Nature likes eyes so much that it's found several different ways to equip animals with them.

EYE SEE THE LIGHT

Of course, what constitutes "seeing" depends on the eye and how complicated it is. If you're a clam, your eye sees differences between lightness and darkness; if you're a human, your eye can see the difference between Dennis Franz and Antonio Banderas (and that's a good thing). But at the basic level, all eyes allow their organisms to be sensitive to light.

THE OLD FISH-EYE

The wavelengths of light that eyes are sensitive to is something nearly all eyes have in common. We see "visible light" because it's those wavelengths of the electromagnetic spectrum that are able to transmit through water; frequencies just above and just below the visible light spectrum hardly transmit in water at all. All varieties of eyes evolved first in water, so it makes sense that eyes would be sensitive to wavelengths that actually can be seen in water. The next time you curse your lack of X-ray vision, blame a fish and the evolutionary processes that caused you to be descended from one.

AND EYE DON'T MEAN "SIX PACK"

Here's another thing that eyes seem to share in common: Pax-6. It sounds like a superhero league ("Say your prayers, Council of Evil! Here comes the Pax-6!"), but it's actually a gene that regulates eye

Chow dogs have black tongues.

development across a range of animal species. If something goes wrong with this gene, you'll have a problem. In humans, a corrupted Pax-6 gene can lead to a condition known as "aniridia," which keeps the iris from forming completely. In fruit flies, a bad Pax-6 gene can cause eyes to grow out of your legs (and you thought flies looked creepy already).

The fact that the same gene is used across various animal species doesn't mean that all eyes are evolutionarily related. Even animals without eyes have the gene. And it's useful in other, non-eye-related developmental processes. In each case of evolution, the emerging eye could simply use the existing gene that best suits its needs—sort of like if you need a hammer and there's one in your toolbox already, it doesn't make much sense to forge a new hammerlike tool from scratch. You just use the stupid hammer.

SEEING EYE-TO-EYE
All complex eyes have lenses (to capture and focus light) and retinas (to hold photosensitive cells that transmit light information to the brain). What they don't have in common is how their major parts evolved and are created during fetal development. The tissues that make up retinas and lenses, and the design of their parts, differ substantially from animal to animal.

LOOK INTO MY EYES...
Let's start with the eyes we have—the same sort of eyes you'll find in other vertebrates, from trout to T. rexes to Tasmanian wolves. The eye of a vertebrate animal (which is how we're classified because we have a spine) is one organ, but it's made out of two different types of tissue. The lens is made from epidermal cells (which is to say, your cornea is heavily modified skin), but the retina is made out of cells that come from your central nervous system—and that's to say that your retina is basically a direct extension of your brain, connected by the thick cable known as the optic nerve. On your retina, your light-receiving cells are in the back of your eye. They're known as ciliary photoreceptor cells. Your retina also has other types of cells laid on in layers.

OCTOPUSES' EYES
Now let's look at the eye of a mollusk—your average squid, let's say. A squid eye or an octopus eye doesn't look all that different

from your eye—bigger and freakier, perhaps, but not completely unrecognizable. However, that eye is made entirely differently. Unlike vertebrate eyes, mollusk eyes are out of purely epidermal cells: retina and lenses both—no direct brain extensions here. On the retina, the light-receiving cells are facing front and are an entirely different type of cell, called microvillar photoreceptor cells, all in a single layer. So while the design and function of the mollusk eye is similar to our own, the parts that make up the eyes come from other systems of the body and use different cells to accomplish the same tasks.

EYES BUGGING OUT
And now for something completely different: bug eyes. Put a fruit fly eye under the microscope, and you'll see how little it has in common with either vertebrate or mollusk eyes (though, like mollusks, their retinas are made from epidermal cells). The most obvious difference stares back at you, unblinking: It's a compound eye. Instead of having one lens per eye, it has hundreds, and each crystalline lens is essentially a self-contained unit, sending information back to what passes for a fruit fly brain. If you remember your horror films, you'll recall that when the scientist with that big fat fly head moved toward the screaming woman in the beehive hairdo, the point of view from the human fly was of hundreds of tiny screaming women instead of one image. Well, this is actually incorrect (proof of why getting your science from horror films is a bad idea). The image a fruit fly sees is more like a mosaic or a dot pattern, not unlike a black and white newspaper picture.

THE EYES HAVE IT
So, you see: Three different types of eyes, all evolved in different ways, formed from differing tissues in the body. And if you think three different evolutionary paths to the same function seems a little much, consider this: Some biologists think that eyes may have evolved independently in various animals up to 65 separate times across the entire animal kingdom. That tells you just how important eyes really are—and why nature keeps an eye on them.

The only animal evidence admissible in American courts is from bloodhounds.

HIGH HOPES FOR HEMP

Hemp growers have to explain it all the time: They're not growing hemp for smoking. Just as the majority of garden-variety poppies don't provide opium, garden-variety hemp doesn't produce THC, the active ingredient in marijuana. Growers with a healthy respect for the courts and jail terms go to great lengths to ensure that it doesn't.

One of the beauties of hemp is that growing it doesn't require herbicides, insecticides, or fertilizers—it actually pours nutrients back into the soil. As testament to that, hemp plants are being used successfully to speed detoxification of the contaminated land around Chernobyl. So why is it a crime to grow the innocent kind of hemp in the United States?

OLD-TIME RELIGION
Hemp was old when Methuselah was young, especially as a food. Over a three-year period, Buddha himself lived on one hemp seed daily, something Weight Watchers might want to think about. Shinto, a Japanese religion that predates Christianity, still has a place for the hemp seed in its dietary teachings. On the Asian mainland, the Chinese have been using it for 9,000 years.

FOR THE BIRDS
Yes, hemp is nutritious. But until recently, the seed was imported to the U.S. primarily for birdfeed. Now the seeds and their oil have become significant ingredients in quite a few health foods, included in everything from power bars to ice cream. Some organic power bars, in fact, taste like birdseed stuck together with honey, but, hey, maybe Buddha knew something we didn't.

READY TO WEAR HEMP
In the 18th and 19th centuries, hemp had other uses. The male plant, which doesn't generate seeds, was found to have a remarkably tough fiber. These were the days before King Cotton and way before denim. In Europe the earliest textile mills turned out hemp cloth for off-the-rack buyers. Hemp pants went as well with laborer's clogs in those days as they do today with Birkenstocks.

The only bird that can fly backward is the hummingbird.

TAKING IT TO THE BANK

Business boomed in Britain. Demand for hemp fiber to feed clothing and cordage mills was so great at the turn of the 19th century, that Canadian farmers were offered a bonus of five guineas per acre if they grew it. That was a nice chunk of change in those days to plant a crop that needed no cultivation, withstood erratic weather, and was easily harvested. Hemp would grow just about anywhere—in clay, sand, swamp, or gravel; sow the seeds in a forest or on a sand dune. Hemp farmers were giggling all the way to the bank because Britain was importing 30,000 tons annually and begging for more.

WE, THE PEOPLE...

Canada's American neighbors grew it, most notably gentlemen farmers George Washington and Thomas Jefferson. Given that, it should come as no surprise that drafts of the Declaration of Independence were written on paper made from hemp fibers.

A COFFIN MADE OF COTTON

Hemp's heyday was over once mechanization in the textile industry gave cotton a tremendous boost. By the 20th century, commercial growing of hemp for the textile industry had fallen dramatically, except in eastern Europe and parts of France. Some American farmers still toughed it out, but they were selling most of their crop for the manufacture of twine.

If cotton was hemp's coffin, sisal from the leaves of the Mexican agave was the nails in it. It was just as tough and a lot cheaper, and soon edged out hemp as the fiber of choice for twine and other cordage.

DIGGING A HOLE FOR THE COFFIN

By the 1930s International Harvester, the company that manufactured hemp machinery, mothballed their blueprints and machinery, followed the trend, and went with cheaper sisal, too. Then came the '40s and the low-budget movie *Reefer Madness*, which dashed any hope hemp growers still had.

CONSPIRACY THEORIES

There's a theory that DuPont needed to guarantee a market for nylon and that the company helped stir up the public furor about the "demon weed" that led to anti-hemp/marijuana legislation. If anything, of course, DuPont would have been beating up on King Cotton, not its poor, nearly bankrupt country cousin.

The current conspiracy theory, which may be a lot more than just a theory, is that the soy lobby (which is not a section of your local health food store) has aimed all its guns toward stymieing efforts to lift the prohibition on growing hemp in the U.S. Hemp fans like to point out that, next to corn, soy may be the most genetically modified food commodity that North Americans consume. Take that, tofu-eaters!

WEARING NEW THREADS

Today upscale boutiques sell casual hemp clothing. It's not exactly as stylish as the fall line from Versace, but it appeals to growing numbers of environmentally conscious consumers who like to wear their labels on the outside.

GOOD FOR YOU

Meanwhile, hempsters eat hemp butter, hemp burgers, and those power bars, and drink hemp milk and hemp beer. Nutrition research shows that, ounce for ounce, hemp offers far more across the board than soy on its best day. Dr. Udo Erasmus, author of *Oils That Heal, Oils That Kill,* ("His Oiliness" to his fans) has termed hemp oil "nature's most perfectly balanced oil." Hemp oil contains something called gamma-linoleic acid, an essential fatty acid otherwise found only in fish oil (a favorite of health-foodies).

THEY CAN IN CANADA

America's less-paranoid neighbor to the north has legalized the growing of industrial hemp (though the practice is highly regulated). The only sign of progress in the U.S. is in Hawaii, where they've OK'd small test crops for farmers.

Meanwhile, most of the seeds that are imported into the U.S. come from mainland China and are meant to be eaten by birds. The seeds and oil meant for human consumption are presumably the pick of the crop. We can only hope.

There are leech farms and the average leech costs $7.50.

SEEING STARS

There are all kinds of stars out there, from super bright hotshots to tiny, burned-out dwarfs and all kinds of mystery objects.

OUR SUN—AN AVERAGE JOE STAR

Our sun is a pretty typical star. At 5,000 million it's about halfway through life. Its regular yellow color is caused by its pretty average surface temperature of 9932°F (5500°C). A star's color depends on its temperatures, which in turn depends on its mass. The sun's energy (light, heat, and radiation) comes from continual thermonuclear reactions, like millions of hydrogen bombs going off in slow motion. It takes the energy produced at the core 30 million years to get to the surface.

WHAT'S IN STORE—THE RED GIANT

Red giants are ancient stars that started out life similar to the sun. After 10,000 million years they begin to run out of the gases that fuel them. The outer gases cool off to a red color and expand. The outer gas can expand by 100 times. When the Sun does this, it may engulf Earth. (Mercury and Venus will definitely be toast.) At the same time as the outer layers of gas are expanding, the core of the giant compacts and burns hotter and brighter than ever before. Red giants are very bright, despite being cooler on the outside. Look for Betelgeuse in the constellation Orion. On a clear night, you can see its red color.

GOING OUT WITH A WHIMPER—THE WHITE DWARF

White dwarfs are the last stage in the life cycle of a medium-sized yellow star like ours. The outer gases of a red giant eventually expand so much, they drift away. Sometimes they form beautiful, illuminated gas clouds called planetary nebulas. The core is left behind—tiny, dense, and still burning white hot. This is a white dwarf that continues to shine until it runs out of gas and beyond; it takes millions of years to cool. (They change color as they cool, but are always called "white.") White dwarfs are so dense, a matchbox full of matter from one would weigh several tons.

BIG BANGS—THE BLUE GIANT

These are the super heavyweights of the universe. They are huge

---

South America has earthworms up to 8 feet long, 3/4" around, and over one pound.

(25 times heavier than the sun) and incredibly hot (144,032°F [80,000°C]). They burn fast and go out with a real bang.

A blue giant starts with more fuel than any other star, but tears through it in just 3 million years. When running out of gas, it first swells up to a colossal supergiant (that would fill our solar system right out to Jupiter!), then "supernovas," exploding with incredible violence and brightness. (Past supernovas have been visible on Earth during the day.) The giant collapses in on itself, leaving a field of gravity so intense that not even light can escape—a black hole.

AWKWARD IN-BETWEENS—NEUTRON STARS AND PULSARS
Size does matter! Stars big enough to supernova, but not big enough to collapse into black holes, become neutron stars. These are little island-sized globes so dense that a pinhead of their matter would weigh a million tons! The first neutron stars were identified in the 1960s by the energy they give off. It's not usually light, but X-ray radiation. Unlike the constant light of visible stars, the radiation from many neutron stars pulses regularly as they spin (up to 30 times a second), hence the name "pulsar."

ODD BALLS—QUASARS
These are the mystery characters of the universe. Quasars ("quasi-stellar objects") are among the most distant objects astronomers have found and much about them remains a mystery. They produce staggering amounts of light. So much that although some are on the edge of the known universe, they can be seen by telescope from Earth. Astronomers have discovered that they are not stars, but the cores of extremely violent galaxies. They are the brightest objects ever found and, together with their close cousins the "radio galaxies" (which send out intense radiation instead of light), are also the biggest—as big as twice the distance between the Milky Way and our neighboring galaxy, Andromeda. That's over 4 million light years across!

It's pretty hard to believe, but astronomers are sure there are even weirder things out there, just waiting to be found…

THE ORIGINAL LOVE BUG

You're driving along a highway when something splats on your windshield, leaving a white streak. Followed by another splat, and another. Pretty soon, you can hardly see out.

Every summer, the deep American South swarms with harmless flies called lovebugs. Why "lovebugs?" Because they fly around while mating.

AN INSEPARABLE COUPLE
A mating pair of lovebugs look like a fly with wings at both ends. The large one is the female. As the male hangs on for dear life, going about his business, which is fertilization, the female continues to fly around, going about hers. After all, she only has three days to live, and she's likely to spend a third or more of it mating! Who can blame her? As the lovebugs fly around, the male just grabs the first female it can get its legs on and—bam!—they're a couple. If he can't find a lone female, he's not above breaking up a pair of mating lovebugs if he's larger than the other male.

THE ULTIMATE PROVIDER
The male provides for her in more ways than one. While they're flying around, he also provides a steady stream of proteins and carbohydrates along with his sperm. They both feed on pollen and nectar while they are on their—er—honeymoon.

Her most important item of business is to find a place to nest. Dead twigs, grass, and leaves are an ideal home for them, which she finds by their smell. If she's lucky, she'll find an appropriate nesting place to lay her eggs and happily set up housekeeping. Once that's done, though, she soon dies. But don't feel bad for her. She had a good life, a long life—for a lovebug.

UNLUCKY IN LOVE
The unlucky lovebug, on the other hand, is drawn to a nearby highway by her sense of smell. (To her, old exhaust fumes smell a lot like dead grass and leaves.) She senses a large expanse of ideal nesting ground, but only finds hot pavement. As she hovers in confusion, she eventually splats into a speeding windshield.

ARCHIMEDES—
THE GREEK STREAK

*Those crazy scientists. This one got so excited at his
discovery he ran naked through the streets.*

Archimedes (c. 287–212 B.C.), the Greek inventor and
mathematician, had just returned from studying in
Alexandria, Egypt, (a favorite hangout for scholars),
when King Hieron II of Syracuse summoned him. The king
wanted to know whether or not his crown was made entirely of
gold, and he figured that a brain like Archimedes would be able to
find out. Archimedes was at a loss. The king had given him strict
instructions not to damage the crown during his investigation.
How the heck could Archimedes determine the volume of the
crown without taking it apart?

THE NAKED TRUTH
As he was turning the problem over in his mind, Archimedes
decided to take a bath. And as he was sitting in the tub, he
noticed that the amount of water that flowed over its edge was
equal to the amount by which his body was immersed.

Archimedes had discovered the principle of buoyancy.
He then leaped out of the tub and (since he was in a public
bath) rushed to his home—naked. As he ran, he repeatedly
shouted "Eureka!"

ALL THAT GLITTERS
The story has an unhappy ending, but not for our hero. When
Archimedes measured the volume of water that the crown had
displaced, he found it was greater than the volume of water
displaced by a lump of gold of the same weight. This told him that
the goldsmith had substituted some of the gold in the crown with
a less dense material, probably silver. For his crime, the sneaky
goldsmith was executed.

MEAN MOUNTAINS

What makes some mountains so deadly? And so irresistible?

They're nature's beautiful—and brutal—endurance tests. Sometimes they offer the challenge of conquest, of going where only a select few can ever go; other times they offer only a punishing chance to cheat death. Climbers continue to struggle to the top of the world's meanest mountains, and every year, some die in the attempt.

ASCENT INTO GLORY

In 1953, Edmund Hillary and Tenzing Norgay were the first to reach the summit of Mt. Everest in the Himalayas—and the world thrilled to their accomplishment. By the late 1980s, amateurs were getting into the act, and by the 1990s, climbing was a chic way to spend one's time if one had the money. Wealthy amateurs could conquer famous slopes while guided by the best mountaineers in the world. They could also supply themselves with the latest in clothing and tent gear, not to mention cell phones that would call in rescuers if needed.

THE MOUNTAIN GODS STRIKE BACK

But in 1996, mountaineering came full circle. The world was once again jolted by news from Mt. Everest. This time, though, eight climbers had died in a storm there, including two famous mountaineering guides, Rob Hall of New Zealand and Scott Fischer from the U.S. As stories of the tragedy hit the global media, so did the collective realization that some mountains remained as unforgiving and deadly as ever.

DANGERS OF THE HIGH LIFE

What's so dangerous about the high life? For one thing, the glaciers. As they're pulled down toward the valleys by gravity, they crack, forming deep crevasses that can be hidden under snowfall, waiting to swallow up unwary climbers. Of course, all this moving ice and unstable snow also cause avalanches, rockfalls, and icefalls—just as dangerous.

Then there's the weather, which ranges from awful to lethal. For example, Mt. Washington in New Hampshire has recorded winds of over 231 mph (372 kph), the highest surface station recordings on the planet. (On some days, climbers who reach the summit of Mt. Washington have to hold on to the summit sign for dear life—literally—to avoid being blown about by the gales.) Even when there's no windstorm or blinding blizzard, the same temperatures that form glaciers can freeze a human to death.

HUMANS GO HOME

Up there, at over 6,000 feet (1,829 m), some people will experience mountain sickness: nausea, loss of appetite, exhaustion, and shortness of breath as the body tries to acclimatize to the lack of atmospheric pressure (or thin air) at high altitudes.

At 10,000 feet (3,048 m), about 75 percent of climbers succumb to it. Acute mountain sickness means less oxygen is in the bloodstream, which puts a strain on the heart and lungs, and means less oxygen is available to the muscles and the brain.

At 17,000 feet (5,182 m), you won't see plant or animal life—and human life isn't exactly welcomed either. Here's where the body begins to deteriorate through muscle wasting and weight loss. Breathing problems interfere with sleep. The higher you climb, the more deadly acute mountain sickness becomes. Sometimes it kills directly with high altitude cerebral edema—a leaking of the blood vessels in the brain—or with high altitude pulmonary edema, when the blood vessels leak into the lungs, filling them with liquid. Other times, a climber's oxygen-deprived mind simply gets so fuzzy that he or she will make stupid—and fatal—mistakes.

DEATH ON MT. HOOD

In May 2002, millions of TV watchers saw the lethal potential of mountaineering play out. Mt. Hood, Oregon's highest mountain, rises 11,240 feet (3,426 m) and attracts hundreds of climbers to what's known as a "beginner's climb." This is not to say it's easy. Over the past century the mountain has killed more than 125 climbers.

On May 31, three separate parties of climbers ascended the mountain. Members of each group were carefully roped together so that if one slipped, the others could pull him up. The highest climbers were about 800 feet (244 m) below the icy summit when one man slipped. Instead of being pulled to safety, his fall yanked his companions down the glacier. They slammed into three roped climbers below them, and the chain reaction continued. Seven men slid downhill before they collided into the third group. Soon nine men were skidding down icy slopes until they all disappeared into a crevasse that was 20 feet (6 m) deep.

Three of the climbers died, several were injured, and even the rescue (covered live on TV) took a disastrous turn when a helicopter airlifting the survivors was caught in a gust of wind and crashed. Somehow its crewmen survived, even though the helicopter rolled 1,000 feet (305 m) down the snowy mountain.

THE EIGER SANCTION

With these kinds of nightmares on a "beginner's" mountain, imagine what the "wall of death" is like. At 13,000 feet (3,962 m), the Eiger looms like a snow-covered spear above Grundwald, Switzerland, in the Bernese Alps. The word "eiger" is German for ogre and the Eiger's Nordwand (northern face) has an ogre's reputation because it's killed some of the world's best mountaineers. The route is so dangerous that for many years locals declared that anyone crazy enough to climb the north face was such an idiot that he wasn't worth rescuing.

Even Hollywood was clued in. In *The Eiger Sanction*, Clint Eastwood's character says that the mountain's north face might save him the trouble by killing his quarry for him. The Nordwand is a 6,000-foot (1,829 m) vertical slab of unstable rock and ice. Falling rock is such a common problem that most climbers scale the mountain only when freezing temperatures hold the rocks more firmly in place. As they cling to the steep slab, searching for firm holds in its crumbling rock and rotten ice, climbers are courting exposure to the Nordwand's continual avalanches and fierce *foehnsturms*—windstorms that can blow at over 100 mph (31 kph).

Some pros will tell you that the worst dangers of the Eiger are psychological. There's a history of tragic deaths that's too easy to remember while you're hanging on to an unstable rock over an abyss. As long as there are climbers who want to confront their ultimate fears, the Eiger will continue to hold a fascination—or idiocy depending on your point of view.

THE TOP OF THE WORLD

They call the Himalayas the "roof of the world"—does that make Mt. Everest the chimney top? At 29,028 feet (8,848 m), the world's tallest mountain remains the ultimate summit, the Holy

Laughing provides an aerobic workout for the body's diaphragm.

Grail of climbing. The statistics keep changing, but at present they stand at about one death for every six people who make it to the top.

In addition to the usual dangers, Everest's sheer height makes it deadly. At 26,000 feet (7,925 m) humans enter what's known as a "death zone" where humans can only stay temporarily. Nothing functions well there, including the heart, the digestive system, the lungs, and the brain. The body screams for rest and descent to a lower altitude, but there's still more than 3,000 feet (915 m) of hard climbing to the summit.

Along with skill and physical strength, good weather and luck are essential to make it to the top. Any setback that strands climbers in the death zone for too long can spell disaster, like the storm that killed Fischer and Hall in 1996, especially since a storm on Everest can mean hurricane-force winds and temperatures of −100°F (−73°C).

FAMOUS LAST WORDS

So why do they do it? George Leigh Mallory, the most famous pre–World War II mountain climber was on the lecture circuit, talking about his unsuccessful but hair-raising attempt to climb Everest in 1922 and trying to raise money for another foray. He managed to raise the money and tried again in 1924. Again, unsuccessfully, but this time he didn't live to talk about it. He and his partner were never seen again.

But Mallory's words live on. When someone in the audience in one of the lecture halls asked him why he wanted to climb Mt. Everest, he gave the famous answer, "Because it's there."

* * * * *

I have rivers without water,
Forests without trees,
Mountains without rocks
Towns without houses.

Answer: a map

I run through hills;
I veer around mountains.
I leap over rivers
and crawl through the forests.
Step out your door to find me.

Answer: the road

You dream an average of five times a night with each successive dream lasting longer.

LEAP SECONDS

The sky may not be falling, but Earth is slowing down.
We can't even trust it to tell the time by anymore.

Precise time measurement is essential. Without a universal time, global navigation and communications for cell phones or radio and TV broadcasts wouldn't work. The systems must be synchronized to the nanosecond. Keeping perfect time is the job of the U.S. Naval Observatory's Master Clock, which averages the time of extremely accurate atomic clocks worldwide.

TIME AND TIDE
The problem is that the earth's rotation isn't accurate enough to tell time by anymore. Over a century, the braking action of the ocean tides slows the earth's time by about two milliseconds per day (which makes our day two milliseconds longer than in 1900). What happens is that time measured in the traditional way, by calculations based on both rotation and the Master Clock's atomic time, tend to drift apart. (If you had a watch that lost a second every day, after a year it would be more than 6 minutes behind.)

YOU'VE HEARD OF LEAP YEARS?
How do we keep our time level with the Master Clock's universal time? The leap second—a whole extra second the Master Clock has to add to its day now and then, when its time and the earth's time are more than .9 seconds apart. If you were watching the Master Clock on a digital readout, it would look like this:
    ...11:59:59, 11:59:60 (!), 12:00:00 a.m., 12:00:01 ...
The exclamation mark is to draw your attention to the :60 seconds, because as a digital clock ticks past midnight (or any hour), it just goes :59–:00. The leap second is the :60.

   Leap seconds are not regular events, like leap years, because they depend on minute variations in the earth's rotation. Declaring leap seconds is the job of the International Earth Rotation Service. Usually, leap seconds are inserted on January 1 or July 1. Sometimes they happen annually (1992, 1993, and 1994 all had one in July). In the past years there have been fewer (1997, 1999).

   There'll be another soon, though—it's just a matter of time.

The computer was *Time*'s "Man of the Year" in 1982.

THE YEAR WITHOUT SUMMER

For most of the world, the summer of 1816 was more like winter.

It was so cold that year it drove some normally rugged New
Englanders to abandon their frozen crops and migrate to the
relatively balmy Midwest. No one suspected that what they
called "Eighteen hundred and froze to death" was caused by the
deadliest volcanic eruption in recorded history.

THE BIG BANG
Why should anyone connect the two events? Mount Tambora had
erupted more than a year before, on the other side of the world in
the Dutch East Indies. The first explosion was heard 1,000 miles
away. For the next few days, the mountain belched smoke. Five
days later, three columns of fire rose from the crater and combined
into one huge flame. Hurricanes of ash blasted through nearby
towns, blowing away houses and uprooting trees. The lava
engulfed two towns and 8,000 islanders. Thousands of survivors
fled to neighboring islands.

The huge, gray clouds drifted west and covered the downwind
islands with a blanket of ash two feet thick, killing all vegetation.
In total, some 82,000 people died of starvation and epidemics in
the months after the eruption. The fallout—over a million and a
half tons of dust and debris—took one year to spread globally.

THE REST OF THE WORLD
In 1816 Europe, temperatures plummeted. It rained or snowed
almost daily. Crops were ruined. Hunger was widespread and riots
broke out in Britain, France, and Switzerland. In Ireland, a cold
rain fell 142 out of 153 days and 65,000 people died of hunger and
from an ensuing typhus epidemic.

MONTPELIER, VERMONT
New England recorded its coldest year in 200 years. By June 8, the
streets of Montpelier were covered with a foot of snow. By August,
the Green and White Mountains were both white—with snow.

THE OTHER MONTPELIER
After Tambora's more famous neighbor, Mount Krakatoa, erupted

in 1883, researchers in Montpelier, France, measured a 20 percent decline in solar intensity. When they finally figured out what had caused the decline—a thin veil of volcanic dust—they zeroed in on Krakatoa. Even so, they never thought to link Tambora to the year without a summer.

AHA!

Finally, in the 1970s, a scientist studying ice cores in Greenland found a layer of acidic ash and matched it to the ash that had fallen with the snow of 1816. More scientists measured Tambora's humongous crater—almost four miles across and more than a half mile deep—and estimated that the volcano must have exploded with the force of a billion tons of TNT, or 60,000 times the force of the bombs dropped on Hiroshima.

LOOK IT UP IN THE INDEX

On the geologists' Volcanic Explosivity Index, which runs from zero to eight, Tambora scored a seven. On another scale, the Dust Veil Index (DVI), which measures how heavy an impact an eruption will have on the climate, Tambora scored an extremely high 1,500. Contrast Tambora's DVI with that of Mt. St. Helens, which had a DVI of a measly 1, indicating a light impact on the climate.

"I'VE CREATED A MONSTER!"

Three Europeans who had plenty to eat that year were Lord Byron and his friends Mary and Percy Bysshe Shelley. They whiled away that famous summer at Lake Geneva in Switzerland. The weather forced them to stay inside, and they passed the time thrilling each other with ghost stories. All of which inspired Mary Shelley to write her masterpiece, *Frankenstein*, which was published in 1818.

* * * * *

YOU WOULD THINK...

That woodpeckers would break their little necks, pecking away at trees all day. If you tried knocking your head against a tree trunk like the woodpecker does, you'd be in serious need of a brain surgeon. So why doesn't Woody get whiplash? The secret is, of course, that the woodpecker is custom built for a life of head banging. He's got an incredibly thick neck, a stronger than normal skull, and a cushioning space between the heavy outer membrane and the brain that protects him like a crash helmet. (And to top it all off, he's even got fine bristle feathers to protect his nostrils from wood dust.)

A half-ounce of gold can be stretched into a wire 25 miles long.

MAKE YOUR OWN ZOMBIE

If you thought zombies were just a bit of folklore, think again.

ZOMBIES

In 1982, a Canadian ethnobotanist named Wade Davis went to Haiti, where he met a man who claimed he'd been turned into a zombie and forced to work on a sugar plantation. Davis tracked down a *bokor*, a "voodoo wizard," who claimed to be able to make "zombie powder." The powder was sprinkled on the doorstep of the victim, who would absorb the powder through his feet and die. The bokor would dig the person up and—voila—a zombie.

Eventually Davis managed to get eight samples of the powder, which he ran through the gamut of scientific testing. His tests found a neurotoxin called tetrodoxin, which you can get from puffer fish, or *fugu*, found in Haitian waters. Tetrodoxin can paralyze you, making your breathing so shallow it would be easy to miss. Davis gave the powder to a pathologist, who tested it on rats. After 24 hours, the rats revived with no ill effect. The final step in creating a zombie requires something to scramble your faculties. Davis believes the secret is a hallucinogenic drug called datura. These findings made Davis something of a celebrity. He wrote a 1985 bestseller, *The Serpent and the Rainbow*, which he sold to Hollywood. The resulting horror movie belittled the voodoo religion. Some are skeptical of Davis's theory. Two tetrodoxin experts, C. Y. Kao and Takeshi Yasumoto, tested Davis's samples, but couldn't find enough tetrodoxin to have any effect.

VAMPIRES AND WEREWOLVES

In 1985, Canadian biochemist David Dolphin fingered a blood disease called porphyria as an explanation for vampirism. People with congenital erythropoietic porphyria are extremely sensitive to light, sometimes have psychological problems, and supposedly their symptoms worsen if they eat garlic. Porphyria sufferers have been down this road before. In 1964, it was said that porphyria caused lycanthropy—the delusion that you're a werewolf. While people with porphyria may not turn into vampires or werewolves, they do turn into kings and queens. The genetic disease worked its way into many of Europe's royal families, including Britain's.

I'VE GOT YOU UNDER MY SKIN

WARNING! The following information is not for the squeamish! We're going skin diving—literally—and we're going to meet creatures guaranteed to make your skin crawl. When you wake up screaming in the middle of the night, don't say we didn't warn you.

CALLING AGENT MULDER
The botfly has found a perfect nest for her larvae—and you're it! A native of Central and South America, the botfly uses mosquitoes and warm-blooded creatures to hatch her little baby botflies. Here's how it works: The female botfly glues her eggs to a mosquito's abdomen. The mosquito bites you, stabbing her way into your skin. As she sucks out your blood, the mosquito's body heat hatches the botfly eggs. The botfly larva crawls into the fresh mosquito bite and burrows into your skin. As it grows, it produces a painful, visibly wriggling, *X-Files*–type boil under your skin. After six weeks, a one-inch-long (2.5-cm-long) botfly, in its pupa stage, crawls out, leaving a nasty sore.

THE WORMS CRAWL IN...
Love those barefoot strolls on the beach? You may want to keep your sandals on, especially in Florida, which has the highest incidence of this creepy crawler in the U.S. Hookworms from dog or cat feces thrive in warm sand. Step on the larva and it quickly penetrates your skin. As the larva migrates through your skin, it leaves an extremely itchy, raised, red, snakelike track. The most commonly affected areas are the feet, hands, buttocks, and genitals. (So much for nude sunbathing.)

...THE WORMS CRAWL OUT
You'll be happy to know that by 1998, most of the 78,000 cases of guinea worm were from Sudan. Unless, of course, you live there. If you do, don't drink the water. If you ingest the guinea worm larvae, they stay in your stomach for three months, after which they mate and the male dies. The female bores her way through your body, usually heading for your lower legs or feet. Once she's

ensconced there, she grows to four or five feet long. It's now a year since you drank that contaminated water. You try to relieve the pain of the blister on your ankle by putting your foot in water, but the blister breaks and hundreds of thousands of tiny larvae are released. The nearly dead female worm now emerges from your foot through the open sore, which takes a few weeks.

OPENING MORE CANS OF WORMS

There is a four-inch-long worm that can cause your legs, arms, and genital areas to swell up several times their normal size. The disease is called elephantiasis because the afflicted limbs resemble those of an elephant. Again, the mosquito is to blame. Its bite injects larvae that lodge in the lymph system. As your immune system fights the invaders, the affected area becomes swollen, red, and painful. Medication will kill the worm but the damage is permanent. The lymph ducts remain blocked and the disfiguration caused by the excess tissue and fluid can only be reduced through surgery. Elephantiasis is a disease of the tropics that affects 117 million people in India, China, Indonesia, and Africa.

MORE TROPICAL WORMY THINGS

The tropical flatworm kills 200,000 people annually. You can become infected by swimming, bathing, or walking in flatworm-infested water. The larva of the flatworm attaches itself to your skin, bores through, and starts swimming in your blood vessels. The worm itself does little harm, but the thousands of eggs it produces can lead to internal bleeding and life-threatening lung and liver damage. The disease is called schistosomiasis and is common in the tropics and East Asia.

EYE SCREAM

Another parasite worms its way into your eye. The bite of a tiny black fly injects the larva of a parasitic worm, *Onchocerca volvulus*, after which the larva grows into a threadlike worm that slithers under your skin. The worms produce more larvae that migrate into the eye. The resulting statistics are sadly eye-popping: 350,000 people in Africa, Latin America, and the Middle East are blinded annually due to a fly bite.

GRILL IT TO KILL IT

Still with us? You're tough, but this might make you squirm. Half of all humans are infested with some sort of parasitic worm. Take the fairly common tapeworm. Their eggs or larvae can get into your gut when you eat raw or undercooked fish, beef, or pork. They attach themselves to the wall of your intestines and absorb some of your food. No wonder some of the symptoms are unexplained hunger and weight loss. Tapeworms can live in your intestines for 25 years and grow up to 30 feet (9 m) long! You may want to reconsider that order of sushi or steak tartare.

BOIL IT TO FOIL IT

There's nothing like the great outdoors and the delightful taste of water from a sparkling mountain stream. Think before you drink. You wouldn't drink from your toilet, and the answer to that oft-asked question, "Does a bear 'go' in the woods?" is yes. Which means that that sparkling mountain stream has probably been used as a toilet by some deer, bear, or beaver—or even a fellow hiker. Animal and human feces have contaminated much of the fresh water worldwide with an intestinal parasite called *Giardia lamblia*. (That includes those pure mountain streams in America's national parks.) *Giardia* is the most common cause of nonbacterial diarrhea in North America; two percent of the population of the U.S. is infected at any one time. *Giardia* causes diarrhea and stomach cramps that can last from a few weeks to a few months—or longer if it goes undiagnosed. The solution: Don't drink that water until you boil it for at least five minutes to kill all the critters.

THIS "MITE" SURPRISE YOU

We'll leave you thinking about a parasite that everyone has and that you can do nothing about. Your skin is inhabited by follicle mites, cousins of the spider. They live in your pores and hair follicles; they're all over your forehead, nose, cheeks, chin, and particularly in the roots of your eyelashes. They're only a hundredth of an inch long and can only be seen through a microscope. They crawl mouth-first into a follicle and embed their scaly bodies upside down in the skin to eat skin cells. Don't worry. Unlike the other parasites mentioned, they're harmless. That's a relief, huh?

**For more fun with parasites,
see "This Mite Surprise You" on page 188.**

BEAUTY OR BLIGHT?

One out of every twenty people has some sort of birthmark.

A small birthmark can seem mildly interesting, or even exotic—like the patch on Mikhail Gorbachev's head. At worst, it can blot out most of a face, like King James II of England, who was nicknamed "James of the Fiery Face."

IMPROVE YOUR VOCABULARY

We've got a new word for you: In most cases a birthmark is what's called a "nevus" (plural "nevi"), a clump of overgrown blood vessels under the skin. And yes, it's called a birthmark because a baby is born with it—the mark grows along with the child. To this day nobody really knows what causes a nevus. It doesn't seem to be genetic. But—probably because the effects can be so dramatic—there's been plenty of speculation in the past.

ACCORDING TO THE UNINTELLIGENTSIA

Both Aristotle and Hippocrates—a couple of supposedly brainy guys—thought that a pregnant mother could cause birthmarks in her babies by getting overexcited. And because people trusted Aristotle and Hippocrates, this view held sway for about 1,500 years. Mothers' fears, fantasies, and cravings got the blame.

Then, instead of getting better, it got worse. In medieval Europe, birthmarks were said to be the signature of the devil; a woman who had one was declared a witch, which could mean death by drowning or burning at the stake.

A GIRL JUST CAN'T WIN

Even if a birthmarked girl wasn't dunked or incarcerated (or worse) for witchcraft, she was still regarded as tainted. At a time when marriage was a girl's only possible "career path," few men would take a girl with a nevus. Even a small nevus on the neck of Anne Boleyn, Henry VIII's second wife, was enough for her to be accused of witchcraft, as well as the adultery she was beheaded for.

EEK!

Just as a lot of people used to believe that a harelip was caused when the path of a pregnant woman was crossed by a Belgian hare (which is where the "hare" came from), being frightened by a mouse was thought by country people to be the reason for bearing a child "stained" with a nevus. Another brilliant idea.

THE COMMONSENSE APPROACH

Then along came the "Father of Scientific Surgery," an English surgeon named John Hunter. He was a close friend of composer Franz Joseph Haydn, and really, really wanted to remove a harmless, but ugly, birthmark on Haydn's face. The composer refused—hard to blame him, since there were no anesthetics in those days. Haydn's refusal prompted Hunter to conduct the first scientific survey into birthmarks. Of course he found out that maternal imagination couldn't possibly be the cause of nevi. It didn't stop other medics from disagreeing, though, and articles arguing the opposite continued to be published in supposedly "learned" journals throughout the 19th century.

EGYPTIAN PRESCRIPTION

To this day, when pregnant Egyptian peasant women crave watermelons, grapes, or exotic vegetables, they are immediately given them. The cultural conviction is that the craving is the clamoring of the unborn child itself. If—the belief goes—the demand isn't satisfied, the child will be born with a birthmark shaped like the fruit or vegetable in question. The unfortunate father is responsible for giving his wife whatever she wants, no matter how difficult it is to find the groceries in question.

OUT, DAMNED SPOT!

For people who don't like their nevi, most can be removed or greatly improved with laser treatment. The lasers produce a short pulse of intense light that passes harmlessly through the outer layers of skin and is absorbed by the darker pigment. This disrupts the pigment, which the body's immune system eventually gets rid of. Studies have shown that most unwanted birthmarks require, on average, six to eight treatments to achieve a satisfactory fading.

* * * * *

"There are in fact two things, science and opinion;
the former begets knowledge, the latter ignorance."
—Hippocrates

DINOSAURS: HEY, WHAT HAPPENED?

They don't fit easily into a nutshell, but we're gonna try.

Dinosaurs first appeared in the Triassic period (about 220 million years ago) and disappeared at the end of the Cretaceous period (about 65 million years ago). Homo sapiens didn't show up until about 25,000 years ago, so it wasn't our fault. Who can we blame it on? There are two camps: the gradualists (who argue that the dinosaur population just declined and finally died out) and the catastrophists (who like to think that it was one disastrous event).

THE GRADUALISTS
Biological changes: Anything that made dinosaurs less competitive with other organisms, especially the mammals that were just starting to appear.
Overpopulation: The theory is that they might have eaten too much, destroying their food supply and thus starving to death.
Mammals: Hungry animals ate so many dinosaur eggs that dinosaurs couldn't reproduce enough to survive.
Disease: Everything from constipation to rickets.
Changes in climate: Drops or rises in temperature, rainfall, atmospheric pressure, etc.
Volcanic eruptions: If big enough, they would cut off UV light. (See the Catastrophists below for further elaboration.)
Continental drift: Related to shifts in the earth's axis, orbit, and/or magnetic field.

THE CATASTROPHISTS
This gang might have an edge, based on the discovery of a 110-mile-wide crater in the Yucatan Peninsula that's been dated to about 64.98 million years ago, made by a theoretical six-mile-wide extraterrestrial object. The dust and debris thrown into the atmosphere would have reduced sunlight enough to kill off most plants and have a domino effect on all organisms in the food chain.

THE BOTTOM LINE
Some experts argue that extinction is a natural result of evolution. (More than 90 percent of all species that ever existed have disappeared.) Has anyone thought that maybe after 150 million years, the dinosaurs just got bored and went away?

Zenith Radio developed the first TV remote control in 1950 and dubbed it "Lazy Bones."

SOMETHING FISHY ABOUT THE FUGU

Like fish? Some menus include fish that are so deadly your face could be on the table before you finish your meal. And they don't come with a Surgeon General's warning.

Fish and rice are the two staples of the Japanese diet. And the fugu fish, even though it packs a poison 1,200 times more powerful than cyanide (one to two milligrams can kill the average diner), is a particular favorite in the fish department.

NOT YOUR AVERAGE JOE BLOW

The fugu looks pretty much like an average fish most of the time. But it can swell itself up with water when it's threatened by predators, hence its generic name, "blowfish." Of course, if the predator happens to be a bubble-brain and makes lunch of the fish, it pays the ultimate price for its folly.

ONE FISH'S POISON...

Fugu, puffers, blowfish, globefish, swellfish—nearly a hundred species swim in the world's oceans, lakes, and rivers, most in tropical and subtropical waters—and almost all are poisonous. The poison is called tetrodotoxin, which works somewhat like curare. If there's an antidote, no one has discovered it.

All the same, the Japanese (who may pay the equivalent of $400 U.S. for one meal) consume about 25,000 tons of these lethal fish every year, the majority purchased from a small wholesale fish market in the city of Shimonoseki. Most of the fish stay in the country, but demand has lately been growing elsewhere.

YOU ARE WHAT YOU EAT

The fugu is a carnivore with teeth strong enough to chew coral and shellfish. In fact, its diet is the source of its poison—it doesn't contain toxin unless it eats tissue from toxin-producing fish such as the Xanthid crab, angelfish, goby, horseshoe crab, or the blue-ringed octopus. The fugu also ingests some microorganisms and bacteria that produce toxin, all of which concentrates in the fugu's liver, skin, ovaries, and certain muscles—and all of which must be

---

Pong was the world's first video game, released in 1972. Its creator went on to found Atari.

carefully removed before the fish can be eaten. Despite careful preparation, fugu accounts for about 50 deaths in Japan annually.

BACKACHE BEGONE!
Apart from having more gourmet cachet than Beluga caviar, the fugu is also enjoying some fame as the stuff of scientific break-throughs. Fugu toxin in a diluted form is being used to deaden the pain of arthritis and rheumatism. Wait—don't throw away your copper bracelets or flush your glucosamine. Deadening the pain is not the same as effecting a cure.

IT'S IN THE GENES
Japan's fugu—the torafugu, or rubripe—was the first vertebrate after humans to have its genome sequenced. The fugu earned this honor because of what the Fugu Genome Sequencing Consortium describes as "sequencing as a cost-effective, more genes-for-the-buck shortcut to a vertebrate gene set."

LONG LIVE THE EMPEROR!
So why do people eat the fugu? Some say it's the best-tasting fish in the universe. Others see it as an extreme sport, like snowboard-ing down Mount Everest. Some swear it's an aphrodisiac. Then there's the ego aspect—for the Japanese perhaps a powerful incen-tive, because eating the fugu is the one way the Japanese have to one-up the emperor. By decree, the emperor and members of the royal family are forbidden to so much as taste the fugu. Long live the emperor! And he probably will if he stays away from fugu.

* * * * *

STRENGTH IN NUMBERS—OR NOT
About 80 percent of all species of fish form schools that swim parallel to each other in synchronized movements. Individuals can be more easily picked off by predators. Being in one massive group does have some disadvantages. Large schools are easier to see from a distance. The fish in the middle of the school may become disoriented when a predator strikes, and some experts believe that in a large school, the trailing fish suffer from depleted oxygen levels in the water, leaving them more open to attack. Then there are the megapredators, like whale sharks, who'll take in the whole school in one mighty gulp. In that case, skipping school wouldn't be so bad.

ACCIDENTAL DISCOVERIES

Some of the biggest scientific breakthroughs have been the result of mistakes, coincidences, accidents, and even incompetence. Here are a handful of scientific bloopers that have changed the world for the better.

CLOSE THAT WINDOW!

Dr Alexander Fleming had spent most of 1928 working in a cramped laboratory in a London hospital. While working on the influenza virus he had filled his lab with culture dishes containing staphylococci bacteria. Exhausted from too many late nights, Fleming decided to take a holiday, giving strict instructions to his assistants on how to care for his precious specimens. On his return, however, Fleming was annoyed to find that someone had left a window open the previous night. The result? A foreign mold had flown in through the window and settled on the culture dishes. They were now useless. A devastated Fleming began collecting the dishes to dispose of when something caught his eye—while moldy patches were growing all over the plates, there were rings of clear space around these patches where there were no bacteria at all. Looking closer, Fleming saw that the bacteria closest to these clear rings were either shriveling or dissolving. The ever-astute doctor began experimenting with this strange mold that appeared to eat up bacteria. After years of research he was able to extract from it a drug—penicillin—that has gone on to save millions of lives. And it was all because someone forgot to close the window.

SNAKES ALIVE!

Nineteenth-century German chemist Friedrich Kekulé had a problem that had been nagging at him for years. He studied organic compounds (chemicals containing carbon atoms) and had found one compound—benzene—that behaved in a totally unpredictable way. Why it did this and what was the structure of its atoms consumed Kekulé's every waking hour. One evening in 1865 it also consumed his sleeping hours. Kekulé had what has

---

It takes over half a million trees to supply North Americans with their Sunday newspaper.

been called the most important dream of all time when he saw, in his mind's eye, atoms dancing in midair. The atoms formed chains that danced around like snakes. Then one of these "snakes" formed a circle with its head chasing its tail. In the next instant Kekulé awoke. He spent the rest of that night sketching in his notebook and making calculations. What he came up with was a revolutionary new proposal to explain the nature of benzene—rather than lining up in chains like other organic compounds, the atoms in benzene joined each other in a circle, just like the snake in his dream. This started a scientific revolution in which chemists combined organic compounds in new and exciting ways, allowing them to produce new products such as durable fabrics, more efficient fuels, and a host of lifesaving medicines.

SPILLING HIS GUTS

Dr. William Beaumont was a frustrated army surgeon. Stationed on Mackinac Island in Lake Huron as part of a peacekeeping force in 1822, he felt that his surgical skills were being wasted. With nothing to interrupt the tranquility of the island, Beaumont had little call for his talents. That was until one day when a drunken man accidentally discharged his rifle into the torso of a fur trader by the name of Alexis St. Martin.

Beaumont rushed to the young man's side to find a massive hole where his belly button had been. Part of the stomach was actually spilling out. Expecting the man to die, Beaumont cleaned the wound and applied a dressing. St. Martin did not die. Instead his stomach healed in a very strange way—the stomach attached itself to the wall of his chest while the hole remained open with a loose flap of lining hanging over it like a curtain. By pushing this aside people could actually see inside the man's stomach.

Dr. Beaumont immediately recognized the opportunity this presented. He could be the first man to study and examine a living digestive system. Convincing St. Martin to cooperate, Beaumont began experimenting by tying tiny bits of food on silk threads and inserting them in St. Martin's stomach. Periodically he would remove them to observe the state of digestion. Such experiments continued for a dozen years, leading to a new branch of science—the study of human digestion—and making celebrities of both Beaumont and St. Martin (whose tummy window stayed open for the rest of his life).

The earliest horse was about the size of a fox terrier.

A CLOSER LOOK

Hans Lippershey was a 17th-century maker of eyeglasses. One morning, having just completed a pair of lenses, he stood in his shop doorway and inspected his work for imperfections. As a final test he held both lenses up to the light and checked for minute flaws. What he saw next caused Lippershay to stagger back in amazement. Shaking his head in disbelief, he put the lenses up to his eyes once more. Again it happened—the church tower in the distance leapt out at him!

Hans had stumbled upon a way to make distant objects appear as if they were right in front of you. Lippershey had looked through two lenses at the same time—one concave (curved inward), the other convex (curved outward). Seeing a quick buck, he mounted the two lenses on a board and charged his customers to take a closer look at the distant church tower. After some experimentation he mounted the lenses inside a hollow tube, dubbing the nifty device his *kijkglas* ("look glass").

We know it as the telescope.

* * * * *

"People think of the inventor as a screwball, but no one ever asks the inventor what he thinks of other people."

—*Charles F. Kettering*

"There is a correlation between the creative and the screwball. So we must suffer the screwball gladly."

—*Kingman Brewster*

"Accident is the name of the greatest of all inventors."

—*Mark Twain*

Galileo made the first thermometer in around 1600.

BALANCING ACT

*With all the different forces acting upon us, you'd think it would
be a major task just to keep our balance. So why is it so easy?*

Everything has a center of gravity. If you balance something
lengthwise across your finger (say, a pencil or a yardstick), its
center of gravity is just above where your finger is.

Your body has a center of gravity, too. It's about two inches (5
cm) below your navel and inside you about halfway between your
front and back—it's the point where gravity is pulling the
strongest. (Of course, it's imaginary, like the equator.) You may
not know it, but you're constantly adjusting and readjusting your
balance as you stand, while your body makes the most minute
corrections. Ask any yoga student.

YOUR LEFT FOOT
How does your body know how to make these adjustments? Your
sense of balance comes from three sources: the eye, the inner ear,
and kinesthetic senses (what your other senses tell you is your
body's position in space, like—without looking—where your left
foot is). If one source disagrees with the others, you get dizzy.

YOU'RE OBLIVIOUS
Let's go behind the scenes for a moment, inside your inner ear,
where three tiny semicircular canals reside—you remember hearing about them in school. What you might not remember are the
two very small sacs behind them. Both the canals and the sacs are
filled with fluid and lined with hair cells. Also in there are tiny
grains of calcium carbonate and protein called otoliths (a.k.a. ear
stones). They roll back and forth, responding to things like gravity, speed, and motion. Their movement bends the hairs, which in
turn sends impulses to the brain so it can determine body motion
and position, taking into account the force of gravity, the wind
direction, and any other factors that could affect your balance—all
in a split second. And without you knowing.

Among the many ingredients found in dynamite are peanuts.

WALKING TALL

*The day that your ancestors decided to walk upright
was the day that your back problems began.*

D o you get backaches? If so, you're not alone. Former
Surgeon General C. Everett Koop estimates that 80 to 90
percent of the population will suffer at least one debilitating episode of low back pain (LBP) in their lives. And 100
percent of us can blame it on Mother Nature.

STAND UP AND BE COUNTED

We started out as quadrupeds, and somewhere along the human
evolutionary path our ancestors developed the ability to walk
upright and we never got back down to earth again. One of our
ancestors was very likely the *Australopithecus africanus*, who first
stood up on the African plains over 2 million years ago.

Fossil remains show that *Australopithecus africanus* (let's call
him AA for short) had a spine similar to a human's. Some anthro-
pologists believe that as Africa's climate grew hotter and drier, its
forests shrank, so Grandpa AA's ancestors were forced to come
down from the trees and learn to hunt on open ground, where
standing upright was an advantage in spotting food or prey.

DISHEARTENING NEWS

Being upright had its disadvantages. For one thing, bipeds had to
work harder than quadrupeds just to get around. (Try chasing your
dog sometime and your disadvantage will become obvious.) And
walking upright made blood circulation more difficult. Simply put,
if you're on all fours, your heart (along with your liver, lungs, and
other organs) wouldn't be that much higher, if at all, than your
hips. But if you're standing upright, your heart can be a couple of
feet above your hips, so those muscles in your legs have to pump
blood two feet farther up.

THANKS, MOM!

To give us the ability to walk upright, Mother Nature fitted us
with bigger lower vertebrae (the bones of the spine) to support the
weight of the upper body. She also gave us plenty of tendons and
ligaments to tie the vertebrae together and keep them from falling
over each other.

TALKING BACK TO MOM
But the problem is that these ligaments are smaller down at the lower part of the spine, even though they're the ones that have to support more of the weight of a standing biped. Another problem is that the blood supply to the lowest vertebrae and spinal discs is smaller than the blood supply to the higher vertebrae. Not a great engineering job.

MORE BACK TALK
And it's not just your poor lower back that has design defects. Becoming a biped changed the position of the arm bone in the shoulder girdle so that the cartilage there wears out prematurely. By the time you're 35, your shoulder cartilage has seen its best days. Bipeds like us also put extra stress on knees, ankles, and feet. As the years go by, the stress causes damage there, too.

BACK TO THE DRAWING BOARD
Scientists who study aging think that a few changes in our basic body design would help us have longer, healthier lives. If we were shorter, we'd have a low center of gravity. If we had a forward-tilting torso, it would relieve pressure on our spines and prevent ruptured or slipped discs. If we had thicker discs, stronger tendons and ligaments, and bigger hamstring muscles in our legs...

IT'S NOT ALL BAD
But wait. There are benefits: When you're not walking on your knuckles, it's easier to use your hands to make tools, and toolmaking helped develop human intelligence. Being bipedal also made it easier for males to carry food longer distances and deliver it to their chosen females and their offspring. Females could forage faster; the odds of infant survival increased. All of which contributed to the survival of the species.

And if being a smart, family-oriented biped doesn't do it for you, what about sex? Continuous sex, that is. Walking upright was the first step away from the kind of sex that nonhuman primates have—based on when a female goes into heat—and the first step toward continuous, any-old-time, sexual activity.

So there you have it. Granny and Gramps *Australopithecus* traded the potential of plenty of sex for the likelihood of a bad back when they began to walk tall. Can you blame them?

It takes seven minutes for the average person to fall asleep.

ASK UNCLE JOHN: IN THE BATHROOM

We spent time flushing the toilet so you wouldn't have to.

Dear Uncle John:
Is it true that water in sinks and toilets swirls in one direction in the Northern Hemisphere and in the opposite direction in the Southern Hemisphere? And what happens to the water in the toilet bowl if you're on the equator?

If you flush a toilet on the equator, the toilet will actually explode. So don't do it! Ah, we're just messing with your head. The idea that sink or toilet water swirls one way or another depending on what hemisphere you're in is pretty much completely wrong.

The belief in differently draining water goes back to the Coriolis force, which is caused by the rotation of the earth, and affects large weather systems. For example, hurricanes and cyclones in the Northern Hemisphere rotate in a counterclockwise direction, while those in the Southern Hemisphere rotate clockwise.

(So what happens to a hurricane when it moves from one hemisphere to another? Nothing, because hurricanes don't leave their hemispheres of origin—in fact, they don't even form within five degrees of the equator, because the Coriolis forces at the equator are too weak to allow it to happen.)

The earth's rotation doesn't do the same thing to your toilet water. The effect of the Coriolis force in the average toilet is less than a millionth the force of gravity. In real life, it does almost nothing to your sink or toilet water that counteracting forces like the shape of your toilet bowl or your dog lapping out of the john can't overcome. Your water drains in all sorts of directions, from Perth to Peoria.

Dear Uncle John:
I get into the shower, and after a few minutes, my shower curtain starts attacking me. What's up with that? Is it possessed?

This is one of those things that everyone's wondered about for years, but the explanation for this weird, clingy shower curtain

---

Over 75% of all of the world's countries lie north of the equator.

behavior didn't come about until 2001—and it required some pretty intense physical modeling on computers to figure it out. Now, you may ask, who spends his time modeling the physics of a clingy shower curtain? The answer: David Schmidt, a professor of mechanical engineering at the University of Massachusetts.

Here's what Schmidt did. First, he created a computer model of his mother-in-law's bathtub. No, really. Having done this, he filled the virtual bathtub with thousands of computerized "cells" that measured pressure and velocity. Then he turned on the virtual showerhead to see what would happen.

What Schmidt discovered was that a typical shower creates a miniature, spinning weather system, caused in part by the aerodynamic drag that water droplets encounter when they spritz out of the showerhead. In the center of this tiny weather system is a low-pressure area that sucks on the shower curtain. The top of the shower curtain is held in place by the curtain rod, but the bottom of the curtain is free to wander. And so it does. No, it's not earth-shattering science, but it is one less thing for you to wonder about.

Dear Uncle John:
I was told that if you put soap on your bathroom mirror and then wipe it off after it dries, the next time you shower, your mirror won't fog up. Is this true, and if so, how does it work?

It should probably work, and the reason is because in addition to getting your hands and body all germ-free and squeaky clean, soap has another quality as well. It acts as a "surfactant." What surfactants do, basically, is lower the surface tension of water, making it "wetter" and less able to form droplets. Surface tension is an important element in fogging up your mirror because it lets water droplets form and grow on the mirror's surface. Coating your mirror with soap and then wiping it off leaves a bit of soap residue on the mirror's surface, so later, when you shower, water that collects is unable to generate the surface tension that allows it to bead. Instead, it just slides down the mirror. There you have it, no misting.

But when you're soaping up your mirror, do remember the important "wiping off" step. If you don't, your mirror won't steam up, but you still won't be able to see through it because you have a layer of dried soap on your mirror.

10 THINGS SCIENCE FICTION GOT WRONG

*We realize that in the phrase "science fiction,"
"fiction" gets equal billing with "science," but come on!*

Most of the time we're willing to shovel down the popcorn and watch Yoda lift X-Wings out of the swamp using nothing but the Force and a smattering of questionably parsed English, or let Jean-Luc Picard get the *Enterprise* out of a scrape by the convenient discovery of yet *another* type of particle beam. But every once in a while we just have to vent about some of the truly egregious "fiction" in science fiction.

1. Sounds in space: The tag line from *Alien* got it right: "In space, no one can hear you scream." The reason no one can hear you scream is that sound needs air to travel in, and there's none in space. Most of space is a hard vacuum, with a molecule or two of hydrogen floating around in every cubic meter—not nearly enough to transmit sound. Every sound in the movies, from photon torpedoes and laser beams to exploding starships and hyperspace booms, would never happen in real life. For that matter, you'd never see laser beams in space either, since in a vacuum there's no medium to reveal them. So a real-life laser dogfight in space would be really boring to watch.

2. Faster-than-light travel: Warp drives and hyperspace are very useful in science fiction, but there's one catch. According to Einstein, the speed of light isn't just a good idea, it's the law. Nothing can go faster than the speed of light in a vacuum (that's about 186,000 miles per second). Even inching toward the speed of light is difficult—immense energy is required to get to even a fraction of the speed of light, and the closer you get to the speed of light, the more energy is required. The amount of energy you'd need to achieve the speed of light is infinite (i.e., more than you've got, even with those supercool long-lasting batteries). So just tossing in a few more dilithium crystals into the warp drives isn't going to make it happen.

There *are* loopholes in our understanding of physics that make faster-than-light travel *theoretically* possible. For example, it's theoretically possible to create a "bubble" of space that breaks itself off from other space and moves faster than light relative to that space (all the while everything inside both "spaces" moves no faster than the speed of light). This is known as an Alcubierre Warp Bubble. The catch (there had to be one) is that these bubbles require the existence of exotic matter that has negative energy, and wouldn't you know, there's not really any lying around, and it's not clear that any actually exists.

3. Laser bolts you can dodge: Aside from the issue of Imperial Stormtroopers being unable to hit the side of an AT-AT, let's review a fundamental fact of light (which is what lasers are): It travels at 186,000 miles per second. So the idea of ducking before the laser hits you is just plain silly. Not to mention, of course, the idea of a laser bolt being visible as a streak that has a beginning, a middle, and an end. If you were zapped by a laser from a laser gun, it'd look like a single stream of light, with one end attached to the barrel of said gun and the other end attached to whatever portion of your head hadn't melted yet (assuming you're having your laser battle somewhere where there's enough air around to illuminate the entire beam). Most "laser beams" in science fiction movies travel slower than bullets do today. Let's see Obi-Wan whip his lightsaber around fast enough to stop the spray from a Mac-10 (and let's not even *begin* to talk about all the things wrong with a sword made of light).

4. Human-looking aliens: This is endemic on the various *Star Trek* series, where creatures from entirely different sectors of the universe look just like humans, except for the occasional bulging ridge on their foreheads. Yes, this is the result of having only humans at casting calls, but in a larger sense, all these "humanoid" variations ain't gonna happen. Look, humans evolved on Earth and share a basic body format (four limbs, one head, side-to-side symmetry) with just about every other vertebrate on the planet. It's a form that works fine for this planet, but not even every vertebrate sticks with it (see: snakes, whales, seals, etc.). Given that any planet with life on it will have that life evolves in its own way, the chances of the universe being stocked with chesty alien princesses who crave human starship captains is slim at best. Related to this is the following.

5. Half-breed aliens: Humans don't even interbreed with other species here on Earth. Our DNA is simply too different from other species to allow such a mating to produce offspring. Given this, what are the chances of successful mating with an alien species that may not even have DNA as its genetic encoding medium? Also, going back to the idea that aliens probably won't look like humans, how would you do it, anyway? It's not exactly the "Insert Tab A into Slot B" proposition it would be here at home.

6. Brain-sucking aliens: Ditto aliens that control your body by using your brains, or gestate in your chest or whatnot. Let's posit that any creature that controls the brain of any other creature (not that any exist here on Earth) does so only after a few million years of what's called "speciation"—i.e., one species eventually enters into a symbiotic relationship with another species. This relationship would have to be pretty specific, as symbiotic relationships are here on Earth. Which is to say, just because you're in a symbiotic relationship with one species doesn't mean it transfers over to another species, especially an alien species, whose body chemistry, DNA, brain wiring, etc., isn't even remotely close to your own. So don't worry about the "Puppet Master" scenario too much, or that you'll be nothing more than a glorified egg sac for some nasty breed of space monster.

7. Shape-shifting aliens: Shape-changing aliens are all very well, but there's a tiny problem in having a roughly human-sized lump of alien protoplasm turning itself into, say, a rat, to scurry around in the ventilation shaft: Where does the rest of the alien go? You can't just make 99 percent of your mass disappear into thin air (or reappear, as the case may be); it has to go somewhere. Unless that "rat" is running around with the highly compressed mass of a human-sized object (which presents its own problems), shape-shifting into different-sized objects is not very likely (one of the smart things about *Terminator 2* was that the T-1000 only shape-shifted into things of roughly the same mass, like human beings or a floor).

8. Time travel: Got an itch to spend time in Arthurian England? Or perhaps Gettysburg during the Civil War? The same relativistic principles that keep us from going faster than light also keep us from traveling backward in time and messing with the past. It's possible to *slow down* time—the closer you get to the speed of light, the slower time moves for you relative to your original frame of reference—but to get the clock spinning in the other direction would require you to go faster than light, and you can't do that. Again, there are theoretical loopholes that could allow it—wormholes, actually, which are "tunnels" in the fabric of space-time

The smallest single cell in a man's body is his sperm.

that could possibly allow travel back in time. But once again, keeping these wormholes open would require exotic matter with negative energy. Got any? Neither do we.

9. The planetary gravity scam: Everywhere you go in science fiction, people are walking around like they weigh just what they do on Earth. Chances of that happening in the real universe? Slim. Consider our own solar system. On Mars, a 180-pound man would weigh 70 pounds; on Jupiter, 424 pounds (not that you can walk on Jupiter, which has no solid surface). That man on the moon? Just 30 pounds. The man's mass is the same, it's just that different planets have different gravitational pulls. The idea that all the planets that humans might visit would exactly match Earth's own gravitational profile is a little much. As is, alternately, the idea that all alien creatures would be as comfortable in our gravitational field as we are.

10. The planetary sameness principle: The desert planet of Tatooine. The ice planet of Hoth. The jungle planet of Dagobah. What do these planets all have in common? One planetary-wide ecosystem. Which isn't too likely. Our own planet has varying zones and ecological areas: desert, tundra, jungle, and so on; other planets in the system also show marked zones of varying atmospheric and weather patterns. Mars has ice caps as well as (relatively) temperate zones; Jupiter has distinct weather systems based in different areas on its globe. The planets that show a sameness are the ones we couldn't live on. Venus is all desert, but that's because a runaway greenhouse effect makes it hot enough to melt lead. Pluto is all ice, but it's so far away from the Sun that its atmosphere freezes for most of its orbit. There may well be purely desert or jungle planets, but most planets we'd want to live on would probably be able to accommodate both.

* * * * *

"If they put one man on the moon,
why can't they put them all there?"

—*Anonymous*

"The marvels of modern technology include the development of a soda can which, when discarded, will last forever—and a…car, when properly cared for, will rust out in two or three years."

—*Paul Harwitz*

Catgut, used in tennis rackets, comes from sheep and not cats.

FRANKENFOODS

Available at your local supermarket.

Scientists who manipulate genes in plants will tell you that they aren't doing anything different than what farmers have always done. And it's true. For centuries, they've used traditional breeding techniques to change crops in order to get bigger apples, better-tasting melons, heartier wheat, fluffier popcorn, and redder roses. Farmers did it by practicing old-fashioned sexual methods of mixing the pollen of similar plants in the same (almost) way that plants themselves had been doing all along.

A FLY IN YOUR PEA SOUP?
In most peoples' minds, traditional plant breeding is a whole different ballgame from what scientists can do now. Molecular biology has given researchers the power to ignore sexual reproduction when it comes to plant breeding. They can take specific genes from one plant and insert them directly into another plant, or even take genes from a completely different organism like an animal or bacteria and put those genes in a plant. The resulting plants are what we call "transgenic," or genetically modified (GM). This has been going on for about 25 years.

PSSST! DON'T ORDER THE POTATO SURPRISE
The first famous genetically modified crop was the FlavrSavr tomato. It was designed to resist bruising to increase its shelf life. But the FlavrSavr wasn't a true transgenic plant, because no new genes were added—some of its existing genes were turned off.

The first real GM crops came in 1983 with petunias and tobacco. Potatoes and soybeans followed in 1987, and then corn in 1990. Since then, over 50 types of transgenic crops have been developed. As you can imagine, lots more are currently hanging around labs and greenhouses, being tested.

Guess we've been eating them all along and didn't know it.

I'LL HAVE THE FRANKENBEANS
Why do scientists make transgenic crops? One obvious reason is that a lot of them work for agribusiness corporations that want to sell these new crops to farmers around the world. Beyond that, they want to create crops with greater and more nutritious

Rats are easy to poison because they cannot vomit.

yields—like wheat with increased gluten to make better bread, potatoes with extra starch, or beans with more protein.

FROZEN TOMATOES
Scientists also want to create crops that can thrive in unusual environments—like extreme cold. There are tomatoes, for example, that have been altered with genes from an Arctic flounder to make them resistant to frost.

CROSSING APPLES WITH...MOTHS?
Scientists want to create crops that are resistant to disease and pests so farmers can use less pesticide. They're working on altering apples with a gene taken from a moth to make the apple tree resistant to fire blight, a disease that destroys millions of dollars worth of apples worldwide every year.

BOLL WEEVIL BEWARE
Corn and cotton have been transformed with genes from a bacterium to make them poisonous to destructive insects.

WE'RE DOING IT FOR YOUR OWN GOOD!
Other reasons to transform crops are all about marketing and farming:

Did you know it's possible to grow coffee beans that are already decaffeinated?

We could also have smart crops transformed with a gene from a lightning bug that would glow when they need water.

More ambitious plans include transforming apples so they contain a vaccine for childhood diseases; an apple a day really would keep the doctor away.

All these goals sound, by and large, like good things, but there's still a lot of controversy over genetically altered crops.

BRAND X
The major concern about GM crops is the unknown. Transgenic plants are new. Nobody knows what the long-term results of genetic alterations could be. They'll almost certainly mean a loss of diversity among crops if agribusiness corporations gain complete control of the commercial seed market.

SOMETIMES YOU FEEL LIKE A NUT, SOMETIMES YOU DON'T
Allergies are a big concern, too. If you're allergic to peanuts and

peanut genes are used in corn, eating that corn could trigger an allergic reaction. And if scientists start switching genes between plants without supervision, there might be no way to know what allergen genes are in the food you're eating.

In the mid-1990s, soybeans altered with Brazil nut genes to increase nutrition were removed from the market because the soybeans could trigger reactions in people allergic to nuts.

POOR BUTTERFLY
Another concern about GM crops is that genes might escape from the altered plants into the environment where they could have unintended consequences. This has already happened. The most famous case of gene escape was Bt corn, which had been transformed with a gene from a bacterium—*Bacillus thuringiensis* (Bt). The bacterium creates a toxin that kills a pest called the corn borer. The transformed corn makes the same toxin, so when the corn borer chomps on a leaf, it gets a mouthful of poison and dies. But the pollen from Bt corn blows around, as pollen does; it settles on milkweed and kills harmless Monarch butterflies.

SHOPPING AT UN-SAFEWAY
Opponents of genetic modification point to these problems as an example of science gone wild. Some consumers refuse to buy these products in the supermarket, more so in Europe than in America. Of course that assumes you know GM food when you see it—it isn't like you can squeeze it or thump it to find out. In fact, over 50 percent of processed foods in American stores already contain altered soybeans, canola, or corn. Some people want to outlaw GM foods, or at leaast require labeling so you know someone's added flounder genes to your BLT.

ATTACK OF THE GIANT CUCUMBERS
Despite the protests, it's likely that GM foods will continue to be developed. Unless, of course, there's some major disaster like an army of intelligent but evil cucumbers emerging from fields across this nation. But that probably won't happen.

Or will it?

SILLY GOOSE

Did someone say "silly?"

The goose may have a dimwitted image, but here are a few reasons why they deserve a closer gander.

GIMME A V!
Geese fly together in a V formation for a reason: It adds a 71 percent greater flying range than if each bird flew alone. The uplift the V creates adds that much momentum. The goose who flies at the front doesn't benefit from this; he's the hardest-working goose in the gaggle. When he gets tired, he falls back into the formation and the bird behind him takes over for a while.

Meanwhile, in the middle, the rest of the geese act as cheerleaders. They honk regularly to spur on the hard workers at the front. And if one of their ranks gets sick or injured and has to drop to the ground, he isn't abandoned. Two "nurse" geese follow him down and look after him until he's ready to take to the air again or until he dies. They'll then wait for another V formation to pass by and join its ranks.

While most birds travel at relatively low levels when they migrate, the goose knows that higher altitudes mean more favorable winds. Mountaineers in the Himalayas have seen geese flying over their heads at heights of up to 29,500 feet.

AT HOME WITH MR. AND MRS. GOOSE
Geese mate for life. They practice monogamy and cooperation in raising the kids. And protective? Just try going near their goslings; they're not afraid of anything, which, come to think of it, might be a little stupid.

CAUTION: GEESE AT WORK
Anyway, this overprotectiveness extends to any place they consider their turf. That's why the U.S. Army's 32nd Air Defense Command in the Federal Republic of Germany has recruited a gaggle of 900 geese to watch its communications, radar, and air-defense equipment.

ON THIS FARM HE HAD SOME GEESE...
A variety of the white Chinese Cotton goose works California cotton farms; they love weeds but ignore the cotton plants. The cost of using goose labor is about $9 an acre compared to $75 an acre for human labor.

The amount of carbon in the human body could fill about 9,000 pencils.

SUCCESS IN SPORTS CAN DEPEND ON DE FEET

Looking for a way to get better at sports and aerobics? Look down.

If we weren't so used to them we'd probably think of our feet as miracles. Mobile, complex miracles made up of 26 bones, 33 joints, and 112 ligaments, not to mention all the nerves, blood vessels, and tendons that combine to form your personal transportation network. Your feet balance, support, and propel you through sports. Whether it's rock climbing, softball, bowling, soccer, boxing, or basketball, you've got a lot riding, er, standing, on your feet.

A MIRACULOUS FEET OF ENGINEERING
On a mile run, your amazing feet endure about 1,500 heel strikes at a force over two times the body's weight. To a climber, they're grippers and levers. To a skater, they're accelerators, steering mechanisms, brakes, and shock absorbers. To a high jumper, they're levers and launching pads. Yet for all their versatility, your remarkable "feets" of engineering may never have been intended to hit the ground at all.

A BRIEF FOOT NOTE IN HISTORY
Recent fossil discoveries in Latvia and Estonia indicate that one of our earliest ancestors crept out of the sea on four stubby fins (not feet). Fossil remains of our likely hominid ancestors show that their feet were suited for grasping, climbing, and "hanging out" in African trees. Your feet are kind of an evolutionary afterthought.

ARC D'TRIUMPH
Watching Tiger Woods swing a golf club, you may not notice how well balanced he is on the balls of his feet. When Michael Jordan leaps to dunk a basket, few people comment on Jordan's feet as carefully placed levers that launch him into high-flying dynamics. Similarly, when Serena Williams smashes a tennis ball over the net at Wimbledon, you're probably not concentrating on the way her feet pivot as she moves side to side or cuts to the net for a

return volley. But in golf, basketball, and tennis, as in most other sports, feet are the literal foundation of an athlete's performance.

Your feet are comprised of three bony arches: a tall one along the inner edge of the foot, a smaller arch on the outer edge, and the curve that runs the width of the foot between the ball and heel. Together they form an arched vault that not only distributes your weight, but is also flexible enough to help you move.

A MOVING TRIBUTE

The ligaments that bind the bones of your arch are elastic, so they can flatten out, then spring back to shape. When you take a step, your foot rolls outward and your arch flattens and stiffens into a lever to push your foot off the ground. Then your arch springs back to a curve with an added bounce that propels you along. When you set your foot down, your arch rolls outward and becomes flexible to absorb impact.

With every step your foot propels you, stabilizes you, and absorbs shock—all while supporting your weight. How difficult is this? The footwear industry has spent millions researching shoes stiff enough to stabilize your foot and cushioned enough to absorb shock. They're still searching for the perfect combination.

IF THE FOOT FITS

Every foot is unique. A key to athletic success is hooking up the right athlete to the right sport, and even small structural differences in our feet can determine whether we can be a star at the 100-meter hurdles or a powerhouse on the tennis court.

TOE-TAL ATHLETIC ABILITY

Talent scouts who are searching for speedy quarterbacks, sprinters, or base-stealing ballplayers, might do well do examine a candidate's big toe. For most of us, the big toe isn't as long as the next one. But some people have big toes that protrude out beyond the second toe. These fortunate few have an advantage over the rest of us when they need speed. They can lean their weight onto their big toe to push off and get a fast start. The second toe is not as strong and can only exert about half as much force.

Other lucky athletes might not have extra inches on their big toe, but they have a unique advantage in the first metatarsal bone, which is attached to their big toe. If the first metatarsal bone hangs lower than the other metatarsals (the bones to the other

Astronauts cannot be over six feet tall.

toes), then the big toe will also hang lower than their other toes. Athletes with a low first metatarsal can also put weight on their big toe, pushing off for a "toe-tally" fast start.

THE FEET SMELL OF SUCCESS

If your big toes are "just average," don't fret. There are other ways to take advantage of the sports equipment attached to your ankles.

Do your feet tend to roll outward and make your arch more stiff and rigid? You might want to try out for track or volleyball. Rigid feet are good levers that make running and jumping easier.

Perhaps your feet tend to roll inward and your arches are extremely flexible. That could give you an advantage at tennis or aerobic dancing. Flexible feet are better at handling constant changes in direction with quick, short pivots.

People who've been told they have flat feet are often wary of participating in sports. But most flat feet are just feet with lower arches—and they have their own advantages. They usually fall in the category of flexible feet with good range of motion. Even just plain big feet can be an advantage in swimming (think flippers).

NEGLECTING YOUR FEET CAN LEAD TO "DE FEET"

Both rigid and flexible feet have their downsides. Rigid feet don't absorb shock well, which can lead to bruised and even broken bones. Flexible feet can lack stability, which puts added strain on feet, ankles, and legs; this can cause sprains, charley horses, and shin splints. In fact, just as feet can give you an extra advantage in sports, neglecting them can mean even more.

Close to 600,000 people a year in the U.S. make a trip to a hospital emergency room because of basketball-related injuries. Most often, the injured parties are playing on an uneven surface and their foot twists, which in turn flips (and sometimes breaks) their ankle.

WHEN FEET GET NAKED

Nowhere is the miracle of the foot more obvious than when running—especially if the runner is barefoot. In 1960, at the Rome Olympics, Abebe Bikila of Ethiopia shocked the world when he won the marathon and set a new world record—in his bare feet! Zola Budd of South Africa, another great barefoot runner, once held the women's world record for the 5,000 meters.

Sports scientists are paying more attention to the performance

Chickens are the closest living relative of the T. rex.

and health of barefoot runners. Research has shown that the bare foot—which has sensitive sensory mechanisms for judging impact and absorbing shock—can do a better job of avoiding impact injury than cushioned running shoes.

Since there are so few barefoot joggers, there haven't been any controlled studies of whether bare feet are really better than shoes. But over 50 years ago, a study from the *Journal of Chiropodists* (foot doctors) reported that rickshaw coolies (who spent long days running and pulling passengers on hard roads) had healthier feet than shoe-wearing, sedentary Westerners!

NO FEET DOESN'T MEAN DEFEAT

Despite everything we've said so far about the importance of feet, we have to mention one superathlete who has no feet at all.

In 1998, Tony Volpentest's 100-meter world record of 11.36 seconds was less than 2 seconds behind the Olympian Donovan Bailey's world record of 9.84 seconds for the same distance. The difference was that Volpentest, who was born without hands or feet, ran in the Paralympics (for people with disabilities) on carbon-graphite feet bolted to carbon-composite sockets that encased his legs. These prosthetics were designed to give Volpentest's artificial feet stiffness and springiness while absorbing the shocks of impact.

Pretty much like nature designed our feet.

* * * * *

"Feets don't fail me now." —Anonymous

"The human foot is a masterpiece of engineering and a work of art."
—Leonardo da Vinci

According to the American Podiatric Medical Association, the average person takes 8,000 to 10,000 steps a day, which they estimate add up to 115,000 miles in a lifetime—four times the circumference of the globe.

The left nostril is controlled by the right side of the brain and vice versa.

IT'S NOT JUST COLD AND WET

Your dog's nose knows more than you know.

For centuries dogs have used their noses to communicate, to find food, and to survive under tough conditions. The dog inherited his incredible schnozz from his ancestor—the wolf. Scientists are learning that man's best friend has such a smart olfactory sensor that he can sniff out criminals, drugs, explosives, and gasoline leaks, as well as land mines and even cancer! That's a lot of power for one cool, little nose.

THE NOSEY INTELLIGENTSIA

Dogs don't just smell odors, they can figure out what those odors mean. The local telephone pole is actually a canine gossip center. Just by smelling a drop of urine, one dog can figure out another dog's sex, what it had to eat for breakfast, its health, and even its emotional state! A dog's nose is so sensitive it can detect some odors at one particle in a trillion.

SUPER SNOUT

A dog's nose works the same way yours does, but it works much better. Though your pooch's brain may be smaller than yours, don't get too smug. A dog's olfactory lobe (the part of his brain connected to nerves in the nose) is four times the size of a human's. Both humans and dogs inhale odor vapors into their nose; these odor vapors are dissolved into mucus-coated olfactory receptors located behind the bridge of the nose. A human has about 50 million receptors; a dog has over 200 million—four times as many as his nasally challenged owner. With the aid of all those receptors, a dog can do amazing things.

DOGS SMELL GOOD

Ever since people realized that dogs were nosy geniuses, they've been trying to take advantage of it. Early hunters used dogs to pick up the scent of their quarry and chase it down. Today, search-and-rescue is one of the most important uses of a dog's ability to "track" quarry and "sniff it out." In British Columbia, they train

---

When a cat rubs up against you, it is marking its territory.

search-and-rescue dogs to follow a 45-minute-old track of one person through a rural environment that includes: a dead end, two road crossings, other human tracks, distracting animal scents, and gravel areas that don't hold scent well.

SCENTS AND SCENTSIBILITY

Tracking is mostly picking up scents from the ground, but dogs can also pick up a scent simply by sniffing the air. Within 20 minutes, the aforementioned search-and-rescue dogs of B.C. can sniff out a person concealed in a rural area larger than 160,000 square yards. How do they do it? Scientists now believe that objects send out smells in a plume that flows in swirls and contains patches of dense odor and areas of faint odor. A dog uses his nose to quickly scan the scent densities until he locates the source of the smell.

WHEN DOGS SMELL TROUBLE

While some dogs search for victims lost in the wilderness or trapped under debris, other dogs are looking for trouble. You've probably seen them at airports or border crossings. They sniff out drugs for the U.S. Customs Service, detect explosives and weapons for the Bureau of Alcohol, Tobacco, and Firearms, and sniff out pests in foods (like the dreaded gypsy moth larvae) for the Department of Agriculture. Some dogs can even detect smuggled bank notes from the paper and ink used in U.S. currency!

VIRTUAL NOSINESS

In Afghanistan, 130 dogs work six dangerous days a week to detect land mines by sniffing out the TNT molecules that leak from a mine into the soil. Meanwhile, in cozy labs, some neuroscientists are trying to build their own doggy schnozzes! Scientists from Tufts, for example, are building "virtual dog noses" to find the estimated 50 to 100 million land mines still buried around the world. Linking a computer with chemical sensors, the scientists then use a hose to "inhale" scent molecules. When odors meet the chemical sensors, the sensors change colors and the computer "reads" them to identify the smell.

So far the virtual nose, which can pick up the land mine explosive odors at 10 particles per billion, is only a tenth as sensitive as a good dog nose. Machines, ferrets, honeybees, and even wasps have all been used to sniff out explosives, but the dog is still king—by a nose.

DOGGY DOCS

If you still doubt a dog's abilities, think about this. That mangy mutt down the street could someday be your doctor! That's right, dogs are now practicing medicine—pathology, to be exact.

In one case, a woman's nosy dog kept sniffing at a skin lesion, and finally bit at it. Turned out the lesion was cancerous, and the dog was trying to save her life. Other dog owners with malignant melanoma were similarly diag(nose)d by their pets.

One dermatologist in particular learned a lot about diagnosing cancer from his colleague George—George the schnauzer, that is! George had nearly 100 percent accuracy nosing out skin cancers in laboratory experiments. George even found a malignant mole on a patient who had been declared cancer-free!

Dogs can accurately warn their epileptic owners of a coming seizure 40 minutes in advance. Though it's presently not known if it's his nose that gives a dog the ability to predict seizures, medical researchers are still betting on your dog's sniffer as a diagnostic tool for disease.

And if medical researchers have their way, dogs will soon be diagnosing other diseases. Researchers are teaching dogs to nose out TB bacteria in saliva samples and detect prostate cancer in urine samples.

So quit calling your bowzer "Goofy" and treat him with respect. He's Dr. Goofy to you.

* * * * *

"GIVE ME YOUR (SOUTH) PAW"

Ever notice that a dog prefers to "shake" with the same paw each time? According to tests made at the Institute for the Study of Animal Problems in Washington, dogs, like people, are either right- or left-handed—they favor either their right or left paws.

IS IT TRUE THAT CHOCOLATE IS TOXIC TO DOGS?

It isn't chocolate but a naturally occurring compound found in chocolate that's poisonous to dogs. Theobromine causes different reactions in different dogs. Size is a major factor—the smaller the dog, the more affected it'll be. It also depends on the kind of chocolate, too. Dark chocolate is ten times more toxic to dogs than milk chocolate.

THEIR NAMES LIVE ON— IN DISEASES

You've heard of them all: Messrs. Bright, Hodgkin, Parkinson, Down, and Alzheimer. Here's how they became household names.

BRIGHT IDEAS
We don't suppose Richard Bright (1789–1858) planned on being remembered for a nasty kidney disease that causes the whole body to swell up because the blood vessels serving the kidney are inflamed. But that's what he did.

After medical school in Scotland and England, Bright took off for continental Europe to see the sights. He happened to be in Belgium during the Battle of Waterloo in 1815, where the casualties were no doubt pleased to see him because he decided to stop and practice his professional skills there for a few weeks.

Back in Britain he went to work at Guy's Hospital in London. This is where he did his kidney research and worked out the causes of what we now call Bright's disease, or nephritis, that inflammation of the kidneys mentioned above. That, and a medical textbook he cowrote with Thomas Addison (who has an adrenal gland disorder named after him), did big things for his reputation. When Queen Victoria came to the throne at age 18 in 1837, Bright was appointed as her personal physician—about the biggest job a medico can aspire to.

U.S. President Chester A. Arthur died of Bright's disease at age 56.

ANOTHER GUY'S GUY
Guy's Hospital was the place to be at the cutting edge of medical research (literally—they did a lot of dissection and surgery there in the 19th century). A younger colleague of Bright's, Thomas Hodgkin (1798–1866) became curator.

He spotted that swollen lymph glands can cause malignant, progressive anemia and gave his name to the condition that's still called Hodgkin's disease. No one knows what causes it, but radiotherapy and chemotherapy are used to treat it. Dr. Hodgkin also founded the Aborigines Protection Society (Australian Aborigines). He lived his last years in warm and sunny Jaffa, Israel. The man got around.

Robert De Niro played a baseball catcher who contracted Hodgkin's disease in the film Bang the Drum Slowly.

THE NAME'S PARKINSON. JAMES PARKINSON.
James Parkinson was a Londoner who studied Latin, Greek, natural philosophy, and shorthand (all of which he considered the basic tools for a physician). He took over his father's general practice, but still had time to be an outspoken social reformer who wasn't afraid to voice his opinions on war, the military establishment, poverty, civil disobedience, revolution, and—not to forget—medical education. In his spare time, he played at geology and paleontology.

His 1817 "Essay on the Shaking Palsy" gained him immortality in the annals of medicine; the palsy in question soon came to be known as Parkinson's disease. But it wasn't until more than a hundred years after his death that it was discovered that Parkinson's disease happens because brain cells are irreparably damaged by the lack of a chemical in the brain called dopamine.

Muhammad Ali and Michael J. Fox suffer from Parkinson's.

DOWN AND HIS SYNDROME
John Langdon Haydon Down (1828–1896) spent his life working with retarded children. An enlightened type, he was one of the first to believe and argue that developmentally disabled people might have a bit of potential, so it wouldn't hurt to encourage them to develop and improve.

On the other hand, he had some odd ideas about the causes of the genetic defect we now call Down's syndrome. He thought that deformity involved having the physical characteristics of another race, and in 1866 Down was the one who coined the word "mongoloid" (which is what Down's syndrome people used to be called).

The French actor Pascal Duquenne, who won a Best Actor award at Cannes in 1997, has Down's syndrome.

A SHREWD SHRINK
Alois Alzheimer (1864–1915) was born in Bavaria and worked at asylums and hospitals all over Germany. His name lives on in the

all-too-common, incurable dementia we call Alzheimer's disease.

In 1906 Alzheimer read a paper before the South-West German Society of Alienists (which is what psychiatrists were called back then, crazy people being so alien, we guess) in which he described a peculiar disease of the cerebral cortex that brought on symptoms of disorientation and impaired memory that increased gradually to hallucinations and a gradual loss of higher mental functions.

He based it on a case he'd been studying: a 51-year-old woman who had died in the Munich mental asylum. Because she'd been so young (and because her brain showed the same atrophy as senile dementia patients), the disease was long considered a form of presenile dementia. Today the experts don't limit the name to younger sufferers. Now you can be pushing 90 and if you get it, you've got what's called Alzheimer's.

The 2001 film Iris *depicts brilliant novelist Iris Murdoch's losing battle with Alzheimer's.*

* * * * *

"A doctor can bury his mistakes but an architect
can only advise his client to plant vines."
—Frank Lloyd Wright

"The art of medicine consists of amusing the
patient while nature cures the disease."
—Voltaire

"Never do anything that you wouldn't
want to explain to the paramedics."
—Anonymous

"I got the bill for my surgery. Now I know
what those doctors were wearing masks for."
—James H. Boren

In its lifetime, a cow produces close to 200,000 glasses of milk.

HEH, HEH, HEH.
YOU SAID "URANUS"

*Stop that. You're not 13 anymore. And besides,
Uranus is possibly the best planet ever. Really.*

LOOKING AT URANUS

Gaze for a moment, if you will, on the featureless disk that is Uranus (stop that). The discovery of Uranus ranks as one of the top scientific finds of history. (I mean it. Don't *make* me come back there.) In fact, we can safely say that science today would be entirely different, if it weren't for Uranus…

I can wait until you're *done,* you know.

WHERE URANUS CAME FROM

"Uranus," of course, has nothing at all to do with your terminal excretory sphincter. First off, it's pronounced "yooor-ah-nus," not "yer anus," as folks are so wont to do. Second, the word refers to one of the oldest characters in Greek mythology, the personification of the heavens, who with Gaia, the personification of the earth, sired the Titans, a.k.a. the Elder Gods. They in turn sired the Olympian gods, whose names (in the Roman versions) grace the other planets, excepting Saturn, who was the most important Titan, and our own little Earth, the most boringly named, probably from the Old English "earthe," meaning "earth."

THE IMPORTANCE OF URANUS

When Uranus was given its name, it was to imply the majesty of the vast reaches of the universe. Its present status as the butt of butt jokes is an unfortunate and cruel irony.

Uranus is exciting because for most of our existence, humans didn't know it existed. It was the first new planet observed by humans since we looked up and noticed some "stars" were moving against the static backdrop of the sky. Mercury, Venus, Mars, Jupiter, and Saturn were bright enough to see in the night sky. (Venus, in fact, was originally thought to be two separate planets, depending on whether it was visible in the evening or morning sky.) Uranus, on the other hand, was too far away from the Sun—1.8 billion miles or so—to reflect enough light to be seen.

FINDING URANUS

It had to wait until 1781 to be discovered. English astronomer William Herschel was doing a survey of the night sky, looking for stars down to the eighth magnitude of brightness (about five times dimmer than most humans can see with the naked eye) when he came across a disk just plopped down there in the middle of a star field. Stars are too far away to present a disc shape, and since it had no tail and a slow, regular motion across the sky—it had to be a planet. And so it was.

The discovery of Uranus led directly to the discovery of the next planet, Neptune, after discrepancies in Uranus's orbit suggested there was yet another planet out there. Neptune's discovery in turn suggested the existence of yet another planet—Pluto. It was like getting three planets for the price of one.

URANUS LOOKS FUNNY

This would be enough to qualify Uranus for Best Planet Ever—but wait, there's more. Every member of our solar family has its odd quirks: Venus has a day that's longer than its year, Jupiter has its Red Spot, Saturn, its rings, and Earth—well, Earth's got us.

But Uranus has got some truly freaky things going on. First, the planet's axis of rotation is tilted some 97 degrees, which means that, relative to all the other planets (whose axes are more or less perpendicular to their orbits), Uranus is on its side. It's fallen down and it can't get up. Its magnetic poles are additionally skewed by nearly 60 degrees from the rotational poles, and—get this—the magnetic core of the planet is offset from the actual planetary core by 30 percent. So don't bother to bring a compass.

OTHER STRANGE THINGS ABOUT URANUS

And there's more, like the fact that Uranus produces anomalously small amounts of internal heat for a gas giant, and the fact that spectral analysis reveals the planet to be mostly various types of ice. But you get the point: Uranus is just a big mess. If any planet in the system could be a metaphor for the freakish, off-kilter, and frankly inexplicable universe we all live in, this would be the one. And if we end up making fun of it because of its name, well, it's just that kind of universe, isn't it?

CALLING DR. GREEN!

*Just as we rediscover the healing power of forgotten plants...
many of them are about to leaf us.*

"Save the yew! This means you!" Conservationists are sounding an alarm that plants are in big trouble. As malls, freeways, condos, and subdivisions sprawl across what once was wild land, more and more trees, shrubs, and flowers are losing their habitat, that is, they're becoming extinct. At least 34,000 species (one out of every eight known plant species) are in danger. Some people think that saving a bunch of wildflowers and weeds is a big yawn. But medical researchers know better. They're warning us that if we snooze too long we may wake up and find that we've lost a key to the cure of a lot of diseases.

OLD WAYS, OLD DAYS

Herbs have been curing people for over 4,000 years. Ancient Egyptians, Babylonians, and Native Americans all practiced herbal arts. The oldest-known written list of medicinal plants came from China and dates all the way back to 3000 B.C. It was in the 1600s that herbs and medicine began to go their separate ways. At the time, some herbalists believed that every plant had its own "signature"—so that a plant's color, shape, and scent were the key to its use. For example, herbalists prescribed pansies for heart problems because the petals of pansies were heart-shaped—a prescription that probably didn't help much. Other herbalists consulted the stars, connected plants to the constellations, then dispensed cures according to a patient's astrological sign. Which probably did worse than the pansies.

THE SCIENTIFIC METHOD

Along came a generation of new scientists like Francis Bacon, who emphasized experimentation and objective results instead of unproven theories. Physicians started to spout anatomy instead of astrology, and medicine took a scientific path that left the herbalists behind. Today there are disputes between medical doctors and alternative health practitioners over the prescription of plants and herbs for illness. But herbal cures and mainstream

---

Pearls can dissolve in vinegar.

medicine never divorced each other completely, otherwise you wouldn't be able to take an aspirin when you had a headache. Three thousand years ago, when the ancient Egyptians suffered from rheumatism and backaches, they cured their pain with an infusion of dried myrtle leaves. In ancient Greece, Hippocrates prescribed juice from the bark of the willow tree for fevers. Both myrtle and willow bark contain salicylic acid, and today the ancient remedies sit in your medicine chest in the form of *acetyl-salicylic acid*, or aspirin.

THIS WON'T HURT A BIT
Aspirin isn't the only synthetic drug derived from plants. Hate those novocaine shots the dentist gives you? Try chewing coca leaves; novocaine is an anesthetic derived from cocaine, which in turn is derived from the coca plant. Cocaine's numbing power was discovered by an assistant of Sigmund Freud (not surprising, since Freud was an addict and probably had lots of it lying around).

DR. GREEN'S PHARMACY
Familiar drugs that are natural substances taken directly from plants include: (bullet following)
- The painkillers codeine and morphine are found in the milky fluid of opium poppy seed pods.
- The bark of the cinchona plant is the source of quinine, a remedy for malaria.
- Native American medicine men and women used the tuberous roots of a plant called the mayapple for a lot of ills, including as a salve for treating warts and tumorous growths on the skin. Centuries later, our modern version of medicine men (that's M.D. to you) also prescribe a cream containing resin from the mayapple for cancerous tumors and polyps.
- One of the most amazing plant cures involves the anticancer properties of the rose periwinkle, which boosted the survival rate of childhood leukemia from 20 to 80 percent!

SORRY, THERE'S NO YEW TO CURE YOU
Modern medicos have learned that plants can heal. But what happens when those plants are nearly extinct? In 1991, doctors had great news. They'd discovered a new drug called taxol that could help women suffering from ovarian cancer, even after other treatments had failed. Taxol also helped fight breast cancer. The

Almonds are in the same family as peaches.

bad news was that the only source was the bark of the Pacific yew, a very scarce tree found only in declining old-growth forests of the Pacific Northwest. The tree produces a beautiful wood that's popular with furniture makers, hence the scarcity. In 1991, a complete taxol treatment for one woman meant harvesting six 100-year-old trees. If doctors prescribed enough taxol to help women battle cancer, they'd force the Pacific yew—the very source of a possible cure—into extinction. But there is more good news: French scientists developed a semisynthetic form of taxol from the needles of the yew tree, and these needles are a renewable resource. Good news for cancer sufferers, but what about everybody else?

HERB GOES INTO BUSINESS
Health seekers are popping ginseng to increase energy, slathering aloe vera on sunburns, and brewing pots of echinacea tea whenever they have a cold. Herbs may be "alternative" medicines, but they bring in mainstream profits in the billions. The popularity of herbs has encouraged traditional medical researchers to look again at their healing power. New studies demonstrate that echinacea can relieve flu symptoms. Ginger appears to be just the thing for nausea—with very few side effects. Feverfew can and does relieve migraines. But just as medical science is discovering their power, a lot of herbs are getting too popular for their own good. Lady's slipper, for example, is a rare wild perennial that grows in the U.S. and Canada and is used to treat nervous anxiety. It was harvested until the plant became so threatened that it was given official protected status. Overharvesting, shrinking habitats, and the introduction of nonnative species are threatening the wild populations of herbs like goldenseal, echinacea, and ginseng.

SAVING DR. GREEN
Chemists screen about a thousand types of botanicals for every one that becomes the basis of a useful drug. The extinction of 34,000 plant species could mean the loss of 34 helpful—possibly lifesaving—medicines. We can only hope that pharmaceutical and herbal companies that are going back to nature for medicines take their eye off the bottom line long enough to see to it that the plants we all need don't shrink to extinction.

EYE STANDS FOR INSPIRATION

Humans had to invent things like bifocals and windshields to help us see better. But some lucky animals are equipped with their own eye improvements, all of which help them survive.

Bifocals: The eyes of *Anableps*, a freshwater fish, are divided horizontally into two parts by a band of skin. When it swims along the water's surface, the upper halves of its eyes scan the sky while the lower parts remain submerged and look underwater. This way, the four-eyed fish searches for food below and at the same time keeps an eye—or, better yet, two eyes—out for hungry water birds above.

Windshields: The speedy duck hawk has a crystal-clear third eyelid that can take the buffeting of a 180 mph (290 kph) power dive.

Storm windows: The eye of the conger eel has a layered retina: five layers of photoreceptors (the cells that sense or receive light) are plastered one on top of the another (though it only uses one at a time and seems to keep the others in reserve).

Photogray sunglasses: The yellow eel undergoes dramatic changes as it migrates. Its eyes grow and its eye pigments change for optimal vision in the changing light of the ocean.

Window shades: The American Southwest's Gila monster digs through rough sand for water and the eggs of other animals. Its tiny eyes, ringed with beaded scales, are shielded by thick third eyelids that resemble heavy white satin.

Periscopes: The burrow-hiding North American prairie dog has widely spaced eyes high on its head, like many other hunted creatures. The eyes can focus full circle without telltale movement.

Sunglasses: That same prairie dog's eyeball has an amber-tinted lens that filters the glare of the plains, so it can focus on any predators that may be prowling around.

One in 1,000 oysters and one in 3,000 mussels contains a pearl.

GIVE ME S'MOHS

Or, why you wouldn't want to powder your baby's butt with diamonds.

Okay, so let's say that in your left hand, you've got a rock. And in your right hand, you've got another completely different type of rock. Your job is to figure out which rock is harder than the other. How do you do it?

A) Take the rocks down to the nearest earth sciences lab and spend lots of time and money painstakingly examining the internal crystalline structure of the mineral to determine structural integrity, and ultimately present your findings in consultation with the nation's finest geologists and mineralogists.
B) Bang 'em together and see which one scratches first.

The answer: B, more or less. (You wouldn't want to actually bang them together, mind you. A simple scratching will do just fine.) Scratching one rock against another is a legitimate way of doing science—and in fact, it's the basis of the Mohs hardness scale, the most common scale to determine the hardness of the various minerals we see around us every day.

MEET MR. MOHS
No, really. Back in 1812, German mineralogist Friedrich Mohs assembled a series of minerals, from talc to diamonds, and set about pitting one against the others to see which minerals would scratch which other minerals.

In a scratch test (we're talking a real scratch here, not something that can be wiped away with a little window cleaner), the harder mineral will always scratch the softer material. Scratch enough minerals against each other, and eventually you'll have them all lined up from the weakest, most pathetically scratchable stuff to the hardest, meanest, most positively impervious mineral that can be hauled up from the earth's crust. It's not very elegant, but, hey, it works.

Mohs ranked all his minerals on a scale of 1 to 10, from weakest to hardest. To give you an idea of how it works, here's each level and some representative minerals therein.

Mohs Level 1: Talc. Scientists call it magnesium silicate hydroxide; you call it baby powder. You could scratch this stuff with your fingernail, if someone hadn't already powdered it for you.

"Carat" comes from a Greek word for "carob," whose seeds were once used as weights.

Level 2: Gypsum. A primary ingredient in plaster; a particularly fine-grained version is known as alabaster and is used for statues—and to compare to complexions of *really* pale people. You can still use your fingernail to scratch this, but it takes a little more effort.

Level 3: Calcite. This is better known as a primary component of limestone and of true marble—much of what's known as "marble" in a commercial sense is any carbonite rock that polishes up real good. Don't be fooled! Calcite is also present in forms of onyx, which is frequently carved to make groovy-looking bookends or animal figurines. You can scratch this stuff with a penny.

Level 4: Fluorite. Here's a mineral with some interesting qualities, including thermoluminescence in a variety called chlorphane. Hold it in your hand in a dark room until it's warmed by your body heat. You'll see it give off an eerie glow (bad news is it only works once). Other fluorites show off other types of fluorescence, and no, it's not a coincidence that "fluorescence" and "fluorite" look a lot alike; the former word is derived in part from the latter.

Level 5: Apatite. A mineral that shows off a number of pretty crystal forms, but at a hardness level of five, isn't particularly hard—it can be scratched with a metal knife—so it doesn't make a very good gemstone. Instead, it's used as a source of phosphorous for fertilizer. Fun fact: The enamel of your teeth has a Mohs hardness level of five as well. Why? Because the enamel is made mostly out of apatite crystals. So don't chew on anything harder than this level—you'll regret it.

Level 6: Orthoclase. This is a crystallized form of feldspar and has been a primary ingredient in glass though the years (although regular window glass is slightly less hard than orthoclase, with a Mohs hardness value of about 5.5).

Level 7: Quartz. Now we start getting to some gemstones you've heard of, mainly because at this hardness level, you stop being able to scratch these minerals with household tools. Level 7 gemstones include amethysts, citrines (rare in nature, but which can be produced by heating amethysts), and all sorts of quartzes, including collector favorites like rose quartz and smoky quartz. The quartz in your watch? Level seven hardness all the way.

Level 8: Topaz. Here we have the topaz, which is usually thought of as a smoky brown gem, but which actually exists in a whole spectrum of colors, depending on tiny impurities (the purest

On or under the ocean floor are coal, sand, oil, gas, and diamonds.

topazes are so brilliantly colorless that they're often confused with actual diamonds). Topazes can also reach huge sizes—some have topped the scales at several hundred pounds! And that's a lot of gemstone. Emeralds can also reach this level of hardness.

Level 9: Corundum. Here are rubies and sapphires—both different-colored variations of the same mineral, known as corundum. Rubies are the red corundums; sapphires, while commonly thought of as blue, also come in gray, yellow, pink, green, orange, violet, and brown. Corundum is the second-hardest mineral known.

Level 10: Diamond. Finally, we come to the diamond, the hardest naturally occurring mineral we know about. Scientists have whomped up a substance known as beta-carbon nitride that could theoretically be harder, but there's not enough of that around for a definite test. But, hey, you say, if a diamond is harder than any other substance, how can it be cut by jewelers? The answer: The diamond's atomic structure allows it to be cleaved in four directions. While you can't scratch a diamond with anything (except a more pure diamond), it can be shaped—and it can be shattered. So be careful when you're showing off that diamond ring.

DIAMONDS, BABY BUTTS, AND BANGING ROCKS
The Mohs scale is a relative scale, so it doesn't mean that a diamond is ten times harder than talc. It's actually 1,600 times harder than the stuff you use on your baby's butt, which is probably a good thing for the baby butt in question. Diamonds are also some 1,600 times harder than graphite, which is made from exactly the same stuff diamonds are—carbon. Think about that the next time you're banging rocks together.

* * * * *

Sneaky Mnemonics Geologists Use to Remember Some Important Stuff like The Mohs Hardness Scale for Minerals

Talc, Gypsum, Calcite, Fluorite, Apatite, Orthoclase, Quartz, Topaz, Corundum, Diamond

- Terrible Giants Can Find Alligators Or Quaint Tigers Conveniently Digestible.
- Toronto Girls Can Flirt And Only Quit To Chase Dwarves.

The largest flower is the giant rafflesia, which grows up to 3 feet (105 cm) across.

WHAT THEY MEAN IS

The science behind some very familiar—but maybe confusing—sayings.

ONCE IN A BLUE MOON

A neat description of "not very often," it refers to the second full moon within a month—a rare thing indeed. Full moons happen about every 29.5 days, and since a typical month runs between 30 to 31 days, the likelihood of two in a month is slim. But over the course of a century there'll be 41 months with two full moons, so once in a blue moon really means—if you want to get literal—once every 2.4 years.

MAD AS A HATTER

Today we know enough to keep clear of mercury, but hatmakers once used it to make the brims of hats. When absorbed through the skin, it could wreak havoc on the nervous system: tremors, fatigue, not to mention behavioral dysfunction—that is, crazy behavior. Just think of Lewis Carroll's Mad Hatter from *Alice's Adventures in Wonderland.*

RAINING CATS AND DOGS

In 1600s England it was common practice to discard any waste into the streets—even dead household pets. Once it rained so much that the now-deceased Tabbies and Fidos became buoyant and floated along the streets, thus inspiring writer Richard Brome in 1651 to record, "it shall rain dogs and polecats."

SAVED BY THE BELL

Before modern medicine, it was hard to determine if a person was really dead or simply in a really, really deep sleep. As a precaution, the presumed dead were buried with a string that ran from the corpse's finger to a bell. If there was a mistake, the person could twitch the finger and thus be saved from being buried alive.

THE ACID TEST

Gold Rush miners tested possible gold nuggets in acid. Unlike other metals, gold won't corrode in acid, so if the nugget didn't dissolve, it passed the acid test and therefore must be pure gold. If a person passes the figurative acid test, they're telling the truth, as opposed to the literal acid test, which would be quite painful, not to mention corrosive.

Fruit eaten as vegetables include eggplant, peppers, pumpkin, and tomatoes.

IN THE LIMELIGHT
Theater stages used to be illuminated by heating lime (calcium oxide) until it glowed brightly. Lime has a high melting point, and when heated, gives off a brilliant white light. The light was then focused into a spotlight, so if an actor was in the limelight, he was certainly the center of attention (and probably very hot as well).

DOG DAYS
The ancient Romans noticed that the Dog Star, Sirius, rose at the same time as the Sun on the hottest days of the year, so they made the natural assumption that Sirius in the sky added to the heat of the day. Today it's generally accepted that the "dog days" of summer are July 3 through August 11. But they have nothing to do with Sirius.

CHEW THE CUD
If you figuratively chew the cud, you're chatting with an acquaintance. If you literally chew the cud, you're regurgitating food from your stomach to be chewed a second time (don't even try it). Cows are ruminants—this means that to properly digest grass to pass through their four-chambered stomachs, they need to rechew it. Consequently, a cow's mouth seems to go nonstop, just like a person who is "chewing the cud."

DON'T LOOK A GIFT HORSE IN THE MOUTH
In other words, don't be ungrateful when someone gives you something. You can tell a horse's age by looking at its teeth, particularly the incisors, but if someone gave you a horse as a gift, it would be considered rude to examine its teeth. (This would be like looking for the price tag on a present.)

THE BEE'S KNEES
It's 1920s slang for something wonderful—but why would the knees of the *Apis mellifera*, the common honeybee, be something to be excited about? Well, when bees find pollen they carry it back to the hive on pollen baskets located on their hind legs near their knees (yes, bees have knees). The pollen is then used to make honey.

COLD TURKEY
To completely abandon an addictive habit is to go cold turkey. As a result, the habit-kicker may experience cold sweats and goosebumps as blood rushes from the surface of the skin to internal organs. That bristling gooseflesh looks like the skin of a plucked goose (which looks quite similar to a plucked turkey). And doesn't it sound better to go cold turkey than to go cold goose?

The largest recorded cabbage weighed 124 pounds (56 kg).

EVERYTHING I KNOW I LEARNED FROM A FRUIT FLY

Drosophila melanogastor is the fancy Latin name for the common fruit fly that you've seen flitting around the overripe bananas on the kitchen counter. They're gnats. Pests. Annoying. But they've helped us learn more about biology than you have.

BECAUSE THEY'RE CHEAP AND WE HAVE LOTS
The fruit fly has been under the microscopes of more researchers than you can count, particularly researchers interested in genetics. Why the fruit fly? First, they're cheap. They'll live in jars and they're not fussy about food—a little banana mush and they're happy. And if they die, a quick trip to the garbage provides enough fruit flies for an entire semester of research.

Plus, fruit flies are particularly important to scientists studying heredity and genetics because they mature quickly, mate often, and have a lot of kids. This gives you multiple generations with large populations to compare and contrast. It also turns out that fruit flies have large and relatively simple chromosomes that make it possible to observe changes in them from one generation to the next, a fantastic advantage in studying developmental genetics, heredity, and gene function.

THE ORIGINAL FLY GUY
The scientific value of the fruit fly was discovered in the 20th century by T. H. Morgan. His labs at Columbia University (and later, CalTech) were known as the "fly room."

One day, Morgan noticed mutated flies with white eyes instead of the normal red color. Hey, he said to himself, how did this happen? He started searching for the cause, and eventually his research showed how traits were passed along from parent to child depending on the location and activity of genes situated on the chromosomes. A very big deal in the scientific world.

The largest seed is the double coconut, which weighs up to 55 pounds (25 kg).

Beyond that important concept, his work led the way to an understanding of sex-linked traits, that is, how some hereditary traits can be passed along only from the mother or the father. This was very important for the study of certain hereditary diseases like hemophilia, which passes from the mother.

OTHER FLY GUYS

Morgan trained a whole generation of fly-loving geneticists who went on to use the humble but annoying insect to discover more basic biology.

- A. H. Sturtevant created the first chromosome map.
- C. B. Bridges recognized that genes were actual physical parts of chromosomes and that the order in which they were lined up was vital to proper gene operation.
- H. J. Muller followed up on Morgan's mutation work; he used X-rays to induce stable mutations (mutations that can be transmitted unchanged). His work established that radiation and some toxins were carcinogenic.
- G. W. Beadle came up with the concept that each individual gene was just a set of instructions for the creation of a particular protein, and this idea has formed the basis for much of the modern fields of biochemistry and molecular biology.
- E. B. Lewis discovered that mutating certain genes changed the way the fly embryo developed.

And no, we have no idea why every single one of them goes by his first two initials. They must have had a club or something. Or maybe it's a homage to T. H. Morgan, the man who started it all.

Anyway, all these fly-borne concepts are things they're teaching in high school biology today, but they were ground breaking science in the middle of the 20th century. And these are just a sampling of the important work that came out of research on *Drosophila*.

Another thing that the fruit fly has produced is major awards. At least four of the researchers listed above won the Nobel Prize.

FLY GENES? MY GENES? WHAT'S THE DIFF?

More recently, fruit-fly science has had an impact on brain research, biological clocks, and the transmission of insect-borne diseases. *Drosophila* has also played a major role in trying to solve one of the great mysteries of biology, that is, how does a fly embryo know to develop into a fly instead of, say, an alligator or a human? This may be a question that's never occurred to you, but now that it's been asked, how *does* a mass of cells that's developing into an organism know where to put legs or eyes or livers?

MAKING MONSTERS

This is the question of how certain "control" genes set up the actions of other genes and make them behave properly, like parents do with children. Some enterprising researchers actually took some of these (parental) control genes from the embryos of flies and mice and exchanged them. Just to see what would happen. Know what? They still triggered proper development, even though they were in the wrong animal. (Weird, huh?)

But weirder than weird are the results of other controlled gene "shuffling." How about fruit flies with legs growing out of their heads where their antennae should be? Scientists hasten to assure us that this is not pointless Frankensteinian tinkering to make monster fruit flies, but important work that demonstrates the function of genes.

STAND UP AND TAKE A BOW!

But perhaps the most important role that the humble fruit fly has played and still plays is to show us how similar all forms of life are at their most basic chemical and molecular level. Every living organism on this planet works essentially the same way, whether it's a fruit fly or your Uncle Sid.

* * * * *

IS IT TRUE THAT TOMATOES ARE A FRUIT?

Botanically, yes. Legally—at least in the United States—they're a vegetable. The question was officially decided in 1893 when a food importer sued to recover taxes he'd paid under the Tariff Act. The act called for payment on vegetables, but not fruit. The Supreme Court interpreted the act based on the ordinary meaning of the words "fruit" and "vegetable" as opposed to the botanical meaning. The importer lost his case. Still, technically, tomatoes are the fruit of a vine. That means that other "vegetables" that aren't sweet, but which are used (and thought of) as vegetables fall into the same category: cucumbers, squashes, avocados, peppers, peas, and even pumpkins are, botanically speaking, fruit.

Insects comprise 85% of all species on earth.

DIRTY SNOWBALLS IN SPACE

*People have always thought of comets as burning masses of gas
with tails of flame and smoke. Uh-uh. The truth is very different.*

Comets aren't hot. They're mostly made of frozen gases, or
sometimes water, and rocks and minerals left over from
the formation of the solar system—all held together neatly
by gravity. Astronomers sometimes call them "dirty snowballs."

WAGGING THEIR TAILS IN FRONT OF THEM

And another thing, they don't jet around the universe with their
tails behind them. The tails only develop when they get close
enough to the Sun, which heats up and melts the frozen gas. The
tail is the matter of the comet itself boiling away into space. The
nearer the comet gets to the Sun, the longer its tail (up to a
billion miles at its nearest approach!). The tail is fanned by the
solar wind (the wind that comes off the Sun), so it's always
streaming out in front of the comet. This means that on its trip
away from the Sun, it's actually chasing its own tail.

I WAS IN THE NEIGHBORHOOD...

Obviously, comets are only occasional visitors, some regular, some
not. They orbit the Sun, but not in the neat, circular way of the
planets. The comets we see follow elliptical orbits, zooming in
very close to the Sun, then slingshotting right out to Pluto and
beyond. The farther away they go, the less often they visit.

Halley's Comet, a "short period" comet, comes by every 76
years; Hale-Bopp is a "long period" comet. It should be back in
4,200 years, if you care to wait.

RUNNING OUT OF GAS

Once a comet has been pulled into orbit around the Sun, its fate
is sealed. The quicker it orbits, the quicker it melts. Gas and water
drift away into space, but the dust is left behind, sometimes passing visibly into Earth's atmosphere as meteor showers.

Some shrews and the duck-billed platypus are the only known poisonous mammals.

HALLEY'S HALF-LIFE

Halley's comet has been with us for 175,000 years. It's been described and recorded throughout history, often as a bad omen. It was once much brighter than it seemed during its last visit in 1986. Every time it passes the Sun, it sheds millions of tons of water. Halley's is about halfway through its predicted life; it's already passed the Sun 2,300 times and has been reduced from 40 to 20 miles across. It'll eventually either be reduced to a tiny core of orbiting rock (an asteroid) or melt away completely.

CHARLIE'S COMET

As many as ten new comets are found every year, but most of them are too small to be visible to the naked eye. Amateur and professional astronomers are constantly naming new ones. So keep looking up (with a powerful telescope and infinite patience), and if you're lucky enough to spot one before anyone else does, our next comet might be named after you, Charlie!

* * * * *

YOU WOULD THINK...

That snow on mountaintops would melt a lot faster because hot air rises.

Yes, heat rises, but only near the ground's surface. As we go up, the temperature gets colder. So, while at ground level the air temperature might be, say, 59°F (15°C) at an altitude of seven miles (11 kilometers), it can plummet to –85°F (–65°C). Why? Almost none of the energy from sunlight is absorbed by the higher air—it all goes to warm up the air right next to the ground, so the higher air stays cool. And while that warm ground air is going to rise, it's going to be intercepted by wind currents before it gets high enough to have any effect.

TWILIGHT TIME

Without twilight, complete darkness would set in
immediately after sunset—as if a
lightbulb had been turned off.

What does it take to make a twilight? As the Sun sets on Earth, it continues to light the upper layers of the atmosphere, which reflect this light back to us as twilight. As the Sun sinks farther below the horizon and illuminates less of the atmosphere, darkness gradually settles in.

The Moon, for instance, has no twilight because it has hardly any atmosphere. And we don't mean ambience or the fact that it's a desolate, rock-strewn purgatory of a place. It just doesn't have what it takes—the nitrogen, oxygen, and so on—that Earth's atmosphere is crammed with.

HEY, WHO TURNED OFF THE LIGHTS?
Even on Earth, you have to live at the right latitude to get a twilight of any decent duration. Near the equator, where the Sun sets almost vertically, it "travels" below the horizon so quickly that its rays don't touch even the highest layers of Earth's atmosphere. Not much twilight to speak of. At higher latitudes, the path of the Sun is more slanted, so the Sun takes longer to "descend" below the horizon and twilight is longer.

TWILIGHT TAPS
The gradual changeover from day to night gives plants and animals, including humans, a time of adjustment. Some plants fold their leaves and flowers; others open them. Some animals quiet down and head for their nests and lairs to sleep; others wake up and get ready to prowl the night.

It's a signal for us humans, too, to gather up our stuff and go inside. Or maybe to get all dolled up for a night on the town.

The brindled bandicoot has the shortest gestation period—12 days.

PASS THE POPS

The next time you reach across the table for the butter and slather it on that piece of dry toast…here's something that might give you a figurative sharp slap on the hand.

Some scientists collect samples of animal tissue, insects, or earth. But Kevin Jones, a professor of environmental science at Lancaster University in the United Kingdom, buys a stick of butter instead. Why? He's found that persistent organic pollutants such as DDT eventually end up in the butter we buy and eat.

POPs: THEY SOUND SO CUTE…
The butter-borne problem has to do with scary toxins known as persistent organic pollutants (POPs). POPs are chemicals with an inordinately strong staying power; though some of them have been banned for decades, the residue sticks around like a clueless party guest. They've even been appearing in remote places in the world, spreading havoc in the form of cancer and reproductive problems. Some of them just linger in air, water, or earth; others decompose into other toxic chemicals. And all the while that they hang around, they steadily and stealthily work their way into the tissues of living creatures. Like you and polar bears.

SHE-BEARS, HE-BEARS, AND BOTH-BEARS
Scientists have traditionally studied POPs by sampling body fat. In the 1990s they tracked the spread of polychlorinated biphenyls (PCBs) PCBs—industrial chemicals that cause infertility and sexual deformities—all the way to the Arctic, where they found the nasty chemicals in polar bear fat. So it wasn't any surprise when Arctic researchers began reporting incidences of hermaphroditic polar bears. That's right—bears with both male and female sex organs.

As you can imagine, getting a slab of polar bear fat is easier said than done. Even similar studies that target less belligerent animals, like fish or seals, are a worry to scientists who don't want to destroy animal habitats or affect natural behaviors.

Weighing up to 485 pounds (220 kg), the gorilla is the largest primate.

BUT BUTTER IS BETTER

So scientists studying POPs needed a better way. And in 2001, the previously mentioned Kevin Jones found it. Now, instead of heading outdoors for field samples, Jones and his team of environmental scientists just stop by the dairy section of local grocery stores.

After all, what is butter but a glob of animal fat? It's composed of about 80 percent milk fat, from cows that are as vulnerable to POPs as anybody. When cows consume POPs that have accumulated in grass, the chemicals collect in the fat of their bodies. When they give milk, they pass the POPs right along.

THE INTERNATIONAL SPREAD

Jones and company used high-performance, liquid chromatography to analyze the presence of POPs in butter from 23 nations. They found that heavily industrialized regions (like North America) produced the most contaminated butter. Even though contamination levels in general were still relatively low, some measurements showed alarmingly high levels of contaminants. For instance, one sample from India—where DDT is still used to kill malarial mosquitoes—measured 0.25 milligrams per gram, or about 2 grams to a pound of butter (or 250 milligrams per kilo). That's an awful lot of passed-along DDT, particularly in a country where almost everything is cooked in a clarified butter they call "ghee."

DON'T PASS THE BUTTER

So the scientists found more to worry about than ever before. Though current concentrations of PCBs in most areas are still measured in parts per trillion, even such tiny amounts can be dangerous over a lifetime. Butter, lard, and stuff like Crisco appear to be the main source of POPs.

Kinda makes that dry toast look a little more appealing, eh?

* * * * *

"Eat butter first, and eat it last,
and live till a hundred years be past."

—Old Dutch proverb

Butter is "the most delicate of foods among barbarous nations, and one which distinguishes the wealthy from the multitude at large."

—Pliny

WE'RE OFF TO SEE THE WIZARD

The Wizard of Menlo Park, that is.

N early everyone knows that Thomas Edison invented the light bulb, but what most people don't know is that one of his greatest inventions was figuring out a better way to invent things—the research laboratory.

A BRIGHT STAR IS BORN
Thomas Alva Edison was born on February 11, 1847, in Milan, Ohio. It was soon apparent that Al (as he was called) was very bright because he was one of those kids who was always taking things apart to see how they worked.

The family moved to Michigan when Al was seven, and by the age of 12 he was selling newspapers and snacks on a train that ran between his hometown of Port Huron and Detroit. At 15 he was *publishing* the newspaper he sold, the first paper ever to be published aboard a moving train.

STOP THE TRAIN, I WANT TO GET OFF!
He got off the train, but he stayed in motion. After learning telegraphy, he traveled the country as a telegraph operator. It was during this time that he created his first important invention, a telegraphic repeater that automatically transmitted messages over a second line.

PATENTS PENDING
In 1868, he invented an electrical vote counter and got his first patent for it. In 1869, he designed an improved stock ticker and then set up a company to manufacture it. In 1874, he invented the quadruplex telegraph, which could send up to four messages simultaneously. By 1877, he had earned $40,000 from his inventions and decided it was time to expand—and refine—his invention process.

MUCKING ABOUT IN NEW JERSEY

To that end, he built his first laboratory in Menlo Park, New Jersey. He was all of 30 years old. He wanted to bring together the people and materials that he needed to tackle more difficult challenges. Edison called his assistants "Muckers" and they referred to him as the "Chief Mucker."

They usually had several projects going at once, and it wasn't long before they started churning out one invention after another—including such revolutionary devices as the phonograph and the electric light, no less.

TAKING NO CHANCES

To ensure the commercial success of his electric light, Edison and his Muckers also invented all of the generating and delivery systems to make electric power available to businesses and homes. A very smart move.

During this time Edison filed over 400 patents and became known around the world as "the Wizard of Menlo Park."

THE RIGHT INGREDIENTS

The lab was successful because of Edison's inventive genius, his dogged determination, and his ability to inspire his assistants' loyalty and dedication by working hard alongside them—and relaxing with them.

The lab even had a pipe organ, and often after a long day of work Edison would sit down to play it while the gang sang along. The people who worked with him during those years have said that those were the happiest days of their lives.

SHOW ME THE MONEY!

Edison's goal was to create a small invention every ten days and a big invention every six months. His most important consideration when deciding on a project was to determine the ultimate practical commercial application—in other words, how he could make money from it. Edison once said, "I always invented to obtain money to go on inventing." For him, the money wasn't really the goal; it was just a way to ensure that he could continue his work.

THE WIZARD OF WEST ORANGE

Eventually the gang (and Edison's ideas for the future) outgrew the lab at Menlo Park, so the Wizard began building a new laboratory complex in West Orange, New Jersey. He hired a much larger and diverse staff, consisting of more than 200 machinists, scientists, craftsmen, and laborers. One associate recalled that when a new employee asked him if there were any rules, Edison replied, "There ain't no rules around here. We're trying to accomplish something."

The staff was divided by Edison into as many as 10 to 20 small teams, each working simultaneously for as long as necessary to turn an idea from a prototype to a working model that could be manufactured.

MORE WIZARDRY

Edison himself would move from team to team, advising and motivating them. When an invention was perfected, he quickly patented it. With such extensive facilities and a large staff, Edison managed to turn out new products on a timetable and scale that dwarfed his earlier accomplishments at Menlo Park. At the West Orange complex, they invented an alkaline storage battery, the movie camera, the first talking pictures, the mimeograph, the fluoroscope, and made major improvements to the phonograph.

SHOW ME MORE MONEY!

Rather than sell the patent rights or royalties to his inventions, Edison knew that the real money was in selling products. So he built large factories next to his laboratory complex to mass-produce them. Not only did he manufacture movie cameras and projectors, but he even built a movie studio for making motion pictures. The building had a roof that opened up to let the sun in and the entire structure was on a turntable that could be rotated to keep the sun pointed at the stage throughout the day.

THE BIRTH OF R&D

The laboratory and factory complex eventually employed nearly 5,000 people. His research and development labs were the first of their kind anywhere—they revolutionized the process of technological research. Edison's vision led to a new era in which innova-

Pandas spend most of their lives alone, only meeting other pandas in order to mate.

tion proceeded at an unprecedented rate; it brought with it great improvements in the quality of life and sweeping changes to society.

THEN AND NOW
In 1892, the Edison General Electric Company merged with another small research and development company to form General Electric. Since then, GE has grown into a diversified technology, manufacturing, and service corporation with 250 manufacturing plants in 26 countries. GE employs 313,000 people worldwide and in 2001 had revenues in excess of $125 billion.

THE LATE, GREAT WIZARD
Edison worked at his West Orange laboratory complex for 44 years. He died in 1931 at the age of 84, and millions of people from around the world mourned his passing. Among the many awards he received during his lifetime was the Congressional Gold Medal "for development and application of inventions that have revolutionized civilization in the last century."

They called him a genius, but as he was fond of saying, "Genius is one percent inspiration and 99 percent perspiration."

* * * * *

A LOAD OF CRAP

Did Thomas Crapper really invent the flush toilet? Although his name has long been associated with the device, he was not the man who invented it. Crapper was the proprietor of a sanitary engineering company and did sell and install water closets. But it was the silent valveless waste water preventer that got the toilet business really moving and it was patented by an Albert Giblin in 1898. This device allowed the disposal of waste with a single pull on a handle. Crapper immediately recognized the commercial value of the invention and bought the patent rights from Giblin, thereafter advertising the new and improved flush toilet extensively. Thus his name became forever associated with toilet waste, which is quite fortunate for us. After all, going to the bathroom for a Giblin just doesn't sound right, does it?

A species is counted as extinct if it is not found in the wild for 50 years.

FIRE DOWN BELOW

Coal fires are burning out of control. Can they be stopped?

W e've all heard of Hell. Hell is supposed to be below the earth. It's evil, hot, full of flames, and stinks of brimstone. But wait a minute! Unbearable heat, fumes, and flames—is that Hell or is that an underground coal fire?

A BURNING ISSUE

In Centralia, Pennsylvania, the trees are eerily bleached and dead, burned off at the roots. The ground is hot, the streets are cracked, and foul gases and steam gush from the earth. Take a deep breath and you'll smell noxious sulfur vapors. Take another few breaths and the fire's toxic gases, like carbon monoxide and sulfur dioxide, can give you a headache or nausea. In places the baked ground is sinking; in 1981 a huge sinkhole opened up, nearly killing a man.

There's coal burning under your feet in Centralia. The fire started in an abandoned open-pit mine that was used as a garbage dump; a trash fire was ignited to reduce the trash and kill rodents, and it spread to an underground coal seam. Forty years later, the underground fire still burns and Centralia, the former hometown of over a thousand people, is now a ghost town of fewer than 20.

COAL ON FIRE

Coal, a natural, nonrenewable source of energy, lies under the earth in layered deposits, or seams. Given the right conditions of heat and exposure to oxygen, coal can spontaneously ignite. It may also be set alight by lightning and by natural or manmade fires. Once it gets going, a hot-burning coal seam can keep setting nearby seams alight so that the fire blazes on for centuries. On Burning Mountain in New South Wales, Australia, hot sulfur gases escape from underground, where coal has been burning for over 5,000 years.

ENEMY MINE

Though coal fires can occur naturally, mining has sharply increased their numbers. Mine tunnels and mine openings expose coal deposits to oxygen, and coal reacts to oxidation with a rise in temperature. As the coal gets hotter, gases like carbon dioxide are produced, and if the coal's temperature continues to rise, it will eventually reach a "flash point" and catch fire.

Food spends three to five hours in the stomach and six to 20 hours in the large intestine.

Mining does more than bring oxygen to coal seams. It also creates coal rubble and dust, which combust very easily and then ignite underground deposits. Sparks from mining jobs like welding, explosives, and electrical work can turn mining gases into flames.

FIREY FIRE WATER

Abandoned mines still face the danger of careless manmade fires, like that garbage fire in Centralia. In China, local miners start underground fires by using abandoned mines for shelter while they burn coal to keep warm. In India, people have accidentally started fires by using abandoned mines as illegal stills for making alcohol!

Nearly every country that mines coal has experienced coal fires. Thousands of underground fires are blazing in abandoned mines across the world. China (the world's largest coal producer) has underground fires in the north that steadily burn about 200 million tons of coal a year. That's five to ten times the amount of coal that the country annually exports, and it's all going up in sulfurous smoke.

IS GOVERNMENT FIDDLING WHILE COAL BURNS?

In the battle between mankind and coal fires, coal fires are winning. Pouring water on a coal fire can create explosive gases, so when firefighters go after coal fires, they douse flames in other ways. In the U.S., coal fire experts drill holes into the ground, then they inject the holes with heat-resistant grout, inert gas, or smothering foam to snuff out the oxygen and kill the fire. In China, surface fires are smothered with three feet of dirt.

When a fire can't be smothered, ditches are dug to isolate it from other seams. Sometimes those ditches need to be hundreds of feet deep. Whatever the method, fighting coal fires can cost hundreds of millions of dollars, with no guarantee of success.

In Centralia, Pennsylvania, firefighters dug trenches, then used fly ash and clay seals to block off the oxygen and put out the fire. But in 1983 the fire was still advancing, and the town was told that more trenching would cost over $600 million, cut the town in half, and might not put the fire out. Eventually the government bought out the town for $42 million. Reluctantly, even people who loved their hometown relocated—though a few still refuse to leave.

A GAS PROBLEM

For many years underground coal fires were considered a natural phenomenon like the weather—people complained, but nobody did much about them. When environmental scientists finally began investigating the global impact of spreading coal fires, the news wasn't good. Underground fires burn up nonrenewable resources. They spew toxic gases into the air. The heat of coal fires starts grass and forest fires, destroying thousands of acres of trees.

Most worrisome of all, the carbon dioxide emissions from burning coal contribute to greenhouse gases. Coal fires are possibly increasing global warming. Fires in India and China have a global impact, and China's fires alone produce two to three percent of the pollution from the world's fossil fuel burning. The fires send nearly as much carbon dioxide into the atmosphere as all the cars in the United States.

COOKING THE CHICKEN AND THE EGG

And if underground coal fires might be contributing to global warming, there's also the fear that (in a chicken-and-egg scenario) global warming will cause more coal fires. When the earth warms and drought hits areas like the western United States, the water table sinks and the air temperature rises. Abandoned, flooded mines are suddenly drying out, heating up, and being exposed to oxygen. These mines can erupt in flames—and spew out more warming carbon dioxide.

TECHNOLOGY IS HOT

Just when coal fires seemed to be sending us down for the count, technology brought firefighters a new weapon. Scientists and governments are using heat-sensing satellites to monitor coal fires from space. These satellites are so sensitive that they can pinpoint hot spots where coal fires are starting underground. And they can spot a fire before it causes extreme surface temperatures. Using the satellites to monitor coal-producing areas, scientists will be better able to catch—and put out—new fires before they can intensify enough to become unstoppable.

Scientists are also teaching mining companies techniques that inhibit fires. For example, they urge careful removal of coal rubble so that it will not spontaneously ignite near a seam. By isolating old fires, stopping new ones, and using safer mining techniques, scientists hope to someday tame the underground hell of coal fires.

But that day is still far in the future. Meanwhile, Centralia is still burning, and it could keep burning for another 100 years.

BEDTIME STORIES

*Why you can't run away from your nightmares,
but you can walk in your sleep.*

For humans, lack of sleep can cause problems with memory, blood pressure, and breathing.

CATCH THE WAVE
While we're awake and relaxed, our brains generate alpha waves. When we're both awake and alert, we generate faster beta waves. During sleep, two slower brain-wave patterns take over: theta waves and even-slower delta waves that show up in deepest sleep. By placing electrodes on a snoozer's scalp, researchers can record and measure the brain's electrical activity during different phases of sleep, a procedure called electroencephalography, or EEG.

FIELD OF DREAMS
In 1953, Eugene Aserinsky, working at the University of Chicago, noticed that the eyes of sleeping babies were moving beneath their closed eyelids. That observation led to the discovery of REM (rapid eye movement) sleep periods, which occur roughly three to four times a night and can last as long as 45 minutes. When measured by EEGs, REM sleep was found to include a high amount of brain activity and the most vivid and easily remembered dreams.

WHAT A NIGHTMARE!
Dreams come from your unconscious, but aren't necessarily caused by it; some nightmares have a physiological explanation. For instance, during REM sleep, a dreaming brain experiences visions, sounds, and feeling, but the body is paralyzed—this is nature's way of keeping you safe in bed. When a dreamer becomes aware of this paralysis, it can trigger anxious nightmares, like falling through space or being unable to run from a deadly pursuer. See?

WAKING UP WITH ALIENS
There's an actual disorder called "sleep paralysis." It occurs in the few seconds of transition between REM sleep and waking up. If the brain fails to switch off the REM paralysis, the person feels "frozen stiff" upon awakening. Sleepers often hallucinate. They see

---

Melanin is the pigment that gives skin its color; an uneven production of it is causes freckles.

a terrifying presence in the room, standing over or attacking them. The visions of sleep paralysis so closely resemble the testimonies of people who claim they were abducted by aliens that some doctors cure "alien abduction" with the same treatments used for sleep paralysis—medication in severe cases, but otherwise helping the patient establish good sleep habits and eliminating caffeine.

There are sleepers who can't stop moving. Sleepwalking occurs when the brain fails to release the chemicals that paralyze the body. A sleepwalker gets out of bed with open, glassy eyes and walks or even runs while still asleep. Treatment can include hypnosis or sedatives, but one thing it doesn't include is waking the sleeper up. That's a no-no. Sleepwalkers are so disoriented that they may flail around or attack the person awakening them. It's best to take them gently by the elbow and lead them back to bed.

EATING YOUR WAY TO OBLIVION
Some sleepwalkers, particularly young women, suffer from what's called "nocturnal eating disorder." Maybe they're just hungry or dreaming about food, but these "sleep noshers" get out of bed to munch on anything (literally!) they can find. Taste obviously isn't an issue because some of their sleepy-time snacks have included sandwiches filled with coffee grounds and cigarettes covered in peanut butter. Obviously, the disorder can result in more than unwanted weight gain.

A GOOD NIGHT'S SLEEP
Sleeping accounts for—or *should* account for—nearly one-third of your life. Seven to eight hours of sleep is a necessity, say the experts, even though most people only get six hours or fewer. Here's what the sleep specialists say are the answers to healthier sleeping:

1) Reserve the bedroom for sleep and sex.

2) Sleep in the same comfortable location every night.

3) Avoid vigorous exercise, caffeine, nicotine, alcohol, or large meals before bedtime.

4) Establish a nightly relaxation routine, including a hot bath.

Oh, and don't forget to wish yourself sweet dreams.

Your fingerprint patterns are formed months before your birth.

MOTHER NATURE, WEATHER GAL

Did the TV forecast call for sunglasses instead of the umbrella you really could have used? Did the weatherman advise snowshoes when you needed flip-flops? Maybe it's time to throw away that newspaper, turn off the Weather Channel, and try predicting the weather yourself.

"Red sky at morning, sailor take warning. Red sky at night, sailor's delight." The French, Chinese, and Italians all have their own versions of it—you can even find it in the Bible!

And it's not hokum, either; it's based on scientific truth. In the midlatitudes (which includes most of North America, Europe, and China), changes in weather can show up in the western skies as the sun sets. Red sunsets are created by high-pressure systems and clear western skies that predict dry weather. When the sky burns red at sunrise, light is often shining on moist clouds that signal wind and rain coming in from the west.

RATTLED BY THE WEATHER

But if you're not an early riser, or live in a place where a good view of a sunset is hard to come by, there are other ways of predicting what kind of weather is on the way.

If you want to know the temperature you can always use a rattlesnake. A rattler won't rattle when the weather is at freezing (32°F), but every degree above freezing increases his noisemaking by 1.5 rattles per second. So if your rattlesnake is rattling at 30 rattles per minute, add 66% of 30 to the temperature of freezing (32 + 20); you'll know it's time to grab a sweater 'cause it's a cool 52°F. Of course, rattlers do their rattling just before they bite, so along with that sweater, you might also want a doctor. Or at least a snakebite kit.

Maybe a safer way is by listening to a field cricket. You can figure out the temperature by counting the number of chirps in 15 seconds and adding 37. That's the temperature! (In Fahrenheit, of course.) The snowy tree cricket and the katydid have slightly different formulas, but are just as accurate.

The tip of the index finger is one of the body's most sensitive parts.

WHETHER BAD WEATHER IS ON THE WAY

To predict the weather, you need a barometer to measure air pressure, the weight of the air in one small area. Falling air pressure is a sign of storms.

There's a natural barometer in North Dakota called the Wind Cave. Low air pressure produces a wind that wails out of the cave and practically announces, "Hey, don't forget that umbrella today!"

In Yellowstone National Park, "Splendid Geyser" only erupts when air pressure is low, so when Splendid shoots hot water over 100 feet in the air, bad weather is on the way. If you can't make it to the geyser, there are plenty of other signs of falling air pressure: Smoke rises from a chimney at a flattened angle instead of rising straight up; birds, bats, and insects fly lower than normal; organic matter bubbles up in ponds to form scum. Who needs a fancy barometer when you can read pond scum?

And don't forget the aches in Grandpa's bunions and Grandma's joints. The decreasing atmospheric pressure makes the gas in their bodies expand. Even younger folks with old injuries are tipped off by aches and pains right before it rains.

SEE HUMIDITY WITH SEAWEED

And Mother Nature has her own ways of measuring humidity.

Pinecone scales absorb moisture and swell up, effectively closing the pinecone and protecting the seeds from coming rain.

The Brits who hang seaweed in a sheltered place aren't just being typically eccentric—they're trying to predict the weather. Seaweed is hygroscopic, meaning it absorbs moisture. So here's another weather rhyme to add to your collection: "Seaweed dry, sunny sky; seaweed wet, rain you'll get."

And if Grandpa and Grandma start their belly-achin' again—jeez!—it's because the humidity is making their tissues swell.

BUGGY PREDICTIONS

Even bugs know what the weather's going to do.

Bees are good forecasters of coming rain. They don't venture out of the hive when wet weather is on the way. Dung beetles buzz their wings when storms are imminent. But when cicadas make noise, the sun will soon shine because cicada wings can't vibrate in high humidity.

Ninety percent of all volcanic activity occurs in the oceans.

Bugs are said to feed more actively and bite harder before rain. If you're the scientific type you can test this out with a bare arm and some mosquitoes...or maybe you'd rather just trust us.

BIRD-BRAINED PREDICTIONS

Sailors often looked to the birds to figure out the weather, as in this old rhyme: "Seagull, seagull, sitting on the sand; it's a sign of rain when you are at hand." In general, birds roost in anticipation of bad weather, so sailors who were afraid that a hurricane was on its way weren't all that happy to leave shore if they saw gulls sitting on the beach.

Gardeners paid attention to the rhyme: "When the swallows fly high, the weather will be dry." Insects fly higher when the air pressure is high (an indication of fine weather) so the swallows fly higher to catch them.

In the American West, hawks are good predictors of heavy rainstorms; they go hunting just before the storm to catch the mice and other small animals that are moving to higher ground.

FISHY PREDICTIONS

A fish called the "weather loach" is so reliable at predicting weather that he's kept in household aquariums all over the world. Scientists think his talent has to do with the genetic memory of his native habitat in India, where the annual rainy season is also the loach's spawning season. When air pressure drops, the loach gets ready to spawn. He gets all excited and jumps around because he thinks it's his favorite time of year. Even though he's in a fish tank, a drop in air pressure will still get him all excited, and he'll splash around just like he used to.

HERE COMES WINTER

Centuries of observation have made native peoples experts at interpreting animal forecasts. Alaskan Indians know that when snowshoe hares leave wide tracks, it means extra fur on the hare's hind feet and a snowy winter ahead.

When black bears sleep close to their den openings, winter will be balmier.

If Mongolian nomads see the deer and elk that live in the high mountains come down to lower slopes, they know the winter will be harsh.

The oceans cover 71% of the Earth's surface.

LEAF WEATHER PREDICTIONS TO THE PLANTS

The scarlet pimpernel—the plant, not the old swashbuckling movie—closes its petals when relative humidity is high so that the rain won't damage its pollen. Centuries ago so many people in England used the pimpernel to predict the weather, that it became known as the "poor man's weather glass."

Other plants with weather-predicting reputations are chickweed, dandelions, and tulips—they all fold their petals before a storm. Watch for it.

YOU, TOO, CAN PREDICT THE WEATHER!

Although rain itself has no odor, trees and plants give off aromatic oils that are absorbed by the earth and then released when moisture in the air increases.

And chemists have discovered that certain types of clay soil give off a strong smell called "petrichor" when rain is about to fall. So wrinkle up your nose, breathe deep, and take time to smell the petrichors.

PHIL? PHORGET IT!

No discussion of weather prediction would be complete without mention of Groundhog Day (February 2), when, in Punxsutawney, Pennsylvania, if their resident groundhog, Punxsutawney Phil, emerges from his hole and sees his shadow, there will be six more weeks of winter. The truth is that Phil—and his descendants—have been correct only about 40 percent of the time, which means he's not even as good as you would be if you tossed a coin.

Ironic, isn't it? Mother Nature's worst predictor of the weather is the most famous. Goes to show, doesn't it, that all you need is a good press agent.

* * * * *

"Nature has no mercy at all. Nature says, 'I'm going to snow.
If you have on a bikini and no snowshoes, that's tough.
I am going to snow anyway.' "

—Maya Angelou

TO YOUR HEALTH! PART I

Doctors of the past had some pretty strange ideas about treating disease. Take this quick quiz to see how you'd have stacked up against the best medical minds the profession once had to offer.

1. Which of these was NOT a popular 14th-century explanation for the bubonic plague?

a) An earthquake had released foul, disease-laden fumes from deep inside the earth.

b) A struggle between the planets and the oceans had caused fish to die—the fish contaminated the air and gave rise to the plague.

c) Fleas and lice carried the plague around the countryside, encouraged by the filthy, unhygienic conditions.

d) The plague was caused by a particular alignment of the planets Saturn, Jupiter, and Mars on March 20, 1345.

2. In the Renaissance, smoking was considered:

a) A filthy, unhygienic habit.

b) A sophisticated pastime for men of breeding.

c) An especially good way of protecting oneself from disease.

d) A money-wasting frivolity.

3. Which of these was NOT a popular 18th-century cure for syphilis?

a) Tying a dead chicken inside one's pants.

b) Drinking a soup made of boiled ants' nests.

c) Applying an ointment made of earthworm sperm.

d) Drinking a dose of mercury.

4. In 1948, typhoid was ravaging London. Scientists began a desperate manhunt to find who was spreading the disease in their feces. How did they find the culprit?

a) The police went door-to-door testing people for the disease.

b) They offered a large bounty to anyone who could help them find the carrier.

c) They tested every sewer, crawling through the pipes until they located the toilet that the carrier had been using.

d) They gave out do-it-yourself stool-testing kits.

ANSWERS: 1. (c) Which, of course, is the correct explanation for the spread of the plague; 2. (c); 3 (d) But mercury had been the treatment of choice back in the 16th century; 4. (c).

10 SF BOOKS EVEN
NONGEEKS WOULD LOVE

Are these the greatest science fiction novels ever?
Maybe, maybe not. But they are SF novels that even
people who don't like science fiction can actually enjoy.

The question of which science fiction books are the best ever is a pointless one for most people, since many of the "greatest science fiction novels" are books that no one but science fiction fans will read. A better question to ask might be: What are the best science fiction books that you don't have to be a hard-core science fiction fan to enjoy? We scanned our library and came up with these 10 (well, 12) books that not only provide great SF fun, but also are approachable enough for the casual reader. Some old, some new—but all good reads.

Dune, **by Frank Herbert:** David Lynch made this book into a 1984 film that was so incomprehensible that the actual novel— 600 pages on the future of religion, politics, desert ecology, and drug trafficking—looks positively streamlined in comparison. When the book came out in the mid-1960s its multiple story threads were daunting. But (ironically) thanks to shows like *The X-Files* and even *The West Wing,* in which several things are happening all at once, people got used to following intersecting story lines. The result is that Herbert's magnum opus now comes across more like an epic historical novel that happens to be set in the future, not the past. Herbert wrote several *Dune* sequels of varying quality. More recently, Herbert's son Brian teamed up with SF author Kevin J. Anderson to write a trio of prequels that Uncle John doesn't think are on par with the rest. Stick with the original.

Earth, **by David Brin:** Scientists in the near future create a tiny black hole and—oops—allow it to sink into the earth's core; in the process of digging it out, they discover there's *another* black hole down there, and that one's origin is a mystery—and a problem. This plot line is the skeleton on which author and real-life physicist Brin hangs some fascinating episodic story lines that involve problems the world faces today (global warming, privacy, energy crunches), carried out to their possible outcomes 50 years from now. Originally published in 1991, *Earth* has already pegged a couple of items correctly (such as a version of the World Wide Web and the idea of futzing with old movies using new computer graphics). Plus, scientists have begun trying to generate tiny little black holes in labs. So imagine what else Brin might (eventually) be right about.

***Ender's Game* and *Speaker for the Dead,* by Orson Scott Card:** Supersmart child-warriors are used by the military to battle an invasion of buglike aliens. That's the setup of *Ender's Game;* the meat of the story comes from the struggle of one of these extraordinary children (named Ender) to keep a grip on his humanity even as he's being turned into the perfect killing machine. Card sets up a lot of questions about morality, war, and man's purpose in *Ender's Game;* in the sequel, *Speaker for the Dead,* these questions get a payoff as the grown-up Ender finds himself in a position to save a new sentient species or allow it to be destroyed. Proof that interesting philosophical questions can be asked (and even answered) in the form of a purely entertaining story.

***Grass,* by Sherri Tepper:** Like *Dune,* this is a large tale involving nobility, religion, politics, and the fate of the human race—but for a change, the hero is a heroine. Marjorie Westriding is dispatched with her family to a far-off planet to find a cure for a plague, but she ends up confronting questions of original sin among aliens. Lots of philosophy, and even some sex (well, sort of), but also lots of action, plus a group of purely malevolent creatures who love nothing better than to toy with humans. Hand this to someone who enjoys those massive romantic epics for a change of pace.

***Hitchhiker's Guide to the Galaxy,* by Douglas Adams:** Earth is destroyed to make an intergalactic bypass, launching the interstellar travels of one completely ordinary and befuddled human being named Arthur Dent. Geeks love this one, but for the right reasons—namely because it'll make you laugh so hard that you may vomit involuntarily. Note that this is humor of the distinctly British, Monty Python–like variety, so if you're not into that, you may wonder what the fuss is about. But if you ever laughed at

Monty Python and the Holy Grail (or even *A Fish Called Wanda*), you'll be laughing at this one, too. *Hitchhiker* has several sequels, each progressively less funny than the one before (but still worth a chuckle or two).

Hyperion and Fall of Hyperion, by Dan Simmons: It takes guts to snatch the format of *The Canterbury Tales* and use it to crank out epic science fiction, but the extraordinarily talented Dan Simmons (who also writes bang-up horror and action novels) is just the guy to do it. Over the course of these two novels, Simmons creates a galaxy-wide human civilization that's pitted against a mysterious enemy. *Hyperion* uses the overlapping stories of a clutch of pilgrims to paint the picture of this future civilization; *Fall of Hyperion* describes its downfall, as seen through the eyes of a clone of the great Romantic poet John Keats. Great storytelling, great action, great plotting; not just a couple of the best science fiction novels ever, but two of the best adventure novels in a long time, period.

The Martian Chronicles, by Ray Bradbury: This one shows up on a lot of high school reading lists, and for good reason. It's a fine combination of science fiction and fantasy and an increasingly neglected literary form—a series of short stories, hung together with a single thread: they all take place on Mars. The stories include encounters with real live Martians (who may or may not be happy to see humans), the stories of the humans who leave Earth to come to Mars, and, in the end, the stories of the humans who are left behind, each short enough to be read in a single sitting. It's Bradbury at the top of his form, which means these are some of the better short stories you'll find almost anywhere.

Perdido Street Station, by China Miéville: The perfect book for anyone who thinks that science fiction can't be literary and/or adventurous in form. Miéville's genre-buster of a novel is not unlike what you would get if you spliced together the genes of Charles Dickens and horror master H. P. Lovecraft and raised the resulting creature on the writings of Orwell, Huxley, and Philip K. Dick (the fellow who wrote the story that was the basis of the movie *Blade Runner*). It's difficult to describe the novel, except to say that it involves mad scientists, interspecies romance, vampiric moth creatures, Tammany Hall–like urban politics, the

The longest cave system is Mammoth Caves in Kentucky—348 miles (560 km).

value systems of alien species, interdimensional spiders, and a rip-roaring final action scene that takes place on the rooftops of a city you really can't imagine. All written by someone who uses the English language like Yo-Yo Ma uses a cello. Fabulous writing, regardless of genre.

Snow Crash, **by Neil Stephenson:** William Gibson's *Neuromancer* may be considered the first "cyberpunk" novel, but the fact is, it's kind of a deadly bore. *Snow Crash,* on the other hand, is a real hoot right from its first scene, which involves a madcap pizza delivery and is written with the same sort of delirious cinematic urgency that you'll find in the best novels of William Goldman (*Marathon Man*). The novel's plot involves a computer virus that (get this) dates back to Sumeria, but it doesn't really hang toge-ther, so instead, enjoy the book for its great portrayal of both an insanely Balkanized America and a huge cyberworld so vividly imagined that a whole bunch of Internet companies bankrupted themselves in the 1990s trying to create a world just like it. Also, any book that features a large Aleutian with a nuclear bomb in a motorcycle sidecar and the words "Poor Impulse Control" tattooed on his forehead is one you know you're going to have fun with.

Stranger in a Strange Land, **by Robert Heinlein:** The expiration date for this novel and its ideas regarding love and sex and human transcendence has sort of passed (people used the novel for years as a foundation for their own desire for hippie polygamy, and now they don't so much), but it still makes for a good read for two reasons. One, Robert Heinlein wrote damn fine dialogue, which makes him more fun to read than most other writers today (and how sad is *that,* since Heinlein's been dead coming up on 15 years now). Two, Heinlein thought seriously about the nature of God and the interrelationship between God and His followers, which is interesting to contemplate even if you're not interested in the polysexual hijinks. Also, Jubal Harshaw, the cranky old man who counsels the "Stranger" like a dyspeptic Yoda advising an extraordinarily horny Luke Skywalker, is one of the great curmudgeons of 20th century writing, and you don't want to miss out on a character like that.

Butterflies don't spin cocoons; moths spin cocoons.

REALITY BITES ASTRONAUT

*What you see on TV is a bunch of astronauts yukking it up
while they float around the cabin of their spacecraft.
Here's what's really going on.*

NASA may not advertise it, but they're intensely studying
what happens to an astronaut's body during weeks or
months in space. They've found that the least dramatic,
but most insidious danger comes from the lack of gravity.

THE GRAVITY OF THE SITUATION
Earth's gravity hurts—you feel it every time you carry something
heavy or try to climb a long flight of stairs. It's more than a force;
it's also a signal that tells your body how to act. Zero gravity looks
like fun, but it causes a lot of not-so-funny changes in the body.

Muscles
On the earth, gravity tells your muscles and bones how strong
they have to be to hold you up. In zero-G, the body doesn't need
muscles, so they start to weaken and they do it pretty quickly. The
muscles we use most to fight gravity—like those in our legs and
spine—can lose up to 20 percent of their mass at a rate as high as
five percent per week in space.

Bones
For bones, the loss can be even more extreme. In space, bones
atrophy at a rate of about one percent a month. It's predicted that
for long stays in space, the total loss could reach 40 to 60 percent.
These bone-weakening effects of zero-G could also lead to permanent tooth loss during long space missions.

Blood
Right now, gravity is pulling your blood down, so your heart has to
beat harder to push blood up toward your head. In space, where
that familiar pull is missing, blood pressure equalizes throughout

---

There is as much ice in Antarctica as the Atlantic Ocean has water.

the body. This is not good—higher blood pressure in the head raises an alarm that the body has too much blood. Within two to three days of weightlessness, astronauts can lose up to 22 percent of their blood volume.

Heart
Meanwhile, the heart becomes deconditioned because it doesn't have to work as hard pumping blood to the head. The lower blood volume makes it worse. If you have less blood, your heart doesn't need to pump as hard, so it's going to weaken further.

Kidneys
There's also a higher risk of developing kidney stones. Astronauts take in less fluid than the average person, so they generally have significantly higher levels of calcium phosphate in their urine. Calcium salts are more likely to crystallize and grow into stones.

RECOVERY
Astronauts must be in good shape during and after landing to respond to any emergency. Because of all their body's changes, they're usually suffering from low blood pressure, dizziness, and weakness. Once they've touched down, their bodies have to be reconditioned. The body restores blood volume within a few days, and the heart recovers with it. Muscle mass can be recouped within a month or so. It's bone recovery that's the problem. A three-to-six month space flight might require as much as two to three years to regain lost bone—if it comes back at all. Some studies have suggested that it doesn't.

THE PRESCRIPTION
NASA scientists prescribe lots of exercise—and not just before takeoff. Exercising in space is difficult because of a lack of resistance. Russian cosmonauts tried strapping themselves to a treadmill with bungee cords, but it didn't provide enough resistance. Solving the problem of zero gravity could lead to improved therapies for people who don't use gravity properly on Earth. Aging is the perfect example. Zero-G living mimics closely the effects of old age. Like astronauts, the elderly fight gravity less. They're more sedentary, which triggers the loop of muscle atrophy, bone atrophy, and lower blood volume.

Ice covers 10% of the earth's surface.

LIFE WITH A ROBOT

*In the near future, you could be kicking the tires
of a shiny new household robot.*

Robots are evolving on a path much like the evolution of animal intelligence—only they are doing it about 10 million times faster.

BABY'S FIRST STEPS

In the 1990s, robots could walk down a hallway, go into a room and out again, and—most importantly—know where they were at any given moment. Robots did this by building two-dimensional maps of their surroundings. They took in data and processed it statistically. But the data had a lot of "noise" (unnecessary information) that made for misleading readings. Robots had to combine thousands of readings to make a fairly reliable map, and even then they got confused. They'd get stuck in a corner or wander down the wrong corridor.

The domestic robot that arrives at your house in about 2010 won't make the same mistakes because it will build a three-dimensional map with about a thousand times as much data as a two-dimensional map (using about a thousand times more computer power).

PAPA WAS A ROLLING VACUUM CLEANER

Prototypes for future domestic robots are available now as small robotic vacuums. When these smart little guys are turned on in a new place, they explore the property and build three-dimensional maps that include height and depth for stairs and such. As they work, robot vacuums constantly build and edit their map, comparing it to the one they made when they first arrived.

Some robots can even find their way to a docking station and recharge themselves! Like we said, smart. But these guys (and the 1990s robots) can only do specialized tasks like vacuuming. They aren't nearly as brainy as the first-generation universal robot that is expected to hit the market within the decade.

Icebergs have a four-year life span and begin entering shipping lanes after three years.

GUESS WHO'S COMING TO STAY

Universal robots aren't specialized; they can do a variety of tasks. Hundreds of thousands of them will be working in commercial industries some time after 2005; by 2010 a universal domestic robot could be slaving away at your house while you put your feet up! The initial generation of universal domestic robots will probably be human in scale. They'll have multiple hands, arms, and sensors that recognize small objects. But "first gen" won't be your best friend. It'll have the mental wattage of a lizard.

Your first robot will do everything his application program tells him to do in one exact sequence. Any new problem will stymie this inflexible guy. He's a slave to programming, and he can't learn anything new. But first gen will still do many rote tasks more cheaply and efficiently than humans because he's not distractible in any way. Inflexibility has an upside.

ROBOT SCHOOL

Around 2020, the replacements for first-gen robots should come to a store near you. Brainpower-wise, the second-generation robot will move up from lizard to mouse. Second gen's application programs will give this choosy fellow several ways to perform the same task. For example, he could pick up a package with his right arm, left arm, or third arm! Each option would be associated with a weight (a number that defines the desirability of doing a task a certain way). This weight will change on the basis of the robot's experience. In other words, this guy can learn!

Second gen's learning curve will rely on programs called "conditioning modules" that give punishment and reward signals for different actions. A punishment signal reduces the desirability weight of an action; a reward increases the weight. The higher weight of desirable actions will be updated in the robot's programming. These updates will allow your robot to become more useful as it "learns through experience."

YOUR ROBOT WILL BE ONE-OF-A-KIND

Your robot will be keyed to your voice and will understand certain words (like "good" as an encouragement to pick up an object with the right hand, and "bad" as a signal not to). Your robot will learn to be different from the same model that lives next door. For example, your guy might learn to be quiet during certain hours of the day. During those same hours, your neighbors might tweak their robot's programming to play loud music!

Second gen will still be a slow learner, making lots of mistakes before he gets some tasks right. Not to worry. The robot industry will eventually fix that.

YOUR ROBOT CAN MONKEY AROUND

The new and improved third gen will arrive around 2030. The improvement will be a simulator. The third generation of robots will try out behaviors in simulation before actually doing them physically. By the time this robot does a task, he'll have simulated it enough to have a good chance of getting it right. In simulating, your robot will learn the cultural aspects of your world—he'll know the difference between paper and other kinds of money, so he won't use the money in your wallet to start a fire.

When you think third gen, think monkey. Your crafty new robot will learn by imitation; he might learn how to tie a knot simply by watching somebody do it. (Monkey see, monkey do.) But gen three will still have mental limits. He'll only know about specific objects, places, events, and people. For example, he'll know a lot about your house, but nothing about the outside world.

MEET MR. PERSONALITY

Third gen will also have a definite personality. To keep its psychological simulator up to date, it will interact with you. Your robot might ask you, "How do you feel today?" You'd be expected to provide a little feedback, like, "I feel great," or "I'm depressed." The conversation will help your robot describe its own behavior in psychological terms. Eventually, your robot could tell you, "I'm having a bad day today," or "I'm behind schedule." Experts think we'll treat third-generation robots like conscious beings with pleasant personalities. Robots will interact in helpful ways for one simple reason—profitability. A helpful robot would be recommended to others, selling better than a surly, selfish robot.

MEET MR. BRAINIAC

When fourth gen arrives, in about 2040, say good-bye to your monkey and say hello to an inferiority complex. This robot will be capable of very powerful reasoning like the chess-playing computer that beat world champion Gary Kasparov in 1999.

Actually, the fourth generation robot should be able to beat you at a lot more than chess. It will do everything third gen could do—only better. Fourth gen will be a third generation robot with general-purpose reasoning grafted onto it. It will be able to infer ideas. At that point, robots will become much more like humans.

For example, fourth gen might be able to figure out (by running several examples in simulation) that if it turns a container of liquid without a lid upside down, the liquid will spill out of that container. Our old pal, third gen, would need to learn not to turn a glass over, then not to turn an open jar over, then not to turn a pitcher over, and so on. Fourth gen would infer that a jar and pitcher should stay upright after it saw what happened when a glass of juice spilled.

Fourth-generation robots will be able to do complicated tasks—and do many of them better than humans, because really deep reasoning involves long deductive chains and keeping track of a lot of details. Human memory is not that powerful.

NOT A PARTY ANIMAL
There's one area, though, where robots will probably find it hard to catch up to humans. Because we've always lived in tribes, we're good at judging the probable behavior of the other members of our tribe. We have a powerful social intuition. Some of our social knowledge is hardwired in our brain and some we learned growing up. We probably use close to the full processing power of our brain—the equivalent of a hundred trillion calculations per second—just to get along with people.

Though it may take a long while before robots catch on to the social interactions of humans, maybe that's for the best. After all, we wouldn't we want our robots to party hearty with lampshades on their heads. Hey, that's our job!

* * * * *

A CLONE AT LAST

If you push a sponge (the underwater kind) through fine silk, it will break up into thousands of tiny pieces. Then each piece will clone itself into a tiny new sponge, exactly like the original.

WHAT THE HECK IS THAT THING?

New species of all kinds are being discovered every day! Let's meet a few.

There's nothing scientists love more than discovering something new. And it happens in every ecosystem—land, sea, or air. These examples were discovered in the last decade.

PLANT ME NOW, DIG ME LATER
How do you miss a plant? It's not like it can run and hide (unless of course it's a Triffid). Scientists have identified a new orchid in Southeast Asia and several new species of tea trees in Australia. And these are only a teensy example of the new plants that show up all the time.

ANIMAL PLANET
It's truly amazing, but there are still big—and we mean big—animals being found:

• A new camel was found in a remote part of China's Xinjiang Province. It has a genetic difference from Bactrian camels, but the only visible difference is slightly hairier kneecaps. And it lives by drinking salt water.

• Several new monkeys, including the Manticore marmoset and the Acari marmoset, were both found in the Amazon basin, sometimes kept as pets by locals.

• There have even been reports from China's Shanxi Province about a new species of panda, but it hasn't been confirmed.

WATERWORLD
Bodies of water are literally swimming with new species:

• New catfish have been discovered in drainage ditches in Indonesia.

• A new bass has been found in similar ecosystems in the American South. You'd think if anything had been thoroughly explored, it would be bass in the South.

• Scientists have actually found new coelacanths (which were long thought to be extinct before they were rediscovered early in the 20th century). Now, not only are they not extinct, a whole new species has been found in the waters off Indonesia.

• Perhaps more amazing is the discovery of a new beaked whale off the coast of California. Most folks would've thought we knew everything swimming in those heavily traveled waters—and certainly with a highly studied creature like the whale.

• A new squid was found in the deep sea. It's probably a magna-pinnid (which means "big fins"), but scientists aren't sure yet. What they are sure of is that it's a (and we quote) "very weird-looking thing."

• There are 116 recognized species of electric fish (or electric eels) and 32 undescribed ones that are already in museums; forget about the ones that are still swimming in the Amazon undiscovered—along with the three new species of piranhas that were recently identified in Brazil and Venezuela.

In fact, the deep, deep ocean will soon start producing more new species than we can count because we're just getting to where we can explore that inhospitable place.

WATCH THE BIRDIE
New bird species are being discovered all the time, which may be because there are so many knowledgeable people watching them—when experienced bird-watchers see a new one, they know it. Some of the most recently discovered species include the Nicobar scops-owl in India, the cloud forest pygmy owl in South America, and of course the short-toed nuthatch vanga in Madagascar. These are only a few of the new birds that show up in people's binoculars every year.

CRAWLING AROUND EVERYWHERE
Like birds, new bugs are always crawling over some scientist's shoes in a jungle somewhere. Take Sri Lanka, for instance, which has produced over 1,000 new species since 1970, one of which was a whole new genus of wasp that acts more like a bee. (Trust us, this was pretty exciting to entomologists.)

A new butterfly showed up in Ireland, the first new butterfly seen in the British Isles in the last 110 years. And in Tennessee, they found a giant 18-inch-long earthworm. The big worm is still

Most fish are in the Southern Hemisphere because these waters are less exploited by man.

under consideration to see if it's a new species or just a freakishly big example of an existing species.

VIETNAM: DID ANYONE EVER LOOK HERE BEFORE?

There have been so many new animals and plants discovered in Vietnam in the last few years, including big mammals, you'd think they were purposely hiding them up until now. Scientists found two new large deer and there have also been reports of two civet cats and a pheasant.

Big plants, too. A new genus of conifer tree was recently discovered, which they named *Xanthocyparis vietnamensis*. In fact, not only is it a new genus, but a new family, and it's caused some reshuffling of well-known trees around the world. The yellow spruce of the American Northwest had to be redesignated into the new genus *Xanthocyparis* because it was the nearest known relative to the new Vietnamese species.

THE OLD LINH DUONG TRICK

Vietnam also gave us an example of one of the pitfalls facing scientists who discover and name new species, that is, getting it wrong. In the early 1990s, scientists discovered weird horns in marketplaces in Vietnam and Cambodia. Locals told them the horn came from an animal called a "linh duong," which was sort of like a mountain goat or an ox—nobody was quite sure.

The scientists had never seen a horn like it, nor had they heard of the linh duong. With nothing more than horn in hand, they claimed discovery of a new species called the *Pseudonovibos spiral*. Well, some other scientists ran DNA tests on the mysterious horn and found out it was a regular old horn from a regular old cow. The horn had been heated and worked and carved by locals. There is no such thing as a *Pseudonovibos spiral*. The scientists had fallen into the old "weird horn and folklore" trap.

THE WONDERS OF SCIENCE

Still, the fact that there are new deer and camels and whales and trees out there hints that there could be even more weird creatures that we've never seen.

Does this mean there is a Bigfoot or Loch Ness Monster yet to be discovered? No.

Does it mean there isn't? No.

See? Science answers all your questions.

Fish species endangered by overfishing include tuna, salmon, haddock, halibut, and cod.

MY OZONE'S GOT A HOLE IN IT

Is the hole in the ozone layer getting bigger? Should we all buy stock in Coppertone or start building underground cities?

As far back as 1985, newspapers and television have been briefing us about the ozone hole over Antarctica—that ultraviolet thingy caused by hairspray and global warming. Isn't that what it is? Well, sort of.

THE HOLE AT THE BOTTOM OF THE WORLD
Ozone itself is actually a type of oxygen molecule. The ozone layer is part of the stratosphere, and it protects us by absorbing most of the Sun's ultraviolet rays. The layer is definitely thinning out, no doubt about it. During some months, it disappears entirely near the South Pole. It's a really big hole, too; in 2001 it measured 10,000,000 square miles—twice the size of Antarctica and pretty much the size of the entire North American continent. Big.

FERNS WITH SUNBURNS
Remember what the ozone layer does, how it absorbs ultraviolet (UV) radiation? Well, without it, rates of skin cancer will go sky-high. And more: UV radiation also contributes to cataracts and doesn't do our immune systems a whole lot of good. And these are just the effects on humans—it's harmful to plants and animals, too. They need the same UV protection that we do.

YOUR OLD FRIDGE
The bad guys of the scenario are airborne chemicals, particularly chlorofluorocarbons, or CFCs. In the old days we used to think they were our pals. They made aerosol cans spray nice and evenly, which was very important in the days of bouffant hairdos. CFCs were used as insulation in refrigerators—mostly in models made during the 1980s. When those fridges are junked (about 8 million of them a year), they're shredded for scrap metal and the insulation releases CFCs into the air. Once CFCs reach the stratosphere, about six to 30 miles up, they become chlorine compounds, and that's where they break down ozone.

WHAT'S UNDER THAT PARKA?
But why is the hole over the South Pole? Good question. It's not like they're all wearing bouffant hairdos under their parka hoods

---

The ocean's total salt content would cover the continents to a depth of five feet.

down there. The layer is thinning out all over the globe, but the hole appears only in the south because the ice clouds around Antarctica trap more CFCs.

This doesn't happen up north in the Arctic, because winters at the North Pole are highly variable, whereas it's always cold in Antarctica in the winter. This doesn't mean that scientists don't worry about ozone depletion up north. It could happen, but it would have to be a uniformly cold winter in a year of high volcanic activity.

WHAT ARE WE DOING ABOUT IT?

The U.S. banned aerosol cans in the 1970s. And a lot of countries signed the 1987 Montreal Protocol, committed to reducing CFC production by 50 percent by the year 2000. Since CFCs can last in the stratosphere for 100 years, they won't be completely gone until late in the 21st century. Studies by the National Oceanic and Atmospheric Association indicate that the size of the hole has stayed fairly constant over the last few years.

Some optimistic experts predict that the hole will close up in 50 years. Not such a terribly long time. But if a deal on a lifetime supply of sunblock comes your way, grab it.

* * * * *

Myth: A lit match contains more heat than an iceberg does.
Fact: Well, not exactly. An iceberg contains more heat than a match does. The total heat energy of the iceberg—meaning the total kinetic energy of all its molecules—is greater than the heat energy of the match. It's the temperature of the match that's greater.

IS IT TRUE THAT HOT WATER FREEZES FASTER THAN COLD WATER?

It can. If the water container doesn't have a lid, some of the water will evaporate. The water lost in evaporation may diminish the mass enough to compensate for the greater temperature range it has to cover to get to freezing. Also, evaporation carries off the hottest molecules, which lowers the average kinetic energy of the molecules that are left. That's why blowing on your soup cools it. It encourages evaporation by removing the water vapor above the soup.

Feet contain approximately 250,000 sweat glands and excrete up to a cup of moisture daily.

RED HOT MAMA

*Gushing over geysers, hooting for hot springs, flushing out fumaroles:
It's geothermal grandeur galore!*

Geysers are the most dramatic members of the geothermal-
emissions family. Their close relatives, the hot springs, are
kinder and gentler and don't get as much press. The rough
and smelly side of the family is represented by the fumaroles and
the least-attractive members of the family—the ne'er-do-well
brothers-in-law, if you will—the mud pots.

RED HOT MAGMA

Hot rocks, hot water, and good plumbing: Put them all together,
they spell geyser. Geysers form in volcanic areas where magma
(molten rocks) is relatively close to the surface—just one or two
miles down. Of course, they need lots of hot water. The geysers in
Yellowstone National Park spew a stupefying 75 million gallons of
water into the air every day. The water comes from the rain and
snow that have percolated down through the earth into the
geyser's plumbing system. This trickle-down effect takes a long
time—centuries, in fact. The water that shoots out of Yellowstone's geysers today is 500 years old. Geysers also need a special
rock known as geyserite and underground channels with one or
more constrictions near the top. The magma heats the water to
500°F (260°C) or more. (The water doesn't turn to steam because
of the immense pressure it's under.) The pressure continues to
build until the water rises, spilling some into the geyser's pool at
the surface. This sudden decrease in pressure triggers a violent
chain reaction. The superheated water bursts through the
constriction and the geyser erupts. Hot springs are geysers without
the constriction. The boiling water gurgles to the surface into a
bubbling pool. It's that simple.

WHAT A GAS, MAN

Fumaroles are basically steam vents—holes in the earth that are
blowing off steam; what little water there is rises to the surface
and boils away. Instead, fumaroles pass gas, hydrogen sulfide to be
exact, which produces a horrible "rotten egg" smell. Mud pots

Eating spicy foods is a common cause of stinky feet.

form when hydrogen sulfide (a.k.a. "sewer gas") bubbles up through the water and is eaten and metabolized by bacteria that convert the hydrogen sulfide to sulfuric acid. One of Yellowstone's mud pots, in fact, is as acidic as battery acid. The acid dissolves the rock into a mucky clay that boils, burps, and throws lumps of mud on unwary observers. Even when it isn't converted into sulfuric acid, hydrogen sulfide can be lethal at high levels.

LOCATION, LOCATION, LOCATION
Yellowstone National Park has the most geothermal features in the world: 300 geysers—more geysers than the rest of the world combined. New Zealand is a distant second. Geysers are found on every continent except Antarctica. Outside of Yellowstone, only Siberia, New Zealand, and Iceland have significant numbers. *Geysir* is an Icelandic word meaning "spouter" or "gusher" and is actually the name of a particular geyser in Iceland. Considering that geologic time is measured in millions of years, geysers are babies. The oldest geyser in the world—thought to be Castle Geyser, just a short walk from Old Faithful—is between 5,000 and 40,000 years old (geyserology being an inexact science). Old Faithful is roughly 300 years old.

MORE GRISLY THAN GRIZZLIES
Don't get too close. At Yellowstone's altitude, water boils at 199°F (93°C); some hot springs spike up to 205°F (96°C). Lovely to look at, but lethal. At least nineteen people have accidentally boiled to death in Yellowstone's hot springs, more than have been killed by its bears.

MAKING A COMEBACK
Geologically speaking, geysers don't last long. They've been known to explode, blowing out their plumbing systems and becoming mere hot springs. But there have been cases where hot springs have suddenly become geysers because of the intervention of man. Solitary Spring in Yellowstone was channeled many years ago to provide hot water for a swimming pool, but when the water level decreased, Solitary Spring became Solitary Geyser. More geysers and hot springs are "spouting up" all the time. One rookie is Parking Lot Spring, discovered one day by a Yellowstone ranger in—you guessed it—one of the parking lots.

One quarter of all the bones in your body are in your feet, which have 52 bones.

THE AIR UP THERE

Clear as air. What could be simpler? When you look up, it's as if there's nothing between you and outer space. But it's more complicated than that; there's really a lot to the air.

Go outside (and take this book with you for further instructions). Now look up. What do you see? Unless something massive is plummeting toward you at great speed, chances are good that what you're looking up at is the sky—or, more accurately, Earth's atmosphere. It's understandable if you thought the atmosphere consisted of two parts: the mostly clear part near your house (unless you live in Los Angeles or Mexico City—then it's brown), and the blue part. There's more to it than that.

So take a deep breath. Hold on, here we go.

TROPOSPHERE: Ground floor. This is where every human lives (except the occasional wacky millionaire balloonist). Here the atmosphere is at its thickest—75 percent of the atmosphere's mass is in this level. It's a cocktail of gases that's about 78 percent nitrogen, 21 percent oxygen, a little less than one percent argon, and traces of carbon dioxide, methane, ammonia, nitrous oxide, hydrogen sulfide, helium, neon, krypton, xenon, and bus fumes.

The troposphere goes up four to five miles at the poles and up to eleven miles high at the equator, which means every part of the exposed surface of the earth, even the Himalayas, is swaddled with it. Nearly all clouds and weather systems are also contained within the troposphere. The temperature is fairly comfortable at the bottom where we are, but it quickly gets colder and thinner the higher up you go (ask any mountain climber). At the top of the troposphere, temperatures can go as low as –70°F (–57° C). Did you bring your sweater? And an oxygen mask?

STRATOSPHERE: Things called "stratospheric" are really high, so you may be surprised to learn that the stratosphere is only the second-lowest level of the atmosphere. It extends from the top of the troposphere to a height of 30 miles (48 km), which is high enough for most of us nonastronauts. One of the interesting things about the stratosphere is that it's warmer than the higher levels of the troposphere below. The temperature can reach nearly 32°F

(0°C), positively toasty compared to the –70°F (–57°C) of the higher troposphere. Why this relative heat wave? Ultraviolet (UV) radiation rains down on Earth from the Sun but gets blocked in the stratosphere, thanks to that famous ozone layer. When UV light gets blocked, heat is released. Without the ozone in the stratosphere, you'd need SPF 2,000 sunscreen, so be glad it's there, even if it is thinning out.

A volcanic eruption spews uncountable tons of microscopic dust particles into the stratosphere, where they get trapped and circulate for years, eventually spreading over the entire stratosphere. There they block light from the Sun, dropping Earth's overall temperature.

MESOSPHERE: This portion of the atmosphere goes from the top of the stratosphere to about 53 miles up. Temperatures begin to drop again, all the way down to about –130°F (–90°C). The mesosphere has much less water vapor than the atmosphere's lower levels, and a higher concentration of ozone. Pretty boring as atmospheric layers go, sort of like a bus station at 3 A.M.

THERMOSPHERE: In contrast, the thermosphere is a hopping place. This is where the International Space Station, the space shuttle, and lots of satellites orbit. And where auroras occur. It starts at the top of the mesosphere and goes up to about 370 miles (595 km); the higher you go, the higher the temperature. At its warmest, the thermosphere gets to above 3,000°F (1,649°C).

Why? Because there's not enough air to screen you from the Sun. If you think that'll cook your cookies, think again. This heat can't be compared to that of other layers. The high temperature means that each air molecule is really hot, but there aren't many molecules in the thin air, so you don't absorb a lot of heat. Wear a muffler if you're leaving the space station to go for a walk.

EXOSPHERE: Satellites orbit here, too, but the atmosphere is so thin that "exosphere" is just another word for "vacuum in denial." Here, lighter elements like hydrogen and helium float away from Earth's gravitational field and wander off. The exosphere extends from the top of the thermosphere and sort of fades out into the interplanetary medium—a fancy way of saying "space." If you've followed us all the way up, congratulations, you're now floating somewhere between Earth and the Moon. Don't look now, but is that a spy satellite sneaking up on us?

Streaks on iris petals guide bees to the flower's nectar.

WAITER! PUT MORE FLIES IN MY SOUP!

Eating bugs. It's not just for frogs anymore.

In some parts of the world it's the "other" white meat. When lovingly prepared, the skin is tender and crisp and the sweet, inner flesh has a delicate flavor reminiscent of almonds. Hmmm. There's nothing like a delicious plate of fried grubs!

PEANUT BUGS AND JELLY

Many of us think of insects as dirty, disgusting creatures, and we'd only eat them if we were stranded in the wilderness without a pocketful of trail mix—or trying to survive on a show like *Survivor*. But the truth is, bugs often show up in your lunch without you knowing it. In grain mills, the occasional beetle or weevil is ground into the flour that makes bread and pastries. Worm-infested apples are made into cider, and ants get picked with the grapes that are fermented into wine.

In fact, the U.S. Department of Health and Human Services has a maximum allowable insect level for ordinary foods. Take peanut butter, for instance. The maximum amount allowed by law is 60 insect parts per hundred grams.

If you've just lost your appetite for peanut butter and jelly sandwiches, consider how enjoyable it is to dine on flower nectar that's eaten and regurgitated by bees. We call it honey. And, just like honey, bugs can be a delicacy.

EATING INSECTS CAN BE DIVINE!

The scientific term for "eating bugs" is "entomophagy," and it's been going on since prehistoric man started digging termites out of hollow logs. No less an authority than the Old Testament gives a thumbs-up to this four-course meal in Leviticus 11:22: "Even these of them ye may eat: the locust after his kind, and the bald locust after his kind, and the beetle after his kind, and the grasshopper after his kind." Not to be outdone, the New Testament reports that John the Baptist survived in the desert on locusts and wild honey. And Muslims talk about Mohammed's wives sending him trays of locusts as presents.

The peacock's fan, which is called a train, is not its tail; the real tail holds the train up.

THE OTHER RED MEAT

It's not only religions that consider bugs a blessing; researchers like them, too, as a way to combat worldwide hunger. Since insects like locusts and termites migrate in the millions, their sheer abundance makes them an efficient food source. Insects are nutritious. Three and a half ounces (100 g) of lean ground beef contains 27.4 grams of protein, while the same amount of small grasshoppers has a protein value of 20.6—and bugs are much cheaper to raise than cows. Termites are higher in protein than beef and have enough fat to make them a good source of calories for people who need (pardon the pun) "beefing up."

Bugs can supply amino acids, vitamins, and minerals. Grasshoppers are a good source of calcium; crickets have lots of riboflavin. And if you're feeling run-down, try feasting on giant water bugs—they have over 13 milligrams of iron in a serving, compared to a paltry 3.6 in beef!

EASY PICKINGS

The benefits of insects did not escape the notice of native indigenous peoples. At the Great Salt Lake in Utah, for example, swarms of grasshoppers were often blown into the lake. After they'd washed ashore and dried in the sun, the Native Americans of the Great Basin gathered hundreds of pounds of them to grind into flour for bread.

In South America during the "swarming season," the Amazons gathered edible ants by the basketful. Australian Aborigines gorged on huge amounts of Bogong moths, which tasted so good that they were sometimes ground into a paste for cakes. Move over, Duncan Hines!

BUGGED ABOUT BEEF

Eating animals consumes a lot of the earth's resources. For example, only four percent of the grain that cows consume is converted to actual body mass; insects convert grain nearly ten times more efficiently. Environmentalists like to point out that if more people ate insects, the application of insecticides around the world would diminish—along with the danger of pesticide use.

Of course, the truth is that none of these arguments has as yet sent everyone looking under a rock for their next meal. Most of us are reserving judgment—eating bugs may be good for us and great for the earth...but hey, how do they taste?

BEE WORLDLY AND SOPHISTICATED

Except for those fancy French snails, in the United States and most of Europe, insects and food are not supposed to mix. But in a lot of other places, insects are considered pretty much luscious. They say that beetles taste like apples and wasps taste like pine nuts. Fried termites have been compared to fried pork rinds—and everybody loves pork rinds! Don't they?

Some favorites from around the globe:

- **China:** In some areas, fried scorpions are a delicacy.
- **Colombia:** Leaf-cutter ants are toasted and served in movie theaters. We hear they taste like bacon.
- **Japan:** Restaurants in Tokyo serve *hachi-no-ko,* or boiled wasp larvae. Fried wasps mixed with boiled rice, sugar, and soy sauce was a favorite dish of Emperor Hirohito.
- **Mexico:** Chocolate-covered bees are a gourmet item.
- **Nigeria:** Kanni, a caterpillar, is dried in the sun and boiled in vegetable soup.
- **Philippines:** Grasshoppers are an all-around favorite, especially in soup.
- **Sweden:** Ant pupae are used to flavor gin.
- **Thailand:** A favorite is *takkatan,* or grasshopper, prized for its shrimplike flavor.
- **Santa Monica, California:** Wait a minute! Santa Monica? In America? Yup, the trendy and highly praised Typhoon Restaurant serves dishes like deep-fried scorpions in sweet and sour sauce. And a side order of ants sprinkled on potato strings gets consistently fabulous reviews.

WORMS HAVE GERMS

In a campaign to tempt the world to go buggy, entomophagy experts have put forth tempting (well, sort of tempting) tips on eating our many-legged friends. First of all, don't just go hunting under a rock for your next meal. Some insects are poisonous; others may be contaminated with pesticides.

While you might want to entertain your friends by chewing live worms, forget it. Insects can contain germs and parasites, so they should always be fully cooked and cleaned. For the brave-hearted and iron-stomached, there are safe sources of clean, pesticide-free insects—take, for example, the crickets and mealworms sold at pet stores.

Bon appetit!

A flamingo gets its pink color from the algae and shrimp it eats.

TOOL TIME

Benjamin Franklin called us humans "tool-making animals"—and the only tool-making animals. As it turns out, some animals use tools, too. And they don't just grab anything at hand.

Cactus spines: Woodpecker finches on the Galapagos Islands like to eat grubs that live inside trees. They pry out their food with a sharp cactus spine. While they eat, they tuck the cactus spine under one foot, saving it for the next job.

Rocks: Vultures and buzzards go after ostrich and emu eggs in their own ways. Some throw the eggs at hard places; others do the opposite and bomb the eggs from overhead with rocks.

More rocks: Sea otters dive to the ocean floor for mollusks like mussels, clams, and abalone. They bring the food—and a rock—back up to the surface. Then, while they float around on the surface, they smash the shellfish against the stone until it opens.

Cars and trucks: Seriously. Some seagulls open their shellfish the old way—they drop their catches onto rocks to smash them open. But others have caught on to a neat trick. They drop their shellfish on the road and wait for oncoming traffic to break them open.

Leaves, twigs, etc.: Chimpanzees use leaves as handkerchiefs or toilet paper. They also use chewed leaves (which work like sponges) to soak up water from tree hollows. Twigs become toothbrushes, and branches are digging tools for poking into burrows to see what's in there and for getting fruit that's out of reach.

Anything they can get their paws on: In an experiment in captivity, a psychologist put some tasty bananas just out of reach, and left a lot of stuff lying around for his chimpanzee subjects to use: wooden boxes, sticks of different lengths, and so on. The chimps dragged the boxes around and stacked them up, then stood on them to reach higher. They used the sticks as clubs, rakes, and climbing poles. One even stuck the end of one bamboo pole inside another to create a longer pole.

Praying mantises eat their victims alive.

HEAR YE! HEAR YE!

That rounded top.
Those curves. Oooh.
Those interesting nooks and crannies…

We're talking about your ears, of course. Why the heck are they so funny-looking? Why do they have those curves and crinkles?

THE DECORATION THEORY

The ancients thought the outer ear was little more than a set of spirals that offset and added interest to the domed shape of the head. Later, some deeper thinkers conceded that it might double as an inefficient ear trumpet, something to "catch" sounds. But all in all, it was generally accepted that the outer ear served no useful purpose whatever.

ALL THE BETTER TO HEAR YOU WITH

It turns out that those crinkles and furrows are complex channels that add a slight reflected sound, or echo, to anything you hear. The echo varies with the different angles that sounds originate from. For example, if you hear a sound above you, the tiny echo added by your ears' crinkles will differ from the echo of a sound coming from below or behind you.

COME AGAIN?

The echo enters your ear a fraction of a second after the main sound does. Your brain then analyzes the sound and the echo and instantly tells you the direction the sound came from. It all happens so quickly that you're not even conscious of it.

Of course, a sound coming from your right reaches your right ear before your left ear and vice versa, which also helps you figure out the direction it came from.

LITTLE BIRDIE IN THE SKY…

This way, you know where to look when you hear the knock-knock of a woodpecker or the tweet-tweet of a bird perched in that tree right over your head.

If a chameleon is angry its skin turns black.

WHAT ARE YOU WEARING?

The cavemen huddled together for warmth, begging the gods of winter for mercy. Seized by an idea, Og leaped up and skinned the deer they'd just caught. He flung the warm (but bloody) pelt around his shivering woman. Ogga yelped in outrage, but quickly silenced when she realized how warm it was. Together, she and Og huddled under the pelt while the other cavemen looked at the first fur coat with awe and jealousy.

We wear clothing for a lot of reasons—not just to keep warm. Our duds are meant for modesty (or not) or to make statements about ourselves. Are we flashy or reserved? Formal or casual? Even when we buy a new coat, we're usually more concerned with how it looks than with its weather-repelling qualities.

We've come a long way since people wore bloody pelts—and animal-rights activists aren't the only ones who are happy about it. Let's look at what the stuff we wear is made of—starting, of course, with man-made fabric.

THE ALL-NATURAL TEAM
If a plant or tree produces a fiber, there's a good chance that someone has tried to weave it. Here's how we get the fibers of the ones that worked best for us.

Cotton: We like cotton. It feels nice, it's cool to wear. It comes from small plants that are covered with bolls (cotton balls that kind of look like the ones you can buy at the drugstore except they're filled with scratchy seeds). To get at the cotton, we spray chemicals on it that eat away the leaves (Why not? We'll plant again next year, anyway). Then the cotton gin comes along and picks the bolls off the plant. The bolls are passed along something rough (like a toothed cylinder or a leather-covered roller), which combs out the cotton strands.

Wool: It doesn't only come from sheep. It also comes from Angora goats, Kashmir goats, alpaca, vicuña (a South American camel), and llamas. To get the wool, we simply shear it off. But since it came from animals, the wool is loaded with dirt, perspiration, and lanolin (which is used in lotions). All of this is cleaned

---

Seven out of 10 of the first domain names registered went to universities.

out using solvents. Next, the wool fibers are actually sorted according to length and factors such as crimp (curl) and how well it will "felt" (yes, wool is used to make the felt that covers pool tables and Shriners' heads).

Silk: Unquestionably the most luxurious natural fiber. In ancient Rome it was literally worth its weight in gold. The famous Silk Road went from the Middle East to deep into the interior of China. But silk has a humble origin—it comes from the cocoon of a silkworm. To get the fibers, we boil it to soften the gum that holds it together, and then simply unwind the cocoon. We can get 2,000 to 3,000 feet of filament from a single cocoon!

Linen: The oldest natural fiber, it comes from the stalk of the flax plant. The stalk is left to rot—or ret, as they say. After a few days of this, the stem has softened, making it easier to get at the fibers. The fibers are removed, cleaned, combed, and sorted. Hemp fibers are obtained using the same process.

IN A LEAGUE OF ITS OWN

Rayon: The first manufactured fiber, rayon was developed in France in the 1890s and was originally called "artificial silk." Unlike most man-made fibers, rayon isn't synthetic—it's made from wood pulp, a cellulose-based raw material. As a result, rayon is more similar to cotton or linen than to the thermoplastic, petroleum-based synthetic fibers such as nylon or polyester. To which we turn next.

THE OTHER TEAM

Man-made fibers come from chemical compounds that are spun into fibers. First, the materials are liquefied, then forced through a sort of showerhead called a spinneret. The holes in the spinneret vary in size depending on the thickness of the fiber desired. As the liquid comes out of the spinneret, they solidify very quickly. If you've every seen a cotton-candy vendor at work, you're familiar with the process.

The most common man-made fibers are acetate (fake silk), acrylic (fake fur), nylon (which is used in everything from panty hose to flak vests), polyester (the bane of the 1970s—and the fashion statement of the 2000s).

Then there's that all-time favorite: Spandex, the stre-e-e-tchy fabric that makes skirts and bathing suits and all other clingy clothes cling so nicely.

THE MOUSE THAT ROARED

Eat Douglas Engelbart's dust, Walt Disney!
A scientist creates a mouse that's even more famous than Mickey.

One day in 1950, Douglas C. Engelbart was driving to his job at Ames Research Center (which, by the way, later became NASA) in Mountain View, California.

Just the day before, he'd asked his future wife to marry him. The realization came to him "that getting married and living happily ever after was the last of my goals." He then calculated how many minutes of working life he had left in him (he was only 25 at the time) and came up with about five and a half million. He wondered how he could maximize the use of that time, for himself—and for mankind.

THAT'S DOCTOR ENGELBART, BUDDY!

For Engelbart, the answer was computers. By the following year, he was enrolled in graduate school at the University of California at Berkeley, where they were conducting a project to build a general-purpose digital computer. He earned his Ph.D. in electrical engineering in 1955.

THE WIZARD OF MENLO PARK

Unlike a lot of engineers, Engelbart was a guy who liked to look at the big picture—and we mean the *really* big picture. As he saw it, society and its problems were becoming increasingly complex, requiring new ways of thinking, new ways of processing information, and new ways of sharing ideas.

He found the perfect outlet for his agenda at the Stanford Research Center (an independent think tank) in Menlo Park, California, where he set out to create new tools for working with words and ideas. He eventually came up with just such a tool, which he dubbed the NLS (oN Line System).

USER UNFRIENDLY

Since the digital computer's birth in the 1940s, its main work had

---

The first Space Shuttle astronauts selected M&Ms as part of their food supply.

centered around crunching numbers. Power was more important than speed, and "ease of use" was unheard of. Computers required operators to enter programs and data slowly, by hand, on paper cards or paper tape. The operators would put the cards into a "reader," then wait 20 minutes or so for a result. No one imagined that computers could work instantaneously.

And no one, it seemed, could see the benefits of devoting a computer's power to tasks such as writing and outlining documents. But this was exactly what Engelbart's new system of computing—the NLS—was designed to do.

WHAT A MICE IDEA!
By the early 1960s, Engelbart had succeeded in building a "writing machine"—in essence, a word processor—that would let someone revise and reorganize text and ideas on the fly.

There were two parts to the machine. The first was a new kind of one-handed keyboard, or console. The user typed in information by hitting combinations of five keys, kind of like playing a piano chord. The other component was a chunky, square wooden box with two metal wheels and a single button, tethered to the computer console with a chord.

In the lab, Engelbart and his colleagues had called it a "mouse" after its tail-like cable—and the name stuck. With his mouse, Engelbart could select (or highlight) text, move it around, and otherwise manipulate it.

HE DOES WINDOWS, TOO!
In 1964, Engelbart's first prototype computer mouse was made to use with a graphical user interface (GUI) system that he referred to as "windows." He received a patent for the mouse in 1970.

VIRTUALLY A REALITY
Today, the descendants of his NLS, with its mouse and graphic display and "writing machine," sit on millions of desks around the world. And with the arrival of the Internet, e-mail, and "groupware" systems that allow people to communicate and communally organize their ideas with incredible speed and flexibility, it would seem that Engelbart didn't waste even one of those five and a half million minutes.

MENU ON THE MOON

*With a full belly, man can overcome almost any challenge,
even the challenges of outer space.*

Throughout history, intrepid adventurers and successful armies of conquest have marched on their stomachs. The wagon trains and cattle drives that opened the American frontier would have stalled without Cookie and his chuck wagon. Camp cooks have always ruled their little kingdoms, be they isolated lumber camps, mine operations, or construction projects.

All of which NASA researchers took into consideration as they prepared to breach the frontiers of space.

MERCURY POISONING?
Unfortunately for the early Mercury astronauts, Buck Rogers and Isaac Asimov had more influence on their meals than Martha Stewart might have. The menu consisted of unidentified snacks: cubes textured like dog biscuits, freeze-dried powders as appetizing as Mojave Desert dust, and tubes of glutinous matter resembling toothpaste but not nearly as flavorful. The cubes crumbled, the powders wouldn't dissolve, and those tubes—they were the first to go. Fit fare for Martians, maybe, but not for humans.

NAME THAT FOOD
Gemini astronauts had it better. Packaging improved. The ever-adventurous food scientists at NASA now dared to identify the food for their astronauts—for example, shrimp, chicken, apple-sauce. This was one step for mankind, but still a long way from the real thing. Maybe that's why astronaut John Young smuggled a corned beef sandwich aboard a Gemini flight in 1965. Gus Grissom ate it, but Young was officially reprimanded (the first astronaut to be reprimanded for anything).

THE AGE OF TANG
Grissom may have washed down that sandwich with a swig of Tang. Pillsbury/General Foods had been trying unsuccessfully to foist the powdered orange drink on a highly suspecting public for three years. But once Tang qualified for the space program, sales shot up. Everybody wanted to try the "drink of the astronauts."

THE END OF HIGH-FLYING HASH

As the Apollo program went into orbit, NASA's faith in the skills of their astronauts improved. This time it actually provided them with spoons—another leap forward. But special containers had to be designed to overcome the near-weightlessness of the cabin. Nobody wanted their pea soup stuck to the ceiling any more than they wanted to have to chase after shrimp that had floated off their dinner tray. Another boon was hot water to rehydrate those powders; that meant fewer lumps and better flavor. Still, no one in orbit was getting fat.

PLEASE PASS THE POTATOES

Skylab, launched in 1973, changed everything—it had an actual dining area, with a table and chairs (that diners had to strap themselves to). Utensils now included not only a knife, fork, and spoon, but also a pair of scissors for opening food packets. A refrigerator and a freezer completed the homelike atmosphere. With things looking up on the equipment side, the food side got better, too. Astronauts could now select from 72 items. They seemed to have everything but a maître d' and a decent wine list.

EATING LIKE EARTHLINGS

Given the confined dining space, an astronaut's food choices were more contingent on the development of packaging, preparation, and serving equipment than on available foods. The concoctions were already available. Earthbound, we've got egg substitutes, hamburger extenders, chocolate bars without cocoa, artificially flavored and colored fruit, and so on. In space, so do the astronauts—but they've had to wait for suitable packaging.

PACKAGING THE MOVABLE FEAST

Space shuttle meals limit each astronaut to one pound of packaging waste daily, a day's food supply having a gross weight of 3.8 pounds, including snacks (this means that more than 25 percent of a meal package is meant to be thrown away—and if you think that's a lot, have a look at almost any frozen dinner available to us nonastronauts).

Months ahead of a flight, astronauts plan their own meals. Engineers review their choices to make sure they won't weigh too much (the meals, not the astronauts). Then nutritionists review the menus to ensure the shuttle won't be harboring a junk food

---

The hardest substance made by your body is tooth enamel.

addict or a budding anorexic. Too much packaging and too much waste food (what we Earthlings call leftovers) could screw up the garbage compactor. Just prior to the flight, the food packages are individually color-coded and stored in the shuttle galley.

A MEAL THAT STICKS TO YOUR...TABLE
To an astronaut, the single most important technological advance for space flight wasn't all-purpose duct tape or crazy glue, it was Velcro. The individual packages containing a full meal could be Velcroed to a tray and all opened at the same time. Previously, packages had to be opened one at a time and consumed before the next was opened. Otherwise, the first package could float away while the astronaut snipped at the top of another. Shuttle crews can now have a full-course hot meal reconstituted in a recognizable form and on a dinner tray within 35 minutes. Not bad.

KITCHEN WIZARDRY
NASA chefs were no slouches. When the tricks of conventional cookery didn't work, they invented some of their own. Many of their offerings were provided with varying amounts of water removed from them. "Add water and eat" or "Add water, heat, and eat" were about the only directions astronauts needed. Breakfast was a breeze: cereal, sugar, and powdered milk in a single pouch. Add water, and voila! It would snap, crackle, and pop with the best of them, even if it didn't come with a prize.

You can taste some of this handiwork in commercially available camping and trail foods. (And we can thank NASA impetus for those small, full-panel pull-off lids on cans—they thought of them first.)

THE LONG HAUL
And all that while, NASA was gearing up to feed astronauts for prolonged periods. The orbiting space station has facilities to provide frozen, refrigerated, and thermostabilized food (heat-treated to kill off the bad stuff).

NASA had to give up its passion to just add water—the space station couldn't generate enough—which meant that astronauts could finally eat fresh food. Moreover, every four astronauts had their own microwave/convection oven; no more line ups to liquefy and heat those first cups of morning coffee.

With all these technical advances has come a quantum

expansion of the menu. Astronauts can choose from nine different cereals, some with fruit; nine different chicken entrees; ten different vegetables; four flavors of yogurt; regular, decaf, or Kona (excuse me!) coffee—and that's just for starters.

CHECK, PLEASE!

The menu on space flights seems to have reached such gourmet standards that private citizens are paying millions for just a short hop. Of course, there's still no wine list, but when tourists can plan their own menus months before tying on the bib—that gives NASA lots of time to procure the best ingredients, not to mention using the acumen of expert chefs and the latest technology to ensure optimal quality and freshness.

CHIX IN SPACE

NASA knows that accessing remote space frontiers may require space flights that last for years, so they've started to figure out ways to fashion a self-contained, self-sustaining food system— shades of *2001: A Space Odyssey*, not to mention *Silent Running*.

The cities in space that cosmologist Stephen Hawking talks about will require the same approach. NASA has already sent (unplanted) tomato and mung bean seeds into orbit, as well as chicken embryos, just to find out what effects, if any, space travel would have on them. As it turned out, the effects were negligible. And NASA scientists have been fiddling with hydroponic (that is, grown only in water) lettuce in space simulation labs.

Help in this regard has come from the private sector: The tomato seeds courtesy of H. J. Heinz, and KFC footing some of the bill for the "Chix in Space" experiments. (We were getting kind of bored with "spacecraft metallic" anyway: Make way for billboards in space!)

* * * * *

"Everyone is a moon, and has a dark side,
which he never shows to anybody."

—Mark Twain

When you sleep your brain is more active than when you are watching TV.

OLD AS THE HILLS

*You've probably never heard of them. But you
(and Uncle John) probably wouldn't exist without them.*

If you were asked to name some of the world's oldest living creatures, you might mention the cockroach, the horseshoe crab,
the crocodile, or the shark. If you were a biology major or have
spent any time in New Zealand, you might cite a large reptile
called the tuatara. But something called a stromatolite?

SOMETHING CALLED A STROMATOLITE
They're ancient creatures with two claims to fame. They
contributed to the oxygenation of Earth's atmosphere, and to this
very day they exist not only as one of the oldest recorded fossils,
but also as living organisms (how's that for old?).

BEFORE LIFE BEGAN...
If we could go back about 3.5 billion years, we'd find stromatolites
all over the place. Unfortunately for the stromatolites, the oxygen
they produced made it possible for life to appear on the earth.
And what happened? That very same life ate the stromatolites—a
typical example of "biting the hand that feeds you." Fortunately,
by then plants had taken over the role of helping to oxygenate the
atmosphere, so other forms of life could grow and prosper.

In fact, stromatolites were the dominant life form on the
earth for over two billion years.

CONSOLE YOURSELF
Few people have ever heard of them. But the people who live
near Hamelin Pool in Shark Bay, Western Australia, are well
acquainted with them. That's one of the few places in the world
that stromatolites exist as both fossils and living organisms. Western Australia also has the oldest known fossils of stromatolites—
3.45 billion years old.

Stromatolites still survive in Hamelin Pool because the water
is far too saline for other forms of life—the same forms of life that
would eat the stromatolites if not for the saltiness.

ROCKS OF AGES

Stromatolites don't have a lot of curb appeal. They look like lumps of cone-shaped rock scattered on the sand. They don't move or blink, and you'll never see one on TV, eating peanuts out of Jay Leno's hand. They don't even grow very fast. The Hamelin Poolites (Hey, somebody! What a great name for a band!) grow a maximum of 0.3 millimeters a year.

SO WHAT THE HECK ARE THEY EXACTLY?

Okay. A stromatolite is a layered deposit, mostly of limestone, that is built by the growth of primitive one-celled organisms (bacteria) that trap and bind the layers of sediment together. And because they "breathe in" carbon dioxide and "breathe out" oxygen, these small, and pretty much boring, stromatolites aren't so boring after all; they're probably responsible for the oxygenation of Earth's atmosphere in the first place. That's all.

* * * * *

MORE MNEAT MNEMONICS

Geologic time periods (from most recent to oldest):
Holocene, Pleistocene, Pliocene, Miocene, Oligocene, Eocene, Paleocene, Cretaceous, Jurassic, Triassic, Permian, Pennsylvanian, Mississippian, Devonian, Silurian, Ordovician, Cambrian
• How Peter Prudently Managed One Evil Problem: Calculating Jacobians Trivially, Peter Performed Many Devious Slimes Of Course!

Periods of the Paleozoic era (from oldest to most recent):
Cambrian, Ordovician, Silurian, Devonian, Mississippian, Pennsylvanian, Permian
• Come On, See Daring Men Play Polo.
• Campbell's Onion Soup Does Make People Puke.
• Can Oscar See Down My Pants Pocket?

Periods of the Cenozoic era (from oldest to most recent):
Paleocene, Eocene, Oligocene, Miocene, Pliocene, Pleistocene
• Phooey! Even Old Men Play Polo.
• Put Eggs On My Plate, Please.

There are 3 fruits native to North America: blueberries, Concord grapes, and cranberries.

A SALTY TALE

Aye! So ye want to know why the sea is salty?
Gather 'round, me buckos!

The sea. It's dark, it's deep, and it holds vast mysteries—such as why when a wave knocks you in the face while you're bodysurfing, you have to swallow the contents of a salt shaker with the gallon or two of water that is suddenly sliding down your throat. Where the heck did all that salt come from, anyway? Fresh water—that is, water flowing into the oceans from rivers and streams—doesn't have that kind of salt in it. Right?

PASS THE SALT, PLEASE

Right, but it does have some salt—and not just salt (or sodium chloride, which is the salt we have on our tables) but also other salts and minerals. Take a glass of water from the Amazon, the Mississippi, or the Nile, and you'll find a veritable chemistry set of elements swimming in the H_2O—stuff like iron, calcium, magnesium, potassium, sodium, and chloride, as well as compounds like silica, nitrate, and bicarbonate. These elements are leached out of the land by the water through rain and other means, and eventually all that mineral-laden water washes out into the ocean.

Every year, almost 750 million tons of sediment and dissolved minerals are flushed into the seas from the U.S. alone.

THOSE SELFISH SHELLFISH

Once that water makes it to the ocean, much of the mineral goodness is sucked out of the water by, of all things, oceanic life. Plankton known as diatoms use the silica to make shells; shrimp, crabs, and lobsters use calcium salts to make theirs. Calcium is also used by sponges, clams, oysters, and other creatures.

However—and this is important—no sea creature extracts sodium from the water; it stays in the water (even sea creatures know too much sodium is bad for the diet). This is one of the reasons why sodium and chloride are only 16 percent of the dissolved minerals in river water, but a big 85 percent of those found in seawater.

The ocean's plant life makes up 85% of all of Earth's greenery.

SALTY WATER EVERYWHERE

That doesn't explain why seawater is saltier than river water; it just explains why there are fewer other minerals in the seawater. What happens is that the salt becomes more concentrated when water evaporates off the surface of the ocean and is carried away. The water evaporates, but the salt doesn't—it's left behind to make the remaining water ever so slightly saltier. The water that's evaporated goes off as clouds, some of which drop their rain over solid ground. That water courses through the earth, picking up salt and other minerals, and makes another trip to the sea, where the whole process starts over. Do this long enough—a couple of billion years or so—and the sea becomes noticeably saltier.

BUT NOT A DROP TO DRINK

How salty? On average, in every ton of seawater, there's about 70 pounds of salt mixed in. Some seawater is saltier than others. The saltiest seawater in the world is in the Red Sea, which is in a hot, dry area of the world that encourages lots of evaporation. See how that works? If you travel north to the chilly Baltic Sea, you'll find that it's up to eight times less salty than the Red Sea. Roughly speaking, warmer climates have saltier seas than cooler areas of the world.

Even if you've been floating in a lifeboat for a week, parched by the sun, thirsty as all get-out—don't drink the water! It's a diuretic that will end up taking more water out of you than it puts back—it'll dehydrate you even more.

THAT'S SALT, FOLKS!

Over four billion tons of salts make it to the ocean every year, so it's fair to wonder if the seas are eventually going to become a sludgy slurry of salt. The best answer seems to be no; while those billions of tons of salts enter the seas every year, it's estimated that a similar amount falls out to become a sediment on the ocean floor, some of which might even eventually become part of dry land (Bonneville Salt Flats, perhaps?). For now, at least, the oceans are as salty as they want to be.

Polecats are nocturnal European weasels, not cats.

SCRATCH AND SNIFF

Throw away those personals ads. Fire your matchmaking service.
Just take a deep breath—through your nose.

Scientists first stumbled onto nose power when they studied pheromones in animals and insects. The word *pheromone* comes from the Greek words *phero* "I carry," and *hormone*, which means "to excite"—so the word literally means "I carry excitement." And they do. Pheromones are chemicals that create signals between members of the same species. In animals and insects, pheromones can "command" sexual arousal or sexual receptivity. Humans have more of a choice. (Or think they do.)

Though pheromones are supposedly odorless, mammals detect them by an organ inside the nose—called a vomeronasal organ (VNO)—a pair of microscopically tiny pits on the skin inside the nostrils. When the VNO picks up a chemical order from pheromones, get out of the way!

THE POWER OF PHEROMONES
Here are some findings from the animal kingdom:
- Male mice emit pheromones so potent they actually promote the sexual development of nearby female mice.
- A male moth can detect the pheromones of a female moth from over a mile away, and has no choice but to fly toward her.
- If a sow sniffs the pheromones in a male pig's saliva, she'll freeze—that's it, she's ready to mate.
- Male cockroaches may be the most pheromone-crazy creatures of all. When a glass rod is doused with female cockroach pheromones, the males try to mate with the rod.

GUYS IN SWEATY T-SHIRTS
Humans aren't sows, and they certainly aren't cockroaches, so how does this apply to us? Human love is deep and spiritual—right? Skeptics claimed that the VNO wasn't functional in adult humans; it couldn't possibly react to pheromones. Here's what the research showed:

- Underarm sweat has a pheromone component produced by the chemical androstenol. An experiment showed that exposure to

There are over 6 billion dust mites in an average bed.

androstenol (a chemical in underarm sweat with a pheromone component) made females more inclined to have social interactions with males (easy, boys, that's "social" interactions).

- When women were asked to smell unwashed T-shirts worn by different men, they liked the smell of men whose immune systems were different from their own. Since different genes emit different smells, the women may have automatically been sniffing for an evolutionary advantage—the combination of immune system genes that are better at fighting off infections.

- Extracts of skin cells with pheromones sitting in open flasks in a lab made the lab workers (male and female) warmer and friendlier. When the flasks were closed, the camaraderie faded.

- Pheromone-laced perfume increased women's sexual attractiveness. Women got more requests for dates and sexual intimacy.

- A set of female twins—one doused with pheromones, the other with witch hazel—secretly traded places at a singles' bar. The one wearing the pheromones was approached nearly three times as often as her witch hazel–wearing sister.

- Men "under the influence" of pheromones found plain women more attractive—and beautiful women less attractive.

STOP PAYING THROUGH THE NOSE
There are lots of pheromone products on the market—but are they really the "love potions" they purport to be? Scientists aren't sure. One thing they agree on is that the nose plays an important part in mating. People who are born blind, deaf, or dumb engage in "normal" sexual behavior, but people born with no sense of smell tend to have diminished sexual behavior.

THE TURN-ONS AND TURNOFFS
In more research—this time in pheromone-free zones—it was found that men were most aroused when they caught a whiff of lavender combined with pumpkin pie. Women went wild over licorice and cucumber. Women were definitely turned off by the scent of cherries and barbecue smoke. What smell turned men off? Well, nothing actually. It seems as if it's pretty tough to discourage a guy who's got love on the brain. Or is it on the nose? (Or maybe somewhere else.)

ASTRONAUTS DO IT SITTING DOWN

Astronauts can spend months on a space shuttle. Have you ever wondered, like we have, exactly what the "amenities" consist of?

They call it a WCS, not for "Water Closet Something-or-other," but for "Waste Containment System," and it makes the bathroom on a 747 look luxurious.

SPACE-AGE DECOR
It's actually a little bigger than a bathroom on an airplane, but instead of cornball wallpaper and rounded plastic edges, a WCS is all sharp edges, metallic, and studded with bolts, gauges, clamps, and strange-looking machines. And handholds and footrests. The overall effect is torture-chamber modern. The most inviting and familiar sight is a white toilet seat that sits on a metallic platform.

NUMBER ONE
First, let's look at the urinal arrangement. Each astronaut (and astronette) has a personal funnel that is attached to a hose for urinating. Fans suck air and urine through the funnel and hose into a waste water tank.

NUMBER TWO
For actual sitting on the john—and don't forget we're in zero gravity—the astronauts have to unscrew the lid first and position themselves on the toilet seat, attaching themselves to leg restraints and thigh bars. Like the number one arrangement, the toilet waste matter is sucked into the commode by vacuumlike fans.

FURTHER AMENITIES
The bathroom also contains dry and wet wipes to wash hands and faces. Curtains close off the area for privacy, so it's also used for changing clothes and taking what can't be very luxurious sponge baths.

THE BUG IN THE SYSTEM
The current "extended duration" or EDO WCS was designed for longer shuttle flights, and despite all those nuts and bolts, has leakage problems. Funny. You can send whole gangs of people into space, but designing a nonleaking toilet—now that's a challenge!

The average beard grows five inches (140 mm) per year.

TO KEY OR NOT TO KEY

If you would not be forgotten,
As soon as you are dead & rotten,
Either write things worth reading,
Or do things worth the writing.
—*Benjamin Franklin*

Okay, so Ben Franklin wasn't a great poet. But boy, could he do things worth the writing! Perhaps his most famous exploit was the kite-flying incident. You know how it went: stormy night, kite with metallic wire, and a key tied to the end of the string with a silk ribbon. Lightning strikes, Ben has harnessed electricity.

GET OUTTA HERE!
Oh, puh-leeeze, says the Boston Museum of Science. They think if Franklin actually performed this experiment (which they have some doubts about), he was too smart to do it the way the legend says he did. He knew that if he flew a kite, with a key attached, in a thunderstorm—and touched it—he'd cook like a cod in a deep fryer. So, doubts about the incident and strong misgivings about the key. Although, maybe it's just a little intercity rivalry—after all, Ben fled Boston when he was 17 and ended up in Philadelphia, where the (ahem) Franklin Institute has no misgivings about the story.

THE EXPERT
Franklin first wrote about electricity in 1747 and followed that up with a whole book, *Experiments and Observations on Electricity*, in 1751. The kite experiment came the year after. See, says Boston. A man who could write a whole book on the subject wouldn't be so stupid.

IT WAS A DARK AND STORMY NIGHT
As the story goes, in 1752, Benjamin Franklin set himself up in a shed with his 21-year-old son William and the kite. (All the illustrations show Franklin out in the storm, but notice he isn't even wet, and in most of them William is nowhere to be found.)

Earth's automobiles are multiplying three times faster than the human population.

SMART ENOUGH
Franklin was trying to prove something that we take for granted—that lightning was an electrical current in nature and was, in fact, electricity. He was smart enough to know that a bolt of lightning must be an awful lot of the stuff, and that it must take a long time to amass in the storm. Therefore, he thought, I'll fly my kite early in the storm before the lightning gets too close.

OUT THE WINDOW
Here's where the story gets dubious. Supposedly, when Franklin—still in the shed—saw loose threads on the kite string stand up, he put his hand out the window and grounded his makeshift insulated conductor by touching his knuckle to the key. The spark that passed between his knuckle and the key presented the final proof of lightning's electrical nature. Yes, but…

A MIRACLE!!!
Almost all accounts call it miraculous that the charge wasn't strong enough to kill Franklin. So how do we know that Franklin actually did it?

Well, he never wrote about it himself. All that we know about what happened that night (and we only know the year, not the day) comes from an account written by Franklin's good friend Joseph Priestley, published 15 years later. Priestley (most famous for the discovery of oxygen) must have shown the manuscript of his *History and Present State of Electricity* to Franklin, who must have given Priestley the precise, familiar details.

Priestley calls Franklin's evening in a thunderstorm "the greatest (discovery), perhaps since the time of Sir Isaac Newton." And he bases his account on "a few particulars which I have from the best authority." The authority being Franklin.

OKAY, NOW YOU TRY IT
So that's where the story came from, Franklin telling the tale 15 years later. If we're to believe it, our hero got away with it. The electricity only raised the hair on his knuckles.

The story would be more believable if the next two investigators who tried it hadn't been zapped. Killed. Dead. Deceased.

Then again, they weren't Ben Franklin.

KEEP ON MOVIN'

Ever feel like you're going a million miles an hour? Maybe it's because you are. Learn all the ways you're moving, even when you're standing still. Hold on to your hat.

Stand still. Just for a second. No, on second thought, forget it. You can't stand still. As long as you're on this planet, you're in a constant state of motion, sliding across the face of the earth, spinning around its axis, and zooming through the universe. Look, you're doing it right now. Have a seat and we'll explain all the ways you're on the move.

1. Plate tectonics: You probably know this better as "continental drift"—how the huge, overlapping plates that form the surface of the planet are constantly rubbing against or diving under each other. Most of the movement goes unnoticed, but every once in a while a plate will do a quick jerk and slide. We call those "earthquakes." These plates move anywhere from a half inch to about four inches a year. Not a lot, but it adds up over a few million years.

2. Rotation: Unless you're standing directly on top of the North or South Pole, you're rotating around the axis of the earth in a counterclockwise direction as viewed from above the North Pole. How fast you're rotating depends on how far you are from the poles. Someone standing at the equator, where the earth's circumference is 25,000 miles (40,233 km), is moving at about 1,040 mph. From there, the closer you get to the poles, your speed decreases from that speed by the multiple of the cosine of your latitude. Don't worry about the math. Excluding Alaskans and Hawaiians, all Americans south of Canada and north of Mexico can expect to be rotating around the earth's axis at speeds between 760 and 940 mph. It's like breaking the sound barrier without even getting up from your La-Z-Boy.

3. Chandler Wobble and nutation: The earth doesn't rotate perfectly on its axis; it "wobbles" a little in a counterclockwise motion every fourteen months. How much of a wobble? Oh, about six inches worth every day. It also nutates, or "nods," on its axis, about nine arcseconds every 18.6 years. This nutation is due to the influence of the Moon, whose orbital plane precesses (see below) around Earth once every 18.6 years (it's not a coincidence). But speaking of precession...

4. Precession: The Chandler Wobble and nutation are little wobbles. The Precession of the Equinoxes is one really big wobble, in which the axis of the earth swings in a counterclockwise direction at the rate of one cycle every 25,800 years. How will you notice precession? Simple. Head over to the nearest time machine, pop yourself in, and jump forward 14,000 years. Get out and look at the North Star. It won't be Polaris, the current North Star, it'll be Vega. Now get back into the time machine and hurry home before the Morlocks eat you.

5. Axial tilt: Chandler Wobble, nutation, precession—why can't the earth's axis just stay in one place? Apparently not, because on top of all those other movements, the axis's angle of tilt cycles between 21 and 24 degrees (currently 23.5) over 41,000 years. The good news is that's the last of these annoying axial wiggles we'll have to deal with.

6. Revolution: Enough with the slowpoke wobblings and noddings. Let's get some real speed going! Earth is cruising along in an orbit around the Sun that has an average radius of 93 million miles, an orbit it completes in a little over 365 days. That's a lot of space to cover in one year—enough space that Earth has to cover over 1.5 million miles a day, or 66,000 miles an hour. That seems pretty fast, but it's not as fast as some planets move in their orbits. Mercury, the closest planet to the Sun, tears around in its orbit at nearly 108,000 miles per hour.

7. The Sun's orbit around the galaxy: 66,000 miles an hour making you yawn? Yearning for a little more speed? Buckle up—while Earth is zipping along in its orbit around the Sun, the Sun is doing a little orbiting of its own, slowly rotating around the center of the Milky Way galaxy once every 225 million years. If the trip takes that long, then it would seem the Sun is taking its own sweet time to come around in a circle—until you realize that the Milky Way galaxy is 100,000 light years in diameter (to put that in miles: 5,865,696,000,000,000,000). To get around once every quarter billion years, the Sun has to move at the speed of 135 miles a second: 486,000 mph. That's fast enough to puff out your cheeks when you stick your head out the car window.

8. The Milky Way's movement through the universe: The Milky Way isn't some slacker galaxy. It has things to do and places to go. Where is it going right now? Stretch out your arm in the direction of the southern constellation of Centaurus and point with your finger. See where your finger is pointed? That's the direction we're going. Don't blink or you'll miss something. We're moving in that direction at 1,000,000 miles an hour, every day, all the time. No, there aren't any rest stops. You should have gone before we left. It's too late to stop now.

* * * * *

"With every passing hour our solar system comes forty-three thousand miles closer to globular cluster 13 in the constellation Hercules, and still there are some misfits who continue to insist that there is no such thing as progress."

—Ransom K. Ferm

MICROPROCESSOR EVOLUTION

Processor	Speed in Megahertz	Year of Introduction
8088	4.77, 8	1978
286	8, 10, 12.5	1982
386	16, 20, 25, 33	1985
486	25, 33, 50, 66	1989
Pentium	60, 66, 90, 100, 120, 133, 150, 166	1993
Pentium Pro	150, 200	1995

If you live to age 75, it is estimated you will have slept about 23 years.

BUBONIC PLAGUE? TRY DENVER

Coming soon to a city near you.

Of all the diseases in the universe, the bubonic plague might strike the most fear into the most hearts. It was eradicated a long time ago. Right? Well…

RIGHT OFF THE BOAT
The plague first came to America in 1899, like everybody else did back then: by boat. This particular boat from Asia was bound for San Francisco, which is where the first outbreak occurred. Since then all the states west of the Mississippi have reported outbreaks.

YOU DIRTY RAT!
At first it was rats that spread the disease, but there have been no rat-related outbreaks since 1924, when 31 people died of plague in Los Angeles. The bacterium that causes bubonic plague can still be carried by rats, but it's also carried by various kinds of squirrels, rabbits, deer, chipmunks, bobcats, and your cat Fluffy.

DO NOT FEED THE SQUIRRELS
Nowadays, infection comes from the fleas of wild animals, but Denver, Colorado, had a case where the tree squirrels in a public park were found to be infected. In fact, wild ground squirrels and rock squirrels bring the bacteria with them when they come into cities to eat garbage.

WHAT PLAGUE?
There are around 16 cases of plague infection a year in the U.S., but modern antibiotics have improved your chances of survival. The mortality rate of 60 to 100 percent has been reduced to 5 to 15 percent. Of course, plague is already resistant to penicillin, and like other infectious diseases, could potentially develop strains that are resistant to other antibiotics.

Public health authorities tend to keep quiet about outbreaks. Even if the majority who are infected are treated successfully, people might understandably get nervous if they learned that the guy next door had come down with a mild case of the Black Death.

Blood travels 60,000 miles (96,540 km) a day as it circulates through the human body.

GENOMES:
FROM YEAST TO YOU

Biologists get billions of dollars in grant money to study genomes.
But the people who own the genomes get nothing. Is that fair?

The genome has been a sizzling-hot topic for the last decade—a whole new science has been built around it: genomics. Some researchers think the genome is the key to a whole new world. You're one of the lucky people who has a genome! And so does the waitress who serves you coffee. And the guy who holds the SLOW/STOP sign at the construction site outside the coffee shop. And that guy's cat. And the bacteria living inside the cat. Everything that's alive has a genome.

WONDERFUL YOU

Every cell in your body has DNA—if you took the trouble to unwind it all, every cell has about six feet of it! DNA is made up of a long, long sequence of genes—your hereditary blueprints. A genome, then, is a complete list of those genes inside any particular organism, a list of everything that makes you the wonderful person that you are.

FASTER, FASTER...

A decade ago, just studying one gene was a time-consuming and painstaking process. Compiling a list (called sequencing) of all the genes of an organism, even a simple one like a bacterium, seemed decades away. But it wasn't.

Technology speeded everything up—in 1995 scientists announced that they'd sequenced the genes of a bacterium. That opened the floodgates. Soon, other bacteria were sequenced, and then yeast. In 1998 the first multicellular beast was sequenced: a microscopic worm called a nematode. Ever since, the race has been on to uncover the genomes of any and every living thing—from rice to people.

GENOME FEVER

At the same time, the Human Genome Project was underway. Everyone thought it would take years—if not decades—because

On average you will inhale 75 million gallons of air in your lifetime.

humans must be so much more complicated than bacteria or nematodes. Supercomputers and automated DNA sequencers speeded up the process. To everyone's surprise, a rough draft of the human genome was announced in the year 2000. It turned out we're not much more complicated than bacteria or nematodes.

YOU AND YEAST HAVE A LOT IN COMMON

Humans have about 40,000 genes, compared to 6,000 in a yeast cell, 19,000 in a nematode, and 13,600 in a fruit fly. A mouse has about the same number as a human. About 30 percent of the genes in yeast are also present in humans; it's close to 50 percent with fruit flies. That means for half the genes in a fruit fly, scientists can find a similar gene in a human that does a similar job.

OKAY, NOW WHAT?

Of course, just because we have a list of all the genes in an organism doesn't mean we know what to do with it. It's like having a copy of *War and Peace* that has no punctuation or capital letters, and all the sentences and paragraphs run together in a 1,000-page string of letters. And it's in Russian. And you don't know how to read Russian. (No, you don't throw it away; you're a scientist. You have to apply a little scientific method here.)

Maybe you have smaller books where some of the words have been translated and some of the punctuation has been inserted. With time and effort, you start chipping away at it, finding words you recognize, trying to figure out words you don't know from the context, and slowly but surely you go beyond individual words and start to read whole sentences and paragraphs and maybe eventually get a sense of what the whole story is about. (And it's a darn good story, too—long, but good.)

A WORK IN PROGRESS

So that's what the genomics people are up to right now. Poring over this mass of information and trying like hell to decipher it.

Once they're done, the information they manage to extract will allow us, at the very least, to fight and prevent disease. It will also—no doubt about it—alter our lives in a myriad of ways we can't even begin to imagine.

ALL TOGETHER NOW

*Some groups of creatures work so well together that they
don't seem like separate animals. And in every way that
really matters—they aren't.*

Ants, termites, and some kinds of bees and wasps live together in large colonies that can include millions of individuals. Since every bug in the bunch is born for a specific job, they all know exactly what they're supposed to do, as if the whole hive is one weird creature directed by—or perhaps making up—a single brain. They at least occasionally get away from the group in the course of their duties, but down in our planet's deep and mysterious seas—and in some fresh waters, too—lurk some creatures that don't ever, ever disengage from their neighbors. Let's meet a few.

MEET THE POLYPS

Allow us to introduce you to polyps, the individual critters that make up what are known as "colonial organisms." These polyps are connected to each other by pores or cells, and their movements and behavior are as well coordinated as a team of circus acrobats. No matter whether they stay put or wander around, polyps do everything together.

TRYING OUT FOR THE CORAL GROUP

The many-splendored coral reefs you see in pictures—or while diving, if you're the active type—are made up of millions of little animals. At first, a coral polyp is a free-swimming larva. But once it lands on something solid, it stays there, just eating and making more coral polyps, either by sprouting a bud or by releasing eggs and sperm into the water. About the size of a pencil eraser, each coral polyp has a body, tentacles, a mouth and gullet, and a cord-like connection to the next polyp. After they die, their skeletons remain in place, adding to the reef's size by about an inch per year.

POLYPS MAKE THE MAN

The Portuguese man-o'-war—a jellyfish look-alike—is actually a colony of four different kinds of polyps. The big one on top is a translucent pink, blue, or violet bubble filled with gas (nitrogen, oxygen, and argon). The bubble is usually three to twelve inches long and it can stick up as much as six inches out of the water.

Mosquitoes prefer blondes to brunettes.

This polyp is both a float and a sail, and it's the whole gang's only means of locomotion.

Meanwhile, clusters of polyps hang in long tentacles underneath this floating balloon. Again, each type has a special job—dactylozooids catch food, gastrozooids eat, and gonozooids reproduce. The man-o'-war's multipurpose tentacles can trail out as far as 165 feet. And this critter's stinging nematocysts can zap you with a neurotoxin almost as powerful as cobra venom. For people who are especially sensitive to the toxin, a man-o'-war's sting might do more than spoil a beach party. It can cause fever, shock, and the disruption of heart and lung activity.

Portuguese man-o'-war balloons are often seen floating along together in clusters or even large swarms. But the biggest of their kind lurk beneath the ocean's surface.

THE MONSTER WITH MORE THAN 1,000 STOMACHS

The Portuguese man-o'-war and its closest relatives are siphonophores. Rather than floating around on the waves, many siphonophores travel vertically, like an elevator—from deep in the ocean to near the surface and back again. Some have been recorded on video at 1,500 feet down. Their "bodies" consist of the usual series of polyps—floaters, swimmers, eaters, breeders, and venomous stingers—strung like a necklace on a hollow central stem. Some are just a few inches long. Others are almost unimaginably big and strange.

IT'S A LONG STORY

A siphonophore species, *Praya* sp., is the largest animal in the world—at least, if you measure it lengthwise. And it surely must have more stomachs than any other creature. Not that anybody has counted a *Praya*'s stomachs—but figure it this way: A six-foot siphonophore can have more than a hundred stomach-polyps on its string, and a *Praya* can be as large as 130 feet long (bigger than the biggest blue whales). Even at its maximum length, the colony is perfectly coordinated. But *Praya* are only as thick as a slender finger, and are so delicate that they can be broken up by something just brushing against them. Whenever scientists try to collect *Praya* or any other large siphonophores in nets, they end up with nothing but goo.

Now, thanks to remotely operated submersibles, we're getting a better look—and finding lots more of these strange colony creatures than anyone had ever suspected were down there.

Over 99.9% of all animal species on Earth were extinct before man's arrival.

IN ONE END AND OUT THE OTHER

Aaah. Having just dined on a plate of fried chicken, you wash it down with a can of beer and contemplate that life doesn't get any better than this. Ever wonder what happens next? Well, we've got the answer. And like it or not, we're about to tell you.

IT'S ALIMENTARY
Your plumbing system consists of a series of organs called the alimentary system. It all begins with your mouth.

THE GAPING MAW
The digestive process begins as soon as you pop that fried chicken into your mouth. As you chew on it—called mastication—you break it down into a pulp that's easily swallowed. Your tongue mixes the food and your saliva has already kicked in, helping to break down the pulp as well.

GULP!
When you swallow, the food passes through the pharynx. Part of its function is to cover your windpipe during swallowing so you don't drown in your own food. It also pushes the food into the esophagus, which is next in the chain.

DOWN IT GOES
When the esophagus receives food, it starts contracting, pushing the food down toward your stomach. This is why you can drink a glass of water while standing on your head—what goes down can also come up. To get a good idea of how strongly the esophagus muscles contract, just think about the last time you vomited.

The mucus glands that line the esophagus help keep the food lubricated on its way down. Here the food encounters the first of a few sphincters (rings of muscles) that push the food along—this one into the stomach—while preventing it from coming back up.

The water content of 10 inches of snow is equivalent to one inch of rain.

YOU WOULDN'T WANT TO DRINK THIS JUICE

Fortunately for you, your food has made it to the stomach, where it belongs. Here, a bath of hydrochloric acid, more mucus (the body is never in short supply of mucus), and digestive enzymes make up the gastric juices. The mucus lines the stomach, protecting it from the corrosive action of the rest of the juice. The enzymes act on certain foods, such as protein, fats, and milk. The hydrochloric acid helps the enzymes digest the food.

MIX WELL AND POUR

The stomach mixes the food in the gastric juice until it's in a semiliquid form. Now it's called chyme (pronounced "kime"). Some parts of the food—like corn husks—can't be broken down; they just continue on their way as is. Other stuff, like the alcohol content of the beer you just swigged, is absorbed directly into the bloodstream from the stomach. When the mixture has reached a satisfactory liquid state, another sphincter opens and allows the chyme to slowly pour into the small intestine.

A LONG JOURNEY

Contrary to popular belief, this is where most of the action takes place. The small intestine is in charge of sucking the nutrients out of the chyme. It's about 23 feet long and is folded into your abdominal cavity like a very flexible hose.

A SECOND HELPING OF JUICE

As the chyme is pushed along, the digestion process continues, now joined by bile and juice from the liver and pancreas. The pancreatic juice does most of the work, breaking down starches, carbohydrates, fats, and proteins. The bile breaks the large fat globs from the fried chicken into smaller globs, which the pancreatic juice can more easily digest. The intestine itself adds some juices to the mix, which assist in digesting the fats and proteins and converting digested food into sugar.

SUCK IT UP

As it's digested into a form that the body can receive, microscopic, fingerlike projections called villi absorb nutrients from the chyme into the bloodstream. How much do the villi absorb? You eat and drink about two to two-and-a-half gallons of food and liquid a day. By the time it passes out of the small intestine, only about 12 ounces remain!

There are 10^{15} ants living on the earth at any given moment.

FORK IN THE ROAD
The small intestine is connected to the large intestine, which is about five feet long. The first half of the large intestine absorbs the liquids and sends them into the bloodstream. Eventually they visit the kidneys, where they're purified; since something has to wash the impurities out of the kidneys, a portion of the blood that flows through the kidneys actually becomes urine, which is sent through the ureters to the bladder, effectively carrying the impurities out of the body.

Meanwhile, back at the large intestine, the solids that were left behind are compacted into feces. At this point, all that's left of the original food is protein, fat, indigestible roughage (those corn husks), as well as by-products from the body itself, such as digestive juices and dead intestinal cells.

THE OTHER END
At the end of the large intestine, the feces collect in the rectum against yet another sphincter muscle (the most famous one). When enough pressure builds, it triggers—yoo-hoo!—nature's call. That's when you know it's time to head for the nearest john.

* * * * *

IS IT TRUE THAT RICE THROWN AT WEDDINGS WILL GET EATEN BY BIRDS, SWELL UP IN THEIR STOMACHS, AND MAKE THEM EXPLODE?

Patently untrue, according to the *Birdwatcher's Digest*. But this is one urban legend that's been taken to heart by most modern brides and grooms, who have replaced rice with birdseed as the postnuptial projectile of choice. Which has, in turn, spawned another urban legend, that of the bridegroom who went to his doctor with a severe pain in his ear. A brief examination came up with the cause. A piece of birdseed had lodged in the bridegroom's ear and had sprouted in that warm and moist environment.

The body's only bone not attached to another is the throat's hyoid; it supports the tongue.

IF YOU COULD BOTTLE THOSE BUBBLES

They said it couldn't be done. Hah! Them's fightin' words to an inventor.

Nathaniel C. Wyeth was born in 1911 in Chads Ford, Pennsylvania, on the family homestead of his father, the painter N. C. (Newell Convers) Wyeth. While his more famous brother Andrew and his less famous sisters followed in the artistic footsteps of their father, Nathaniel was the kind of kid who took clocks apart and made gadgets out of scrap metal.

HE DID DYNAMITE WORK
Wyeth graduated from the University of Pennsylvania and jumped at the chance to work for the DuPont Corporation, where one of his first inventions was an elaborate machine that manufactured dynamite cartridges automatically. The gizmo was a real break-through—it meant that workers would no longer be exposed to poisonous nitroglycerin powder.

ALL BOTTLED UP
He started working on his best-known invention in 1967. After wondering out loud why plastic wasn't used for carbonated beverage bottles—conventional glass bottles were, after all, heavy and breakable—he was told that plastic bottles would explode.

Harumph, said Wyeth. He went down to a store and bought a bottle of detergent, replaced the detergent with ginger ale, sealed the bottle, and put it in the fridge. The next morning, the bottle had swollen up so much that it was wedged solidly between the refrigerator shelves. Wyeth didn't give up—he just set his sights on making a stronger plastic container.

PET PROJECT
The challenge was to stretch plastic so that its molecules would align in two dimensions, rather than just one. He came up with the idea of creating a mold for the bottle that resembled a test tube with threads running, not in a single spiral, but in a diamond crisscross pattern. When the plastic was pressed, or "extruded,"

Reptiles have scales, shields, or plates and their toes have claws.

through this mold, the molecules aligned just the way he wanted. His next improvement was to replace the polypropylene material he'd been using with polyethylene terephthalate (PET), which has superior elastic properties.

A HOLLOW VICTORY
The development of the PET bottle, however, didn't go all that smoothly. Wyeth recalls showing the results of an early experiment to the laboratory director at DuPont, who wondered why Wyeth was spending so much money on such a "terrible-looking bottle." Wyeth was unfazed—he was just happy that the thing had turned out hollow.

Wyeth said that he used his "failures and the knowledge of things that wouldn't work as a springboard to new approaches." Eventually, he produced a plastic bottle that was light, clear, resilient, and safe—a complete success.

STEPPING ON YOUR PET
He patented his bottle in 1973. Though recycling wasn't a major concern to Wyeth (or hardly anybody else) at the time, PET bottles were first recycled as early as 1977.

In fact, they're now the most commonly recycled household products. Recycled PET is used mainly as "fiberfill" (man-made fibers used as filling material) or as synthetic fabric. Today, about half the polyester carpet made in the U.S. comes from recycled PET bottles.

* * * * *

World's Top Five Soft-Drink Consuming Countries
Annual Consumption Per Capita in Quarts

Switzerland:	111.0
Barbados:	86.0
Bahamas:	79.3
United States:	78.4
Australia:	78.1

Source: Beverage Marketing Corporation

Amphibians have moist skin and their toes lack claws.

HALF BREEDS

What do you get when you cross a goat with a spider?
You're about to find out.

L et's make this simple. By and large, you can't breed one
   species of animal with another. You can't just shove a goat
   and a kangaroo into a room with mood lighting and Barry
White albums and expect baby goat-a-roos to hop out a few
trimesters later. The reason for this is the reason that there are
different sorts of animals in the first place. It's called speciation,
and it occurs when a population of animals, for various reasons,
evolve to a point where they can't interbreed successfully with
other related animals ("success" in this case meaning making more
of themselves).

THE END OF THE LINE, EVOLUTION-WISE
This can happen when an animal population is cut off from other
animals like it and adapts to its new surroundings ("adaptive
radiation," which has nothing to do with plutonium), or when a
random mutation spreads through one group of animals, eventually cutting it off genetically from other animals to create a new
species ("quantum speciation," which has nothing to do with
quarks and leptons). Once you're in a new species, that's pretty
much it. Genetically speaking, you stick to your own kind.

GET THAT SKUNK AWAY FROM ME!
Humans, who are either ignorant of the complexities of the
genetic process of speciation or—as is so frequently the case—not
willing to let a simple thing like evolution get in the way of their
fun, have tried over the millennia to mix and match their animal
species to see what they can get out of it. (Usually, two agitated
animals that want nothing to do with each other).

I GIVE YOU THE COCKAPOO, E.G.
The one reason to do this is to take advantage of a concept called
"hybrid vigor"—the idea that the interactions of the genes from
two different animals will make the resulting animal hardier than
either parent. This has been proven to work between different
breeds of a single species. Humans have been breeding dogs this

way for hundreds of years to accentuate desired traits, giving us a species of animal whose sizes range from toy Chihuahuas to Great Danes (theoretically, you could breed a Chihuahua with a Great Dane, although, depending which is the male and which is the female, the process could be either painful or humiliating).

STUBBORN AND STERILE
The successes of mixing different species of animals are few and far between. The single most successful example of a species crossbreed is a mule, which is what you get when you cross a male donkey or ass (also known as a "jackass") with a female horse (a mare). Humans have been breeding mules as pack animals for over 3,000 years. Almost all mules are sterile. Incidentally, if a female donkey and a male horse breed, the resulting offspring is called a "hinny." Hinnies are considered to be less hardy than mules, so there isn't much call for them.

TIGONS AND LIGERS AND...OH, NEVER MIND
Another famous crossbreed is a "liger," which is what you get when you breed a male lion with a female tiger (female lions and male tigers—you get a "tigon"). Ligers and tigons are exclusively created through human meddling, since lions and tigers in the wild don't share much in common in terms of habitat or behavior (lions live in groups, tigers work alone). Like mules, ligers and tigons are almost always sterile, although there have been cases of females who are able to breed.

ALL IN THE FAMILY
In the cases of mules and hinnies, and ligers and tigons, the cross-breeding takes place within species families. Horses and donkeys belong to the same genetic family of species called Equidae (which also includes zebras, which are sometimes bred with horses to create—wait for it—"zorses"), while lions and tigers are in the family Felidae, which also includes cheetahs, pumas, leopards, jaguars, and your own domestic housecat (attempting to breed your cat with a lion or tiger is a fine way to get your cat eaten, so don't do it). There's been no successful attempt at crossbreeding species outside of genetic families. No crossing horses and tigers, or bears and dolphins, or whatever.

OR, SHOULD WE SAY

That is, not until humans began to master the art of genetic manipulation. Now that humans have begun to crack the DNA code, we've started to mix and match genes from one animal species with others, creating genetically engineered animals with genes that span not just genetic families, but across entire animal phyla.

GOT SILK?

For example, in an attempt to generate massive amounts of spider silk that could eventually be used to create superstrong fabrics, scientists have taken genes from orb weaver spiders and placed them into goats, which then produce spider web proteins in their milk, which can in turn then (theoretically) be processed out. The goats look and act like normal goats—no eight-legged goats spinning webs or cocooning the scientists in silk to eat them later (at least not yet)—but they've got just a little bit of spider in them.

THE GREENMOUSE EFFECT

Scientists have high hopes for these "transgenic" animals. Plans are underway to create cows or goats that are genetically engineered to produce medicines in their milk. Other transgenic animals are of somewhat more dubious utility, unless you can think up of a good reason for putting jellyfish DNA into mice, as a bunch of CalTech researchers recently did, which made the mice glow green under fluorescent lighting.

IT'S A PUPPY! IT'S A READING LAMP!

One major difference exists between transgenic animals and their traditionally crossbred brethren. Transgenic animals pass on their genetic changes to their offspring—the CalTech researchers noted that the offspring of the jellymice had the same fluorescent gene as their parents. Given the pace of genetic development, owning your own glow-in-the-dark transgenic pet may not be too far in the future. Just don't try to crossbreed it with your cat or dog (or your horse). Leave that stuff to the pros.

The French high-speed TGV holds the railway speed record—320 mph (515 kph).

BUG-HUNTING
WE WILL GO

A chimp tries to teach an anthropologist a lesson.

As world-famous anthropologist Jane Goodall watched, one of the chimps she was studying picked a blade of grass and trimmed it just so. Then he stuck the grass into a termite mound, waited a moment, pulled it out, and gobbled up the bunch of termites that were hanging onto it.

Goodall's report—which really shocked the scientific community—was the first observation of an animal actually making a tool. Another (not as famous) anthropologist, Geza Teleki, decided to try termite-fishing himself.

After all, how hard could it be?

HARDER THAN IT LOOKS
Teleki took some lessons. His fishing instructor was a chimpanzee he called Leakey (after British anthropologist Louis Leakey, who had been Goodall's mentor.) Teleki discovered that a termite-fisher must first know where to look for entrances to termite tunnels, a skill that eluded him. The subtleties of tool-shaping were another problem. And even when Leakey pointed out the location and provided the tool, Teleki fished for a lot of hours without getting even a single termite.

IT'S ALL IN THE WRIST
Teleki learned that the probe has to be inserted carefully, to exactly the right depth, then it has to be vibrated to attract the termite's attention. If that isn't done right, the bugs will just bite off the fishing pole and go on their way. Even when termites do attach themselves to the pole, it requires real skill to get the grass blade back out of the hole without losing them all.

TAUGHT BY AN EXPERT
Teleki never did get the hang of it. He wrote of his klutziness thusly: "Similar ineptness can only be observed in chimpanzees below the age of about 4–5 years." He added a special acknowledgment to his chimpanzee teacher: "I am…more than grateful to the patient and tolerant Leakey, whose termite-collecting skills so out-stripped mine."

Chewing gum has over 40 compounds including pine resin, petroleum products, and latexes.

EVER SEE A FULGURITE?

How one of nature's most savage forces
creates one of its most delicate oddities.

Y ou're going to need your rubber-soled boots to follow us into the astonishing world of fulgurite craftsmanship. First, let's get up to speed on the awesome power of lightning.

LIGHTNING 101

Clouds, especially cumulonimbus clouds (the big ones that produce thunderstorms), generate static electricity, just like scuffing your feet on a thick carpet. The cloud has a positive charge at the top (about six miles [10 km] up) and a negative charge lower down (about 3 miles [5 km] up). The ground right under the cloud becomes positively charged; so does the very bottom of the cloud, about a mile and a half (2.5 km) up.

A lightning bolt starts with a small current flowing between the cloud's negative charge and the small positive charge at the bottom of the cloud, in steps of about 150 feet (46 m). This opens up a conductive channel that carries a much bigger charge between the cloud and the ground—or things in contact with the ground, such as trees, tall buildings, or people walking in the rain. Most of the lightning we see is cloud-to-ground lightning, but lightning can also jump from one cloud to another—that's what they call "sheet lightning."

Lightning has a lot of power, about a million kilowatts at peak current flow. About one percent of this is radiated away as light and heat, producing the visible flash; nearly all the rest goes into heating the air the bolt flows through, as high as 54,000°F (30,000°C). This heated air expands faster than sound, producing a shock wave that we hear as thunder.

ZAP!

In the few seconds it's taken you to read this far, some 10,000 lightning bolts have struck the earth. That adds up to about 8.5 million strikes per day. At that rate, it's amazing that we haven't all been zapped with an electric energy boost.

A black panther's a leopard with a dark coat; its spots are a bit darker than the rest of its fur.

So what do the millions of lightning bolts that fail to connect with humans or large objects do for amusement? Well, one thing they do is create fulgurites.

THEY'RE TOTALLY TUBULAR!

"Fulgurite" is from the Latin word *fulgur*, meaning "lightning." The word has been used since 1821 to describe an amazing mineral formation produced when lightning strikes a sandy patch of ground. The intense heat of the electrical discharge melts some of the sand, which forms a long, narrow—and very fragile—tube of glass, smooth on the inside, crusty on the outside. That's a fulgurite, a.k.a. a "lightning tube."

GOING TO GREAT LENGTHS

Because lightning follows the path of least resistance, fulgurites usually have irregular shapes, with tubes and forks or small offshoots protruding from the main stem. Its length is determined by the depth and resistance of the sand, the position of the local water table, and the power of the discharge. Most recovered fulgurites are only a few inches long, but they've been known to extend as far as 60 feet (18 m) into the ground. They follow the path of lightning, so they usually go straight down, like an elevator shaft.

CAN YOU DIG IT?

You can find your own fulgurite, most likely in sandy country that's prone to electrical storms. On rare occasions, observers have seen the exact position of a lightning strike and have found a fulgurite while the ground around it was still warm. But more often, fulgurite-hunters have found their buried treasure where the surface of the sandy ground has eroded away, revealing the upper section of the tube.

Extracting fulgurites from the sand or soil is tricky. The fragile tubes can break into lots of tiny pieces that have to be painstakingly pieced together again.

PSSST...WANNA BUY A FULGURITE?

If hunting fulgurites sounds like too much trouble, you can visit an on-line store where you can either buy a fulgurite or take the proprietors up on their offer to "fulguritize" anything you send them, be it 10,000 paper clips or five gallons of sand from your favorite beach.

The smallest insect (fairyfly) fits through a needle's eye; it's 1/100" long (0.25mm).

SCIENCE IS SO AWESOME, DUDE!

*What do extreme sports like surfing, skateboarding,
and snowboarding have in common besides the board?
It's the excellent science!*

Y̲ou gotta envy them, riding the waves, launching out high above the pavement, or swooping down snow-covered mountains. The dudes (and dudettes) who ride the boards seem so free and wild, breaking all the universal rules that keep most of us stuck in our cars or slogging along on our own two feet.

Surprise, it only seems like rules are being broken. Even the clueless who paddle out on their surfboards, coast "goofy foot" on their skateboards, or hit the slopes strapped to a snowboard are learning to cope with universal laws like gravity, momentum, and rotational motion.

ALL ABOARD
Surfing, the sport that started the board craze, is hundreds of years old. Ancient Hawaiians surfed on big, heavy, wooden boards. In the 1950s the sport caught on in Southern California, where new engineering techniques and materials like fiberglass allowed for lightweight, smaller boards that still supported the mass of the surfer on the water. Spectators flocked to the amazing sight of swimmers standing on seemingly flimsy surfboards while cresting the tops of breaking waves. Most did not know they were watch-ing some totally excellent feats of rotational motion and physics.

YOU NEED BALANCE, MAN
Balance is obviously an important part of surfing. How does a surfer stay stationary (balanced) on a board that's cresting a wave? Along the lengthwise center of the board and slightly toward its tail, where there's extra mass, lies the center of the board's gravity. This point is the board's axis—like the fulcrum at the center of a seesaw. Where the surfer stands in relation to the axis controls his or her board's rotational motion exactly like the up-and-down rotational motion of a seesaw. If the rider's weight moves too far

There are male and female ladybugs.

toward the nose of the board, the board tips (or torques) forward and the nose sinks. Too far backward and the tail sinks. Either way, it's a slam-dunk into the drink. A good surfer straddles the center of gravity with one foot toward the tail and one toward the nose. The two torques cancel each other out, and the radically awesome surfer stands stationary and balanced.

POWER PLAYERS

It takes more than an understanding of rotational motion to make a brilliant surfer. Our genius needs a thorough (if intuitive) understanding of the development of potential energy and how it can be turned into kinetic energy.

A surfer arrives at the top of a wave just before it breaks. By taking up this position, he's gained potential energy (or trouble, depending on how you look at it). Potential energy is the potential product of you and your equipment's weight or mass, and the vertical distance you're about to fall. Our surfer converts this potential energy to kinetic energy when he drops off the top of the wave down toward the flat of the wave. This conversion into energy gives him the power to propel himself along despite the friction of the water currents. The surfer can now ride the wave.

TAKING IT TO THE STREETS

Any surfer also knows that when the wind blows toward the shore, there are no great waves to ride. So during the 1960s some bored surfers started buying boards that were fitted with wheels on the bottom. When the ocean was glassy and calm, surfers could use their surfing skills on dry land, rolling along those hot Southern California pavements.

The first skateboards were unwieldy, with clay wheels that didn't grip the pavement well. One of the earliest improvements was the kicktail, the turned-up end at the back of the board. Now a skateboarder could lean back a little more as he rolled along. Urethane wheels, invented in the 1970s, added mobility and safety; verethane wheels turned a part-time hobby into a full-blown craze. Kids who'd never seen the ocean were zipping down hills and maneuvering around obstacles on skateboards.

GETTING WHEELS

Two more ideas changed skateboarding from a way to get around on pavement into a way to defy gravity and fly through the air.

Ladybugs a.k.a. ladybird (U.K.), flower lady (China), Good News (Iran), Crop-Picker (Africa).

In 1977, a skateboarder named Willi Winkel was riding down a standard quarter pipe (an elevated ramp that led downhill to help a rider pick up speed). Willi thought that two quarter pipes might be better than one, so he put together a *U*-shaped ramp or "half-pipe." Though he probably didn't know it, Willi would soon be using the rules of acceleration and velocity to overcome gravity. His total mass, that is, his weight, was pulled by gravity down the half-pipe creating speed, which gave him the momentum to take him vertically up the other side of the U and even soar out over the lip to "catch some big air" in surfer-speak. Using the laws of physics, boarders were learning to fly.

BIG AIR
In the late 1970s, Alan "Ollie" Gelfand worked on a new move that literally took the power of rotational motion to new heights. As he sped up the vertical incline of a half-pipe, he made a crouching jump while shoving down the kicktail of his board with his back foot, deliberately torquing the back of his board down and causing the front of the board to fly up as the back bounced off the ground. (Remember the seesaw? Ollie had taken advantage of the effects of rotational motion.)

If left to itself, the board would simply have flipped over backward toward its axis—and it probably did the first few times that Gelfand tried it. But eventually, while the board was in the air, Gelfand learned to slide his front foot forward, which put torque on the front of the board and leveled it out before gravity pulled rider and board back down to earth.

Spectators were wowed; it looked as if Ollie's skateboard was strapped to his feet—but it wasn't. The next time you see a skateboarder jumping over an obstacle or up onto a curb, he or she is doing what boarders call an "ollie." Gelfand had mastered the laws of critical mass and rotational motion to seemingly defy the gravity that pulls more timid souls down to earth.

COLD AND BOARD
It was only a matter of time before boards hit the powder. By the 1980s snowboarders were "shredding" the slopes (sliding downhill with their feet strapped to a board); they'd adapted the skills of skateboarding to snow. Like skateboarders, they rode either regular (with their left foot in front) or goofy foot (with their right foot in

front). They even adapted the half-pipe, picking up enough momentum in a high curving trench packed with snow so they could slide up over the top of the lip and catch some awesome—but cold—air.

THE SCIENCE OF SNOWBOARDING
Snowboarders also take advantage of the forces of friction, gravity, acceleration, and momentum. A board speeds downhill pulled, of course, by gravity, but it also melts the snow as it goes, so that it actually zips along on a film of water.

Like all board riders, snowboarders position their critical mass and exploit the board's rotational motion to stay balanced. One side of the board will have more contact with the snow than the other. A rider keeps his or her center of gravity over whichever edge of the board is in contact with the snow (the riding edge). To end a ride, a snowboarder turns uphill so that the force of friction and the force of gravity drag on the momentum and slow the board to a stop.

BOARD EXAMS
Okay, so the next time you see some kid with pink hair—and lots of metal piercing various parts of his face and body—flying along on his board, treat him with a little respect. He knows enough about the universal laws of physical science to ride the waves, the streets, the air, or the snow.

He's like this totally studious scholar, a Dr. Dude Ph.D.

* * * * *

SURFING TERMINOLOGY

clucked: scared of the wave
gnarly: impressive, intimidating
jag: retreat after being thrashed
pucker factor: the impact of a gnarly wave on your ability to relax
sick: first-rate, incredibly cool
thrashed: when a wave opens a can of whupass on you
getting worked: when a wave introduces you to how a sock feels in the washing machine

TO SLEEP, PERCHANCE TO DREAM?

No hot chocolate and antifreeze for these furry guys. Give them some brown fat and they'll sleep for months.

When you think of hibernation, does the image of a sleepy brown bear in a cave spring to mind? Even though bears are the most common animals identified with hibernation, they in fact do not hibernate! Bears just sleep a lot, and that's why their kind of hibernation is now called "winter sleep" or "winter dormancy." Most animals that hibernate in the true sense of the word are rodent-type creatures who don't have as much body surface area.

THE BIG SLEEP

There are hundreds of other warm-blooded (as well as some cold-blooded) animals that nap through the long winter. Dormice, hedgehogs, snakes, bats, squirrels, marmots, and even snails start their hibernation when the weather gets a little chilly.

Their pulse rates drop alarmingly (to just a few beats per minute) and they hardly breathe at all. In fact, they look (and feel) pretty dead. Their skin becomes very cold and some animals can even be picked up or poked without waking them up (try that on a bear!). This supersnooze usually lasts a few months.

THE GLAND SCHEME OF THINGS

How do they stay alive? Well, first of all they stuff themselves with food before going to sleep. And second, well, it's a glandular thing. Animals that hibernate have a "hibernating gland," a mass of brown fat, most of which goes around the shoulders and neck to keep them warm and snug. Brown fat is different from normal fat; it supplies energy and heat directly to the body via the blood. It's kind of like an electric blanket or animal antifreeze. Most animals have it when they're born—even humans! Newborns use it to keep them warm until they start eating and developing white fat, then the brown fat goes away.

Fastest mammal: cheetah—70 mph (240 kph).

DING! DING! DING!

So how do they wake up? Alarm clock? A garbage truck outside the window? Actually, when the air around them rises above a certain temperature, an automatic burst of chemical activity in their bodies tells their brains that it can take over again; this arouses them from their big sleep. A winter with warm spells can be dangerous. The warm weather keeps on waking them up, draining their energy resources each time and often not allowing them to make it through the winter. Another danger for them is all that sleeping can make them vulnerable to predators if they're not tucked away in a cave or burrow.

A BIRD AMONG BIRDS

There's only one type of bird that hibernates during winter, and that's the goatsucker—the nocturnal goatsucker to be exact. It got its rather alarming name from an old European belief that it used its rather large bill to suck milk from goats at night. But it actually just eats insects.

* * * * *

"Perhaps I am a bear, or some hibernating animal underneath, for the instinct to be half asleep all winter is so strong in me."
—Anne Morrow Lindbergh

"Animals awaken, first facially, then bodily.
Men's bodies wake before their faces do.
The animal sleeps within its body.
Man sleeps with his body in his mind."
—Chazal

"Even where sleep is concerned,
too much is a bad thing."
—Homer

LEFT OUT IN THE COLD

What happens to nonhibernating animals when winter comes?
Uncle John was worried, so we checked.

WHAT THE JET SET WEARS IN WINTER
Snow leopards and polar bears are white all year round, but an ermine is just a short-tailed weasel during the warmer months. Once he sheds his reddish-brown coat for winter white—only the tip of his tail stays black—he's officially known as an ermine. It's this time of year that he's most desirable to fur trappers and their hoity-toity clientele.

DIVE BOMBER
The ptarmigan's day is done, so he searches for just the right snowdrift. When he finds it, he dives straight in and uses his beak and feathers to carve himself out some body space. Finally, with the insulation of the snow keeping him warm, he'll happily drift off to sleep.

LUCKY RABBIT'S FOOT
With the approach of winter, the snowshoe rabbit sprouts new white fur on his lucky rabbit's feet. By the time snow is on the ground, his tootsies have been transformed into broad, soft pads that'll carry him safely over even the deepest of snowdrifts.

SNOW BIRDS
Lots of birds migrate, but when the white stork flies from Europe as far south as South America to escape winter, it's the young storks—who may have never left the nest—who lead the way. The yearly trip takes the stork family some 14,000 miles (22,500 km). Just like lots of other feathered migrators, the trip will be almost entirely over water, making it a nonstop flight.

FETAL POSITION
When a blizzard strikes, the white fox digs in his heels and burrows into the snow. Then he simply curls up his bushy tail to cover his nose and goes to sleep—cozy, snug, and contented.

GETTING OUT HIS WINTER COAT
When autumn's in the air, the white-tailed deer sheds his cool summer coat. The hairs on its new winter coat are hollow, providing an extra layer of heat protection in every single thicker strand.

Color-change artists besides chameleons: squids, cuttlefish, flounders, and octopuses.

A WHALE OF A TALE

The shocking true story of whales...
Whales once walked the earth. Yes, that's right, we said walked.

Okay, here's a quiz. Each of these things has something in common. You get to guess what it is. Oh, relax, you're not being graded. This is supposed to be fun. Ready?

Here we go: giraffe, deer, hippopotamus, whale. What do they have in common?

a)   They're all mammals.

b)   They all have a recent common evolutionary ancestor.

c)   If given the opportunity, rock star and bow enthusiast Ted Nugent would hunt each one.

The answer? Well, they're *all* true. But, the one we want you thinking about at this particular moment is b): They all have a recent common evolutionary ancestor. And of course, by recent, we mean as measured by the evolutionary clock. Not last week.

WAIT JUST ONE MINUTE!
Now, admittedly, this is a little confusing. You can see how giraffes and deer could be related to each other, and even possibly how those two could be related to a hippopotamus. They're all land-based mammals with four legs, while your whales (taxonomic order Cetacea, which includes whales, porpoises, dolphins, and narwhals) live their entire lives in water and have no legs to speak of, just two front flippers and a tail (called a fluke). So how do you get from deer, giraffes, and hippos to whales?

How on earth are Bambi and Flipper evolutionary cousins?

WHEN WHALE-SIZED MEANT SMALL
Well, you start out with the staggering realization that 50 million years ago or so, whale ancestors *did* walk on land, and were far closer in size to deer or hippos than they are today—even smaller, in fact. *Get out!* It's true.

One ancestor, called *Ichthyolestes*, was the size of a modern-day fox. Shocking news for the average Joe, but your average

---

Earth's oldest living thing: 4,000-year-old General Sherman tree, Sequoia National Park, CA.

paleontologist has been in on the secret for years. In fact, for your average paleontologist, the question is not *whether* whales are descended from land-walking mammals, but merely what *kind* of land-walking mammals.

One camp maintained that whales were descended from a group of extinct, meat-eating, hooved animals called mesonychians, while the other suggested instead that they were related to artiodactyls ("even-toed" in Greek), which includes several species of animals you know and love: the aforementioned giraffes, deer, and hippos—but also sheep, cows, pigs, and camels.

CASE (PRETTY MUCH) CLOSED

The discovery in 2001 of several previously unknown whale-ancestor fossils in Pakistan seems to have tipped the argument into the *artiodactyl* camp. These whale ancestors have the heads of ancient whales but the ankles of sheep, and if you think that would make for one strange-looking animal, you're right. But there you have it—sheep and whales: evolutionary brethren.

A SHORT WALK TO THE OCEAN

Now that we've placed the whale ancestors back on land, we have to figure out how they made it to the sea—and not just how, but how they managed to do it so fast. The time lapse between the land-bound whale ancestors and the first completely sea-living whale species is, evolutionarily, very short—just a few million years or so. What allowed for such a (relatively) quick dive? Interestingly, it may have less to do with flippers and fins, and more to do with the shape of a whale's inner ear.

SEMICIRCULAR REASONING

The semicircular canals in your inner ear are the place in the body where humans and other mammals work out their balance skills—mess with your inner ear's sense of equilibrium (say by spinning around very quickly or riding the Tilt-a-Whirl at the county fair), and you experience varying levels of dizziness, nausea, and instability, especially while walking (the operative word).

THE ONLY THING THAT'S NOT WHALE-SIZED

Well, about 45 million years ago, the semicircular canals in the whale's ancestors shrank in a truly impressive way. They shrank so much that today your average blue whale, the largest animal that

---

What they provide us: sheep–insulin; cows–smallpox vaccines; horses–serums for tetanus shots

has ever lived, has a semicircular canal smaller than yours. To put this in perspective, a blue whale's heart is bigger than a telephone booth. So we're talking a small inner ear, both objectively and subjectively.

OK, so the whale's semicircular canals are dinky. So what? Here's what: The theory is that most acrobatic land mammals (monkeys and such) have large canals because they need lots of sensory feedback to land in just the right place on a branch or the ground; the whale's semicircular canals shrunk because sea creatures have less mobility than land creatures and their movements are more constrained. As our whale evolved from a land-dwelling quadruped into a swimmer, the canal system shrank very quickly.

FREAKS OF NATURE
When did the whales lose their legs? It was a gradual process—the family with the likely direct ancestor to our modern-day whales, *Protocetidae*, featured species with both flukes and hind legs. Later whale families like the *Basilosauridae* (which are now extinct, since they lived 35 million years ago) showed even shorter, stumpier legs that probably had no use at all. Eventually evolution caused whale legs to disappear—but not entirely. Vestigial leg bones are still found in whale skeletons, and occasionally a whale is born with rudimentary hind legs outside the body. It's a reminder of a life once lived on land—and the fact that the whales didn't lose their legs until long after they left land for good.

* * * * *

FOR TOMORROW WE DIET

If you're trying to lose weight, you will. When the tide rises, each one of us loses a fraction of an ounce! Unfortunately, we regain the weight when the tide falls. (We're affected by tidal pulls because of the water and salt content of our bodies.)

Then again, why bother dieting? Look at the statistics on the blue whale, the largest animal on the planet. The mature blue whale is 100 feet long; it weighs more than thirty elephants combined, over 100 tons. In fact, its heart alone weighs a ton. The blue whale maintains all this weight on a healthy diet of small, shrimplike creatures called krill. Compared to him, you look great!

Harvest from the sea: sulfur, oil, magnesium, bromine, salt, manganese, gold, diamonds.

ISLETS AND INSULIN

*Quick, point to your pancreas. If your finger is hovering
somewhere in the neighborhood of your stomach, you're
probably a medical professional or a diabetic.*

The Greeks named it "pancreas," which means "all flesh,"
because they didn't know what it was for. The islets of
Langerhans (which sounds like an exotic spot for a
vacation, but isn't) are islandlike patches on your pale, rubbery
pancreas. Which is where we'd like to direct your attention.

POP, POP, FIZZ, FIZZ
The pancreas has two jobs. First, it acts as the body's natural
antacid by squirting an alkaline digestive juice onto your food as it
leaves your stomach on the way to your small intestine, so that
when it arrives, the acid content is neatly neutralized. The same
juice helps break down proteins into smaller pieces, called amino
acids, that can squeeze through your intestinal wall into your
bloodstream.

Second, those patches, or islets, produce some pretty vital
hormones, without which you—the owner of this quirky little
gland and the body that houses it—are in trouble.

LET'S SEE, WHAT'LL I CALL THEM?
The first chap to notice these little patches was an observant
doctor by the name of Langerhans. He described them in his
doctoral thesis in 1869, but he didn't know why they were there.
Twenty years later, two researchers in France removed the
pancreas of an anesthetized dog and discovered that the critter
developed the symptoms of human diabetes. Add to that a doctor
at The Johns Hopkins University who noticed that when he
dissected the corpses of dead diabetics, their islets of Langerhans
were always in poor shape.

THE HORMONE OF THE ISLANDS
It was eventually concluded that those apparently unassuming
islets of Langerhans secrete a vital hormone. If you haven't got
it—or not enough of it—your body can't lower your glucose

(sugar) levels. This affects your body's management of all nutrients. The doctors and chemists who were studying it called it "insulin," from the Latin word *insula*, which means "island": the hormone of the islands.

BEST IN SHOW
Diabetes was a fatal disease until researchers could find a way to produce insulin artificially. The breakthrough came in Toronto in 1921, when a research team pumped an extract of pancreatic tissue into dogs whose pancreases had been removed. Their condition improved. A year later came the first experiment in injecting a refined version into human diabetics.

HORMONIC CONVERGENCE
Now we know that the islets of Langerhans secrete not just insulin, which lowers glucose levels, but also glucagon, a hormone that raises it. Together the two hormones act like an accelerator and brake, working as a duo to keep the body functioning evenly.

GOOD NEWS, BAD NEWS
The discovery of artificial insulin was the good news. The bad news for diabetics was that insulin is a protein. If you eat protein, your system doesn't know the difference between it and a mouthful of steak or a Brazil nut. The first thing your body will do is try to digest it by breaking it down, which defeats the purpose. That's why insulin usually has to be injected so that it enters the bloodstream without being destroyed by digestion.

IF YOU CAN'T GO TO THE ISLETS...
Here's more good news/bad news. Thanks to the wonders of modern science, hope has arrived. Diabetic patients who've received islet cell transplants have begun to produce their own insulin within 24 hours of the operation. The bad news is that there aren't enough donors to fill the demand.

Hey, buddy, want to donate a few islets? You've got plenty to spare.

WHAT'S THE FREQUENCY, HEDY?

Gorgeous, sexy, and smart as a whip.

How many movie stars do you know who hold the patent to a significant technological breakthrough? In a story even Hollywood couldn't have invented, Hedy Lamarr—a superstar of the silver screen in the 1930s and 1940s—invented a military communications system that held the promise of bringing a speedier end to World War II.

THE BARE FACTS

Hedy Lamarr (born Hedwig Eva Maria Kiesler in Vienna, Austria, in 1913), was best known for two movies, one of which she never actually appeared in. In the 1933 Austrian-Czech film *Ecstasy*, Hedy shocked European society and caused a worldwide scandal because of a single scene that lasted ten minutes. In it, Lamarr swims nude in a lake and then runs through a forest (without a towel or anything). This sequence—considered the first nude scene in cinematic history—resulted in the film being banned in many countries. In the U.S., the film was either banned or was shown only in a radically edited version.

Although Lamarr made her last film in 1958, she did appear—in name only—in the Mel Brooks western parody, *Blazing Saddles* (1973). Brooks used the running gag of a bad guy by the name of Hedley Lamarr (played by Harvey Korman), who had to constantly correct people who kept calling him "Hedy."

BEAUTY AND BRAINS

At Louis B. Mayer's invitation, Lamarr escaped Austria—and the domineering, pro-Nazi husband whom she had recently divorced. She arrived in Hollywood in 1938, billed as the world's most beautiful woman. She was a looker, all right, but not a great actress. Her career peaked in the 1940s.

What fans of the film goddess could not have known was that, mere months after the entry of the United States into World War II, Lamarr and avant-garde musician and composer George

---

By 1882 Edison had successfully lit one square mile of New York City.

Antheil were granted U.S. Patent Number 2,292,387 for inventing a "Secret Communications System" intended for use as a radio guidance device for U.S. Navy torpedoes. The system, a sheer stroke of genius, was based on the idea of "frequency hopping."

HEDY'S HOPPER

The idea behind frequency hopping is to change the frequency of a radio signal rapidly and randomly so that it is impossible to intercept a torpedo or change its course. The way the composer and the actress proposed to do this drew on their experience in the arts, especially on Antheil's work in electronics and music.

In the 1920s, Antheil had composed a ballet using synchronized player pianos. He thought he could adapt this concept to Lamarr's idea of frequency hopping. The transmitter they sketched used slotted-paper rolls, like those of a player piano, to send a pattern of 88 (the number of piano keys) changing frequencies. The receiver mounted on the torpedo would have a duplicate slotted-paper roll, so it would only recognize signals that matched those sent by the transmitter. Thus, signals could be transmitted without being detected, deciphered, or jammed. Brilliant!

HEDY'S HOPES

Although Hedy had hoped that her invention would help speed the end of the war, the system was never used by the U.S. military. Instead, they let the patent languish in their archives, partly because the technology of the time wasn't up to implementing such an advanced system.

When her patent expired in 1959, so did Hedy's chance to cash in on developing this "new" technology for the cellular phone industry. (The technology is now referred to as "spread spectrum" rather than "frequency hopping," although the basic concept is the same. Spread spectrum allows more cell-phone subscribers to use the existing frequency spectrum.) This was too bad for Lamarr, who could have used some of that money toward the end of her life. It wasn't until March 1997 that Hedy's amazing feat of technological prowess was finally acknowledged. She was given an award by the Electronic Frontier Foundation, an organization devoted to addressing civil liberties issues related to technology. For 83-year-old Lamarr, then a Florida retiree, "It was about time." She died three years later.

The first car ad was in *Scientific American* in July 1898.

DO YA THINK I'M SEXY?

In which various bugs get the surprise of their lives.
And some even live to tell the tale.

NOT THE THUMPING HE EXPECTED
Some kinds of orchid flowers are designed to mimic female bees, flies, or wasps. That's so the insects will spread the orchid pollen around, making more orchids—though contributing nothing to the reproduction of the flying creatures.

The hammer orchid even has a dummy female wasp on a stalk. When the male wasp comes courting, it meets with what must be quite an unexpected experience. The orchid—true to its name—slams the dummy wasp into the real (if dumb) wasp. Again and again, the bug is slammed into the flower's pollen pods, then he's let go to spread the pollen to another hammer orchid. If he's still in the mood for flitting around.

THE INKY-STINKY SPIDER
Smelling sexy works, too. The Australian bird-dropping spider, which is named for its ability to camouflage itself as you-know-what, has a tricky way of hunting, too. At night the spider hangs off the edge of a leaf, with its front legs stretched out wide. It releases a chemical scent—a pheromone—that mimics one released by female moths when they want to attract a mate. Male moths who come to check it out are in for a terminal shock when they get grabbed by those strong spider legs and eaten for supper.

FIREFLY FATALE
And then there's the fatal fakery of the female firefly. All fireflies blink signals, but different kinds of fireflies have different flashing patterns. That's because the species don't interbreed. It's no problem for fireflies—they can recognize signals from their own kind. After breeding, a female gets the munchies. So she reads the signals for a different purpose. She responds to a male of another firefly species, and has him for dinner—literally.

READ A WEATHER MAP LIKE A PRO

Why should meteorologists have all the fun?

On a TV weather report most of the official weather symbols have been replaced with snazzy computerized graphics that represent the weather very clearly for us. Thunderstorms are animated thunderclouds with little lightning bolts shooting out, snow is gently falling snowflakes, and warm and cold fronts are strings of blinking arrows.

Come on! Do you honestly think that's what meteorologists see when they look at their own secret official weather maps—the maps they have to study in order to bring you those snowflakes and arrows and cute little thunderclouds?

Hardly. The maps that meteorologists use are filled with arcane (but about to be explained) symbols that represent every kind of weather condition there is. That's how they find out where to put the snowflakes for the rest of us.

WHY YOU SHOULD CARE ABOUT FRONTS

The place where an air mass of a certain temperature and density meets up with another air mass of a different temperature and density is called a front. Fronts mean funky weather, like thunderstorms, kind of like a battle zone between two weather systems—which is, in fact, how weather fronts got their name. They reminded early meteorologists of the fronts of World War I. (Do meteorologists know how to have fun or what?)

Here's what fronts look like on a meteorological map, and one or two facts about them that will make you more authentic when you go to your next costume party dressed as a weatherperson:

COLD FRONTS: A sweeping line (usually blue) with triangles indicating the direction of the front.

Advancing cold fronts typically move quickly and mean thunderstorms and tornadoes and other messy atmospheric conditions.

WARM FRONTS: A sweeping line (often colored red) with half circles on it—again to point out the direction in which the front is moving.

Warm fronts usually move more slowly and the weather they create is often gentler but lasts for longer periods of time.

STATIONARY FRONT: A line that has alternating half circles and triangles (often in their respective red and blue) on opposite sides of the line.

Occasionally a cold and warm front will meet and then just sort of butt heads against each other, neither making any appreciable horizontal movement at all. This bit of meteorological mule-headedness is known as a stationary front. The storms that can come out of it can be severe, so look out.

OCCLUDED FRONT: A line with alternating triangles and half-circles, this time facing the same direction. The line is also often purple, to represent the merging of the two fronts. This is what happens when a fast-moving cold front kind of sneaks up on a slow-moving warm front plodding along in the same direction. These give you low temperatures and lots of rain and snow.

YOU GOT WEATHER? WE GOT A SYMBOL FOR IT
Now let's get to the smaller but no less important symbols:

Rain: A black dot (relatively small but about the size of a large city on the map).

One dot if the rain is light, two dots (side by side) if the rain is moderate, three dots (in a triangle) if the rain gets heavy, and a diamond of four dots if it's time to start gathering up the neighborhood animals in pairs.

Rain shower: A dot with a downward-pointing triangle underneath it.

Heavy shower: Add a stripe inside the triangle.

Freezing rain: A tilde sign—"~".

Drizzle: A curled single quotation mark. Heaviness of the drizzle works on the same one-to-four system as rain.

Snow: An asterisk or a small x. Again, one for light snow, two for moderate, three for heavy, and four for a mini ice age.

Snow shower: An asterisk with a little triangle underneath.

Heavy snow shower: Add a stripe to the triangle.

Snow is also represented by arrows, and the symbol for blowing snow is two arrows perpendicular to each other.

Hail or ice: An upward-pointing triangle.

Sleet: An upward-pointing triangle with a black dot inside.

Hail or ice shower: Add a triangle pointing down. (It gives the symbol a nice symmetry, but spells trouble for your car's paint job.)

Thunderstorm: An angular, stylized R with an arrowhead attached to a kinked right leg to symbolize lightning.

Severe thunderstorm: The arrowhead gets another kink in it so that it points to the left leg.

Rain and thunderstorm: The R gets a black dot on the top.

Snow and thunderstorm: An asterisk on top.

Hail: An upward pointing triangle on top of the R.

Tornado: A symbol that looks like two brackets placed next to each other in the wrong direction: "]["

Fog: An equal sign with three lines instead of two.

Sand or dust: An S with an arrow through it horizontally.

Smoke or smog: Imagine a straight vertical line with a wavy thing at the top (like a lower-case W) that goes off to the right.

Haze: An 8 lying on its side.

Have we forgotten anything? Oh, yes.

Hurricane: Two single quote marks (one upward and one downward stuck together).

READING THE WIND—AND MORE

You don't need a weatherman to know which way the wind blows (just a wet finger), but a nice weather map can tell you how fast the wind is blowing and how much cloud cover is overhead at the same time. Take that, Bob Dylan!

Wind: The basic symbol for just plain wind looks something like a half note in music: a circle (but a full circle, not a squashed one) with a bar sticking out. The circle represents weather conditions at the point where the wind reading was taken; the bar represents wind speed and direction. Let's turn our attention to the circle.

Clear sky: The circle isn't filled in.

Scattered clouds: A quarter of the circle is filled in. (Ninety degrees of the circle, going clockwise from the top, like from 12 to 3 on a clock.)

Sky half-filled with clouds: Half of the circle is filled in, still going clockwise.

Sky completely covered with clouds: The circle is filled in.

Now back to the wind. That bar we told you about? The one that sticks out of the circle? It points in the direction of wind, so if the wind is moving to the south, the bar points down. Couldn't be easier.

The first parking meter was installed in Oklahoma City, Oklahoma.

Wind speed is determined by adding lines coming out of the bar.
  Very light breeze (1 to 2 mph): No line.
  3 to 8 mph: One short line toward the end of the bar.
  9 to 14 mph: A long line at the end of the bar.
  15 to 20 mph: One long line and one short line.

Long and short lines are added progressively until wind speeds
reach 55 mph, at which point the bars are replaced by a triangle.
More lines are then placed alongside the triangle for higher wind
speeds until you hit 119 to 123 mph, when you get two triangles
and a short line.

  At this point your house has probably wrenched itself off its
foundation, so wondering how many more lines or triangles to add
really becomes more of an academic than a practical issue. Head
to the basement with your saltines, flashlights, and domestic
animals.

  And go with pride—you figured out the weather all by
yourself.

* * * * *

"Man will never be content until each man
makes his own weather and keeps it to himself."
—Jerome K. Jerome,
The Idle Thoughts of an Idle Fellow, 1889

"Don't knock the weather; nine-tenths of people couldn't
start a conversation if it didn't change once in a while."
—Kin Hubbard

"Isn't it interesting that the same people who laugh at
science fiction listen to weather forecasts and economists?"
—Kelvin Throop III

"No matter how rich you become, how famous or powerful,
when you die the size of your funeral will still pretty much
depend on the weather."
—Michael Pritchard

The first commercial color TV show aired in 1921; regular color broadcasts took till 1954.

WHAT'S IN A NAME?

Some interesting facts about some common animals.

When is a cat not a cat?
When it's a ringtail cat; this desert animal is a member of the raccoon family.

When is a bear not a bear?
When it's a koala bear. These cuddly natives of Australia may resemble small bears, but they're actually a marsupial, or pouch-carrying mammal, like the kangaroo.

When is a fly not a fly?
When it's a firefly or lightning bug; it's related to the beetle.

When is a snake not a snake, and a toad not a toad?
When the snake is a glass snake, and the toad is a horned toad—they're both really lizards!

When is a panther not a panther?
When it's a black panther. (Sorry, Mowgli!) The animal is actually a black leopard with even darker black spots.

When is a horse not a horse?
When it's a seahorse, of course; then it's a fish.

You've probably heard of a pride of lions, a litter of puppies, a flock of sheep, and a swarm of bees, but you may not be as familiar with some other funny, but true names for animal groups: a colony of ants, a string of ponies, a murder of crows, a kindle of kittens (but a clowder of cats), a pace of asses, a skulk of foxes, a crash of rhinos, a peep of chickens, a paddling of ducks, a drift of hogs, a skein (in flight) or a gaggle (on water) of geese, a drove of cattle, an unkindness of ravens, a knot of toads, an army of caterpillars, a barren of mules (weren't you paying attention when you read "Animal Crossbreeds"?), a shrewdness of apes, and a parliament of owls.

First functional typewriter was invented 1867; word processors began to replace them in 1974.

OUTBREAK!

*Somewhere in the heart of Africa, there's a reservoir of
Ebola virus carriers…will we find them in time?
Tracing the history of a 20th-century plague.*

Ebola appeared from nowhere in 1976, and since then
medical researchers have been trying to do two things: find a
cure, and find out where it came from. So far, they've gotten
nowhere. The best guess is that it originated in some kind of wild
animal population, but no one can figure out which animal is
responsible. If it can jump to humans, then it can jump to other
animals, too, and isolated cases of monkeys and apes being
infected don't mean that they were the original carriers.

When two people became infected after visiting a bat cave in
Kenya, researchers thought they'd found the culprits. (For more
on this, read "Curious Caves" on page 19.) An outbreak in Sudan
was also associated with bats, that time living in a factory roof.
However, all of the tests on the bats proved negative.
On the other hand, an outbreak that killed 53 people in Gabon in
2002 was traced to an infected gorilla, some of which had been
eaten by local people. How did the gorilla pick it up?

DEADLY SYMPTOMS
Ebola can be fatal in up to 90 percent of cases, depending on the
strain. After being infected, there's an incubation period of one to
three weeks. The first signs are a headache and muscle pains. The
next phase brings on vomiting and a high fever, and then bleeding
from the mucous membranes, usually from the eyes and mouth.
The bleeding can't be stopped, and in a few days it's all over.

EBOLA GOES TO THE HOSPITAL
Because the early symptoms are difficult to identify and because
they take a while to come on, Ebola sufferers often make it to the
hospital before the later attack phase of the disease starts. They're
feeling sick, but don't know what's wrong, so they're admitted for
observation. Some of the worst outbreaks have been centered in
hospitals, with nurses apparently spreading the virus to other

---

Dr. Christiaan Barnard successfully performed the first human heart transplant in 1967.

patients before anyone realizes what's happening. The very first recorded outbreak in 1976 happened in Zaire (now Democratic Republic of Congo). It infected 318 people, 280 of whom died. It started in a hospital and spread to neighboring villages from there. The original infected person who started it was never identified.

EBOLA IN AMERICA?

A primate research center in Virginia had a nasty moment in 1989 when a strain of Ebola was recognized among some macaque monkeys that had been imported into the U.S. from the Philippines. This particular strain of the virus turned out to be harmless to humans, but the government is so concerned about the potential for disaster, they've restricted research on the Ebola virus to certified labs and declared the virus and its component parts "deadly agents that pose a threat to public health."

IF IT HAPPENED HERE

So far, there's no antidote. The only good news is that the hospital-based outbreaks that have taken place in Africa wouldn't have happened in America. African hospitals are rudimentary health-care facilities: They regularly reuse needles and don't particularly follow the commonsense rules that prevent the spread of infection. So, while an outbreak in the U.S. might kill some unlucky people in one wave, it would probably be contained after that.

* * * * *

THOSE CONSIDERATE VAMPIRES

They may be bloodthirsty, but vampire bats are very considerate. They don't puncture the skin to draw blood like Dracula; they scrape the skin with their teeth, and this scraping is so gentle that the bat's sleeping prey doesn't even wake up while the bat is at work!

The first permanent artificial heart transplant was not performed until 1982.

WE'VE GOT YOUR NUMBER

Real or irrational, complex or imaginary, numbers count for something.

What's in a number? Well, depending on which number it is, quite a lot. On a day-to-day basis, most of us only deal with a certain subset of numbers. A few integers here and there, maybe some fractions if we're trying to slice a cake, or some negative numbers if it's January and it's really cold. But outside the confines of daily life, some really odd numbers are lurking. Irrational numbers. Imaginary numbers. Even transcendental numbers. How would you know a transcendental number from an irrational number? We're glad you asked. Forthwith, we provide a list of number categories. Don't worry, they may seem daunting at first, but really, they're as easy as pi.

1. Natural numbers: Let's start off with an easy set of numbers. "Natural" numbers are all the positive numbers: 1, 2, 3, 4, and so on all the way up. See, that wasn't so hard. Only slightly more complex are the whole numbers, which consist of all the natural numbers plus zero (0).

Well, big deal, you say, but just remember that the concept of "zero" is relatively new to Western thought—Europe had to get along without zero until well into the 13th century. The Indians, Arabs, and Mayans had it long before then. So don't get smug (unless you're Indian, Arabic, or Mayan, in which case, go right ahead). Moving on from whole numbers, we arrive at:

2. Prime numbers: A subset of natural numbers. A prime number is greater than 1, and is only cleanly divisible (that is, no fractions) by itself and 1. Early on, we get a lot of these—2, 3, 5, 7, 11, 13—but the further you go down the line, the more these prime numbers space themselves out (because, of course, the larger numbers get, the more likely they are to be divisible by lesser numbers). For all that, primes continue to pop up, even among tremendously large numbers. The largest prime yet discovered (at this writing, anyway) is 4,053,946 digits long. That's a mighty big number.

3. Integers: All natural numbers, plus zero, and then all the negative values of natural numbers: -1, -2, -3, -4, and so on. Sure, negative numbers are a little weird—it's strange to think of something as being less than zero—but since negative integers pop up in everything from thermometers to simple charts, we're used to them.

4. Rational numbers: Uh-oh, here come the fractions. But as far as fractions go, rational numbers are pretty harmless, since they're defined as all numbers that can be expressed as x/y, where both x and y are integers. So, numbers like 1/2, 1/4, 1/8, and so on. Integers are rational numbers since they can be expressed as themselves over 1: 3/1, for example, is 3. Rational numbers also include fractions that endlessly repeat in decimal form: 1/3, for example, which is .3333333333333333...as far as you want to carry it out. See? Nothing to get freaked out about.

5. Irrational numbers: Now things are beginning to get a little weird. Irrational numbers can't be expressed as integers, nor do they present themselves as repeating fractions. The fractions go on forever, but they never repeat their sequence. The most famous irrational number is pi, which is the ratio of the circumference of a circle to its diameter: 3.14159265 is how it starts, and it keeps on going, irrationally, forever.

Which is not to say that people have tried to impose rationality on it. In 1897 a bill was proposed in the Indiana legislature to give pi a specific, finite value. It passed unanimously in the Indiana House of Representatives but was killed in the Senate after Indiana was roundly mocked by everyone else in the world for its poor math skills.

Incidentally, pi is also a member of a particular subset of irrational numbers known as transcendental numbers, whose definition is as follows: a real number that is not the solution of any single-variable polynomial equation whose coefficients are all integers. (We're not going to go there, but you can memorize the definition and impress all the math geeks you know!)

6. Real numbers: Real numbers are all the numbers we've discussed so far: natural, whole, rational, and irrational. Well, duh, you say. If numbers aren't real, what would you call them? We're glad you asked! You'd call them:

7. Imaginary numbers: No, these aren't the imaginary friends of mathematicians who've inhaled too many marker fumes. Imaginary numbers are defined as any real number multiplied by a little something called the "imaginary unit," or "i" in shorthand. The imaginary unit is understood to be the positive square root of -1 (in engineering, i is also known as "j" or the "j operator," apparently because engineers like being different from the rest of us). You probably won't be using imaginary numbers for anything anytime soon, but as it happens, engineers find them useful in determining reactance in electronics.

8. Complex numbers: So, you have your real numbers and you have your imaginary numbers, and what fun would it be if they never actually got together? Why, no fun at all, which is why there are complex numbers, which can be expressed as $x + iy$, where x is a real number, and iy is an imaginary number. Once again, a practical application for these numbers comes from engineering. Complex numbers help to describe electrical impedance. Those crazy engineers. What will they think of next?

* * * * *

SO THAT'S WHAT THOSE ARE!

The ridges on the edges of coins are called "reeds." They were added to metal currency to deter counterfeiting and to prevent people from shaving the precious metals off of the rims. In spite of the fact that coins are not made of pure metals any longer, the reeds remain.

> Dime: 118 reeds
> Quarter: 119 reeds
> Half dollar: 150 reeds
> Susan B. Anthony dollar: 133 reeds

Count them and see if we are right! We dare you.

The first Apple computer in 1976 had 8 bytes of RAM and cost about $700.

HOPPER TO IT

In which an early computer whiz discovers the first "bug" in the system.

Like a lot of great inventors, Grace Murray Hopper believed that "we've always done it that way" was not necessarily a good reason to continue to do so.

AMAZING GRACE
She was born Grace Brewster Murray in 1906—three years after the Wright brothers' first successful power-driven flight and two years before Henry Ford's introduction of the Model T. Maybe that's why she made a career out of being a pioneer.

After scooping up a Ph.D. in mathematics from Yale in 1934—a rare accomplishment for a woman in those days—she went on to join the U.S. Naval Reserve in 1943.

GRACE MEETS HER MARK
She graduated from the Naval Reserve as a Lieutenant Junior Grade and was ordered to the Bureau of Ordnance Computation at Harvard. There she became the first programmer on the Navy's Mark I computer, a true mechanical miracle for its time.

It was love at first sight, and there was certainly a lot for her to love! A glass-encased mass of bulky relays, switches, and vacuum tubes, the Mark I was 50 feet (15 m) long, 8 feet (2.5 m) high, and 8 feet (2.5 m) wide. This modern marvel could store a whopping 72 words and perform three additions per second.

THE MOTH WAS NO MYTH
When Hopper traded up to a new model, the Mark II, she met the computer that would make her famous. She coined the term "bug" when she traced an error in the Mark II to a real moth trapped in a relay. The bug was carefully removed and taped to a daily logbook. Since then, whenever a computer has a problem, it's referred to as a bug.

GOODBYE, MARK
Hopper's love affair with the Mark series (she also worked on Mark III) ended in 1949 when she joined a company that later came to be called Sperry Rand. At Sperry Rand, she turned her

affections toward designing the first commercial, large-scale (and we mean large) electronic digital computer—UNIVAC I (for Universal Automatic Computer). UNIVAC I was a big boy, weighing in at around 16,000 pounds; it used 5,000 vacuum tubes and operated a thousand times faster than the Mark I.

SPEAK ENGLISH!
Faster wasn't good enough for Hopper. She knew that the key to opening up new computing worlds was to develop programming languages that could be used and understood by people who were neither mathematicians nor computer experts—she had the wacky idea that computer programs could be written in English, a pretty heretical notion in the early 1950s.

She eventually developed FLOW-MATIC, a program designed to translate a language that could be used for nonscientific and business applications like automatic billing and payroll calculation. Using FLOW-MATIC, Hopper and her staff were able to make the UNIVAC II "understand" 20 statements in English.

When she recommended that an entire programming language be developed using English words, she was told that it was impossible because computers didn't understand English.

GRANDMA COBOL
Not one to be deterred by such shortsightedness, Hopper and her colleagues went on to develop something called the Bomarc system, which eventually became COBOL (*common business-oriented language*). COBOL made it possible for computers to respond to words rather than just numbers, a feat that dramatically changed the lives of everyone in the computer industry. The first COBOL specifications appeared in 1959. COBOL is still the most widely used corporate computer language in the world. The Navy paid tribute to Hopper's pioneering work by dubbing her "Grandma COBOL."

THE "MAN" OF THE YEAR
In 1969, the Data Processing Management Association honored Hopper as its first-ever "Computer Science *Man* of the Year." (italics ours)

In 1985 she was named the U.S. Navy's first female rear admiral. She was buried with full Naval honors at Arlington National Cemetery on January 7, 1992.

10 THINGS SCIENCE FICTION GOT RIGHT

*From communication satellites to robotic pets,
a few of the things science fiction nailed before they happened.*

Science fiction is supposed to predict future events—and to be entirely honest, some of us are getting impatient waiting for our own rocket cars to the Moon, which we understood we'd have by now. Be that as it may, here are some things dreamed up by science fiction writers that are part of our real world.

1. Moon visits: Lots of science fiction writers had this one covered, but the question is: Who got closest to the real thing first? The best candidate is good ol' Jules Verne, whose 1865 novel, *From the Earth to the Moon,* and the 1870 follow-up, *Around the Moon,* nailed a lot of the minutia of a moon visit, including weightlessness, the basic size of the space capsule, the size of the crew (three men), and even the concept of splashdown into the ocean on return to Earth. In one of those fun coincidences, the fictional splashdown in *Around the Moon* was just a few miles from where the actual *Apollo 8* capsule splashed down (and, interestingly enough, the fictional launch pad was just a few miles from Cape Canaveral).

Verne was tremendously prolific, writing two novels a year for much of his creative life and dying with quite a few novels unpublished. It's not entirely surprising that he's credited with a number of other predictions, including trips by balloon, helicopters, tanks, and electrical engines. One "discovery" he's famously credited for, the submarine, is inaccurate, since submarines existed prior to the 1870 publication of *20,000 Leagues Under the Sea.*

2. Robots (and robot pets!): "Robot" comes from the Czech word *robota,* which means "drudgery"; *robotnik* is a word for "serf." Since today's robots are typically found in industrial settings doing mindlessly repetitive work, this is a strangely appropriate term. The word "robot" was popularized in Karl Capek's 1920 play *R.U.R.,* which stood for Rossum's Universal Robots. In the play, robots were manufactured humans who were used as cheap labor. One day they got fed up with this and decided to have a revolution and kill all the humans, proving once again that good help really is hard to find. One thing people don't seem to know about Capek's "robots" is that they're not actually mechanical—they're made out of synthetic flesh, although that fake flesh was then put into a stamping mill to make the bodies. The concept of robots as mechanical beings came later and was most famously popularized in fiction by writer Isaac Asimov in his Robot series. It's probably not a coincidence that a humanoid robot manufactured by Honda is called "Asimo."

Robot pets, like the Sony Aibo robot dog, have also been a staple of science fiction. The most famous example of this is probably *Do Androids Dream of Electric Sheep?*, the Phillip K. Dick novel that was the source material for the movie *Blade Runner*. The main character in the book is saving up to buy a realistic electric sheep for his lawn, so he'll be the envy of his neighbors (the movie had none of this suburban one-upmanship going on). Woody Allen, of all people, nailed the robot dog in 1973's *Sleeper*, in which we're introduced to Rags ("Hi! I'm Rags! Woof woof!"). Allen's reaction: "Is he housebroken? Or will he be leaving little piles of batteries all over the place?"

3. Cloning and genetic engineering: Humans haven't been cloned yet (so far as we know), but sheep, cats, cows, and rabbits have. And humans have used genetic engineering and gene therapy to improve their bodies. In June 2002, for example, it was announced that genetically modified cells helped to create functioning immune systems in two "bubble boys" who were born without immune systems of their own.

The most famous work of science fiction with cloning and genetic engineering is also one of the earliest: 1932's *Brave New World,* by Aldous Huxley. In it, humans are "graded" into jobs and social classes based on the number of clones that were made from their originating embryos; the higher the number of clones, the less bright they are and the more menial their jobs (this was backed up by a social agenda that assured each level of humanity that they were actually the best, so everyone went along with it).

Forensic entomologists can estimate how long someone has been dead by the corpse's insects.

4. The Internet: Okay, now, who wants to be blamed for this one? There are so many culprits. Author William Gibson is credited with coining the term "cyberspace" in his 1981 short story "Burning Chrome," and kick-started the whole media fascination with computers and the Internet and all that geekiness with his seminal 1984 novel *Neuromancer*. But even before Gibson, John Brunner's 1975 novel, *The Shockwave Rider*, posited a continent-wide information net, "hackers" who broke into the net, identity theft (when someone pretends to be someone else on-line), and most famously, computer viruses and worms—the terminology for these, in fact, comes from Brunner's book. Brunner imagined using viruses and worms as part of warfare—something that worries today's military quite a bit.

It should be noted that in 1975 a proto-form of the Internet did exist, though not in the scope and complexity imagined by Brunner. It existed in the form of ARPANET, a decentralized computer system that the U.S. Department of Defense created and which by 1975 also included several research universities as "nodes." Internet features created by 1975 include E-mail, on-line chat, and mailing lists. The most popular mailing list in 1975? One on science fiction, of course.

5. The World Wide Web—which, despite the propaganda of the 1990s, is not the whole Internet, just a subsection of it—was created in 1991 by Tim Berners-Lee and hit the big time with the creation of the Mosaic Web browser in 1993. The dynamic of the Net had been described before then. In 1990's *Earth*, David Brin imagined streaming audio and video and clickable hypertext links. And in a 1989 short story, "The Originist," based in Isaac Asimov's "Foundation" universe, Orson Scott Card also created a linking system similar today's hyperlinking.

6. Webcams? Imagined (sort of) by every single science fiction author who ever wrote about a picture phone. There are too many of those to bother counting.

7. Waterbeds: Yes, waterbeds. Robert Heinlein used them in 1961's *Stranger in a Strange Land;* the first modern waterbed was created in 1967 in San Francisco by design student Charles Hall, who dubbed it the "pleasure pit" (naughty boy). Heinlein also

---

"Borborygmus," the stomach rumbling sound, is fluid and gas going through the intestines.

The future calls for the introduction of bison, caribou, moose, and musk ox to churn up the mossy tundra and open the way for new grasses to grow. Zimov even hopes to reintroduce the darker side of the old food chain. The region already has wolves, but Zimov would like to bring in Siberian tigers to play the starring predatory role of Pleistocene era lions. (Which means that camping in the park will be pretty much at your own risk.)

The purpose of Pleistocene Park isn't just to see if you can introduce new animals in Siberia (although the local government has visions of ecotourism dancing in their heads); it's an exciting experiment that will put a lot of ecological theories to a new and practical test.

I'LL SHOW THEM WHO'S MAD!

You could have guessed that not everybody thinks the park is a good idea. Some biologists dispute Zimov's basic premise. They think that the changing animal populations didn't cause ecological change, but rather resulted from it. To them, the shifting ice age weather made Siberia colder and wetter and that's why the grazers died off and the land went from grass to moss.

Other scientists are more supportive of the ecological theory behind the park, but still have their doubts. They think that horses and moose are poor substitutes for mammoths and woolly rhinos, and that these modern animals can't tear up enough ground to make a difference.

SOMEBODY OUGHT TO WRITE A BOOK

The eventual success or failure of Pleistocene Park depends on a lot of factors, not the least of which is that the Russian economy is nearly as extinct as the mastodon.

But listen to this: Zimov and his colleagues could solve the pressing problem of not having big enough grazers by hooking up with another group of scientists who are dreaming about using DNA from a frozen mammoth recovered in Siberia to clone a new one. Maybe Pleistocene Park will get some of its original inhabitants back, after all. What a great idea! Then they can turn it into a theme park and people can visit it! But what if the animals go crazy and attack?

A brown bear eats up to 10 salmon before it is full—equal to a kid eating 40 burgers at once.

MEDICAL METEOROLOGY

It's nothing to sneeze at.

About 2,500 years ago, Hippocrates expressed great interest in the effects of climate and weather on human health. But the scientific world pretty much ignored this fascinating field until recently. Here's a look at the ways in which changes in the weather—such as temperature, seasonal changes in levels of light, air pressure, electrical charge, and even the blowing of the wind—can seriously affect both our physical and mental health.

There's a reason why they call it "under the weather."

TEMPERATURE TANTRUM
Humankind has survived long periods of both extreme cold (the ice ages come to mind) and extreme heat. Scientists have discovered just how high and low our body temperatures can actually go, beyond which the human body cannot survive.

HOW LOW CAN YOU GO?
If normal is 98.6°F (37°C), what's the lowest internal body temperature ever tolerated by a living human being? Well, if a person's body temperature falls below 85°F (29°C), the chances of survival are doubtful; at 80°F (26°C), coma usually sets in. Death is pretty much certain once body temp dips to 70°F (21°C).

There are always exceptions, of course. One took place in February 1951, when a 23-year-old woman was found in Chicago, Illinois, frozen stiff and unconscious—but alive. (She'd drunk too much the night before and passed out in an alley.) When hospitalized, her body temperature was recorded at 64.4°F (18°C). She managed to survive, but required amputation of both legs and all but one finger. She lived to see another 23 years.

HALF-BAKED EXPERIMENT
On the high end, body temperatures from 108° to 112°F (42° to 44°C) are considered very unusual, and only a few hotties have survived them. In the interests of science, an associate professor of engineering at UCLA subjected himself to an average *external* temperature of 250°F (121°C) for nearly 15 minutes—without serious results.

Miami's border includes two U.S. national parks: the Everglades and Biscayne National Park.

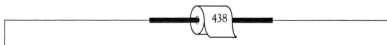

THE SAD SEASON

The decreasing light and colder temperatures during fall and winter affect a significant number of people who suffer from SAD (Seasonal Affective Disorder, also known as "the winter blues"). Those afflicted with SAD are, well, sad. The symptoms can be as serious as severe depression, but as relatively harmless as carbohydrate cravings that lead to overeating and weight gain. Other symptoms include irritability, loss of libido, and various physical symptoms such as joint pain or stomach problems.

SHEDDING SOME LIGHT ON THE SUBJECT

SAD symptoms are at their worst in the darkest months of winter, when the lack of bright light makes things tough on our brain chemistry (even though the exact means by which sufferers are affected by light isn't really known). Researchers have found that by literally shedding some light on the subject—regular exposure to fluorescent light works best—these SAD sacks can experience significant improvement. Sitting next to a light for as little as 15 to 45 minutes per day may be enough to alleviate depression and other SAD symptoms.

NO PAIN, NO RAIN

Remember your eccentric aunt or uncle who used to claim they could predict rain by the increased pain in their joints? New discoveries in medical science have shown that they were probably not as far off their rockers as you thought. Human ailments can predict the weather. A change in atmospheric pressure before it rains can indeed make swollen joints even more painful for people who suffer from rheumatism and arthritis. Doctors now believe that very sensitive pain receptors in the joints are zapped by even the slightest changes in atmospheric pressure.

HUMAN BAROMETERS

A recent study showed that 83 percent of patients with osteoarthritis (the kind of arthritis that's marked by degeneration of the cartilage and bone joints) could foretell a change in the weather from the way their symptoms changed. Other studies of these "human barometers" have shown that dramatic changes in weather can result in even more serious health problems: heart irregularities, respiratory distress, and even seizures.

WHEN IT RAINS IT SPORES

Humidity can affect swollen joints, too, although scientists haven't yet figured out exactly why. Changes in humidity can also

The smallest snake is the blind snake, which could wrap around your fingertip.

bring on asthma attacks. The most dramatic cases seem to take place when thunderstorms are approaching. The increased humidity releases countless microscopic fungal spores that, when breathed in by asthma sufferers, can trigger an attack. In July 1983, a hospital in Birmingham, Alabama, recorded *ten times* the number of asthma admissions after a thunderstorm during which high levels of fungal spores were released.

THE SHOCKING TRUTH
The intense atmospheric electricity that accompanies thunderstorms may also be held accountable for asthma attacks and a lot more. A survey of work accidents in a factory in Munich found that accidents almost doubled during bad weather. German researchers also showed that road accidents rose by 70 percent—and road deaths by 20 percent—during periods of high atmospheric electricity.

A SUNNY DISPOSITION
Sunshine is an important part of our health because it makes vitamin D, which is essential for maintaining a calcium balance to keep bones healthy. Women who spend ten minutes a day in the sun are less likely to suffer from hip fractures in old age because their bones are much stronger. A good dose of sunshine also improves breathing and blood circulation. Sunbathing can even lead to a drop in blood pressure and lower levels of cholesterol—but don't forget the sunscreen!

SUN DOWNER
Of course, it's less easy to measure the effect of the Sun's energy on our mental health. But it's well known that sudden gusts in the solar wind—the stream of electrically charged particles streaming out of the Sun—can wreak havoc on radio communications and send compasses spinning. So why wouldn't it affect humans, too? A recent study found a relationship between visual hallucinations and magnetic solar activity caused by sunspots. Scientists discovered that artificial magnetic fields (as evidenced by the spinning compasses) can affect the pineal gland just below the brain. This gland secretes the hormone melatonin, which some people take in tablet form for jet lag, but which if overused can cause depression and hallucinations.

Another theory holds that sunspot activity can affect ions in Earth's atmosphere, which in turn can disturb certain people. In 1991, an unusually high number of weather-sensitive ailments broke out in America. It was probably no coincidence that 1991was a peak year for sunspots.

BAD BEHAVIOR

High winds have long been associated with negative effects on people's health and behavior. Most teachers know, for example, that their classes can be hell when the wind blows. Children become restless, badly behaved, or even downright obnoxious. Studies of children in the playground of an American school showed that the number of fights doubled when the wind blew greater than force 6 (25–31 mph).

THE SANTA ANAS

The Santa Ana is a hot, dry wind—with gusts of up to 100 mph—that blows from the east across the mountain passes of Southern California into Los Angeles and environs, bringing with it a good strong dose of the heebie-jeebies. As mystery author Raymond Chandler once wrote: "Meek little wives feel the edge of a carving knife and study their husbands' necks." He might be right. One study found that murders rose by up to 50 percent during Santa Anas, regardless of whether they blew in winter or summer.

ARE YOU POSITIVE?

What might be causing these normally quiet spouses to head for the cutlery? One idea holds that, when the wind blows, the electricity in the air changes as a result of a change in the charge of ions—those positively or negatively charged atoms. Normally, air contains negative ions, but dry winds tend to collect positive ions, which are thought to adversely affect the way we feel. In about a third of the population, this includes irritability and anxiety as well as nausea and headaches.

GOOD FOR WHAT AILS YOU

An excess of positive ions can trigger the production of serotonin, the nerve-transmitter hormone. High levels of the stuff are linked with migraines and nausea. Negative ions—which are created near waterfalls, beaches, mountains, and even in your shower—tend to counteract these unpleasant effects and make you feel better as a result.

* * * * *

"Art is made to disturb. Science reassures. There is only one valuable thing in art: the thing you cannot explain."
—Georges Braque, *Le jour et la nuit*

Mosquitoes' small wings vibrate air quickly and make a high whining sound.

TO YOUR HEALTH! PART II

*Uncle John presents—in quiz form—a few of his
favorite oddities from the annals of medical research.*

1. In the 1740s, Doctors John Williams and Parker Bennett disagreed over whether yellow fever and black-water fever were the same. What did they do about it?
a) They tested 50 patients to compare symptoms, the first study of its kind.
b) They wrote scientific papers pooh-poohing each other's ideas for the next 30 years.
c) They fought a duel with pistols in which they both died.
d) They agreed to disagree, then formed a joint medical practice—the Mayo Clinic.

2. German Scientist Robert Koch (1843–1910) proved for the first time that germs cause disease in humans. He did this by injecting mice with dye-stained anthrax to make them sick. What did he feed the anthrax to keep them alive?

a) Moldy cheese
b) The jelly-like substance from the inside of an eyeball
c) Salt
d) Ground hippo hooves

3. Alexander Fleming (1881–1955) was famous for discovering penicillin—but he also discovered a germ-killing chemical in mucus. How did he come across it?
a) One day he had a cold and drippings from his nose fell on some germs and killed them.
b) He was working on a cure for the common cold and produced the chemical in a test-tube.
c) He observed that his lab rats who had colds were able to fight off the germs.
d) He picked up a germ-laden slide with a used handkerchief and observed that the germs turned pink and then died.

ANSWERS: 1. (c); 2. (b); 3. (a)

A bumblebee's larger wings vibrate air more slowly and make a low buzzing sound.

ASK UNCLE JOHN: ZEN QUESTIONS

You don't need to be a Zen master to answer these questions. It's just science!

Dear Uncle John:
What is the sound of one hand clapping?
Easy: Just slap someone. The question is a corruption of what the Buddhists call a "koan" (a question or statement that cannot be answered by mere intellect). You have to feel it, which makes it kind of touchy-feely, but what can you do? The "one hand clapping" bit comes from an 18th century Zen Buddhist named Hakuin, who asked, "In clapping both hands, a sound is heard. What is the sound of one hand?"

The proper answer in the Zen Buddhist tradition is to assume a Buddha posture and then simply thrust one hand out, palm outstretched. This is a deeply unsatisfying answer, since doing this produces no sound whatsoever. But, again, with a koan, not getting an intellectually satisfactory answer is the whole point.

However, this koan is easily solved by experimentation and cursory examination of human physiology. Try clapping right now. Most people clap by bringing together the fingers of one hand with the palm of the other—it's the way to get the most consistent clapping sound. To clap with one hand, all you have to do is bring the fingers of one hand together with its own palm. The tips of the fingers on your hand can easily connect with the lower part of your palm. With a little practice, you can bring down your middle and ring fingers with sufficient force to generate a verifiable clapping sound—a rather weak and quiet clapping sound relative to the usual clap, but as Twain would say, "The remarkable thing about a dancing pig is not how well it dances, but that it dances at all." And you didn't even have to slap anyone. The bad news is that making the sound of one hand clapping does not automatically make you a Zen Buddhist master, ready to transcend the wheel of life to negate one's sense of self in everlasting Nirvana. You still have some other karmic kinks to work out. It's not fair, but no one ever said life was fair (certainly not Buddha).

Dear Uncle John:
If a tree falls in the forest, and no one's around to hear it, does it make a sound?
Of course it does. The proof is evident in the fact you have ears at all. Ears, like every other feature of your body, are an evolutionary adaptation that provides you (and other creatures with ears) the advantage of perceiving vibrations in the air (or other media) generated by physical events—or, to put it another way—sounds.

Smarty-pants people will say that there's a way a tree can fall in the forest without making a sound: if that forest exists in a vacuum. Since nearly every sound humans hear is carried to us through the air, if you remove the air you also remove the medium sounds travel in—therefore, no sound. Nice try, but sound is also carried by solids and by liquids (and faster, too, because the sound waves have less space to travel between atoms—sounds carried by steel, for example, move 17 times faster than through air). So when the tree hits the ground, the vibrations of wood hitting earth will transmit sound, vacuum or no. You'll just need to put your ear to the ground to hear them. Yeah, but what if the tree that's falling in the forest is falling through airless, empty space with the rest of the forest falling at the same time? Well, in that case, there would be no sound, even if someone were there to hear it. But you'd have to admit that would be pretty strange.

Dear Uncle John:
How much wood would a woodchuck chuck if a woodchuck could chuck wood?
Well, first, woodchucks certainly *can* chuck wood—researchers at Cornell who keep woodchucks in captivity report providing the creatures chunks of 2 x 4s for chucking (and chewing) amusement. The real question is whether they *choose* to.

By and large, woodchucks in the wild choose not to. Because, really, why would they? Woodchucks are also known by the other, more popular name of "groundhog," and indeed that second name is more appropriate, since groundhogs typically burrow into the ground, chucking out whatever they have to to build their living quarters (groundhogs are also known as "whistle pigs," a pretty dumb name for any animal, much less for one with two other perfectly good names). The ground groundhogs excavate for their living quarters is typically comprised of dirt, and while there is

The largest giant squid was 20 tons, 20 feet long from tail to beak, and had 35-foot tentacles.

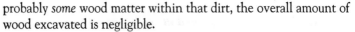

probably *some* wood matter within that dirt, the overall amount of wood excavated is negligible.

However, a naturalist named Richard Thomas once took it upon himself to estimate how much wood a woodchuck would chuck, if the dirt he chucked for his burrow were replaced with wood. It turns out that the average woodchuck burrow is surprisingly roomy, since a woodchuck chucks about 35 cubic meters of dirt in the course of his building activates. A pile of wood with a volume of 35 cubic meters, Thomas estimated, would weigh about 700 pounds. That's a lot of wood chucking.

Dear Uncle John:
What happens when an irresistible force meets an immovable object?
Nothing. You've hit on a genuinely unanswerable question, since the conditions that would allow for one of these items would, by necessity, preclude the possibility of the other. So you could theoretically have one or the other, but not both.

In our universe, there is neither an irresistible force nor an immovable object. In the latter case, it's a fact that *everything* in our universe is moving—the universe is expanding, and as it expands, nearly everything in it is moving away from everything else (the exception from our point of view being objects that are cosmically local to us, say, nearby galaxies, some of which are coming toward us—but even those are moving relative to the rest of the universe). Clearly, in a universe in which everything moves, there are no immovable objects.

As for irresistible forces, there are none of those either—all the forces of the universe that we know of (electromagnetism, strong and weak nuclear forces, and good ol' gravity) are easily resistible with (depending on the force in question) enough distance, shielding, or energy. The closest thing we have to an irresistible force would probably be gravity at the point of a black hole's event horizon. That's when the pull of gravity is so strong that not even light can escape. However, theoretically, even *then* random particles can escape a black hole through a phenomenon known as Hawking radiation.

Nothing is perfect, irresistible, or immovable. You could say that asking what would happen when an irresistible force meets an immovable object is simply a scientific koan.

Extended
Sitting
Section

BIG MOMENTS IN FORENSICS

Who thought of identifying people with fingerprints?
When were blood types first discovered?
When did Quincy go on the air? Soon, you will know all.

Forensics is the science of whodunit. When a crime is committed, forensic scientists pore over physical evidence to discover who did it, when it was done, and how it happened. It's just like the board game Clue, except with more expensive detection equipment, and at the end, someone goes to prison. Like any good science, the science and practice of forensics didn't happen overnight. While the practice of forensics in crime-solving has exploded in recent years, with everything from DNA typing to forensic accountants poring over insider trades, some very basic forensic ideas have been kicking around for years—long before *CSI*, *Crossing Jordan*, or even *Quincy*. Come with us as we pursue the trail of forensics through history, from China to L.A.

A.D. 700: The Chinese use fingerprints on documents and on clay sculptures. Some time before this, ancient Babylonians are also pressing thumbprints into clay documents for business transactions. So at least a few civilizations out there are clued into the idea of fingerprints as identifying marks.

1248: We're in China again—this time for the publication of a book entitled *Hsi Duan Yu* (*The Washing Away of Wrongs*), which told its readers how to tell the difference between someone who had been strangled and someone who had been drowned. What makes this such a big deal is that it offers medical reasoning instead of just saying something like "if they're floating in the water, there's a good chance they've drowned." It's the first time anyone records the medical reasoning being used to solve crime.

1609: The first stirrings of forensic accounting occur when François Demelle of France publishes the first treatise on systematic document examination.

1784: In Lancaster, England, some guy named John Toms had a torn piece of newspaper in his pocket. The bad news for him is that the torn newspaper nicely fit another torn bit of newspaper found in a pistol that was used to commit a murder. The law puts them together—the first instance of physical matching—and Toms is convicted.

1810: Master criminal Eugène François Vidocq is on his way to the Big House when he has an idea. He'll use his criminal skills for the good of mankind instead! In addition to providing generations of comic book, movie, and TV show hacks a durable plot idea, he also forms the first detective force in the history of the world: The Sûreté of Paris. All of the detectives, like Vidocq, are former criminals. Among Vidocq's forensic innovations: making plaster casts of footprints and shoeprints, the use of ballistics, and competent record-keeping (on index cards, no less).

1813: Paris again, where Mathiew Orfila publishes the first treatise that systematically catalogs poisons and their effects. For this, he gets the title of "Father of Modern Toxicology," although there probably wasn't an official ceremony. Orfila also was one of the first to develop forensic blood tests and to examine blood and semen with a microscope for forensic purposes.

1835: Scotland Yard investigator Henry Goddard determines that a butler had staged an attempted robbery when he traces a bullet back to a bullet mold owned by the butler. This is the first example of bullet matching, as well as one of the first actual recorded cases of "the butler did it."

1863: Is that blood or a spot of ketchup? A German scientist named Schönbein creates the first presumptive test for blood when he discovered that hemoglobin will oxidize hydrogen peroxide. Mixing peroxide and ketchup will simply give you inedible ketchup, although it's unclear if Schönbein made this observation.

1879: As police forces started keeping systematic records of crimes and criminals, they found themselves with more information than they could keep track of, especially in big cities. Alphone Bertillon, a clerk working for the Paris police, came up with a solution—measuring a lot of body parts on each criminal. He calculated that there was a one in four chance of two different criminals having one measurement match; by taking eleven measurements, he cut the odds to one in four million. A lot of criminals found policemen coming toward them with calipers in their hands and a gleam in their eyes. Police departments sorted their rogues galleries by the span of their outstretched arms and the length and breadth of their ears. This sounds pretty random, but so are fingerprints, which replaced bertillonage (a.k.a. the anthropometric method) in the early 20th century. Fingerprints were more random, which made them even less likely to be duplicated.

1880: Trouble in Tokyo! There's been a burglary, and an innocent man has been blamed for the heist! In steps Scottish physician and missionary Henry Faulds, who uses fingerprints not only to clear the accused, but also to help bring the actual criminal to justice. Faulds writes about using fingerprints for crime-solving in the science journal *Nature,* and then spends the next couple of decades in a nasty little letter-writing spat with one Sir William Herschel, about which of the two of them thought up the idea first. (Herschel—not to be confused with the *other* Sir William Herschel, the guy who discovered Uranus—concedes the point, finally, in 1917.)

1887: Everyone's favorite fictional master of forensics, Sherlock Holmes, makes his debut.

1892: Sir Francis Galton of Great Britain publishes *Fingerprints,* the first book to codify fingerprint patterns and show how to use them in solving crimes. Meanwhile, in Argentina, police investigator Juan Vucetich develops a fingerprinting classification system based on Galton's work and uses it to accuse a mother of murdering her two sons and then slitting her own throat to make it look like the work of someone else. Seems she left bloody fingerprints on a door post. That'll teach her.

1901: Human blood groups are identified and described by Austrian doctor Karl Landsteiner, who subsequently codified his discoveries into the blood types we know today (for more on this, see "Are You My Type?" on page 130). This discovery was useful in the field of forensics (to help identify criminals by the blood they might leave at the crime scene), as well as in medicine in general, and it lands Landsteiner a Nobel Prize in 1930.

American eels migrate from freshwater streams to the Sargasso Sea in the ocean.

1903: The first academic program for forensic science is created at University of Lausanne, Switzerland, by Professor R. A. Reiss.

1905: Teddy Roosevelt creates the FBI. He was president at the time. He could do that.

1910: Rosella Rousseau confesses to the murder of Germaine Bichon. Why? Because her hair is matched to hairs at the crime scene, a technique pioneered by Victor Balthazard, a professor of forensic medicine at the Sorbonne. The same year, another French professor of forensic medicine, Edmund Locard, helps to create the first police crime lab. The first U.S. crime lab was founded in 1925 by Los Angeles police chief August Vollmer.

1921: The portable polygraph (lie detector) is invented. In 1923, polygraph testimony is ruled inadmissible in U.S. courts.

1925: Blood's not the only bodily fluid you can type, suggested Japanese scientist K. I. Yosida, as he undertook studies to determine serological isoantibodies in other body fluids. He's right.

1960: An arsonist's job gets harder as gas chromatography is used for the first time in a lab to identify specific petroleum products.

1976: *Quincy, M.E.*, starring Jack Klugman as a feisty L.A. coroner, debuts and runs through 1983. The character of Quincy is allegedly based on real-life Los Angeles "Coroner to the Stars" Thomas Noguchi, who presided over the autopsies of Marilyn Monroe and Bobby Kennedy, and played a significant role in the investigation of the Manson family murders. The physical resemblance between Klugman and Noguchi is enigmatic at best.

1977: Japanese forensic scientist Fuseo Matsumur notices his fingerprints popping up as he prepares a slide for examination and tells his friend Masato Soba. Soba would use this information to help develop the first process to raise latent prints with cyanoacrylate, or, as it's more commonly known, superglue. Yes, superglue. Now you know why not to get it on your fingers.

1984: Yes, 1984. An ironic year for the first successful DNA profiling test, created by Great Britain's Sir Alec Jeffreys.

1986: Jeffreys uses his DNA profiling method to help convict the ominously named Colin Pitchfork for murder. Interestingly, in this same case DNA is used to clear another man accused of the crime.

Salmon migrate from the ocean to freshwater streams.

1987: DNA profiling makes its debut in the U.S. and nails Tommy Lee Andrews for a number of sexual assaults in Orlando, Florida. However, in the same year, the admissibility of DNA profiling is challenged in another case, *New York v. Castro*, in which the defendant was accused of murder. This set the stage for many years of back and forth argument on the standards and practices of the labs that perform DNA profiling.

1991: *Silence of the Lambs* is released, starring Jodie Foster as an FBI investigator who uses forensic techniques to track down a serial killer, and Anthony Hopkins as the oddly genteel cannibal who helps her. Foster becomes the first actress to win an Oscar for playing an FBI agent; Hopkins becomes the first actor to win an Oscar for playing a character that has a good friend for lunch with fava beans and a nice Chianti.

1996: In Tennessee, a fellow named Paul Ware is accused of murder, but the only physical evidence is a few hairs. Investigators use those hairs to extract DNA from mitochondria, a small structure within human cells. Mitochondrial DNA is different from DNA found in a cell's nucleus. Since there are quite a few mitochondria in every human cell, the amount of mitochondrial DNA to work with is larger. The mitochondrial DNA in the hairs is a match for Ware's. Ware is serving a life term in prison. It's the first use of mitochondrial DNA to convict someone of a crime.

2001: Not one but two shows about forensic scientists hit the TV: The redundantly titled *CSI: Crime Scene Investigation* and *Crossing Jordan*. None of the stars look remotely like Thomas Noguchi.

* * * * *

"People in general have no notion of the sort and amount of evidence often needed to prove the simplest fact."

—Peter Mere Latham

"Some circumstantial evidence is very strong, as when you find a trout in the milk."

—Henry David Thoreau, *Miscellanies*

Every part of these plants is poisonous: azalea, foxglove, nightshade, oleander, rhododendron.

COOL ASTRONOMICAL TERMS TO MAKE FRIENDS AND IMPRESS PEOPLE

You'll be the life of the party when you explain the difference between an AU and a parsec!

How often has this happened to you? You're walking down the street, and you hear someone imploring, "Can't someone on God's green Earth just tell me what an Oort cloud *really* is?" Well, in about five minutes, you'll be the hero of that particular situation. From astronomical units to wormholes, here are 15 simple explanations of complex and obscure astronomy terms. Collect them all!

1. Astronomical unit: Technically, the length of the semimajor axis of Earth to the Sun, but you can think of it as the average distance of the planet Earth from the Sun; it's a little under 93 million miles (92,955,808 miles, to be precise, but who's counting?). The Astronomical unit, or AU, gets used as a handy way to measure distances within the solar system. Mars, for example, is 1.5 AU from the Sun, and Pluto is 39 AU back. It's not so useful for interstellar distances, however, since the nearest star to our own is more than 275,000 AU away. It's easier to say "4.39 light-years." No, really. Try it yourself. See? Let's move on.

2. Baily's beads: These are an arc of bright spots that are visible during a total solar eclipse, just as the Moon is moving directly in front of the Sun. The reason these spots exist is that the Moon's surface is not perfectly smooth—it has hills and valleys and craters and litter from *Apollo* missions on it. These imperfections allow isolated spots of light to shine through. Enjoy them while they last, because they don't last long.

3. Chandrasekhar limit: So, you're a star, and you've burned through all of your nuclear fuel and expanded and then ejected

of them come from the Oort cloud, a collection of icy debris that stretches to about 50,000 astronomical units from the Sun. The comets that come from the Oort cloud are known as "long period" comets, which means they visit the Sun every few thousand to millions of years (if, indeed, they ever drop down that way again). Shorter period comets frequently come from the Kuiper belt, between Neptune and Pluto.

10. Parsec: The distance of an object that has one arcsecond of parallax when measured from opposite ends of Earth's orbit—but you can think of it simply as 3.26 light-years. Note that parsec is a measurement of distance, not of time, so when Han Solo brags about doing the Kessel Run in less than 12 parsecs in *Star Wars*, it's pretty clear he's messing with Luke's goofy little head. In addition to "parsec," astronomers also use the term "kiloparsec" (3,260 light-years) to describe large distances within the galaxy and "megaparsec" (3,260,000 light-years) for intergalactic distances.

11. Proplyd: Sounds kind of icky, doesn't it? Well, relax, it's not catching. It's just a term that hip astronomers use to refer to a "protoplanetary disk"—a protoplanetary disk being a swirling collection of dust and gas that forms around a young star and from which (if the disk lives up to its name) planets may eventually form. Earth itself came from a proplyd; the Hubble Space Telescope has seen bunches of them in the Orion Nebula.

12. Roche limit: The reason Saturn has rings. The Roche limit marks a boundary, roughly two-and-half times the radius of a planet. Inside that boundary, tidal forces are so strong that any moon inside the Roche limit is literally shredded. We're talking total destruction here. Saturn's rings, which lie inside Saturn's Roche limit, may be the remains of a moon unfortunate enough to have (briefly) formed inside the limit. Now, interestingly enough, there *are* small moons inside Saturn's rings themselves. These moons are too small to be greatly affected by tidal forces. However, if you took *our* moon and put it inside Earth's Roche limit, it would be, literally, dust.

13. Spin–orbit coupling: No, it's not what happens when a couple of Shuttle astronauts try to have a little "quality time."

Hair is straight, curly, or wavy based on if it grew out of a round, oval, or flat hair follicle.

Spin–orbit coupling happens when tidal forces between a smaller body and a larger body cause the smaller body's rotation to match its orbit. For example, the Moon rotates exactly one time for every time it orbits around Earth, but other spin-orbit ratios can exist. Take Mercury: It rotates three times for every two trips around the Sun.

14. Standard candles: If you want to know how far away a star cluster or galaxy is, there's a simple way to do that. Just compare the apparent magnitude of a star in that cluster or galaxy (how bright it looks to you) with its absolute magnitude (how bright it really is). Since the luminosity of an object is related to its distance from an observer, you factor these two data points together and what comes out is distance. One problem: How do you know its absolute magnitude? Well, for that, you use a star of a type whose physical properties are so well known that it acts as an excellent reference. Cepheid variable stars, for example, have been called "cosmic yardsticks," and their brightness grows and decreases in a cycle that's directly related to their absolute magnitude. These types of stars are commonly referred to as "standard candles."

15. Wormhole: Trekkies (oh, fine, fine—Trekkers) know all about these babies. They're "tunnels" through the fabric of space and time that could theoretically allow you to travel vast distances in space (and, interestingly, in time, too) in a flash. Unlike the wormholes in *Star Trek*, however, real wormholes are much less likely to be used for quick jaunts around the universe because: a) they're theoretical, and b) in order to keep them open to use, you'd need negative energy and all sorts of exotic matter. To do that in *Star Trek*, you just hire another writer. In the real universe, alas, it's not that simple.

* * * * *

WHAT SCIENTISTS SAY ABOUT PUSHY PEOPLE

"Give some people an autoparsec
and they'll take 16.093 tera-angstroms!"

Marie and Pierre Curie's notebooks recording their radium experiments are still radioactive.

TAKE YOUR VITAMINS, ALREADY!

Ten very good reasons to take that stinkin' multivitamin every morning.

Vitamins, as you may remember dimly from those health class sessions that you didn't actually sleep through, are a bunch of organic compounds that your body needs to function properly.

The word "vitamin" comes from "vitamine," a word coined in the early part of the 20th century to refer to these life-essential compounds, conjoining *vita*, meaning "life," and *amine*, which refers to certain nitrogen-based compounds that scientists assumed at the time were present in all vitamins. As it happens, not every vitamin has amines in them, so they just dropped the "e," and everybody was just fine with that solution.

Vitamins are also sometimes referred to as "accessory food factors," but probably not by anyone you know or are likely to meet in your everyday wanderings around the planet.

We need vitamins from our food or other outside sources, since by and large our bodies can't create vitamins internally, yet they are still required to keep our bodies healthy. The problem there is that most vitamin-rich foods, like raw leafy greens and lean meats and whole grains, are really far less compelling on a gustatory level than, say, Twinkies, Twizzlers, Slim Jims, and ruffled potato chips so deeply fried that they glisten translucently in the sun and cause your arteries to scream wordlessly in anticipation of subsequent plaquing.

Be that as it may, you really do need to take those vitamins, even if it's only by sneaking a couple of your kids' Flintstones Chewables when they're off at school. To impress upon you the importance of daily vitamin ingestion, we'll now cheerfully terrify you with examples of all the horrible, disgusting, nasty, debilitating diseases and ailments you can get if you don't. Yes, that's right, nature imposes penalties for not treating your body right. You probably knew that. Now you're going to get it spelled out for you. Let's take the vitamins in alphabetical order, shall we?

The highest recorded temperature was 136°F (58°C) in Azizia, Libya, in 1922.

VITAMIN A

What it does for you: Keeps your skin and your eyes healthy; helps you heal your body.

What happens if I don't have it? Your night vision goes out the window, since vitamin A is a component of "visual purple," a protein that boosts your eyes' sensitivity in dim light. Your skin can become scaly and dry. The linings of your mucous membranes can lose their cilia, which will increase your susceptibility to bacterial infections. In severe cases of vitamin A deficiency, you get xerophthalmia, a totally disgusting disease in which your eyes become swollen, your tear ducts shut off, and your eyelids get all full of pus. Unsurprisingly, your corneas are more susceptible to infection and ulceration when your eyes are like this, and it's fairly likely you'll go blind and then fall down some stairs or something.

I'm convinced. Feed me! Vitamin A is in eggs, milk, liver, and green and yellow vegetables. But, be careful, too much vitamin A is not good either. Stick to the recommended daily allowance.

VITAMIN B1 (THIAMINE)

What it does for you: It helps your body break down carbohydrates and keeps your nervous system humming along nicely.

What happens if I don't have it? Then you get beriberi, which despite its mildly amusing name is really a righteously nasty little disease; the name of the disease is taken from a Sinhalese word meaning "extreme weakness." To start off, you lose your appetite and get all slackerlike; you experience digestive problems and numbness in your extremities. That numbness is just your body's way of saying, "Hey, moron, the long nerves in your arms and legs are beginning to atrophy!" From there, you have your choice: "dry" beriberi, in which those long nerves atrophy even more and you experience loss of muscle mass and motor control, or "wet" beriberi, in which you experience edema (i.e., fluid saturating your body), poor circulation, and cardiac failure. They both sound so good. It's really hard to choose. End results of severe beriberi: paralysis or death. Or both.

I'm convinced. Feed me! Milk, liver, peanuts, and pork are all good sources of B_1.

VITAMIN B2

What it does for you: A factor in your body's oxidization of carbohydrates and amino acids and a key ingredient in some critical enzymes.

What happens if I don't have it? Your friends start to think you've become a vampire, because your eyes suddenly develop an increased sensitivity to light. They also wish you would, like, take a bath, because your skin is becoming all greasy and scaly. Your mouth is also in bad shape. Your lips redden and develop cracks at the corners (this is called cheliosis), and your tongue is inflamed and sore (glossitis). Basically, a B$_2$ deficiency makes you look all squinty and puffy, and where's the fun in that?

I'm convinced. Feed me! Get your B$_2$ from green vegetables, liver and other organ meats, and milk.

VITAMIN B3 (NIACIN)

What it does for you: Helps you metabolize carbohydrates and also oxidizes sugars.

What happens if I don't have it? You'll be introduced to pellagra, a perfectly charming disease that hits you with skin lesions that first look like sunburns (thanks to your skin's increased sensitivity to light) but later become crusty and scaly. Then constipation kicks in, alternating with diarrhea—what a lovely combination— and your mouth and tongue become inflamed and sore. Having fun yet? Just you wait, because later stages of pellagra bring dementia in a variety of fun flavors, like general nervousness, confusion, depression, apathy, and the ever-popular delirium. Also, since pellagra is mostly seen these days in drug addicts and severe alcoholics, guess what your friends will be thinking you've been doing in your spare time.

I'm convinced. Feed me! Open up for peanuts, lean meats, fish, and bran.

VITAMIN B6

What it does for you: Helps in the formation and breakdown of amino acids, the breakdown of proteins and fats, and in the synthesis of important neurotransmitters.

What happens if I don't have it? Early on, you'll be sore, irritable, and weak. Later on, you'll experience anemia and possibly seizures.

---

5 most popular fruits worldwide: bananas, apples, oranges, watermelons, and plantains.

B_6 deficiencies are not uncommon among chronic alcoholics—and, interestingly enough, some oral contraceptives can cause B_6 deficiencies, as well.

I'm convinced. Feed me! Chow down on whole-grain cereals, fish, legumes, and liver.

VITAMIN B12

What it does for you: It helps you make red blood cells and is important in digestion and the absorption of nutrients.

What happens if I don't have it? The first thing you might notice is that something's up with your tongue. A B_{12} deficiency keeps those little bumps on your tongue from forming, which means your tongue will be unusually smooth. Really kind of creepy if you think about it. More seriously, you'll experience pernicious anemia, defective function of your intestines (Indigestion! Diarrhea! Constipation! All in one package!), and you might even experience spinal cord degeneration, which is, as you might imagine, a very bad thing. Keep this up, and a vitamin B_{12} deficiency will kill you right dead. Vegetarians take note. Vitamin B_{12} is not available in vegetables. No, not a single one. No, it's not a conspiracy to get you to eat bacon. It's really a true fact.

I'm convinced. Feed me! Eggs, milk, liver. Vegans, take that multivitamin and try not to think too hard about where that B_{12} might have come from. Hey, it could come from fungus or algae.

VITAMIN C

What it does for you: Keeps your connective tissue, cartilage, and bones healthy; keeps your metabolism chugging along.

What happens if I don't have it? Arr, me matey! Ye'll get scurvy, me boy! Arrr! Yes, scurvy, the scourge of sailors, who didn't get enough fruit in their long sea voyages. (Fact: The British term "limey" comes from a lime juice ration provided to sailors to prevent scurvy.) Scurvy is genuinely unpleasant, with sore and bleeding gums, wobbly teeth (they'll spring right out of yer scurvy skull, matey!), stiff joints and extremities, internal bleeding, and let's not forget anemia, shall we? Ah, the life of a sea dog.

I'm convinced. Feed me! Stock up on fresh citrus fruits, laddie! Oranges, lemons, limes, and so on. Also cabbage, bell peppers, and Brussels sprouts.

---

5 most popular vegetables worldwide: tomatoes, cabbages, onions, cucumbers, and carrots.

VITAMIN D

What it does for you: Helps with calcium and phosphorus absorption in your body (these two compounds being essential for bones)

What happens if I don't have it? Well, if you're an adult, not too much. However, if your kids don't get enough vitamin D, they'll get rickets, in which bones soften and bend. This leads to bowed legs, knocked knees, and creepy-looking ribs, not to mention other developmental issues. As if your kids won't already have enough problems getting through junior high.

I'm convinced. Feed me! Have some fortified milk and fish liver oil. Also, get some sun. Your body uses sunlight to create vitamin D internally. Yes, this will work for your kids, too, although a cup of milk here and there for them isn't a bad idea, either.

VITAMIN E

What it does for you: It's believed to help your body deal with free radicals, which may fool around with cellular structure if not watched closely.

What happens if I don't have it? You'll get clumsy, that's what. Vitamin E deficiency can lead to walking difficulties and inhibited reflexes, and may also cause your eye muscles to become paralyzed. How's that for freaky?

I'm convinced. Feed me! Eggs, cereals, and beef liver are all fine sources of vitamin E.

VITAMIN K

What it does for you: Helps your blood clot.

What happens if I don't have it? Hope you like bruises, because you'll be getting a lot of them. And naturally, any cuts or scrapes you get will bleed that much longer because your body doesn't have what it needs to form effective clots. Stay inside. Eat all your food with a dull spoon.

I'm convinced. Feed me! Leafy green vegetables are good. So is liver, which, come to think of it, seems to be the most vitamin-packed organ you can eat. If only it tasted like potato chips.

THE POOP ON DOG BREEDING

Why are bulldogs so gosh-darn ugly?
And Dobermans so scary? It's not by chance.

Scientists speculate that the first dogs separated themselves from the wolf pack about 100,000 years ago. And until a few hundred years ago, dogs pretty much bred themselves willy-nilly with little record of human intervention. That is, until the dawn of...

THE UNNECESSARY DOG

In postmedieval Europe, lower-class dogs pulled carts and herded livestock (and were completely unappreciated for it). But on royal estates, "unnecessary dogs"—the darlings of kings and countesses—were becoming the objects of previously unheard-of emotional attachments. By the mid-19th century, these pampered pets outnumbered the workers in the dog population. And by the late 19th century, dog lovers who were fiercely loyal to particular breeds started forming private registries and kennel clubs so they could just as fiercely protect those prized bloodlines.

DESIGNER GENES

Today, after nearly 100 years of serious breeding, most pedigreed dogs are extremely inbred. The chance that a purebred dog will have a different combination of genes at any given site on a chromosome is very small: 4 to 22 percent. In most mutts it's a healthy 57 percent. Between two members of a typical human family it's an even healthier 71 percent. The degree of uniformity among purebreds means that when a bad trait gets locked in by chance, it tends to stay as long as breeding is confined within the group.

MORE THAN ONE SICK PUPPY

So when you hear the phrase "indiscriminate breeding," it doesn't mean despoiling those pure bloodlines with a doggie liaison outside the breed (horrors!), it refers to the breeding of pedigreed

---

The largest cat breed is the ragdoll, which can weigh up to 20 pounds (9 kg).

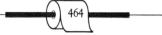

dogs who are known to carry traits that are bad for the breed—mostly physical, but behavioral as well.

A lot of breeders are doing what they can to breed out the bad stuff while keeping in the good. But meanwhile, here's the poop on a few distinctive breeds: where they came from and—because of indiscriminate breeding—the reasons why you might end up spending all your time and money taking them to the vet (or the doggie shrink).

BULLDOGS: THE UGLY SWEETIE-PIE

The dog who looks like Winston Churchill—or is it the other way around? He waddles, he slobbers, and he's the snoring champ of all dogdom.

Origins: Bulldogs were bred to be used in a sport—and we use the term loosely—called "bull-baiting," in which it was the bulldog's job to "take down" a bull by jumping up, biting its face, and hanging on until the bull was pinned to the ground. So the bulldog was bred for a strong lower jaw, a less intrusive nose (so he could breathe while attacking the bull and hang on forever if need be).

After bull-baiting was outlawed in the 19th century, the dog evolved into the shorter, squatter version we know today. But because of all that inbreeding, the bulldog's physique is terribly damaged and distorted.

What they're good for: He's not as fierce as he looks. The bulldog is actually one of the more placid and generally happy breeds. A sweet companion.

Problems: Bulldogs have breathing problems in general and small windpipes in particular. Their pups are often delivered by cesarean because their heads were bred to be so big. They have poor eyesight, are very sensitive to the cold and heat, and don't even get us started on the hip and knee problems. (And probably as a throwback to their bull-baiting origins, they have a penchant for attacking moving cars and vacuum cleaners.)

CHIHUAHUA: THE SHORT MAN SYNDROME

If it weighs more than six pounds, it isn't a Chihuahua—this according to the American Kennel Club (hey, they've got to have some standards). Named after the Mexican state of Chihuahua, it's the oldest breed on the American continent and the smallest breed in the world.

Origins: The modern-day Chihuahua was bred from the Techichi, a small dog kept by the Toltecs and the Aztecs. Both peoples believed the Techichi safely guided the human soul through the underworld, warding off evil spirits until the recently deceased arrived at the Great Taco Bell in the Sky.

Gossip has it that the Techichi was a "prairie dog," that is, not a dog at all, but a burrowing rodent, which the natives raised for food. Then there's the belief that the little ankle-biter came originally from Asia a very long time ago, when the two continents were still joined by the land bridge.

What they're good for: The perfect apartment dog. And not bad as a watchdog, either. An alarm system that doesn't require any batteries.

Problems: Despite their godly status, Chihuahuas are prone to a lot of human-style diseases, including hemophilia, hypoglycemia, and cleft palates. Also, heart, knee, and trachea problems. And don't laugh if you see one wearing an angora doggie sweater—they hate cold weather.

DOBERMAN PINSCHER: THE BAD GUY'S DOG

A triumph of German engineering, the dobie is named for Louis Dobermann (yes, with two Ns), a German tax collector and dog-pound keeper who first bred them at the end of the 19th century.

Origins: In his work collecting taxes, Herr Dobermann sometimes needed to convince reluctant taxpayers to cough up the dough, and also needed to protect himself from bandits on the road. First he tried using tough-looking humans, but eventually decided to create his own breed of dog.

He took a German shepherd for hardiness and intelligence, crossed it with a German pinscher for quick reaction, added a weimeraner pointer for its hunting abilities and coloring, then he threw in a little Rottweiler, greyhound, and Manchester terrier...and voila! A dog that inspired fear and trembling in every taxpayer in the land.

What they're good for: To inspire fear and trembling in everyone who isn't his master. But seriously, folks, the dobie, though a ferociously loyal watchdog, turns out to be very social. He loves being with other people and other dogs (though he can be "aggressive" with the latter).

Problems: This love of being with others means that he demands

---

The body's longest muscle, the sartoris, runs from the pelvis to just below the knee.

THE DRAKE EQUATION

Or, what are the odds the aliens are going to pop by for tea?

Human beings, bless our souls, are optimists. We want to believe that we're not alone in the universe—that somewhere out there, other advanced civilizations exist and are just itching to get to know us and teach us exciting things about life, the universe, and everything. This flies in the face of our actual experience with the only intelligent race we've ever met so far—us—which by and large is content to blast endless loops of *Married...With Children* reruns into space, and whose first contact with new civilizations on our own planet typically boiled down to some guy stepping off a ship and saying to the curious onlookers, "Nice chunk of land you've got here. Got any gold?" before accidentally infecting the lot of them with smallpox.

But like we said, we're optimists. The universe is a big place, and there's just got to be another intelligence or two out there who know how to handle introductions better than we do.

FIGURING THE ODDS

But is there an actual, reasonably logical way to guess as to how many intelligent races exist here in our own galaxy? As it happens, there is, provided by astronomer Dr. Frank Drake, the chairman of the board of the SETI Institute ("SETI" being an acronym for "Search for Extraterrestrial Intelligence"). In 1961 Drake came up with an equation to estimate how many detectable alien civilizations might exist out there in the Milky Way—"detectable" in this case meaning that, like us, they're busy pumping electromagnetic signals into space from their planet (we do this through radio and television broadcasts, among other things).

It's called the Drake Equation, naturally enough, and it looks like this:

$$N = R^* \bullet f_p \bullet n_e \bullet f_l \bullet f_i \bullet f_c \bullet L$$

No, don't run away screaming. It's not nearly as complicated as it looks. Let's break it down to its components and see how it works.

N: This represents the total number of civilizations in our galaxy that we can detect. We get the number N by multiplying together all the variables on the other side of the equal sign.

R*: This variable considers the rate of the formation of stars suitable for the development of life. Not every star is going to be gangbusters for life, after all. For life, you need a star with a fairly long life span (it took four and a half billion years for intelligent life to pop up near our star, after all).

Then you need moderate energy output, so any budding life won't get fried by stellar radiation before it has a chance to make it out of the single-cell stage. That cuts out a wide range of hot, large stars, which burn through their fuel in a mere hundreds of millions of years (or less) and then explode, sizzling up everything in the neighborhood. But small stars might not put out enough energy to create the right environment for life.

The stars you want for life are stars like our own sun: not too big, not too small, but just right for you and me and the green aliens with big heads. These represent a fraction of stars in our galaxy, but there are some 200 billion stars in the Milky Way. Even if only one percent of all stars in the Milky Way are right for life, that's still *two billion stars* to start with.

f_p: So, you have two billion stars that could support life. But life does not live by stars alone. Life also needs a place to put its feet (or tentacles, or pseudopods, or cilia, or whatever). So this variable takes into account the number of suitable stars that actually have planets around them. Up until 1995, the only planets we knew about were the ones in our own solar system—and it was possible, but deeply unlikely, that our planets were the only planets out there. However, in '95 a large planet was spotted around a star called 51 Pegasi, and since then dozens have been discovered, with more popping up all the time. So it seems planets are pretty common after all. Let's say half of our stars have planetary systems. We're down to *one billion stars.*

n_e: Now you have planets. But how many planets can actually support life? This is the question this variable has to take into consideration. In our own solar system, there are nine planets, but most of them, to be blunt, are really awful places to be. Venus is hot enough to melt lead, and Mercury experiences temperature swings of some 700°F (371°C) between night and day. Mars was nice once, maybe, but now it's a cold and dusty fixer-upper. Jupiter, Saturn, Uranus, and Neptune are all gas giants, with no solid surface and with immensely high internal pressures that will squash life flat. Pluto is so cold that its atmosphere actually freezes and falls to the ground. There's only one place in our solar system that life exists: Earth. One planet out of nine. Let's say that half of the star systems have no planets that can support life, and of those that do, there's only one planet in the system that can make it work. We now have *five hundred million planets* to work with.

f_l: Of course, just because a planet can support life, that doesn't mean it does. It could be that an otherwise life-bearing planet has a runaway greenhouse gas problem that turns the planet into an immense Easy-Bake Oven. It could be the planet is whacked by an asteroid that creates a divot the size of the Gulf of Mexico. Or maybe all the ingredients are there to make life happen, and it just doesn't happen. This variable considers the number of planets on which life can appear—and actually does. Let's be conservative and say that life only occurs on one of these planets one time out of five. We're working with *one hundred million planets* at this point.

f_i: Congratulations, you've got life! But do you have intelligent life? You know, the sort of life that does math, plays guitar, makes speeches, and invents handy tools to get to the tasty parts of whatever fruits and animals it might want to eat? That's what this variable concerns itself with, and here's where the numbers really begin to pare down. Consider that there have been millions of different species here on planet Earth over the more than a billion years that life has walked or crawled or slimed around on it—but only one species can be said to be truly intelligent (yes, yes, your dog is smart. But unless he can do geometry, he doesn't make the cut). Let's say that only one life-bearing planet out of a hundred will have a species on it that can work an abacus, or whatever its abacus-equivalent might be. We've got *one million planets* left.

f_c: As any geek in a singles bar can tell you, it's not good enough just to be intelligent. You gotta do something with that

---

The tallest known iceberg, off Greenland, at 550' is 5' less than the Washington Monument.

intelligence—namely, develop a technology that allows your species to broadcast detectable signs of your existence to the rest of the galaxy. Some intelligent species may never do his. Either they're not smart enough, or their variety of intelligence orients them away from doing so, or maybe they're just paranoid and would rather not have you know where they are because you're unclean or something. Or maybe they're just busy with other things and haven't gotten around to it. Whatever the reason, this variable considers the number of intelligent species that will actually do something that lets us know they're there. We'll say that half of them do because, after all, we're doing it now. That's *500,000 planets* leaking electromagnetic signals into the cosmos.

L: Let's face it: Sure, we humans are spewing scads of signals into space—everything from *Father Knows Best* to *The Osbournes* is making its way out to the stars. (What *will* the aliens think of Ozzy trying to work the DVD player?) But consider how often humanity has come close to wiping itself out over the last 50 years (Cuban missile crisis, anyone?), and you'll appreciate what this variable is all about: the amount of time an intelligent species that can broadcast evidence of its existence actually does so. Because just because you're smart enough to let the universe know you exist doesn't mean you're smart enough not to wipe yourself out. Let's say that of the 500,000 planets that can let us know there's someone on them we can talk to, just one out of 50 is actually sending those signals. The rest of them pushed the button somewhere along the way.

HOW DO YOU LIKE THE ODDS?
So with our little run-through of the Drake Equation, we have *10,000 planets* left with intelligent life capable of communicating with us right now. It's a bit of a drop from the two billion stars we started with, but 10,000 is still more than enough to start a good conversation or issue an invitation for a visit. Now all we have to do is find them out there. Rest assured, someone's working on it even now. We're optimists, remember.

The largest pearl ever found is the Pearl of Lao-tze—14 pounds, 1 ounce (6.37 kg).

TRUE STORIES
OF THE ZODIAC

The next time someone asks, "Like, wow, man, what's your sign?" Hit 'em with this stack of information on your zodiac sign. Or just hit them. Your choice.

So, what's your sign? You know what we're talking about here. Whether you believe in astrology or not, you almost certainly know whether you're a Scorpio, a Leo, a Virgo, or one of the nine other classical signs of the zodiac. But here's a question for you: What *is* the zodiac? If the only good answer you can think of is "It's where they keep those signs, man," then it's time to get up close and personal with the zodiac and all the signs in it, from Aries the Ram to Pisces the Fish.

THE DAY YOU WERE BORN...SORT OF
The zodiac is a series of 12 constellations that coincide with the ecliptic, the path that the Sun takes in the sky. The word "zodiac" itself derives from the ancient Greek word that means "animal," because most of the constellations of the zodiac are animals: ram, fish, bull, lion, and so on. Over the course of a year, the Sun spends time in each of these constellations. During that time, the Sun is said by astrologers to be in that particular constellation's "house." Your astrological sign is determined, sort of, by the constellation the Sun is in the day you were born.

THE 13TH SIGN
"Sort of?" What does *that* mean? Well, two things. First, although there are 12 signs, the Sun actually moves through 13 constellations—the zodiac 12 and then also Ophiuchus, known as the serpent bearer (and in fact the constellation is attached to the constellation Serpens, so there you have it). Ophiuchus is wedged in there between Scorpio and Sagittarius, and in reality the Sun spends rather more time in Ophiuchus than in Scorpio. But you never hear anyone saying they were born under the sign of the snake handler, although about half the people born in December (and a few in November) should be saying just that.

OK, EVERYBODY MOVE BACK A MONTH OR SO

Second, the traditional astrological dates in which the Sun is supposed to dwell in any constellation's house aren't accurate. A "wobble" in Earth's movement, known as precession, shifts the constellations eastward over time, so the traditional astrological dates no longer correspond to where the Sun actually is during those dates. On January 1, for example, the traditional zodiac dates say that the Sun is supposed to be in Capricorn, but it's actually in Sagittarius. Compound these fuzzy numbers with the fact that this very book you're holding has far more influence on you (gravitationally, at least) than any of the stars in any of the signs of the zodiac, and you'll understand why, entertainment value aside, it's best to take those astrological attributes of zodiac signs with the proverbial grain of salt.

ACCURACY REARS ITS UGLY HEAD

Be that as it may, each zodiac sign is still interesting from both a cultural and scientific point of view. To prove that, let's take a quick tour through each sign to fill you in on the actual, verifiable details of your sign. This information may or may not be any more useful to you in a day-to-day sense than your horoscope might be, but there's no doubt that it's more accurate. In addition to the traditional dates associated with the signs, we're also adding the actual dates that the Sun can now be located in the constellation.

Aries (the Ram)
Traditional dates: March 21–April 19
Actual dates: April 19–May 13

The story behind the sign: In Greek mythology, this sign represents the flying ram that had the golden fleece, the famous fleece that Jason and his Argonauts made off with. While this ram was still unskinned, it was assigned the role of rescuing the tykes Helles and Phryxus from their evil stepmother, who was planning to kill them (evil stepmoms go back a long way). The rescue was a limited success because midflight, Helles fell off, splashed into the water off the coast of modern-day Turkey, and drowned. The area where she supposedly drowned is known to this day as the Hellespont. This is not a recommended way to become famous.
Astronomical sights: In terms of astronomy, Aries isn't much to look at, but there are two things of note: the star Mesartim, which

---

resolves into a very nice double star in a telescope, and the spiral galaxy NGC 722, also viewable in a telescope.

Taurus (the Bull)
Traditional dates: April 20–May 20
Actual dates: May 14–June 19

The story behind the sign: This sign represents the striking white bull that the Greek god Zeus turned himself into in order to make off with Europa, princess of Phoenicia. One would think that being abducted by livestock would be a traumatic incident (especially when one considers that in the legend, the bull heads to the sea with Europa on its back and swims to Crete, a fair distance away). But Europa recovered her poise well enough to bear Zeus three sons. One presumes (indeed, fervently hopes) Zeus switched out of his bull suit for that.

Astronomical sights: Some really interesting objects in Taurus, including the dazzling cluster of new stars known as the Pleiades, the Crab Nebula, which is the remnant of a supernova that exploded in 1054, and red Aldebaran, the constellation's brightest star, one of the 20 brightest stars in the sky.

Gemini (the Twins)
Traditional dates: May 21–June 20
Actual dates: June 20–July 20

The story behind the sign: The twins represented are Castor and Pollux (which are also, not coincidentally, the names of the two brightest stars in the constellation). In Greek mythology, these were the sons of Zeus and the Queen of Sparta (Zeus got around), and while Pollux was immortal, Castor was not. Well, one day Castor got himself killed as mortals do, but Pollux pleaded with Zeus to share his immortality with his sibling. Zeus agreed, and set them both in the sky. Which is kind of a sweet tale, except for the whole "somebody had to die" part.

Astronomical sights: Those twin stars, Castor and Pollux, of which Pollux is slightly brighter (Pollux was originally the immortal twin, after all). Castor is actually a system of six stars, divided into three binary star systems. There are also several star clusters, M35 being the most prominent, and the Eskimo Nebula, which can be viewed through a telescope, just off the constellation's midsection.

Cancer (the Crab)
Traditional dates: June 20–July 22
Actual dates: July 21–August 9

The story behind the sign: This is supposed to be the giant crab that the goddess Hera sent to harass the mighty Hercules while that warrior was battling the Hydra monster—yes, this is illegal tag-teaming, and it just isn't cool. However, Hercules dealt with the crab by crushing it with his feet, after which everyone probably had crab cakes for a week (he also killed the Hydra by crushing its many heads). What was Hera's problem with Hercules? Well, it turns out that ol' Herc was the son of Hera's husband, but not of Hera. Hera's husband? Zeus, of course. What a goat.

Astronomical sights: Not much going on in Cancer, whose stars are rather dim and uninteresting. But there is M44, which is a nice open cluster of stars; it's also known the Beehive Cluster, which is a rather nicer name than the one given to it by ancient Chinese astronomers: "Exhalation of Piled-up Corpses." Really, that's just icky.

Leo (the Lion)
Traditional dates: July 23–August 22
Actual dates: August 10–September 15

The story behind the sign: Another animal fatality related to Hercules. This was the Nemean Lion, which Herc was required to kill as one of his famous 12 labors (offing the Hydra was one of them, too). The catch here was the lion's skin was impervious to arrows, so Hercules had to wrestle the thing to the ground after which he choked off its air supply until it expired. Herc later famously wore the lion skin as armor, and one has to wonder how he managed to skin the thing if the hide was totally puncture proof. It's probably best to gloss over that little bit of plot inconsistency and just move on.

Astronomical sights: The star Algeiba is a very attractive double star under a telescope. Be sure to check out galaxies M65 and M66, as well—two tilted spiral galaxies that seem to crowd up against each other in your field of view.

Virgo (the Virgin)
Traditional dates: August 23–September 22
Actual dates: September 16–October 30

Largest butterfly: Queen Alexandra's Birdwing has an 11-inch (28-cm) wingspan.

The story behind the sign: It's supposed to represent Astraea, the goddess of justice, who was also, you know, a virgin. Astraea, incidentally, the daughter of Themis and (wait for it) Zeus. Legend has it that when the Greek gods abandoned humanity, which was becoming increasingly wicked, Astraea was the very last of the gods to go. Fine, then. Just *leave*.

Astronomical sights: The constellation Virgo is utterly packed with galaxies—indeed, the Virgo Cluster has more than 2,000 of them, including several prominent enough to be picked up by amateur telescopes. The most famous is probably M104, a flattened spiral galaxy whose distinctive shape earns it the nickname "the Sombrero Galaxy." Real astronomy buffs will also groove to M87, a massive elliptical galaxy that is famous for shooting jets of gas and holding an intense radio source known as Virgo A. The jets of gas and radio emissions won't be visible in your home telescope, however.

Libra (the Scales)
Traditional dates: September 23–October 22
Actual dates: October 31–November 22

The story behind the sign: There aren't any definitive stories that go with this constellation, actually, though there is some intimation that the constellation is related to Mochis, the fellow who legendarily created weights and measures. But no one's sticking their neck out on that one. It's also sometimes identified with the goddess Astraea, and in drawings, the constellation Virgo is sometimes seen holding Libra. Before it was known as Libra, it was known as Chelae Scorpii, "the Scorpion's Claws."

Astronomical sights: Libra's sights are about as unimpressive as its history. Its stars are faint and not very interesting, although some maintain that Zubenschamali, Libra's brightest star, appears green—one of the few stars visible to the naked eye to do so. However, most people typically see it as white. Yeah, we're disappointed, too.

Scorpio (the Scorpion)
Traditional dates: October 23–November 21
Actual dates: November 23–November 29

The story behind the sign: This is the scorpion that was sent to sting Orion, the hunter whose ideas of ecological balance were out

All of your body's functions stop when you sneeze, even your heart.

of whack, since he was in danger of killing off every animal on the planet—thus the reason the scorpion was assigned to whack him. And whack him he did. Legend says that both the scorpion and Orion were set in the sky—but at opposite ends, so they would never be in the night sky at the same time. Seems reasonable enough.

Astronomical sights: First, the constellation actually does look a bit like a scorpion, making it one of the few that truly resembles what it signifies. Beyond this are several very nice clusters, including M6 and M7, which are parked right in the path of the Milky Way, and M4, which at about 7,000 light-years away is one of the closest globular clusters to us.

Sagittarius (the Archer)
Traditional dates: November 22–December 21
Actual dates: December 18–January 18

The story behind the sign: Sagittarius is traditionally seen as a centaur with a bow, and two centaurs have been associated with the constellation. First, there is Crotus, the son of the god Pan (not Zeus, for a change), who was also legendarily the inventor of archery, so you can see how this makes sense. Second, there is Chiron, the fabled tutor of Hercules, who is also and more commonly associated with the constellation Centaurus. Hercules killed Chiron with a poisoned arrow while in a drunken rage. So remember, kids, drinking and archery just don't mix.

Astronomical sights: There are some glorious nebulae in Sagittarius, including the Lagoon Nebula, which can be seen with the naked eye, the Trifid Nebula, with three dust lanes that trisect the nebula, and the Omega Nebula, which features a star cluster within it. There are also several star clusters. Lots to look at.

Capricorn (the Sea-Goat)
Traditional dates: December 22–January 19
Actual dates: January 19–February 15

The story behind the sign: Capricorn is the disguise of the god Pan, who, when confronted with the sea monster Typhon, decided it would be wise to change into an animal and escape detection (and smartly done, since by this time Typhon had already ripped out Zeus's tendons). So he turned his top half into a goat and his bottom half into a fish. Yeah, that's inconspicuous.

Astronomical sights: Capricorn's two brightest stars are both double stars, although the two stars that appear to make up Alpha Capricorni aren't actually tied to each other (one is ten times as far away from us as the other). Beta Capricorni's stars, however, are definitely paired up.

Aquarius (the Water-Bearer)
Traditional dates: January 20–February 18
Actual dates: February 16–March 11

The story behind the sign: The most solid story linked to Aquarius is that it represents Ganymede, a cute young shepherd boy who was kidnapped by Zeus and brought to Mount Olympus to be the cup-bearer to the gods. (Zeus's usual cup-bearer, Hebe, had been put out of commission by a sprained ankle.) Less mythologically, it's been said that Aquarius got its "water-bearing" reputation because in ancient times it was the constellation that was rising in the sky during the rainy seasons.

Astronomical sights: The stars of Aquarius aren't much to look at, but a couple of interesting nebulae, including the Helix Nebula, readily visible in binoculars, and the Saturn Nebula, which looks like it has "rings" when looked at through a large enough telescope.

Pisces (the Fish)
Traditional dates February 19–March 20
Actual dates: March 12–April 18

The story behind the sign: Remember Typhon, that big, bad sea monster that Pan changed himself into a sea-goat to escape? Well, he wasn't the only god bravely running away from that monster. Aphrodite and her son Eros did the same thing, turning themselves into actual fish to flee (much less conspicuous than a sea-goat, you have to admit). Pisces represents those fish.

Astronomical sights: With your bare eyes, you'll be able to observe the Circlet, a ring of stars that define the head of the pair's southernmost fish. Grab a telescope and you'll be able to see M74, a spiral galaxy that faces Earth head-on. It's sneaky, though, and can be surprisingly difficult to find.

ATTACK OF THE MOVIE MONSTERS!

Look out! They're coming your way! And they're hungry!!

Whether they're spawned from radiation, spurt acid blood, or have simply come from outer space to eat your brains and take over your body, we can't get enough of these science fiction film monsters. Here are some of our favorites—and what makes us love to hate (and fear) them.

JAWS SO NICE, THEY HAVE THEM TWICE

Monsters: The Aliens

From: *Alien*, 1979, and three additional sequels

Description: Toothy, reptilian chewing factories with two sets of jaws and acidic blood.

Hobbies: Lurking in shadows, capturing humans to use as incubators, gestating in your chest.

What's their story? They were discovered by a group of space truckers, one of whom had a larval version slither down his throat and then pop out of his chest a few days later. These aliens grow quickly, are always hungry, and like nothing better than to slither up to a human skull and use their second set of jaws like a bottle opener to get at the good stuff inside. In later films we learn that the aliens are part of a hive society, with a big, very nasty queen at the top. Individual aliens aren't particularly smart, but they sure are mean, so often the humans have to get rid of them by detonating entire ships or human colonies. This makes the battle not very cost-effective for the humans.

Can they be killed? Sure, just don't get any of their blood on you, or it'll eat right through your arm.

TROOPER SCOOPERS

Monsters: Arachnids

From: *Starship Troopers*, 1997

Description: Think of a 12-foot-high cross between a crab and a spider with razor blade legs and you're in the general ballpark.

Hobbies: Going to war with humans, impaling humans on their legs like screaming cocktail weenies on a toothpick, and picking said humans' brains (literally).

What's their story? Think of it as a real estate squabble. Humans want more planets to live on, and so do the arachnids, but both groups have apparently forgotten everything they learned in kindergarten about the concept of "sharing." Arachnids are mean and tough and sport cool racing stripes, but more importantly there are more of them than there are of us. One memorable scene in the movie has an incredible panoramic view of thousands of them descending on a couple of dozen humans like hungry conventioneers stampeding toward the hotel breakfast buffet.

Can They Be Killed? Yes, they can, but can you kill all of them before they put you on the skewer?

OOEY, GOOEY, AND YOU'RE WHAT'S CHEWY!
Monster: The Blob
From: *The Blob*, 1958, and a 1988 remake
Description: Gelatinous, amoeba-like, sticky.
Hobbies: Extending pseudopods, capturing unsuspecting creatures, surrounding and ingesting said creatures, terrorizing sleepy mountain towns.

What's its story? It was just your average smear of space goo hitching a ride on a meteor, when that meteor crashed into Earth. The blob looked out (so to speak), adjudged our planet to be a really nice smorgasbord, and started snacking. Tried the humans, found them to be magically delicious. The humans didn't like this, of course, but, look, everyone needs to spend a little time on a middle rung of the food chain. Fortunately for the Blob, it was discovered first by moody teenagers (in both the 1958 and 1988 versions) whose warnings were ignored by adults, thereby giving the blob plenty of time to snack before it had to go away.

Can it be killed? Well, it can be frozen into immobility, which was good enough for the original movie; they froze the Blob and dropped it off at the North Pole. In the 1950s, apparently, no one worried at all about the possibility of global warming.

HONEY, WHAT'S THAT POD THING IN THE BASEMENT?

Monsters: The Body Snatchers
From: *Invasion of the Body Snatchers*, 1956, and a 1978 remake
Description: Before: Large, podlike things. After: Look in mirror.
Hobbies: Refining, to the nth degree, the idea that "imitation is the sincerest form of flattery."
What's their story? Here's what these invaders would say: We're just humble podlike entities, trying to make our way in the world like so many others. We're really more interested in your story. You seem so interesting. And you have such nice things! We wish we could be just like you. No, we don't know why everyone else in town is acting kind of funny. You're just imagining things. You know, you look tired. Why don't you take a nap? Here, we fixed you a nice, warm glass of milk. With some Xanax.
Can they be killed? Not all of them. Stay awake, pal.

FATAL ATTRACTION—A WHOLE NEW MEANING

Monster: The Chick from *Species*
From: *Species*, 1995, and *Species II*, 1998
Description: Totally hot babe, except when she's showing her alien side, in which case she's a totally hot babe with sharp spikes.
Hobbies: Going to clubs, meeting guys, and killing them after she's, um, "retrieved their genetic information."
What's her story? Human scientists get a message from space that says, more or less, "Hi there! Here's the DNA recipe for one of our kind. Combine it with your own DNA for extra fun! It's just like making sea monkeys!" But of course, the end result wasn't like sea monkeys at all. It was like a super-hot babe with an insane biological urge to procreate, who was not above killing a few measly humans who got in the way of her breeding program. Maternal instinct? She's got it, man. The moral: The next time aliens come to your door selling DNA, just say no!
Can she be killed? Sure; the question is whether you killed her before she spawned.

The 3,100-carat Cullinan Diamond was the largest gem-quality diamond before it was cut.

GODZILLA MEETS EVERYBODY

Monster: Godzilla

From: *Godzilla*, 1956, plus too many sequels to count, including a 1998 American remake

Description: Huge, radioactively mutated lizard with fire breath.

Hobbies: Stomping on Tokyo, screeching, belching fire, and battling other large, mutated creatures, preferably near a major population center.

What's its story? In the original 1956 version, Godzilla was a Jurassic-era dinosaur, mutated by nuclear bomb tests carried out by the American military. Godzilla then goes on to wreak havoc on Japan despite the furious opposition of the Japanese military. Really, you don't need a road map to figure out the symbolism there. In innumerable sequels, Godzilla would return, sometimes to wreak havoc, but sometimes to save Japan from some other hideous mutated creature. Hey, Japan is Godzilla's territory, you lousy monsters! Go over there and wreck Hong Kong! In 1998, a souped-up version of Godzilla rampaged through New York and terrorized Matthew Broderick, but it wasn't the same.

Can it be killed? In the original movie, Godzilla was defeated bv a scientist who unleashes a machine called the Oxygen Destroyer. Two dozen sequels make it clear that while you can knock Godzilla down, you can't ever really knock him out.

C'MON! SHOW A LITTLE SPINE!

Monster: The Predator

From: *Predator*, 1987, and *Predator 2*, 1990

Description: Humanoid, technologically advanced, in serious need of first-rate orthodontic work.

Hobbies: Exploring strange new worlds, seeking out new life and new civilizations, and then hunting down members of those civilizations and ripping out their spines as trophies.

What's its story? On a hunting trip to the planet Earth, the Predator comes across a band of U.S. commandos, looks at their weaponry, figures it's not a totally unfair fight, and then wipes out all of them except the one guy who is contractually guaranteed to make it through the film alive (even alien hunters are not immune to movie star contracts). In the sequel, the Predator changes locales and starts hunting humans in L.A., and why not? It was getting crowded anyway. This time the government wants to capture it for its own nefarious purposes. You can imagine how well that works out for the government.

Can it be killed?: Yes, though like the bad guys in the *Alien* films, killing a Predator usually involves a very large explosion.

PEOPLE-SIZED PEOPLE-EATERS

Monsters: Raptors

From: *Jurassic Park*, 1993, and two sequels

Description: Human-sized, genetically reengineered dinosaurs with really big brains, sharp claws, and organizational skills that make Patton look like a lost Boy Scout.

Hobbies: Running, leaping, planning ambushes of overconfident humans, snacking on same.

What's their story? A large, arrogant genetic engineering company decides to bring back the dinosaurs to make a quick buck on a theme park, and in addition to bringing happy, gentle herbivores, also brings back smart, mean, vicious carnivores, because, well, they sure are cute! Anyway, it doesn't take long for these smart, mean vicious carnivores to deduce that humans are soft and chewy, make great snacks—and are easy pickin's. And they're easy pickin's over three separate movies, so you tell us which is the smarter species.

Can they be killed?: Yes, but it helps if a T. rex does it for you.

* * * * *

CLASSIC MONSTERS

An Internet poll of favorite movie monsters ranked the "classic" monsters as follows:

Dracula 32%
Mummy 26%
Werewolf 25%
Frankenstein 17%

The only monster movies that made the American Film Institute's list of top 100 American films of the 20th century were:

King Kong, 1933 • *Jaws*, 1975 • *Frankenstein*, 1931

A worker bee produces only about 1/12 of a teaspoon of honey it its lifetime.

HYSTERICAL SCHOLARS

*Our contributors. Proud members of the
Bathroom Readers' Hysterical Society.
We couldn't have done it without them.*

Lee Bienkowski

Jennifer Carlisle

Wim Coleman

Susan Elkin

Clay Griffith

Kathryn Grogman

Dena Jordan

Vicky Kalambakal

Diane Lane

Jennifer Lee

Christopher Lord

Art Montague

Tia Nevitt

Ken Padgett

Paul Paquet

Pat Perrin

John Scalzi

Joyce Slaton

Stuart Smoller

Stephanie Spadaccini

Rebecca Steiner

Susan Steiner

Johanna Stewart

Steve Theunissen

Diana Vandehoef

Ana Young

INDEX

THE LAST PAGE

Hear ye, hear ye, all bathroom readers! We at the Bathroom Readers' Hysterical Society feel that it is your inalienable right to always have the very best in bathroom reading material—no more shampoo bottle labels with their incomprehensible multisyllabic ingredients (hmm...could there be an article there?), no more already perused magazines, no more desperate gazing at the bathroom wall—just bathroom reading entertainment of the highest quality. Quality of a level high enough to be proudly displayed in all rooms of the house—even in (dare we say it?) the *bookcase!*

Uncle John's new *Bathroom Readers* are already in the works! Join us in looking forward to:

   Uncle John's Ahh-Inspiring Bathroom Reader—the 15th edition
   Uncle John's Ahh-Inspiring Bathroom Reader—the very special
     Limited Edition (available through the BRI website)
   Uncle John's For Kids Only
   Uncle John Plunges Into Great Lives
   Uncle John's Presents series brand-new titles:
     Blame It on the Weather
     Necessary Numbers
   Uncle John's MINIATURE Series (from Running Press Publishing)
   Uncle John's Page-A-Day Calendar (from Workman Publishing)
   And—Uncle John goes global! Uncle John's first foreign editions for
   Australia, Great Britain, and Spanish-speaking nations.

So we once again invite you to take the plunge by joining the Bathroom Readers' Institute. Send a self-addressed, stamped envelope to us at: The Bathroom Readers' Institute, P.O. Box 1117, Ashland, OR 97520.

What's in it for you—where to begin? First, your very own official (and most attractive, if we do say so ourselves) BRI membership card. Then, a subscription to the newsletter for those who want to be in the know (sent via email). Plus: Access to all sorts of very cool official BRI merchandise! Discounts galore when ordering through the BRI! And—(drum roll, please) a permanent spot on BRI's honor roll !

It appears that I've run out of space, and I don't want to make this an extra-time last page, so...when you've gotta go – you've gotta go!

In weird times—always go with the flow...

          —Uncle Al and the
          Bathroom Readers'
          Hysterical Society